GUIDE TO AMERICAN ENGLISH

L. M. MYERS

Arizona State University

GENE MONTAGUE

University of Detroit

PRENTICE-HALL, INC. Englewood Cliffs, New Jersey

Library of Congress Catalog Card Number: 73-177393
Printed in the United States of America

ISBN: P 0-13-369249-3
   C 0-13-369256-6

10 9 8 7 6 5 4 3 2 1

PRENTICE-HALL INTERNATIONAL, INC., London
PRENTICE-HALL OF AUSTRALIA, PTY. LTD., Sydney
PRENTICE-HALL OF CANADA, LTD., Toronto
PRENTICE-HALL OF INDIA PRIVATE LIMITED, New Delhi
PRENTICE-HALL OF JAPAN, INC., Tokyo

*It is not sufficient to know what one ought to say,
but one must also know how to say it.*
ARISTOTLE, *Rhetoric*

FOR ERNIE PARKER, a Guide

CONTENTS

8

DEVELOPMENT OF THE LANGUAGE   94

9

THE PATTERNS OF GRAMMAR   105

10

OUTLINING AND PARAGRAPHING   173

11

CHECKING SENTENCE STRUCTURE   188

12

EXPLAINING   199

13
LETTERS

14
THE RESEARCH PAPER

15
THE CRITICAL REVIEW

INDEX TO USAGE

INDEX

PREFACE

The fifth edition of this book differs from the preceding edition in these particulars:

1. New material on dialects and free writing techniques has been added.
2. The Index to Usage has been brought up to date.
3. A new chapter on the Critical Review is included.
4. The sections on paragraphing and outlining have been amplified.
5. The basic organization of the book has been altered to fit more exactly a natural classroom sequence.
6. New exercises accompany each chapter. We are grateful to Catherine Miles for her help in preparing the exercises.

L.M.M.
G.M.

IN THE BEGINNING

This book contains more material than any one student needs but no more material than an entire class can use. Every chapter does not have equal value for every student; that's one reason for the first word in the title: *Guide*. Some students have been over many of the paths mapped out in various chapters; others have not been there at all. Figuring out which student needs what gives teachers something to do—and gray hair.

No two students are the same, and, barring plagiarism, no two themes are quite the same. That means the teacher has to be a mental acrobat to cope with—and *encourage*—the differences. No book can do that for him. But it can give the student and him useful material to work with.

It can also put that material into useful order. This particular book begins by setting out some assumptions about writing. Then it takes up elementary considerations about your first papers, since one of the oddities of writing courses is that you begin writing before you've been "taught to write." Then the book discusses thinking processes and analyzes the medium of thought: the language, specifically American English. Following that, it takes up problems that inevitably occur in writing, without assuming that any student suffers all those problems, but realizing that in any class all those problems will probably occur. Beyond that come chapters devoted to special writing projects. Finally, there is an Index to Usage, arranged alphabetically and designed largely as a compact reference book.

That is a reasonable and useful arrangement, but any student who finds himself skipping around in the book is doing the right thing because he knows what he needs when he needs it.

One thing he probably needs to know in the beginning is the series of assumptions that lie behind this book.

ASSUMPTIONS

1. **Whether we like it or not, good writing shows up our differences.** In early chapters we speak of the limitations of logic, the provisional nature of truth, the many meanings of *meaning*. If logic were a perfect instrument, truth an absolute, and meaning fixed, there would be no occasion for communication. By efficient programming, most of us could learn swiftly and easily most of what everyone else knows. But things are not like that. Any view of reality is an interpretation of reality, and no two interpretations are quite the same. We write not because we are all the same but because we are all different and because all these differences exist on the same globe.

2. **The object of writing is to communicate with someone other than yourself.** That someone else is always different from you. You must assume, therefore, that you are writing for someone who does *not* share your point of view, your store of facts, your interpretation. Students are often told to regard their classmates as the audience for their writing. In practice, most write for their instructors. There is nothing depraved about that—calculating, perhaps, but not depraved. It doesn't really matter what audience you write for, but it is essential that you know who your audience is. Why? Because any piece of writing proposes to span a gap in time or space or status—to build a bridge between two different individuals or groups. That is called communication. The purpose of writing is to offer material reasons for changing one's mind. Usually it is a two-way bridge: if you change your reader, he will also change you, because you had to consider him while you were writing. In the beginning, therefore, you have to have some idea of what your reader's mind already holds; what you write is determined as much by what you think *he* knows as by what *you* know.

3. **The writing process itself is often a way of discovering what you want to say.** We think in language, but we don't usually think in para-

graphs or themes. Writing something down reveals the weakness of an idea while allowing us to broaden and sharpen the idea. The weaknesses drive us to strengthening. There's more than a little truth in the remark, "How do I know what I want to say until I've said it?" That is why, for example, the first draft of a paper is just a beginning, and why we put such emphasis on rethinking and rewriting.

4. **The teaching and learning of standard English must be a cooperative task.** Otherwise both teacher and learner are going to suffer. Both should recognize one cardinal principle:

> *The idea that only standard English is grammatical and therefore "good" is an outworn superstition that must be abandoned.*

A grammar is simply a set of habitual patterns which its speakers can use to construct and understand new sentences. Without a grammar we could only memorize a limited number of sentences and use them with no variation. Every dialect simply *must* have its own grammar, and there is no evidence that any one of them is better than any of the others. The people who say "Them apples is ourn" use their patterns just as systematically and effectively as the people who say "Those apples are ours." (For a full discussion, see Chapter 3.)

> *The sign of a bad piece of writing is not that the writer has not mastered standard English, but that he is not expressing any interesting ideas, or not arranging them effectively, in whatever dialect he is working with.*

A good man can write beautifully in any dialect that is natural to him; and the Lord knows, it is possible to write miserably in standard without breaking any rules.

All the same, there are two sound reasons for teaching and learning standard English. The first is simply that—however mistakenly—it has a much higher prestige than any of the other dialects, and anybody who does not learn to use it is severely limiting his future. Call the prejudice against the others ignorance, snobbery, or whatever—it exists, and we won't be able to root it out in a hurry.

The second reason is more interesting, and there is nothing either silly or snobbish about it. The English language is not a single, uniform structure. It is a complicated mixture of perhaps hundreds of overlapping dialects, differing in various dimensions—ancestral, geographical, occupational, social, and nobody quite knows how many others. There is nothing shameful about any of them, and no sound reason for trying to drive any of them out of existence. But many of them are comparatively private; that is, they are understood and appreciated only within a limited range. We need— and we have—a public dialect that has a wider currency. We call it *stand- ard English.*

We all learn our first dialect from the people we happen to grow up with. And since these people have different backgrounds, needs, and in- terests, their dialects are not all alike. Moreover, these dialects are con- stantly changing; and if there were nothing to hold them together, it would soon become impossible for their speakers to understand each other. (In Chapter Eight you will find a brief discussion of how far such a splitting process could go when there was nothing to interfere with it.) Six centuries ago the local dialects in England (small as that country is) had become so different that it was often thought necessary to translate a book in order that it might be locally understood.

To overcome this difficulty, Englishmen developed the habit of writing in the dialect of London, regardless of the dialect they spoke. In other words, what had originally been simply a local dialect became standard as an auxiliary dialect for the whole country. At first this was used only by a comparatively small number of writers who made a special effort to learn it. But with the introduction of printing and the wider spread of edu- cation, it gradually came to be considered the official form of the language, and everybody who was anybody was expected to use it.

For the past two centuries our schools have been trying very hard to force everybody to use this dialect for all purposes. Their reasons have been partly democratic—to remove a handicap which could keep many people from leading fully successful lives—and partly moralistic—there must be just one *right* way to talk, and everybody ought to learn it. But their methods have often been stupid, even cruel; and they have probably taught more people to hate "good English" than to practice it.

Nevertheless, some good has come out of their efforts. We do have a standard dialect that most people can understand, whether or not they can use it themselves; and the other dialects have not become as different from each other as they would have if they were not in continual contact with the standard one. We need a *public* form of the language for the whole country as well as a number of comparatively private forms for smaller groups within the country. This statement will strike many people as a half-hearted compromise. Wouldn't it be simpler to have *just* the public language, make everybody learn it, and wipe out all the other kinds? Of course it would—just as it would be simpler to have everybody the same size and shape, and with all the same tastes, so that we wouldn't have to make so many kinds of clothes and shoes. Beautifully simple, but it won't work. And we have centuries of history to prove that one all-purpose language won't work for everybody, either—but an auxiliary dialect can work at least reasonably well.

Most Americans have to make some kind of linguistic adjustment; and the adjustment is much easier if it is not mixed up with a superstition. When teachers tell a boy that expressions that he has used all his life are stupid or shameful, they are likely to do him a good deal of harm. If he believes them he may turn into a prig, and is very likely to suffer from anxiety about his language for the rest of his life. If he doesn't believe them he may develop a permanent resistance against standard English.

A teacher who respects his dialect, and simply points out that some of its forms and patterns are not appropriate in standard English, has a much better chance of helping him. The student knows perfectly well—at least in part of his brain—that he has a good deal to gain by learning the new ways; and he is usually willing to try if the process is not made too unpleasant. And of course he is likely to write much better if the tension is removed and he can concentrate on learning a new skill instead of reforming his supposedly depraved character.

We should emphasize that a desire for social approval and a successful career is not the only good reason for mastering standard English. For although this dialect is not *intrinsically* better than any of the others, its possibilities have been exploited much more thoroughly, simply because it is the one generally used by educated and successful people throughout the English-speaking world. These people are likely to have more to say, to say it more precisely, and to express complex relationships better than the speakers of any dialect of a more limited range. In short, though their language is no better, they are more likely to use it well; and if you want to stretch your mind, you have a lot to learn from them.

5. **You cannot learn much by writing defensively.** Students as well as teachers should take to heart the following "new commandment."

> *Thou shalt rise above adultery.* You should not adulterate your teaching; you should teach over your students' heads, not under their feet. Students should be taught to write and speak as they cannot yet write and speak, not to avoid errors by trying to compose like morons. Some teachers are tempted to instruct their charges to write like small children, in order that they will make no mistakes, but this is the pedagogical sin of sins: to teach the student what he knows already, not what he needs to know. Any young person who produces a composition without error is not trying to do enough; he should be attempting structures which as yet he cannot control, seeking words he does not as yet command, not writing full sentences to avoid fragments.[1]

[1] Charlton Laird, "The New Ten Commandments for Teachers of Composition," *And Gladly Teche* (Englewood Cliffs, N.J.: Prentice-Hall, Inc., 1970), p. 5.

THE FIRST PAPER

WHY MAKE IT HARDER?

Some freshmen can write competently when they come to college. Others are anxious to learn to write, and willing to make the effort required. But a good many students spend more time in fussing, fuming, and general frustration than they do in actual productive work; and even when they are working they often make the job unnecessarily hard by using wasteful methods. It therefore seems worthwhile to begin this chapter with some very elementary remarks—and if you don't need them, you probably have a classmate who does.

If you think the requirement of a certain number of themes is silly, and the particular assignment that your instructor has just given you unbearably stupid, we won't argue. But we will say that you can't afford to think so for more than a moment or two. Make a few uncomplimentary remarks (preferably under your breath), and then get on with it. This advice is not moral, it is practical. Every minute you allow resentment to build up makes the job harder and longer. If you'd rather gripe than write, you're only human. But if you'd rather gripe for one hour and dawdle for another than do the whole thing in forty minutes, it isn't the instructor who is stupid.

DO YOUR ORGANIZING FIRST

Joe Williams begins his paper by writing his first sentence, in the blind hope that it will somehow generate a second, which will in turn generate a third. This method does sometimes work. if the writer is good enough, and if the topic has a built-in organization. But Joe is not that good, and though he has picked his topic, he hasn't decided how he is going to treat it. He simply writes his first sentence, and then looks at it. The second one somehow doesn't leap to his pen. He looks at it again, and then lights a cigarette and looks at it some more. After a while he crosses it out and writes another first sentence. This can go on for hours.

Eventually Joe gets half a dozen sentences written. They all have something to do with the subject, and on the paper they look something like a paragraph. But they don't hang together very well, they don't really cover any part of his subject, and they don't seem to lead anywhere. Joe decides that maybe he has selected the wrong subject. He tears up the paper, takes a drink of water, lights another cigarette, and starts all over again. He begins by writing his first sentence.

It would be painful to follow Joe any further. Let's assume that he finally gets 400 words and a D– for his grade. The important question is, what was wrong with his method? The answer is simple. He put down his first sentence as soon as he had decided what he was going to *write about*. He should have waited until he had decided in some detail what he was going to *say about it*. If he had got the outline clear in his head first, he could have written a much better paper in less time. And if he had actually jotted down an outline, so that he could examine it for completeness and consistency and rearrange it where necessary, he could have done better still. We can reasonably assume that he had been told all this more than once. We can also make a reasonable guess about why he has paid no attention to sound advice. He thinks an outline requires extra time and effort, and he knows it requires extra paper. Perhaps subconsciously, he has indulged in two kinds of false economy. It might have paid off, but the odds were against him.

Let's do it the easy way instead.

SELECTING A TOPIC

The first step in planning a paper is selecting a topic. There are three possibilities.

1. Your instructor assigns you a topic. You may not like it, but at least he has saved you some time. Get on with it.

2. Your instructor gives you a choice of several topics. If one of them appeals to you at once, take it and forget the others. Otherwise, give yourself not more than a couple of minutes to decide, and don't change your mind. It is easier to write on any of them than to decide for sure which is best.

3. Your instructor gives you a free choice of topics. Don't waste an hour trying to find one that you really want to write about. Just let your mind run over some ideas until you find one that you would be interested in talking to a friend about, and decide firmly to write about that. No subject, in itself, is either interesting or uninteresting; but if one interests you, you have a fair chance of making it interesting to somebody else.

Once you have chosen your general topic, the next step is to decide just what parts of it you want to treat. There is always a great deal more that could be said than you are going to have time to say. Even if you started out with something as simple as a burnt match you could go on indefinitely—what it is composed of, how it was made, how it was or might have been used, what an improvement it is over earlier methods of making fire, what changes matches have made in our everyday life, and so on. The idea that you have said all that you possibly can, and are still 150 words short, is a common source of discouragement. It is always false; and the real reason for it is often simply that once you have skimmed over a subject in a paragraph, you tend to look for any excuse that will justify your reluctance to rewrite that paragraph in a longer form. But if your outline indicates that you don't have enough material, you won't mind inserting some more detail.

DEVELOPING AN OUTLINE

One way to give a general topic specific form is to take a piece of paper and list the first things that occur to you. They don't have to be in any particular order—yet. Here are three subjects with possible preliminary listings:

THE DRAFT	BURNT MATCH	TELEPHONES
fear	looks useless	wonderful invention
the Vietnam War	made of pine	different kinds
question of war itself	when invented?	saves lots of time
World War II	flint and steel	sometimes a nuisance
the old system	be careful	salesmen
the new system: lottery	forest fires	calling home
possibility: volunteer army	rubbing sticks	party lines
inequalities	different kinds	talking too long
conscientious objectors	pretty cheap	children on phone
selective objection	chemicals	wrong numbers
exemptions		"you have been
minority groups		chosen"
solution: no wars (!)		public phones
Canada		
registering		
burning draft cards		
prison		
parents favor the		
Vietnam War		

Putting aside for the moment the problems of knowing your audience, what you write about any subject depends on what you know about
it and how you feel about it. Furthermore, how you feel about something
depends to some extent on what you know about it and how you came to
have that knowledge. If you choose to write, for example, on the draft, the
list of impressions you set down will be significantly different if you are
male instead of female, 19 instead of 45, a former draftee rather than an
exemptee, etc.

Writing is not only a process of communicating with someone else, but
a way of discovering and announcing who you are, as we have said. Students don't write themes; individuals, who happen to be students at the
time, do. Even a topic such as "Burnt match" will produce quite different
lists, quite different themes from someone who has had a good high school
chemistry course, someone with no chemistry course, someone with a poor
chemistry course. People don't react to objects objectively. Students who
do not understand this try to "write like everyone else" and often end up
writing like nobody at all.

For the sake of the example here, we either had to invent a personality, a highly artificial way to go about writing, or get ourselves a real person. We selected an apprehensive white male freshman who had not been

drafted, and had not been through a pre-induction physical, but had passed the first semester English composition course.

He made the list headed "Draft." We asked him to organize it into a theme, using what he had learned, and telling us what he was doing and thinking as he went along.

This is a summary of his account.

First, he grouped his impressions.

He put the figure 1 before the first item, "fear." Then he went down the list looking for items that seemed closely related to it. To do that he had to decide what he meant by rather cryptic notes. In a sense, everything on the list can be "feared" except the solution, but there is nothing on the list that corresponds in magnitude or quality to "fear." So he had a single item: 1—fear.

He put the figure 2 before the next item, "the Vietnam War." Then he went down the list and put a 2 in front of items closely related to it. Several suggested themselves. The "new draft system" arose during the Vietnam War, largely as a response to it. The question of "selective objection," objecting to a war, not to War, arose likewise, in the courts. The older system, with its many exemptions, was a hangover from World War II. From an equal-risk point of view, that system was shot through with inequities, or so the U.S. Congress decided when it changed the system.

Thus far, then, he had as figure 2

the Vietnam War
question of war itself
World War II
the old system
the new system: lottery
inequalities
selective objection
exemptions
minority groups

He put a 3 in front of the next open item, "possibility: volunteer army." Then he put a 3 in front of related items. Obviously this category deals with alternatives to the draft. The related items are

conscientious objectors
solution: no wars (!)
Canada
burning draft cards
prison

He put a 4 in front of the next open item, "registering," then a 4 in front of related items. The trouble is, they were already preempted. "Conscientious objectors" is a category of registration, but in the list it doesn't relate to registering as strongly as to alternatives to being drafted.

He put a 5 in front of the next open item, "parents." He couldn't put a 5 in front of related items because everything was preempted.

He had five groups then, three of them with only one item:

1 fear

2 the Vietnam War
   question of war itself
   World War II
   the old system
   the new system: lottery
   inequalities
   selective objection
   exemptions
   minority groups

3 possibility: a volunteer army
   conscientious objectors
   solution: no wars (!)
   Canada
   burning draft cards
   prison

4 registering

5 parents

That was not an outline, but a grouping of impressions. Several things were clear from the grouping. From this list was not going to emerge an objective theme on the workings of the draft. He did not have enough information for that, and most of the items didn't deal with that subject. The prominent items—at the beginning and the end—dealt with the writer's reactions to the draft: fear and his concern for the reactions of his parents. Maybe these two were one; it was hard to say. He assumed they were or were very nearly so.

Now he had to decide what he was going to say about the topic. So far he had succeeded only in getting impressions together in more or less logically related groups. Now the real decision had to be made: Where did he stand? and therefore, What did he want to say?

He read the list again. It was obvious that he didn't like the idea of being drafted, would avoid it if he could, but was almost equally afraid of the reaction of his parents. (Whether that point of view is admirable or contemptible is beside the point. It is a statement to the reader about the writer.)

Now he had to create a thesis sentence: a sentence that summarized what he would say in the order he was going to say it—not a title but a kind of guide and contract between reader and writer: "I hereby swear to develop these ideas in this order."

He wrote a working thesis sentence for this paper: "Because I don't want to be drafted, I have explored the alternatives, but I may choose none of them, since I don't want to hurt my parents."

The thesis took into account the divisions already made.

Now the subtopics had to be put in order.

The only problems were in 2 and 3. In 2 it was clear that "inequalities," "exemptions," and "minority groups" were part of "the old system" and that "the old system" was part of "World War II." This meant that the present order of discussion would not work. And in 3 it was equally clear that "conscientious objectors," "Canada," "burning draft cards," and "prison" went together, but not with "possibility: a volunteer army" and "solution: no wars (!)," although the last two belonged together. He could, of course, have made entirely separate subgroups of the two parts, but it seemed easier to put them in proper order and conjunction:

> burning draft cards
> Canada
> conscientious objectors
> no more wars
> volunteer army

The last item presented no problem except explaining what it meant. Obviously there is a conflict of attitude; that could be easily represented in the outline.

So he made an outline:

> Thesis: Because I don't want to be drafted, I have explored the alternatives, but I may choose none of them since I don't want to hurt my parents.
> I.   My opposition to the draft
> II. The draft in my lifetime
>   A. The Vietnam War vs. World War II
>   1. The old system and its inequalities
>   2. The new lottery system

III. The alternatives
    A. Burning draft card
    B. Canada
    C. Conscientious objector
    D. No more army
    E. Volunteer army
IV. My problem
    A. My parents' attitude
    B. My attitude

Our comment:

The outline could be objectionable on several counts, none of them impressive.

1. There is an A without a B. The "rule" that insists that every A must have a B, every 1 a 2, is based on either (a) a misplaced mathematical theory similar to the notorious "double negative," or (b) a rhetorical theory of balance that may be helpful but is a matter of opinion.

2. A and B under IV are blind topics since no one but the writer knows exactly what will be said there. Precisely. An outline is a skeleton organization, not a theme in miniature. It tells the writer where to go, in what order—nothing more. Readers don't read outlines; only writers do.

Then he wrote the theme—in thirty minutes.

Way Out or No Way Out?

Because I don't want to be drafted, I have explored the alternatives, but I may not take any of them, for a reason I'll explain in a minute.

I think I'm normal. I don't want to kill anyone, and I don't want to get killed. I don't want to lose years of my life in any war, particularly not in a war I don't understand and that I don't think anyone else does either. Maybe I'm a child of the Vietnam War.

That war called into question the morality of war itself. I have no real opinion on that. But the draft system also got called into question. The old system, the World War II system, worked well enough in a "popular" war, but when it was applied to this one, the faults showed up. I don't know all of them, but the old system certainly discriminated against the poor and minority groups by allowing exemptions to the educated and the well-to-do, although the deferments were called Occupational, Educational, etc. So we got the lottery system. It's fairer, in that it's random, but it doesn't solve my problem. For one thing, it doesn't allow selective objection. That is, it doesn't allow me to say, "I don't want to fight *this* war," and make that statement mean anything.

Well, in a way it does. I can say that and stick to it if I want to take the legal consequences. That's a polite name for some of the alternatives I've been considering.

I can burn my draft card; for that I'd probably go to prison.

I can run away to Canada; for that I might lose my citizenship or go to prison if I ever tried to come back.

I could try to get classified as a conscientious objector. I'd never make it. I don't really object to all wars. I don't know anything about all wars. If somebody asks me if I would have fought in World War I or the Spanish-American War or the Mexican War or the War of 1812, I don't know; I wasn't there.

I can dream up solutions. No wars, for example. That's not likely to happen, not here and now and maybe never. A volunteer army. That may happen, but probably not soon, not soon enough for me, because I keep reading that Congress is thinking about it. Congress takes a long time to think and a longer time to act.

All that is daydream. The facts, the two central facts, are that I'm going to be drafted if I don't do something and that I've got parents. My father is a veteran of World War II. Both he and my mother favor the Vietnam War, so much so that they even got upset when I called it the Indochina War, even while I was thinking "the Asian War." They say they understand the war very well. They talk about "halting the spread of international Communism," and I've heard about the "domino theory" until it's coming out my ears. I never met a Communist, and I don't think they have either. I don't see what a silly game has got to do with human life, unless that's a silly game too.

But I love my parents. I wouldn't hurt them for the world. They're *people,* people I know, not like Communists or dominoes or gooks or Congressmen. So maybe I've got to hurt somebody else, and myself, for them.

No masterpiece perhaps, and you may react violently to the content. But the theme is logically connected throughout; it conveys a point of view clearly and forcefully.

PARAGRAPH AND OUTLINE

Notice that the topics and subtopics in the outline frequently do not correspond to the paragraphing in the theme. Paragraphs are thought units, but they are also visual and rhetorical units; they have been since the time when "paragraph" simply meant a mark in the margin of a manuscript. They are not arithmetical units. Readers—except some college instructors—don't count words. They glance at the unit they must digest before pausing or passing on to the next. In this book, a 200-word paragraph is average. In a newspaper, that would be unacceptably long because of the format and the audience: narrow columns, hurried readers.

The idea that correct paragraphing is an exact science is pure superstition. A dozen editors will paragraph the same book in a remarkable variety of ways. Aside from the rigid convention that in dialog every change of speaker requires a new paragraph (and this is an aid to the reader, like most conventions in writing), there are no rules for paragraphing. Especially is there no rule that "every new thought requires a new paragraph"; every new sentence contains a new thought, and, on the other hand, if a piece of writing is connected properly throughout, no sentence begins an entirely new thought.

A reasonable writer will paragraph by reasonable principles:

1. **Paragraphing is first of all a convenience for the reader,** not a hard and fast division of the writer's thought. Paragraphs, therefore, ought to be of convenient size for the audience. What is too long for one audience may be too short for another. Paragraphs ought to be bite-size.

2. **Paragraphing is second a rhetorical technique.** Very short paragraphs call attention to themselves. Use too many and the reader will pay attention to none. When everything is emphasized, nothing is noticed. A biographer of Theodore Roosevelt once said that Teddy killed lions as if they were mosquitoes and mosquitoes as if they were lions. The trouble was that you couldn't tell the mosquitoes from the lions.

Very long paragraphs may irritate and even frighten the reader, even to the point where he delivers the supreme insult a reader can give a writer: he stops reading.

The competent writer considers the division of his thought, the format of his page (typescript, longhand, page print, column print), and his reader. Then he paragraphs for the convenience of the reader, by the visual demands of his format, according to the divisions of this thought. Practicing that is simpler and easier than writing down the principle behind it.[1]

ORGANIZING

It's disturbing to hear a student say, "I can write sentences but I can't paragraph," or "I write beautiful outlines and lousy themes," or "I can write, but I can't outline." Paragraphing, outlining, and constructing sentences all have one thing in common: they are ways of organizing what is going on in your head. Organizing in writing means simply to get things arranged so that the reader can comprehend with the least distress. Dif-

---

[1] Paragraphs do, of course, have internal pattern and organization. For these patterns, see Chapter Ten.

ferent readers are distressed by different things; but it is reasonable to suppose that most readers are most distressed when they can't see the connections between ideas. Outlines, paragraphs, and sentences are simply devices that make organization possible. An organized paper shows the relationship of what comes before to what comes after. An organized paper is a unit. And there is always something *before* that first sentence on paper ("What was I thinking?"), just as there is always something after the last sentence ("What do *you* think?").

There are, of course, mechanical devices that help the reader see what the writer sees; they are guides furnished the reader by the writer, and they ought to be used intelligently, consistently. For example:

1. **The title.** A good title states the subject, limits it, implies the writer's attitude toward it, and therefore prepares the reader. "Narcotics," for example, is a subject heading for an encyclopedia article or a ten-volume research series, not a title for a theme. "Legalizing Marijuana" is a topic, not a title. "My Roommate, Mary Jane" is a title for a theme, as is its less clever counterpart, "Pot and the Lonely Freshman."

2. **The thesis sentence.** A thesis sentence summarizes what you are going to say in the order in which you are going to say it. It assumes that a title exists; the thesis sentence does not repeat the title but refines it.

3. **The format.** Readers judge by appearances; that is all they have to go by. Professional writers are very careful about the appearance of their words on the page. That is why they read their articles and books first in galley proof and then in page proof. At each stage they send back corrections to the publisher and printer that involve not only mishaps in spelling but alignment of the print, quality of the paper, size of the type, and, occasionally, the ancestry of the typesetter. *The reader sees the page, not the individual words alone.* That is the way reading is done, universally—first the reader sees the page, then he works down to the individual words.

For the past century accuracy on the typed or printed page has been part of the *message* the piece of writing sends. What you write is a visual message. A student who doesn't type well hopes his instructor will chalk up his mechanical atrocities to typographical error. The fact is that if you take up the machine, you are responsible for the machine. The reader sees only appearances, whether it is manuscript or typescript, print or etchings. A carelessly produced theme says exactly that about you to the reader. **In the twentieth century there is no difference between a typographical error and a mental error.**

ALTERNATIVES

Possibly you don't want to write on a topic like "The Draft" and therefore our earlier example was not particularly useful. Suppose, then, you choose or are assigned to write on "Telephones." The procedure is the same.

Assume you have made the list headed "Telephones." Put the figure 1 before the first item, "wonderful invention." Then go down the list looking for other items that seem to be closely related to this. To do this intelligently you will have to decide just what you mean by "wonderful." If you are thinking of the technical aspects, you will find "different kinds" and "party lines," and you could add a few more at the bottom, such as "direct dialing" and "coaxial cables." But if you are thinking of the human values, the only two that seem related are "saves lots of time" and "calling home." Put 1's before these, and see if there is anything more you want to write about in this area. Perhaps you might add at the bottom "making dates" and "checking on assignments," also marked with 1's.

Then put a 2 before the first remaining unmarked item, "different kinds," and 2's before the other items dealing with equipment. You could add more related items here, too; but possibly you decide that you are not interested in writing on this phase, and that you will have enough without discussing it, especially if you put in a few examples. Cross out these items, and put a new 2 before "sometimes a nuisance." All the others may seem related to this, and could also be marked with 2's; but "talking too long" suggests a garrulous neighbor who annoys you so much that she deserves at least a paragraph to herself. Mark that one with a 3, and add a few other 3's, about the details. (Of course, if you make your expenses by selling over the phone, or if you like to rush from the bathtub to hear a sweet voice telling you that you have been chosen to receive a tinted, enlarged portrait absolutely free if you'll just buy six small black-and-white ones at the special bargain price of only ten dollars, you will make a different grouping.) Otherwise, your list might look like this:

TELEPHONES

---

1 wonderful invention
~~2 different kinds~~
1 saves lots of time
2 sometimes a nuisance

2 salesmen
1 calling home
~~2 party lines~~
3 talking too long
2 children on phone
2 wrong numbers
2 "you have been chosen"
~~2 public phones~~
1 making dates
1 checking on assignments
3 Mrs. E. talks forever
3 calls at mealtimes
3 has a draggy voice
3 tells all her symptoms
3 if only they were fatal!

The next step is to rearrange these items in something like the order you will use in your paper. Since you have three sets of numbers, it seems logical to divide the paper into three paragraphs: one on the advantages, one on the incidental nuisances, and one on the particular nuisance that you want to treat in detail. There is no fixed rule about which should come first, but it happens that the order just mentioned seems logical—you can begin by conceding that the telephone has some value, go on to a big *but*, and wind up with a heartfelt cry woe. If you want a different emphasis, you will need a different arrangement; but you should decide your line of development now. It will take a little time to rewrite the list, but not nearly as much as it would to keep on going up and down to make sure you were not leaving anything out. You therefore rearrange the list as follows:

A.   wonderful invention
    saves lots of time
    calling home
    making dates
    checking on assignments

B.   sometimes a nuisance
    salesmen
    children on phone
    wrong numbers
    "you have been chosen"

C. talking too long
    Mrs. E. talks forever
    calls at mealtimes
    has a draggy voice
    tells all her symptoms
    if only they were fatal!

Next, decide in what order you are going to take up the points in each paragraph. You want to get the most closely related items together, and to move in a definite direction instead of zigzagging back and forth. Various arrangements are possible, but the following seems reasonable, and can be indicated without recopying:

A. 1 wonderful invention
    2 saves a lot of time
    5 calling home
    4 making dates
    3 checking on assignments

B. 1 sometimes a nuisance
    4 salesmen
    3 children on phone
    2 wrong numbers
    5 "you have been chosen"

C. 1 talking too long
    2 Mrs. E. talks forever
    4 calls at mealtimes
    3 has a draggy voice
    5 tells all her symptoms
    6 if only they were fatal!

Now you can begin to write.

At the first attempt this may seem to be a rather complicated method of working out a paper. Probably nobody needs it every time, and you may not ever need it, but a good many students have found out that it saves time in the long run. You know what you are doing, step by step, and you do your selecting and rearranging in the most economical way. You are not so likely to have to throw away whole pages that have taken a long time to write, or to find yourself tacking on at the end things that should have gone in much earlier.

FORETHOUGHT AND AFTERTHOUGHT

It may seem safer to write about telephones than about the draft. After all, you might irritate your instructor with your opinions on a controversial subject. (You might, of course, put him to sleep with another kind of subject.)

The important point is that people write well about things they care about. If you care about telephones, or about making your reader laugh or cry about telephones, or about awakening him to certain facts about telephones, or about letting him know who you are by using telephones as the subject matter, you can probably write competently about telephones. But, except among the very best professionals, a writer bored with his subject matter writes a boring theme. If a theme is considered merely an exercise in mechanics, it is something less than writing.

This, of course, raises a question we touched only lightly before. What do you do with assigned topics? Consider the other side of the question: Why does an instructor assign topics? Probably for several reasons:

1. Because some students are simply baffled when asked to choose their own, either because they are startled by the unfamiliar permissiveness, or because they have so many topics in mind that they cannot choose among them without enormous waste of time.

2. Because the instructor believes that he can judge where the class stands at the moment by comparing their performances on a given topic.

3. Because the topic is related to something you were supposed to read or investigate and what the instructor is judging is something besides and beyond your prose style.

4. Because the instructor knows that the bright student can find an angle, aspect, or point of view on almost any subject that will be of interest to him and to the reader.

5. Because the instructor knows that much of the writing you will do in college and out will, alas, be on assigned topics; you had better train yourself now.

A FEW RECOMMENDED PRACTICES

Your instructor may give you his own set of instructions about the mechanical rules to follow in writing a paper. If he does, you will be wise to do all your griping about his unreasonableness at one session. Then forget about it, clip the instructions in your notebook, and follow them religiously. It saves so much time. Save your wild, free spirit of independence for more important things. If he does not give you special instructions, those listed below will probably prove satisfactory.

1. **Always leave adequate margins.** An inch and a half at the top and on the left, and an inch at the bottom and on the right is the general rule. Remember that the right-hand margin is the margin of error, especially on typed papers. You need room for an occasional word to go over without running clear off the page or requiring a hyphen where the rules don't permit it.

2. **Leave space between your lines.** On a typewriter, double space. In longhand, use wide-lined paper. If you have only narrow-lined paper, write on every other line.

3. **Don't write too many words on a line.** Even when very compact writing is legible, it has an irritating effect. We become used to reading at a certain rate of speed. If we find we are taking twice as long as usual to read a page, we are likely to feel resentful.

4. **Don't make your writing deliberately difficult to read** on the theory that it will be hard for your instructor to prove you are wrong. You may arouse his combative instinct.

5. **Use a legible writing instrument.** If your instructor says that he will accept papers written in pencil, he means about a number 2 lead. Very soft pencils smudge. Very hard ones are practically unreadable by artificial light. Don't use a worn-out typewriter ribbon. It is even harder on you than on your instructor. You won't notice half your mistakes. He may get annoyed and concentrate on looking for them.

A STRONGLY RECOMMENDED PRACTICE

For some students few of the suggestions made in this chapter are going to be of much use because they do not take into account one obstacle. Call it fear. Some students freeze mentally when faced with paper, pen, and an assignment. Whether that paralysis is a result of unhappy past experiences, an unwillingness to put oneself on public display, a fear of doing things wrong, or a combination of these, it produces the same kind of paper: stiff, unnatural, and quite unlike the everyday speech of the writer—a sort of bad ventriloquism. If part of the benefit of writing is self discovery, no real self is ever going to be discovered in or through that kind of writing.

There is a way to remove that obstacle. It rests on the proposition that a student writes first to discover what he thinks and only second to communicate what he thinks, and it requires the cooperation of the student and the instructor.

The student must agree to write something, at least a paragraph and preferably a page, every day. The instructor must agree not to mark or grade those papers, although he will read them, day by day, and when the student asks advice, the instructor will give it. In effect, the instructor only overhears the papers.

The procedure is this:

1. The student is to select his own topic without worrying about whether he "knows enough about it" or not. The only restriction is that the topic should be one that touches him personally.

2. He is to write down whatever words are going through his head without worrying about spelling, punctuation, sentence structure, or organization.

3. He is to tell the truth as he sees it without worrying about the instructor's agreement or approval.

4. He is not to revise what he has written once he has finished any piece, although of course he can alter anything in the process of writing. If he sees something later that he wishes to change, he should simply make a mental note to avoid that "mistake" in the next piece. This is an exercise in writing, not rewriting.

5. He is to keep his papers after the instructor has read them. After two weeks of writing, he is to meet with the instructor to go over the papers so that both may say what they find good in them. Unless the student requests it, the instructor is not to "correct" the papers. There is to be no talk of spelling, punctuation, etc., but of the speaking voice that comes through the papers irrespective of formal considerations.

If several students in a class have this basic difficulty, some instructors will use the method on a broader scale: the whole class may go to free writing and the audience for the papers can then be the class as a whole. From free writing often emerges the speaking voice and from class reaction—focused in the beginning on the positive aspects of the papers—often comes confidence and the conviction that a private voice from a unique world can be both interesting and valuable. And as students comment on each other's work, the qualities that enable the private voice to communicate effectively—clarity of detail, careful focus, simplicity of language—emerge as the ingredients of good writing. When textbooks say the same thing it is somehow never as impressive.

It should be understood that although this is a remedial process, it is not designed specifically for remedial students in the sense in which that phrase is often used today. The brightest student in a class may have a mental block about writing, especially if he has spent several years being taught to write in one dialect on pre-selected topics of little interest to him and if the response to his writing has been a ritual bloodletting in the margins and at the end of his papers. He may have so warped his own voice that it is unrecognizable, even to himself.

EXERCISES

Imagine that one of the lists below represents your own associations with the listed subject. Continue the process necessary for developing a theme in this manner. (1) Group related items; (2) eliminate those that do not fit easily into the emerging pattern; (3) add new items that are suggested by the emerging pattern; (4) decide on the order in which the groups should appear in the finished theme; and finally (5) arrange items in some logical order within each group. Write the theme only if specifically requested to do so by your instructor.

STARTING COLLEGE

picking courses	moving into the dorms
registration	buying books
paying fees	meeting your roommate
finding classrooms	saying goodbye to parents
learning the campus	meeting new people

THE STUDENT CAFETERIA

expensive	jukebox selections
cold food	hours of service
unfriendly personnel	waiting in line
greasy hamburgers	small portions
noisy	stale desserts

THE HIPPIE-RADICAL-FREAK STEREOTYPE

long hair	lazy
blue denim bells	leftist politics
beards	musical tastes
drugs	Stop the War
the New Morality	courageous

Suggestions for Discussion or Theme Writing

On a topic of current campus interest draw up items in class discussion and list them on the chalkboard. As a class, proceed with steps 1, 2, 3, and 4 as in the exercise above. If the instructor assigns it, write the theme individually, outside of class. Compare results.

AREAS

OF

USAGE

Standard English is the kind of English that is, on the whole, used by people of education and standing in the community; and it is standard simply because such people use it. We will get along much faster if we can manage to get rid of the mysterious idea of "perfect English." There just isn't any such thing. Even our best speakers do not all use the language in the same way, and there are times when we can't possibly satisfy Jones without running into criticism from Smith. But when Smith, Jones, and Robinson all agree that "I saw" is respectable and "I seen" is ignorant, we'll get along with them better if we adopt their practice.

Fifty years ago there was a general, though vague, belief that it was the duty of grammarians to lay down rules for the correct use of the language, and the duty of everybody else (except, perhaps, certain lovable characters who spoke in amusing dialects) to obey them. This belief has not entirely disappeared, but it is no longer respectable. Linguists now generally agree that a grammarian has no more right to say how people ought to talk than a chemist has to say how molecules ought to interact. The laws of grammar are like the laws of any other science, simply generalized statements about what does happen, not directives about what should—and they are subject to revision as soon as any new evidence comes in.

Since this new attitude sounds both scientific and democratic, it would take a bold man to call it wrong; but it takes only a reasonably careful man to say that it has to be analyzed rather thoughtfully before it can safely be adopted for general classroom use. Otherwise we will have no answer for Joe, who takes the logical view that if grammar is based on usage, usage obviously can't be based on grammar—therefore anybody can talk exactly as he pleases; and if he is accused of violating the rules of grammar, he can answer: "Nonsense. If the grammarians don't recognize the way I talk it just shows that their rules are inaccurate or incomplete."

Now, of course Joe can talk exactly as he pleases if he is willing to take the social and other consequences; and of course the grammarian's rules are incomplete. With hundreds of millions of people talking as much as they do, a grammarian cannot possibly analyze more than a very small sampling of the language. He realizes, of course, that there are many varieties of English, and he probably takes a very broad-minded view about them all, because he finds them all interesting. As a scientist he is not in the least inclined to say that standard English is *intrinsically* better than any of the other varieties; and he is certainly not inclined to tell the native speakers of standard that they should change any of their habits to conform to his private idea of what the language ought to be like. But he is in a position to say something like this:

> These are the patterns of standard English. Anybody who is not sure that his own language is standard may use them as models. As a grammarian I can't say that they are better than any other patterns; but as an observer of American life I can say that they are generally believed to be more useful.

USAGE, GRAMMAR, AND RHETORIC

Usage is a very broad term used to cover the complete set of language habits of a person or a group—vocabulary, pronunciation, mechanics, and so forth, as well as strictly grammatical matters. *Grammar* refers to those patterns of word form, word order, "function words" (such as connectives and auxiliary verbs), and intonation which make up the general structural patterns of the language. Thus the difference between "We saw him" and "We seen him" is a matter of grammar, because it involves a structural principle that would apply to many other sentences; but the difference between "The youngsters interfered with the proceedings" and "The punks loused up the works" is one of usage. Grammatically these last two sentences are exactly parallel.

Obviously, standard English involves more than grammar, but in this country grammar is particularly important. Anybody who has seen *My Fair Lady,* or seen or read Shaw's *Pygmalion,* on which it is based, will realize that in England pronunciation is the sacred thing. Eliza can safely use any words or constructions that she cares to, as long as she pronounces them acceptably. An American Eliza could speak with anything from a "southern drawl" to a "midwestern twang" without being suspected of imposture; but if she got tangled up with her verb and pronoun forms, the other ladies would be exchanging meaningful glances.

Rhetoric is concerned with *effective* rather than (or in addition to) "correct" communication. Such rules as "Avoid short, choppy sentences" and "Don't begin a sentence with *and*" are rhetorical rather than grammatical. They are reasonably good general advice, but may be disregarded at any time by a writer who knows what he is doing. Since the effectiveness of a passage depends on the speaker, the audience, and the situation as well as on the choice and arrangement of words, absolute rules about it are never reliable. This does *not* mean that rhetoric is unimportant. A moron can learn grammar by simple exposure if he is lucky enough to be brought up in the right surroundings. It is sound rhetoric that distinguishes a good writer or speaker from a bad one.

COMMUNICATION AND ETIQUETTE

The rules of grammar may be divided roughly into two groups— those that make for clear communication, and those that deal with the etiquette or the language. When we are learning a foreign language we are particularly concerned with those of the first group. We want to be able to understand as accurately as possible things said in that language, and we want to be understood when we use it. If we manage to do these two things reasonably well, we are usually satisfied. Any minor errors we make will probably be forgiven us.

Our emphasis is quite different when we study English grammar. The rules we take most seriously deal with the forms of words; yet it is rather seldom that an incorrect English form really interferes with understanding. Two of the chief reasons for the study of grammar are that it can help us to talk and write in such a way as to gain the respect of those with whom we communicate, and it can increase our self-confidence and peace of mind. Indirectly, this increases the probability of our being understood.

Worrying about our grammar often distracts us from a clear presentation of our ideas; and if our uncertainty shows, or our usage is of a kind not generally admired, people may not listen to us as carefully as they otherwise would.

SHIBBOLETHS

Perhaps the best answer to the theory that etiquette is secondary to communication is a bit of Biblical history. When the ancient Hebrews were engaged in a civil war, one group, on a particularly dark night, had control of a ford. Members of both sides were trying to cross the river, and it was too dark to tell friend from foe. Somebody hit upon the idea of making everybody who wanted to cross pronounce the word *shibboleth*, because it happened that those of the "wrong" group had trouble with the *sh* sound. Anybody who pronounced the word "correctly" as *shibboleth* was allowed to cross. Anybody who pronounced it *sibboleth* was killed. Of course the pronunciation *sibboleth* did not prove anything against his virtue or intelligence; but it did prove that, for the purpose of immediate survival, he had been born on the wrong side of the tracks.

We do not usually act quite so drastically about modern shibboleths; but it is hardly necessary to argue that failure to conform to certain standards can seriously handicap a man's social and business career. We may feel very strongly that this should not be so; we cannot deny that at present it *is*.

Another thing we must realize is that some important grammatical habits have nothing whatever to do with logic. We know from experience that the man who says "I seen" or "them apples" is greeted with more raised eyebrows than the man who misplaces his modifiers or calls anything more complicated than a screwdriver a "doohickey." This is a simple matter of cause and effect. Since word forms have little to do with making meaning clear, they are more often learned by unconscious imitation than by deliberate study. They indicate background rather than ability, which makes them perfect shibboleths.

A shibboleth is by its very nature completely unreasonable. If the other side had held the ford, a different pronunciation would have been the key to survival. The same principle holds true today. "It is me" may get you a low mark in an English class, but "It is I" may get you blackballed by the Elks. Which gives rise to the natural question, "Short of being a chameleon, what is a man supposed to do?"

Actually, the situation is not quite so bad as it sounds. We may find it advisable to shift gears occasionally, but a man who talks "standard

English" comfortably and as a matter of course, without giving the impression that he is smug about his own language or overcritical about that of others, can usually get along as well in an Elks Club or a cow camp as at a meeting of a learned society. And the requirements of standard English are not nearly as numerous or as mysterious as many people seem to believe. We don't really have to worry about offending those precious souls who are upset by anything that a dictionary marks "colloquial." If we master the most important shibboleths, learn something about the structure of the language, and pay some attention to the speech and writing of people whose language habits we admire, most of us can get along very well.

AREAS OF USAGE

As we have already seen, the variety of usage with which grammarians usually deal, and to which educated people in general try to conform, is often called *standard*. The diagram below is intended to indicate the relations of standard to several other kinds of usage. It should be noticed that none of the lines are solid. Many of the words and expressions are common to several of the areas, and even the outer limits of the language cannot be exactly defined. There is also room for unlimited argument over exactly where the inner lines should be drawn. Nevertheless, the areas indicated are, in a general way, recognizable; and if we freely admit the existence of numerous borderline cases, the diagram may be of some use. At least it is more informative than one which indicates only "good" and "bad" English, or one which shows differences only as "levels." We should recognize that one way of saying things may differ from another without necessarily being better or worse.

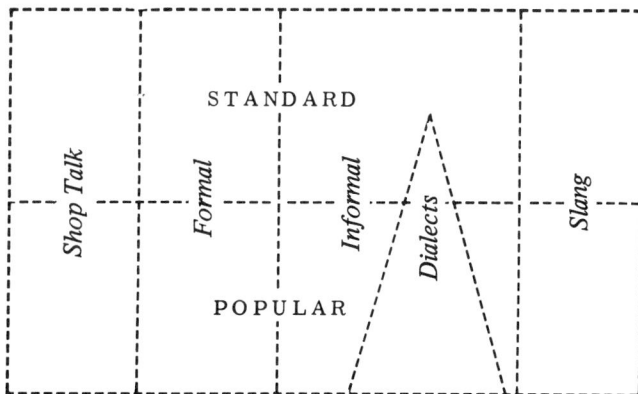

FORMAL AND INFORMAL VARIETIES OF STANDARD ENGLISH

In spite of a few minor differences, the general characteristics of standard English are surprisingly uniform throughout the country. If it is used naturally it will usually be respected in any sort of company. Of course, anybody who uses it with an air of showing off will arouse some resentment. And the man who regards it as a mysterious ceremony, and tries too hard to avoid ever making a mistake, is going to be consistently uncomfortable and occasionally ridiculous. Except for a few uses of verb and pronoun forms, the differences between standard and "popular" English are not nearly so great as is often supposed. They certainly do not justify the very widespread feeling that when there is the least cause for doubt, whatever sounds natural must be wrong.

The curious theory that standard English has to be formal has probably done more harm than any other idea connected with the language. Many of our best books and public speeches, to say nothing of letters and conversations, are definitely informal, and not a bit the worse for being so. The difference between formal and informal English is a matter of style and attitude, rather than of "level." Yet an amazing number of students have clearly been taught that only the formal variety of standard is truly legitimate, and that the term "colloquial" is practically equivalent to "illiterate."

It is impossible to draw an exact line between formal and informal English. In general, formal English is more impersonal. It does not emphasize the individuality of the speaker or writer, and it takes little account of the personal qualities of the audience. It is often rather bookish, and makes use of a larger and more exact vocabulary than we ordinarily meet in general conversation. It avoids shortcuts, such as contractions, abbreviations, and omissions. Its sentences tend to be longer, and their parts are more carefully fitted together. It is particularly appropriate to ceremonial occasions, and to serious communications addressed to comparatively expert audiences. Those who have been trained to respond to it may enjoy the precision and careful construction which are its best qualities.

On the other hand, formal English is likely to lack force and vividness. The very fact that it is formal implies that it depends more on arbitrary conventions than on natural speech habits, and it therefore demands more effort and concentration on the part of the audience. Some of them will find its longer and more complicated sentences confusing. Even people who are pleased by the sound often find it hard to get through to the sense.

In choosing how formal to be on a given occasion, we should consider both the effect we want to produce and our ability to produce it. A speaker who attempts more formality than feels completely natural to him is likely to seem pompous to his audience. An exaggerated informality is equally likely to leave an impression of poor taste.

It seems reasonable to insist on standard usage in a classroom, but to let each student choose the degree of formality that suits his own temperament, so that he can talk to educated people without feeling either incompetent or unnatural. After all, the principal champions of strictly formal English today seem to be the writers of government bulletins and certain kinds of textbooks. If we are to take them as models, the world will become a gloomier place.

POPULAR ENGLISH

If a man says, "I dont have any more of those apples," he is talking standard English. If he says, "I ain't got no more of them apples," he is talking something else, though it isn't easy to decide just what to call it. The terms *illiterate, vulgar,* and *substandard* have been used to describe this sort of speech. The term *popular* English now seems to be gaining ground, and will be used here. In this sense *popular* does not mean "generally liked" but "characteristic of the populace or great mass of the people."

In spite of the general schoolroom attitude, there is nothing shameful about popular usage. It is the normal language of millions of intelligent and self-respecting people (as well as some others), and nobody has ever proved that it is essentially inferior to standard. Nonetheless, a man who uses it is likely to be handicapped in both his business and his social career, simply because we generally associate it with the lower social and economic levels. Most people who have any interest in getting along in life would rather talk standard English if it were not made too hard or presented as too unnatural. About the only ones who make a deliberate effort to use popular seem to be certain politicians and salesmen who think they get along better by making a point of being "plain folks." Some of the most common popular departures from standard usage are pointed out in the INDEX TO USAGE.

DIALECTS

The word *dialect,* as used by a linguist, is not a term of reproach. **It means simply the kind of language used by a limited group.** Since English is not spoken uniformly over the enormous territory where it is used, everybody who speaks it must speak some dialect of it (or some mixture of dialects). Three major dialect areas have long been recognized in American English—New England, Western or General American, and Southern. Linguistic geographers now prefer the terms Northern, Midland, and Southern, with appropriate subdivisions. Whichever terms we use, the most obvious differences between the three are in pronunciation and intonation. We can often identify a man as a New Englander or a Southerner after hearing him say a few words, though we might read hundreds of pages of his writing without being able to guess where he came from.

There are people who regard General American as *the* language of the country, and believe that the other two should be conscientiously driven out. There are others who believe that the New England variety is our only truly cultured form of speech and that it should therefore be extended over the vastly greater areas where the other two varieties are normally spoken. And there are many Southerners who are quite sure that their way of speaking is best, though they usually show no particular desire to improve the habits of the rest of the country. On the whole, however, it is now rather generally accepted (at least by linguists) that the three major dialects are on an exactly equal footing. Possibly they will merge in the future. Meanwhile, we may use the terms *standard* and *popular* English to extend across all three.

Within the three major dialectal areas, there are any number of minor dialects and subdialects, some of which are far from standard. Nonlinguists ordinarily use the word *dialect* only in referring to these, and frequently imply that they are inferior to, as well as different from, the standard language. Some of these minor dialects, such as Pennsylvania Dutch, show a strong influence of the original language of the speakers or their ancestors. This may appear in vocabulary and construction as well as in pronunciation. These characteristics have been preserved by some sort of isolation, either physical, as in the Southern hill country, or social, as in many tightly knit national, religious, or occupational groups.

American dialects have never differed nearly as much as those in many other countries, and during the past fifty years their differences have decreased in both number and degree. This is due partly to such influences as movies, radio, TV, and more nearly universal education; partly to the fact that more people move around the country. Nevertheless, many regional variations remain. They are naturally more marked among people of limited education than among those who, through reading, schooling, and association, have had more experience with standard English; but to some extent they are found in all levels of speech.

A "dialectal" word or expression is therefore one of limited currency. Used in its own area, it is exactly as good as it is thought to be. *Goober*, for instance, is a perfectly good word for *peanut* in Georgia. But it may not be understood in Oregon.

Aside from the question of whether dialect will be understood, using it away from its natural range may have either of two opposite effects. Some people will tend to approve of it as strange and therefore fascinating; others will feel that it is strange and therefore inferior. The general effect probably depends more on the attitude of the speaker than on the proportion of dialectal expressions he uses. Either an aggressive insistence on dialect or an overanxious effort to avoid it is likely to create a bad impression.

SHOP TALK OR TECHNICAL LANGUAGE

Both standard and popular English can be used over the whole range of our general interests. **The term *shop talk* covers a large number of specialized sets of usages in which various groups talk about matters of particular concern to themselves.** These range from the technical *jargon* of scholars and scientists to the *cant* of hobos and criminals.

Shop talk cannot be given a separate level from standard and popular English. It lies alongside them rather than above or below. Some varieties are used largely by people of considerable education and standing, and are quite as "good," within their narrower range, as standard. Others are clearly of no higher standing than popular.

The chief question about shop talk that arises in schools is whether it is permissible to carry it over into nontechnical communications. Some people argue, for instance, that a bank can *loan* money, but that a friend can only *lend* a book. This is carrying a theory rather far. It is usually inadvisable to talk to people in terms that confuse them or give them a low opinion of us. But the standard language is always changing and growing, and shop talk is one of the natural sources of its growth. Each expression must be judged by the effect it apparently has, not by the one it theoretically should have.

SLANG

If there is a man living who can explain satisfactorily why *bonehead* is a slang word and *blockhead* a respectable literary term, he would do a great service by making his explanation public. Until he does, we shall have to agree that although "everybody knows" there is an area called slang, nobody can define it with any certainty.

Slang might be called a novelty language; and like most novelties, slang expressions are likely to be in doubtful taste at the beginning, and even more likely to grow tiresome by too much repetition. It is impossible to estimate how many of them flicker and die out before the general public even becomes aware of them. Even those that sweep the country usually last only a short time. A few years after their vogue they may be completely unknown to the younger generation, and pathetic even to those who remember them. Yet many of them are so effective that much of the sparkle would die out of the language if all slang should come to an end.

At its best, slang is a vivid, cheerful, and often poetical way of speaking. It depends largely on metaphors, usually uncomplimentary ones. Such expressions as *stuffed shirts* and *sob sisters* would be hard to replace from the literary language. Brevity is another common characteristic. This may take the form of substitution of a short word for an unrelated long one (*crate* for *airplane*); of mangled abbreviation (*prexy* for *president*); or of simple shortening (*rep* for *reputation*).

Not all such shortenings are generally considered as slang, and it is impossible to draw a clear line. Perhaps the best test—admittedly not very definite—is whether the reason is simple economy of effort or space (*taxi, phone*), or an attitude that is playful (*prof*).

A slang expression may become so completely a part of the standard language that its origin is forgotten. A good many of our most respected polysyllables can be explained only on the theory that the ancient Romans had a pretty taste for slang—for instance, *recalcitrant* (kicking back) and *supercilious* (having eyebrows). On the other hand, if a slang expression happens to be particularly convenient, it may gain almost universal use in spite of continual opposition. *O.K.* has probably been attacked as unceasingly as any word in the language; and it is certainly now one of the most widely used terms on earth.

Even if it does not win a permanent place in the language, a slang term may enjoy a high social standing during its lifetime. A desire to be in fashion is just as characteristic of hunt clubs as of poolrooms; and a phrase, like a hat, may seem delightful one year even though it is destined to be hopelessly out of date the next.

For these reasons the rather common schoolroom attitude that all slang is an evil to be opposed at all times seems silly as well as hopeless. If used with reasonable judgment, slang can be a valuable ingredient in any but the most formal language—and even there a dash of it is not always out of place. Roosevelt and Churchill both knew this—and even people who dislike their politics seldom deny their mastery of the language.

There are, however, a few tendencies that are worth avoiding:

1. *The lazy use.* Some speakers seem to feel that the plentiful use of slang terms will conceal the fact that they are not saying (or perhaps thinking) anything in particular. It may be no worse intellectually to call everything we approve *swell, slick, cool,* or whatever term happens to be in fashion, than to use such older words as *nice* or *fine* just as loosely; but

the flashy character of the slang terms helps to deceive their users into the belief that they are communicating information.

2. *The show-off use.* Slang is often used to prove that the speaker is an up-to-the-minute insider. The latest phrases are worn like costume jewelry rather than used as language, and whoever can wear most and jangle them most often apparently gets the highest mark. This form of amusement has a natural enough attraction for teenagers, but if retained beyond adolescence it is likely to strike observers as pathetic, and it certainly should not be mistaken for a form of communication.

3. *The apologetic use.* A speaker is responsible for everything he says. If he chooses to use a slang term, he should do it firmly, and not apologize by putting it in quotation marks, either written or suggested by the tone of voice. (Since this is one of the very few places in this book where the writers take a firm moral stand, it is hoped that readers will be suitably impressed.)

4. *The deliberately vulgar use.* Some people use slang not merely in the bubble-pricking fashion which is natural to it, but in a deliberate effort to reduce every statement to its lowest and ugliest terms. This does not necessarily indicate a naturally obscene mind. Often it appears to spring from a fear that the speaker will be considered square if he does not continually demonstrate that he is hip. Since the habit grows out of a feeling of personal uncertainty, it is not likely to impress anybody who does not share the feeling.

EXERCISES

I. Characterize as best you can the *speaker* or *writer* of each of the following statements. Then try to describe the *situation* in which the statements would likely appear, including the listener or reader. Finally, try to assign the statement to an area of usage.

1. Jeez, honey, your fingernails are a mess!

2. When Nancy talked about dating my roommate, I think she was putting me on.

3. When Nancy talked about dating my roommate, I think she was "putting me on."

4. He's down by the pumphouse, eating goober peas an' studyin'.

5. I found him sitting behind the pumphouse, eating peanuts and staring into space.

6. Like that cat come on strong till I eyeballed him, stern-like, and put down that honky jive.

7. In the modern world of today we all must be aware of current events and not evade their consequences.

8. Especially today, no man can evade the consequences of national policy.

II. The point is sometimes lost, in discussions of areas of usage, that any area is distinguished not only by its vocabulary and diction, but by its rhetoric and grammar—that is, by its sentence structure, punctuation, syntax, etc.

Select a theme (or themes) from the last class assignment and reproduce it for the class, either by reading it aloud or dittoing it. Then analyze it in terms of its area of usage. Is it consistent? Where does it move from one area to another? Is there good reason for doing that?

III. One has a right to expect that the first paragraph of this chapter, which deals with standard English, be written in standard English. Look at the paragraph and then:

1. In a paragraph, define standard English by using the first paragraph of the chapter as an example.

2. In a paragraph, attack the first paragraph as nonstandard.

3. Rewrite the first paragraph, using another area of usage.

IV. Discuss the changes in cultural climate that have produced first tremors and then a barely perceptible fissure in standard English.

V. Although standard English is the language of power and control, it may not in some cases enable you to exercise control, that is, to communicate an idea or to move an audience. Words and language rhythms that work in one context may not work in another.

Write three versions of a single paragraph explaining your views on a controversial subject. Envision a different audience for each. For example, you may write a paragraph about women's liberation which you will deliver to your fellow students, to a young all-male blue-collar audience, and to a woman's club gathering at which most of the audience are middle-aged housewives.

PEOPLE,
THINGS,
AND
WORDS

SOME LIMITATIONS OF LANGUAGE

Many people have said that language is the most important of all human activities. Some of them have added that learning to talk is the most remarkable intellectual achievement that most people ever manage. We could devote a number of pages to discussing each of these statements, but we will settle for the simple statement that language is both very important and extremely complicated. We can then examine at our leisure a rather less obvious statement: Although almost everybody learns to use language after a fashion, most people don't do it very well, at least partly because they take it so much for granted that they never give any real thought to how it works.

People use language to talk about things, objects, relations, and actions, and to talk to other people. **Language, then, is a way of connecting people and things, and people and people.** But it can connect them only if it fits reasonably well at both ends. And since the general structure of our language was worked out thousands of years before our present ideas of the human nervous system and the structure of matter were developed, we can hardly expect that a good fit will be automatic.

Let's concern ourselves first with language as a connection between people and things.

Suppose you were a medieval sailor who came across a lemon for the first time, and later you wanted to describe it to a friend. You could tell him how big it was, and what shape, and what color. You could describe the skin and the segments and the seeds. You might even give him some idea of how it tasted by comparing it to other fruits you both already knew. But you could not tell him about its cell structure or its vitamin content, because you would have no way of perceiving these things, or even guessing about them. Naturally there would be no word for vitamin in your language, and the word for cell could not yet be applied to a tiny unit of living matter of a kind which nobody had yet seen through a microscope, or even imagined. **Our language is always *limited by what we know*. And at their best our statements describe not things as they are but things *as we perceive them*.**

WHEN IRON WAS SOLID AND THE EARTH WAS FLAT

When our remote ancestors developed the language from which ours is descended, they were necessarily trying to describe the world *as they knew it*; and they could examine it only with their unaided senses. Their reasoning may have been every bit as good as ours is today, but their data were inadequate. Consider a man of the Iron Age, looking at a bar of the iron for which we have named his period. When he called it solid he meant solid, because as far as he could tell it was a simple, continuous, uniform substance. It was *solid* as a child means the word—and as most of us do, too, when we are not really thinking about it.

Some of the Greeks later figured out that it couldn't really be that solid, because if it were it would be totally indestructible. Democritus said that it must be composed of tiny, invisible particles, which might be rubbed off by enough force, or between which a cold chisel might be forced. But he thought of the particles as *tightly packed, uniform*, and *at rest*. What made the bar iron rather than lead was simply that it was composed of iron particles rather than lead particles. Iron was one substance and lead was another. He had no reason to suppose that the bar would change in the slightest degree, if it was protected from rust and other outside damage.

And he had no reason to suppose that it was not exactly the same as another bar.

Compare this with our current knowledge of iron. *Our* bar is composed of moving molecules, which are an arrangement of moving atoms, which are an arrangement of moving protons and electrons and we don't know how many other kinds of wave particles, all moving at various speeds, some of them practically as fast as light. In this whole rush of activity not a single thing stays still for an instant. In other words, the iron is changing all the time, and as it changes it acts in different ways. If the molecules are made to move faster, the iron will burn you at a touch. If they are rearranged magnetically, the bar will attract other pieces of iron. If they are rearranged in another way the bar will crystallize, and may break unexpectedly. But whether or not the changes in the iron affect it in a way we can notice, they are taking place all the time and at enormous speed. We may still call a piece of iron solid, but we now know—or ought to know—that this means only that it *acts* in certain ways because the particles of which it is composed are comparatively dense, and their movements are confined to certain patterns in a restricted space. The iron *is happening.* If you think this is too academic to be important, try shielding yourself from radiation behind a "solid" sheet of iron. Make your will first.

Because we know more about the structure and activity of metals than our ancestors did, we can make even simple objects such as hammers and knives of a much better quality than they could manage, to say nothing of electronic gadgets and nuclear reactors. And because we have learned something about the way the earth rotates while it revolves around the sun, while the whole solar system is doing something or other in the Milky Way, which in turn—but perhaps we had better stop here. Anyhow, what we have learned about the complicated movements of the earth in relation to other bodies is being used every day in navigation, farming, and many other fields, not to mention long-range missiles and space ships.

Now let's turn for a moment from things to people. Our ancestors thought of thinking as a *nonphysical* process that operated by its own mysterious laws in a vacuum called the mind. Or if the mind was not precisely a vacuum, at least it was a perfectly uniform substance of which each of us somehow had a little part, and which did not affect what passed through it. The speed of thought was supposed to be infinite, and the "laws of thought" were supposed to be absolute and unvarying. If we learned these laws we had only to consider the universe and *think,* and the truth about it would come to us. This theory ran into a few snags, but it was pretty generally believed for centuries, and it has by no means died out today, even among people who ought to know better.

In a world where people and things are as simple as this it is easy to believe in "perfect communication." I see something happen. I frame in my mind a pattern of symbols that exactly and completely reflect this happening, and pass them on to you. Since your mind is essentially exactly like mine, you receive the symbols with no distortion and understand them exactly as I do. If you don't, you must be either stupid or wicked; and since I am a teacher I may ridicule you or pray for you or beat you, all the while exhorting you to think, *think*, THINK. And if you never do get the pattern quite straight it is all your fault, because I know more and better established alibis than you do.

The modern theory of thinking is a little different from this. There is a good deal that we don't yet understand about the process, but we have some pretty reliable evidence about parts of it. For one thing, it takes place not in a mysterious, standardized "mind," but in individual and physical brains, no two of which are alike. Each brain seems to operate rather like a computer though in a far more complicated fashion. It contains millions of short nerve lengths, comparable to wires, and millions of nerve connections, comparable to switches. But the cell structure is such that electrical impulses pass through the circuits at not more than about 400 feet per second; and it is the passage of these impulses that constitutes our thinking. Far from being instantaneous, thought is less than half the speed of sound, and very slow indeed compared with the speed of an electric current passing over ordinary wires (186,000 *miles* per second). That is why computers can be programmed to solve in a few hours problems that would keep mathematicians busy for many years.

Even the simplest thought requires a current to pass over a complicated circuit containing innumerable switches. When an impulse starts, it might follow any one of an enormous number of routes, depending on how the switches click. But once a route has been selected, there is some tendency for the switches to set, so that a second impulse starting from the same point as the first can more easily follow the same route than pick out a new one of its own. It is by this setting of the switches that memory and habits develop. Sometimes it takes many repetitions to make the switches set.

A switch may be set so firmly that another possible connection is blocked out temporarily, or even permanently. For instance, most of us have had the experience of doing a complicated problem of arithmetic, in the midst of which we have made a very obvious mistake, such as multiplying 2 by 2 and getting 2 as the result. We may then have checked it over several times without finding the error—2 times 2 still seems to give us 2. One of our switches has temporarily been jammed in the wrong position. Fortunately, not every passage of a nerve impulse jams a switch; most merely make it easier for the switch to turn one way than another.

There are always a number of impulses passing through different circuits, and these affect each other. The way we think at a given time is therefore guided largely by our earlier experiences—not only the things we have encountered, but the particular paths that our nerve impulses have followed as a result of encountering them. **NO TWO OF US STARTED OUT WITH EXACTLY THE SAME WIRING SYSTEM, AND THE ORIGINAL DIFFERENCES HAVE BEEN INCREASED BY LATER ACTIVITY.**

Now let's consider how language can be used to connect people as we know them now with things as we know them now. A word can no longer stand directly for a thing, because the thing won't stand still. A while ago we mentioned the "laws of thought" which for centuries were regarded as beyond question. The first of these is that "Everything is identical with itself," which may be expressed symbolically as "$A = A$." This may seem so obvious that it is hardly worth saying—but think again. Our piece of solid iron is really an enormous number of particles moving so fast that it is *not* identical with itself long enough to talk about it, and neither is anything else. **The first law of thought is a very useful convention when we are dealing with mathematics, or any problem about abstractions, but it is simply not true about anything in the physical universe.**

It will be easier to accept this if we recognize at once that the word *identical* (along with its common equivalent *same*) is used to express two quite different ideas which we often fail to keep separate. If you take a bite out of an apple, then leave the apple on your desk for a week and take another bite, it is useless to argue about whether it is the same apple. In the sense of continuity it is the same apple; in the sense of identity of structure it is *not,* as your nose and tongue will tell you at once.

Our language-makers saw no reason for making such a distinction, because they thought in terms of "substances" rather than of structure. Since *their* bar of iron was uniform and inert, *continuity implied identity of structure,* and the word *same* covered both things at once. If the bar got to be somehow different—for instance, if it got hot and burned their hands—they would explain that the substance was still the same, but that an *accident* called heat had been added. Of course they knew that many things quite obviously change—for instance, apples mature and decay. But since they did not know *what happened* to bring about these changes, they could not discuss them very accurately. They thought of the world as basically static, with only bits of movement here and there, and they devised their language to describe that kind of world. We *know* that the world has nothing static in it, but we don't usually *think* of it in this way, because we think largely in their language.

THE BANG THAT CHANGED OUR THINKING

Most of us are not very happy about the atomic bomb, but it has had one good effect—it has made millions of people accept, and accept as important, the discoveries of modern physics about the nature of the physical universe. As long as only a few specialists played with cyclotrons in laboratories, J. Q. Public could ignore their theories, and he had some excuse for retaining the old "common sense" attitude of "I believe what I see." The bomb convinced him instantaneously of what he might not otherwise have learned to appreciate for generations—that the nature of the world in which we live is very different from what it seems to be, and that this difference is not merely a matter of academic theory, but a matter of actual life and death.

Since Hiroshima, most literate people have learned to accept the statement that all matter is composed of particles in constant and enormously fast motion. Einstein's relativity, which used to be something between a mystery and a joke, has now been shown to be both true and important. But most of these same people have not really modified their habits of thinking and talking to conform with these important facts. They are rather like many of the contemporaries of Columbus—once he had discovered America, they "believed" that the earth was round (which a number of people had known for thousands of years), but they certainly didn't *realize* it. They still thought of the sun as rising and setting, rather than of the earth as spinning, and they had an uneasy feeling that if they went to the other side—which of course was the "bottom"—they would be in imminent danger of falling off. Many of them were very much upset by the idea. When a feeling of solid certainty was taken from them, life seemed much more dangerous.

Actually, it was all the safer. The better we understand the forces at work on earth, the better we can prepare for them. There is no record of anybody's falling off the earth because it has been discovered to be a whirling ball; but there is plenty of evidence that knowledge of its shape and motion has made for more safety and efficiency in navigation, farming, and a large number of other activities.

The idea that not only all knowledge, but all motion and position, are "merely" relative seems to upset many people in much the same way that their ancestors were upset by Columbus's discovery. They feel that they are asked to give up all their old certainties, with nothing equally stable to take their place. It takes a while for them to realize that their old certainties were merely delusions, and that the new theories not only take nothing away but actually supply useful corrective information.

Our ancestors thought in terms of "substance" rather than of molecular and atomic structure and activity, and the language they invented is full of expressions like "identical objects," "the same thing," and "these are exactly alike." They not only used these phrases, they believed in them, and got into trouble accordingly. We may still use them for convenience, but we should know that we are talking loosely when we do. It is accurate to say that two triangles are exactly alike, because triangles are *pure abstractions*, with nothing physical about them to cause a variation. But if we say that two ball bearings are exactly alike we can mean only that they are so nearly alike that we can *probably* afford to neglect their differences.

Some readers may think it is splitting hairs to insist upon making a distinction between indistinguishable or negligible differences and no differences at all. They are likely to say that for all practical purposes the two things are exactly alike. But the fact is that we can never be sure in advance what all practical purposes will be. If a ball bearing cracks, the difference between it and one that would not crack is obviously important. Possibly we could have avoided the poor choice by a more careful examination. Perhaps we had to take the chance; but it is at least well to know when we are taking such chances, and to bring a few spares along.

There are times when it is useful to *pretend* that things remain identical with themselves (so that they will hold still while we talk about them) and even that they are identical with each other. If you have a problem that begins "Farmer Schwartz has ten cows, each of which gives eleven quarts of milk a day," and so on down to "How much does he get for the butter?" you have to assume a number of identities or you'll never get the answer. It often pays to neglect minor differences in order to simplify a calculation. But it usually does not pay to believe that the differences are not there because you have neglected them. If Farmer Schwartz, for instance, did not recognize that differences in care, feed, and sanitation affected both the quantity and quality of his milk, he would probably not remain in the dairy business very long.

One result of our ancestors' inadequate knowledge of the structure of the physical universe was that it gave them no reason to suspect that *physical things* and *mathematical conceptions* cannot be treated exactly alike. Compare the two following:

1. A equals B.
    C equals B.

    Therefore

    A equals C.

In mathematics or logic the conclusion is indisputably true.

2. A is an apple.
   C is an apple.

   Therefore

   A equals C.

The form of these statements is very much like that of those above, but we are now dealing with physical things—and the truth of the conclusion is not quite so convincing. If we were dealing only with imaginary apples in a school problem, where the only thing definitely said about apples is that "an apple is worth five cents" or "an apple weighs six ounces," the statement that A equals C is just as solid in the second problem as in the first. But if we are dealing with actual physical apples, we know that no two of them are in all respects exactly alike.

But although we actually know this, our language leads us to forget it, and we continually say such things as "an apple is an apple," "all Germans are alike," and "Fords are better than Chevrolets," without paying any real attention to the differences between individual apples, Germans, Fords, and Chevrolets, and with the subconscious assumption that two things wouldn't both *be* apples or Fords unless they were "essentially" alike.

A good many of the words our ancestors invented describe things and conditions that do not exist. Unless we use these words with great care we are likely to make the mistake of thinking that the things they seem to point to are really there. I can still remember the time my baby sister got an "unbreakable" doll for Christmas. She happily tossed it out of a sixth-floor window, and wept bitterly when it smashed on the concrete below. It was her first lesson in the actual relativity of words that sound absolute.

Few of us would make that particular mistake after we had cut our second teeth, but we—or at least many of us—make others that are directly comparable, and perhaps more serious in their consequences. You hear people saying with perfect seriousness that coffee is better than tea. If they mean by this merely that they usually like coffee better than tea, we can hardly argue. But some of them will drink without protest anything called coffee, no matter how weak or strong or stale, and scorn anything called tea in contrast. They often view tea drinkers with dark suspicion. Or they will argue for hours about whether "the dog" really is or isn't "Man's best friend." With one part of their brain they know perfectly well that no two dogs are alike; but with the other—the part conditioned by their inherited language—they feel that any animal that can justly be called a dog must be essentially composed of a sort of doggy substance, so that he is somehow like the others.

Our ancestors did not think they knew all about everything; but they did think: (1) that they knew all about some things; (2) that they could express this *all* exactly in language; (3) that by using language they could transfer information complete and unchanged from one mind to another.

On the other hand we can now see: (1) that nobody knows all about even the simplest thing; (2) that we can indicate what we do know only *approximately* **in language; (3) that since no two brains work exactly alike, we can never get a bit of information complete and unchanged from one brain to another.** It is true that the change may be so small that it does not matter *in a given situation,* but there is always a little loss and change, and it is important to bear this in mind. For one thing, it will save you a shock when a situation comes up where the change does make a difference. For another, it will keep you from beating your brains out attempting the impossible. An engineer who realizes that there is always a little loss from friction will not waste his life and talents attempting to construct a perpetual motion machine.

Language habits that were developed to describe *the world as our ancestors knew it* **have to be adjusted considerably to describe** *the world as we know it.* We describe things and people with words. What changes must be made in the attitudes our ancestors held toward words?

WHAT DOES A WORD STAND FOR?

Most of us think we know what "meaning" means. We may say, for instance, that the word "stool" *means* a chair with no back. If anybody asks us what we mean by "means," we probably say that the word stands for the piece of furniture. In a way this is true, but it needs more examination. Just how is the word connected with the thing?

What happens when you look at a stool? Light waves reflected from it strike your eyes and stimulate a flow of electrical currents over nerve paths leading to your brain. It is in the brain, not in the eye itself, that the effective seeing takes place. If your optical nerve is cut, your eye becomes completely useless; and what you see in your brain is a *partial and not particularly accurate image of the stool.* The people who developed our language did not know this. They "believed what they saw," and they had good reason to, because the human eye was the keenest instrument of perception available. Anything that it could not see could only be guessed at, not measured. But you know that at best your eyes have missed the cell structure, not to mention the spacing and motion of the particles of which the cells are composed. How much else they have missed depends partly on the accuracy of your vision and partly on the *influence of your previous experiences.*

Suppose, for example, that a carpenter and a typist, both with 20-20 vision, look at a stool in a lunchroom. The carpenter may notice the grain of the wood and the way the rungs are joined to the legs—details of which the typist is completely unconscious. But she may notice a roughness that would be likely to snag her stockings—a different detail that the carpenter might not see at all. There is no use saying that they both *saw* it all but only *noticed* parts. We have a phrase for that: certain details "failed to register." We can talk and act only about what does register, accurately or inaccurately. If you don't think this is important, consider the hunters who have shot cows and even wives after clearly "seeing" bucks complete with spreading antlers.

Even the bare act of seeing is not as simple as the passing of a current through an electric circuit. *Secondary* nerve circuits are brought into the action, and these inevitably affect the mental picture that is formed. *Which* secondary circuits are brought in depends on previous experience— that is why the carpenter and the typist see different stools. When you speak of the stool, you may think, and even insist, that you mean "the whole stool," but you cannot mean more than you are conscious of mean- ing (though what you say may mean more to somebody else than it does to you). If you sit on the stool without noticing that the paint is wet, you are not likely to admit that the stickiness of the surface was included in your meaning. The "object" that you see and talk about is a *unique ab- straction,* created by a reaction between your nervous system and the physical process.

You may find it hard to grasp the idea in the last sentence, because you have almost certainly been trained to believe that objects have a re- ality of their own, independent of observers. But the reality of objects is a theory that will not hold in the light of modern science. **What exists is a** *process*—an arrangement of dancing particles. The object that the car- penter sees and feels and calls a stool is derived from this process by the impressions made on his senses and modified by his previous experiences. The object that the typist sees is at least slightly different because her senses and her previous experiences are different. Naturally there are sim- ilarities as well as differences in our nervous systems; and if our back- grounds are also similar, we may derive objects that are very much alike. But no two of us ever see quite the same things.

The stool you talk about, then, is an abstraction—that is, a selection of some of the characteristics of the underlying process. When you speak the word "stool" you almost certainly use it to refer to even less than you have seen. You may, for instance, have noticed a knot in the grain of the seat, a small crack in one leg, a smear of grease on another. But when you say, "Hand me that stool," you have no idea of calling your companion's attention to any of these details. In fact you may already have dismissed them from your own mind. You use the word merely to indicate those characteristics which you assume that he has also noticed and is likely to connect with the word. The word "stool" is therefore a second-level abstraction from the object already abstracted by your senses.

If you use the word to refer to a number of different objects, as in "I don't like to sit on a *stool*," you are using a third level of abstraction; and if you use other words like "seats" or "furniture" or "property," you go higher still—you include more and more different objects with less and less in common. Every time you go up a level you leave out more of the characteristics of the individual object. As a result, the higher you go, the less chance you have of getting your hearer to duplicate the impression in your own mind. If you say, "Hand me that stool," you will probably be adequately understood. If you say, "Get me a stool," he may bring one twice or half as high as you wanted. And if you give him some money and ask him to buy some "attractive furniture," it may mean the end of a friendship.

You may be used to thinking of words as divided into two classes, abstract and concrete; but the evidence shows that **all words are abstract on one level or another.** Moreover, the difference in levels is not a permanent characteristic of the words, but varies with the way they are used. Thus *wealth* is likely to represent a higher level of abstraction than *dollar*. But if I reach in my pocket, pull out a few coins, and say, "Here is my entire *wealth* at the moment," I am using *wealth* on the lowest possible verbal level. On the other hand, if I say, "He is always anxious to pick up an honest *dollar*," I am using *dollar* on a fairly high level. Nevertheless, since *dollar* is usually a low-level word, it will probably make a more direct and forceful impression on the hearer than *wealth* would.

Thinking of *levels of abstraction* may seem much more complicated than the simple division into abstract and concrete words. But it is a great deal more accurate; and once you get used to it, you will find that it straightens out a good many difficulties.

THREE KINDS OF MEANING

As we have just seen, when a man speaks, he uses words as symbols to indicate something that is going on *in his own mind.* His words are directly connected not with the processes in the outer world, but with his own abstractions from those processes. It is this private mental activity that the words mean to *him,* and we may call it *meaning 1.*

When another man listens, the words stimulate some activity in *his* mind. We may call this activity *meaning 2.* If it is very similar to that of the speaker, we say he understands—in other words, *meaning 1* and *meaning 2* are so similar that no noticeable difference appears; but the two meanings can never be absolutely identical.

When there is an obvious difference between the two meanings, it is rather silly to argue about which is the "right" one, but it may be useful to consider which is closer to our *general habits of association,* which we may call *meaning 3.* For instance, if you ask a child for a chisel and he hands you a screwdriver, you may explain the difference between the two kinds of tools and tell him which label is usually applied to each. He will probably accept your explanation; and since you now use these labels in very similar ways, you may avoid future misunderstandings. You have not, however, established the "real" meaning of the word, because *words in themselves have no meanings at all.* It takes a mind to develop a meaning by associating a symbol with something else, and no two minds work in quite the same way.

If you ask for a stool you can expect other people to know *roughly* what you mean. They are not likely to associate the word with a bed or a cat or a chisel. Our habits are enough alike so that a given word *limits* the possible associations within a certain range. But we must be prepared for borderline cases; a low-backed seat, for example, might be called either a chair or a stool. And we must realize that even when there is a complete *verbal* agreement there is still a little misunderstanding because no two of us see exactly the same stool.

It is also important to realize that *meaning 3* or the "dictionary meaning" is merely a generalization derived from the *meanings 1* and *meanings 2* that occur in everyday communication. If you find a puzzling word in a sentence and look it up, a dictionary can tell you something about *how other people have used this word in the past.* This information may give you a definite impression (*meaning 2*) about what the writer means by the word in this sentence (*meaning 1*). You may therefore learn something from the writer that you might otherwise have missed. But you cannot find the true and permanent meaning of the word, because there is no such thing.

PUBLIC AND PRIVATE MEANINGS

The idea that we can all learn to speak exactly alike and use all words with only their universally agreed "correct" meanings is therefore a delusion that we might as well abandon. But we can profitably try to learn: (1) to speak more nearly alike; (2) to become conscious of the probable differences in our meanings.

If you say that a stone weighs ten pounds, a friend may argue with you or want to bet with you. Such an argument or bet may be settled by weighing the stone; when you read the scales you will probably agree about what the stone weighs. On the other hand, if you argue about which of two girls is prettier, there is no way to settle the question satisfactorily.

There is nothing mysterious about this. Some matters affect all of us so frequently that we have had to develop standards of measurement that are as impersonal as possible. We recognize that no scale and no measuring stick is absolutely perfect, and that it is possible to measure inaccurately either by cheating or by carelessness. However, both our commonest measuring devices and our methods of using them are so nearly uniform that most of us will ordinarily accept their readings without protest. Moreover, we are generally conscious of these standards. Consequently, when we say that a stone weighs ten pounds, or that a man is six feet tall, the information conveyed to all our hearers will be remarkably similar. Such statements as these may be said to have public meanings. Anybody knows how to test them; and anybody who does test them will get very similar results. *All statements that have public meanings involve some kind of measurement by generally accepted standards.* The standards need not be universally known, but they must be agreed upon by an appropriate group. Thus the statement that "Roberts suffered second-degree burns" has a public meaning. Anybody with much medical training will know that Roberts had blisters resulting from heat. And anybody who does *not* understand the statement will probably accept the explanation of those who do.

At the other extreme there are meanings which are purely private, because there are no acceptable ways of measuring them. You don't know how cauliflower tastes to your brother, and you won't get very far by explaining that it is "really delicious" if he finds it nauseating.

In between these extremes lies the area of most of our difficulties. You cannot prove that one girl is prettier than another as easily or as definitely as you can prove that she is taller; but there is likely to be a good deal of similarity in the opinions of a given group of people who have lived in the same atmosphere and have interchanged ideas. If we don't exaggerate the permanence or the "universality" of our local and temporary standards of measurement, they can be very useful for communication.

Some people cannot believe that their relative standards are less than absolute. Others feel that if they are not absolute they are no standards at all. But we must use what we have. We can now measure rather accurately many things at which our fathers could only guess; and as time goes on we may learn to do even better.

If we consider the question of meaning in this light, we arrive at the conclusion that a *meaningful statement should suggest a measurement,* considering "measurement" in its widest sense. If somebody says, "It's cold outside," you may want to know what the thermometer reads, or you may simply ask, "Should I wear my heavy coat?" The thermometer reading is a more public type of measurement, but you may not be skilled in interpreting it. Besides, it covers only the factor of temperature, and leaves out wind and humidity. You may find a less precise measurement more useful—for example, an estimate of how thick your clothing should be to keep you comfortable.

There is a widespread belief that some things are subject to measurement and others are not. It seems more accurate to say that **some things are more** *accessible* **to measurement than others.** We have been able to measure height and weight for a long time. Only recently have we begun to find ways of measuring the strength of brain waves and the secretions of the ductless glands. Some of the measurements we should like to make are so complicated and difficult that we may never arrive at a satisfactory method of making them, or reach general agreement about a scale. But unless we can measure a thing—by at least a rough estimate—well, we can make noises about it, but how are we to say anything that has a discoverable meaning?

Alfred Korzybski has compared our statements about things to maps of territories. A good map is drawn to scale: that is, the structure of the map corresponds to the structure of the territory. And a meaningful statement should also correspond in structure to the territory that it describes. This is a very useful comparison, because on the whole we deal with maps rather more sensibly than we do with words. We know, for instance, that a man cannot draw a map of a place he has not measured, whether accurately with surveying instruments or roughly with his eye, and whether directly or by using somebody else's map. And before we depend on a map we want to know some idea of how it came to be made and what kind of measurements were used in making it. Of course we might be deceived by an inaccurate or dishonest map, but we wouldn't believe one that showed rivers running uphill or palm trees growing out of a glacier. When it comes to verbal maps, however, some of us are ready to believe almost anything, because we have never thought of applying the structural test.

For instance, a politician promises to act "in the best interests of all the people," and thereby attracts a number of votes. This sounds like a fine way to act; and it would be, too, if water could run uphill. Unfortunately, some people would gain by having the income tax raised so the sales tax could be eliminated; others would be better off with the sales tax raised and the income tax reduced. If we want to know what the candidate actually plans to do about this issue, we'd better try to get him to talk in map language, so we can examine the structure of the events for which his words stand. He may be unwilling to do this, because as soon as he indicates what things and activities his words refer to he will probably lose some votes; but until he does, his words have no measurable meaning.

Sometimes the relation of a good verbal map to the territory it represents is direct and obvious—for instance, "John is six foot two and weighs over two hundred pounds." Sometimes it is less direct, but still possible to follow with confidence if you know something about the territory. "Murphy sparks the Panthers" might not convey much to some people, but almost any follower of baseball would read it as meaning not only that Murphy fields well and gets his hits when they count most, but that his teammates play better when he is in there. This is a very slight sketch of a complicated situation, but it is map language because the words stand for things that happen.

But when language is related *only to other language*, **it has no value as a map of events, no matter how impressive it sounds.** A faculty does not get anywhere by defining "liberal education" as "the kind of education that develops a broad cultural background." Neither phrase has any map value until the speaker decides what activities it represents. You can't just study "culture." You have to make up your mind whether to learn French verbs or differential equations or appropriate remarks to make after listening to Beethoven's quartets. It is sometimes convenient to have ambiguous map language, so that we may "agree in principle" and then make whatever interpretations we please. But when we want to convey or receive information, we'd better examine the relation between the words and the events they represent.

RHETORIC

So far we have been talking mostly about how language connects people and things. It also connects people and people. **The means by which language is made to connect effectively people and people is called** *rhetoric.* A student once defined rhetoric as "the study of how to get listened to."

Rhetoric is not just the study of how to rearrange parts of a sentence or paragraph or theme for the sake of clarity, nor is it (despite its present bad reputation) simply the study of how to get people to agree with you, whatever the truth of your position. Since no two brains are quite alike, and since every brain deals not only in facts but in inferences and judgments, whims and prejudices, **rhetoric, at bottom, involves publicly acknowledging (1) the complexity of the world the writer is trying to communicate, and (2) the reasonable possibility of other points of view.** Those are the attitudes that underlie the classic definition of rhetoric as the "art of persuasion"; the opposite attitude ("How can I convince these clods that I, of course, am right?") is exactly what has got rhetoric its present evil reputation.

The writer acknowledges the two attitudes noted by the *tone of voice* **he projects.** *Tone* means the writer's attitude toward his subject matter. *Tone of voice* means the writer's attitude toward his subject matter and his reader. Since every writer projects a tone of voice, it is worthwhile to take time to make sure you are projecting the tone of voice you want. The worst papers in any class are those in which the tone of voice fails— as when, for example, a lovable 19-year-old girl, thinking the thoughts of a lovable 19-year-old girl, projects them in stilted diction and convoluted syntax appropriate to an insecure, opinionated assistant professor of education.

Writers too impatient to take the time to consider their tone are making the mistake this chapter was designed to correct. They are, in fact, assuming that "the facts speak for themselves," and that "the information is what counts." The fallacy implicit in both illusions is precisely that the world consists of identical, fixed entities, and that therefore language can be an exact, exhaustive instrument for relaying fixed sets between identical brains.

You can project a tone of voice that the reader will listen to by observing one simple principle:

Don't put your reader on the defensive.

That means that you ought not to insist absolutely on your own judgments and that you ought not to ridicule opposing views. The reader may hold other views. You want to talk to him, not destroy him. It is dead certain he has opinions. Threaten them strongly and he will stop listening, in self-defense.

It also means that you must not show contempt for the reader, because then you make yourself contemptible in his eyes. Also, if your presentation is unclear, incomplete, or mechanically slipshod, you are saying to the reader, perhaps unconsciously, that you couldn't care less about him.

Nobody pays much attention to an argument he cannot understand; nobody pays any attention to a presentation that insults him.

The writer has to guard himself against himself. **One of the important facts and, at the same time, one of the greatest dangers in writing theory is the statement that, "All writing is self-expression."** It is dangerous because people make it mean what they want it to mean. It means objectively that, through tone of voice, any piece of writing conveys a self, a human intelligence complete with limitations. It does not mean, "I write to please myself." Writing is self-expression because it can't escape being that, despite the efforts of some disciplines to eradicate the self by removing all personal pronouns and employing wholesale the passive voice. (The result sounds like evasion, not conviction.)

A psychologist could probably explain how "Writing is self-expression" twists into its opposite: "Whatever I say is important, simply because I say it." Or even "Whatever I say is true, simply because I say it." The selves being displayed in those slogans are not selves the reader will listen to; the polite category for them is egomania.

"Writing is self-expression" doesn't mean "Writing *should be* self-expression" or "The reason *I* write is to express myself." The self is expressed in anything one writes whether he wants that or not; it's inescapable. **The problem is to bring the self that is expressed into line with the self one wants to express.** That requires work. If you don't honestly believe that logic has limitations, that other points of view are not only possible but often as reasonable as yours, and that any paragraph you write puts down your tone of voice as definitely as your fingerprints, your problem in writing goes far beyond a prose style, and your writing is never likely to be read beyond your circle of very close friends.

EXERCISES

I. The following statements are questionable as verbal maps of territories because no clear-cut *structure of events* for which the words stand is presented in them. Present two widely differing sets of circumstances (structures of events) for which each statement could easily stand.

Example: Elmer is deeply interested in the welfare of others.
Possible events (a) He takes nourishing food to the sick people of his neighborhood.
(b) He tries to find out who is receiving welfare assistance from the county.

1. It was an unusual date.

2. I will carefully consider your suggestions at promotion time, Mr. Harvey.

3. This is the most lively and spirited dorm on campus.

4. When you buy a car from Mr. Haley, you know exactly what you are getting.

5. Once you understand how we see things around here, I'm sure we'll all get along fine.

6. There is nothing quite like living in a small town.

7. That history course was just not what I expected.

II. The following statements more closely approximate verbal maps. Rewrite them in general and ambiguous terms.

> Example: If elected, I will lower corporate taxes.
> > Rewritten: If elected, I will work to lower the tax burden which now limits the growth and prosperity of this community.

1. The driver of the luggage cart went to lunch and took the keys with him, so you will have to wait for your luggage.

2. The people in the room you reserved have not checked out yet.

3. Nothing is going to happen concerning your complaints.

4. Dad, I flunked the first two chemistry quizzes.

5. I don't know what I'm supposed to do in this situation.

6. Half of the last shipment of our toasters was defective.

7. One of our keypunch operators mispunched your IBM card and overcharged you.

Suggestions for Discussion or Theme Writing

I. Write a paragraph on the misconception about the relationship of people, things, and words represented in incidents such as the following:

1. In one country, the native word for cancer is never used, for fear the speaker will contract the disease.

2. When the submarine *Squalus* sank, with great loss of life, and then was salvaged and recommissioned, the Navy felt it politic to give it some other name than *Squalus*.

II. Write a theme on the subject that this chapter suggests: If everything is in flux, and if public meanings differ at times from private meanings, how is communication possible?

DEFINITION, CLASSIFICATION, AND GENERALIZATION

WE LEARN BY COMPARISON

The way we learn about anything new is to find out how it resembles things that we already know, and how it differs from them. If a child asked you what a zebra was, you might say something like: "It's a wild animal that lives in Africa, a good deal like a horse, but chunkier and with black and white stripes, and I hear it's much harder to tame." A zoologist would give a more precise, and perhaps a more elaborate explanation, but he would use the same general method—comparison with the known to explain the unknown.

Since we don't have time to make a separate investigation of everything, we soon develop the habit of grouping things that are sufficiently similar, calling them by the same name, and reacting to them in the same general way. This habit is absolutely necessary. It wouldn't really be practical to make a new examination of every potato before deciding whether it was edible—not to mention peas. But since the habit emphasizes the similarities of things called by the same name and tends to conceal their differences, it can be dangerous if not practiced with some care. It is therefore worth our while to give a little thought to three closely related processes that the habit involves—definition, classification, and generalization.

FORMAL DEFINITION

A formal definition must explain two things—the *genus* or kind to which something belongs, and the *differentiae*, or differences from other members of that kind. As you can see, this is quite in line with the first sentence in this chapter—since it tells us what the thing is like and how it differs; but the formal definition must be precise and absolute. Informally, you might explain a regular pentagon by saying that it is like a square except that it has five sides instead of four. Formally, you would have to say that it was a five-sided regular polygon. The word *polygon* puts it in the genus of figures bounded by straight lines connected by angles; the word *regular* differentiates it from all those figures whose lines and angles are not exactly equal; and the word *five-sided* completes the differentiation by excluding all hexagons, octagons, and so forth. A good formal definition leaves nothing to guess about. It says that the thing defined *is* a member of a class, *with* certain differences from other members —and it says so directly and definitely. There are no *likes* or *kind ofs* or *is whens*. And a noun is defined by other nouns, a verb by other verbs, and so forth.

MATHEMATICAL DEFINITION

Formal definitions are indispensable in mathematics and logic. A mathematician can define a square or a circle or an equilateral triangle *completely*, and his definitions will apply exactly to all squares, circles, and equilateral triangles, future as well as past. Suppose, for instance, he defines a square as a plane figure consisting of four equal lines connected by four equal angles. He does not have to worry about whether the angles will be exactly equal in the next square he encounters. They must be, or it will not be a square.

The reason for this certainty and regularity is simple. Since mathematical concepts have *no physical content*, there is no reason for them to vary. A "square" on the blackboard is merely a representation of a true square. And every square is exactly like every other square in its "essential characteristics"—that is, the characteristics covered by the definition (size and position, for instance, are usually left out). *The definition controls the class.*

Of course other mathematicians may refuse to accept their colleagues' definitions, and may make new ones of their own. But if they find his definitions satisfactory they can accept them and use them exactly and uniformly. They may find that a definition implies additional consequences unsuspected by its originator—for instance, that every square can be divided into two equal triangles. But they will not find any irregularities because *there is nothing physical to change or vary.* Consequently, they can talk about "all squares" or "all circles" with complete confidence.

PHYSICAL DEFINITION

When it comes to defining things that do have a physical content we have an entirely different problem. Suppose a zoologist attempts to define a dog. Whatever definition he gives must be based on not quite complete observation of some dogs. No two dogs are the same; no one dog stays the same; and nothing he says about dogs will make them more uniform than they actually are. **His definition does not control the class.** If he chooses to talk about "all dogs" he is certainly going beyond the boundaries of his knowledge, and very possibly making a fool of himself.

A zoologist is very likely to know this, and to act accordingly. Students of some other branches of knowledge frequently fail to realize it. The completeness and regularity of mathematical definitions are so effective and satisfactory that they are tempted to use them even when they are dealing with things that do have physical content. So they define "democracy" or "the psychopathic personality" or "the progressive school" with impressive formality, and then get so impressed by their definitions that they never again take a clear look at the things their definitions are supposed to be about. In a way they lead a very happy life. I know people whose faith in progressive schools is absolutely unshakable, because any school that has faults open to the public view is not "really progressive."

Of course there are times when it is useful to define classes of physical things, and there is nothing wrong with doing this formally, as long as you realize that what you are doing is simply *explaining how you are using words.* If you are going to write a paper about sports cars you'd better let your readers know whether or not you include hot rods on one side and low-slung family cars on the other. But you will simplify things for everybody concerned if you make it clear that you are simply explaining what *you* mean when *you* use the word. If you make the rather common mistake of insisting that your meaning is the only true one, you are wasting time and probably losing friends.

In this connection there are two important things to remember. The first is that it is often better to let the context explain a term than actually to define it. Look at the following paragraph:

> He received his formal education in the public schools of Cleveland and at the University of Michigan, where he majored in economics. But the really valuable part of his education was gained in other institutions— Durfee's Pool Hall, the West Side Democratic Club, and Larkin's Meat Packing Company, where he worked in the summers.

Here the word *education* is used in two quite different ways, and is not defined in either use. But most readers will grasp what is meant by "formal education" and will have a pretty good idea that the "valuable part" of his other education was what he learned about different sorts of people. A definition of terms would be unlikely to make the paragraph any clearer —and it would be very likely to make it dull, pompous, and generally ineffective. You have to give your readers credit for knowing something.

The other thing to remember about definitions is that your readers are not completely at your orders—they have formed their own opinions on some things long ago. There is a very good chance that they are going to continue to interpret words according to their own habits, no matter what you say they mean. If you want to use the term *American* for any inhabitant of North or South America, and *U.S. Citizen* for a U.S. citizen, you have all sorts of good reasons on your side. But no matter how carefully you explain what you are doing, most of your readers will probably think of U.S. citizens every time they see *American,* and react to your writing accordingly. It's wiser to think about what they *will* do, rather than what they *ought* to do.

SOCIAL DEFINITION

Of course the fact that definitions of physical things do not control classes is extremely inconvenient. Consider the difficulties of lawmakers. They define crimes, property rights, and all sorts of other things, and then lay down rules of procedure based on their definitions. Moreover, these rules are workable a good proportion of the time. If a man steals some money in one way, we can call it theft and send him to jail for six months; if he steals in a different way, we can call it burglary and send him up for three years; and if he steals in still a third way, we can call it robbery and send him up for twenty. But no matter how carefully the definitions are framed, some criminal will come along whose actions are not clearly in any of the classes, and there may be a long and expensive trial to decide whether what he did was "really" one crime or another.

Now consider the case of a man who is convicted of robbery—unjustly, he believes—and sent to prison for twenty years. He admits that he picked up a wallet which he saw fall out of another man's pocket, and walked away with it. But he believes that this is simple theft, and that he shouldn't get more than a year in prison. Unfortunately, he happened to be carrying a hunting rifle at the time, and the jury decides that this made the crime armed robbery instead of simple theft. Our criminal argues that this was simply a coincidence, and that he didn't even threaten the victim. But the victim says that he saw the gun and assumed that the criminal would use it; otherwise he would have taken the wallet back. The case might have been decided either way, but it was in fact called robbery, and the criminal is in for a long term. After some years of meditation he may come to the conclusion that in his case the definition *did* control the class.

But the fact is that the definition had no effect on the crime itself. What he did was simply what he did—an action on the borderline between two different things that the lawmakers were thinking of. **What the definition controlled was the court's later *action* about the crime.**

In our everyday affairs we must let our actions be controlled by definitions to some extent, because we haven't got time to investigate every new incident from scratch. Even as simple an action as buying a can marked "Tomato Soup" depends on accepting a definition and making a small investment in the belief that it is probably satisfactorily accurate. But the soup *may* have a peculiar taste, or even give us ptomaine poisoning; and the manufacturer cannot eliminate either of these possibilities by the precision of his definition. All he can do is to be very careful about his materials and processes in order to make his product as nearly uniform as possible.

DEFINITIONS AND CLASSIFICATONS

A definition is appropriate only when we are talking about a *class* of things. There is no necessity for defining a unique thing—we simply describe it. For instance, if we think of the earth all by itself as the place where we live, no definition is necessary. But if we think of it as part of a set including Mars, Venus, etc., we *classify* it as a planet, and *define* planets in such a way as to show *how they resemble each other* and *how they differ from members of other classes,* such as stars.

If we remember that in the physical universe no two things are exactly alike, we are led to see some interesting things about classification:

1. Classification of physical things can never be as exact (and complete) as classification of mathematical abstractions, because there is always the possibility of borderline cases. We may be quite sure that a rose is a plant and that a cow is an animal, but we can't find the exact line between plants and animals. In some of the simpler forms of life, botanists and zoologists disagree. When we realize that classifications are often useful but never perfect, we save a good deal of misdirected energy.

2. There are always a number of different ways of classifying anything, and no one of them is the one right way. Different ways are useful for different purposes. For instance, Mary Pemberton may be classified as a human being, a female, an American citizen, a blonde, a minor, a freshman, a resident of Arizona, and a member of Blue Cross, not to mention a few dozen other things. Our first impression may be that some of these classifications are "real" and others "arbitrary," or that some are important and others trivial. But the fact is that they are all quite real, and any one of them may be important at a given time. If Mary wants to cast a vote or buy a drink, the fact that she is a minor becomes for the occasion more important than the fact that she is female; and if she needs an emergency operation the fact that she is a member of Blue Cross may save her life when neither her sex nor her citizenship would do her any good. Naturally, some of the classifications that can be applied to her are more likely to be permanent than others, and are important on more different occasions. But they are all based on certain similarities with *some* people and differences from *other* people. Even the fact that she is human is not always the most important thing about her. In a war we may be trying to preserve our people and equipment and to destroy the enemy's people and equipment. In a very practical way we classify her with our tanks rather than with their women. She may not think the classification is flattering; but if it means that she goes on living she can hardly deny that it is real.

3. Classifications are *invented by observers* and are based on the similarities and differences that we recognize, not on the ones that "really" exist. It is all very well to define a fair ball in baseball as one that lands between the foul lines; but in practice it has to be one that the umpire *says* lands between the foul lines. Of course if it lands in center field there is not much chance of an argument; but if it lands within inches of a foul line it has to be called one way or the other, and it is what it is called by the umpire that counts.

If this illustration seems trivial, consider the case of Alvin Spivak, who was born in the United States of parents who were both citizens, but who was brought up in a foreign country and did not return to the United States until he was twenty. Theoretically we may argue that Alvin is a citizen; but suppose he has no way of proving or even of suspecting, this fact. If he never gets the privileges of a citizen it doesn't mean much to say that he is one. Or consider Toni Frandl, a native of Switzerland who takes out naturalization papers in the United States. We say he is now an American citizen, but the Swiss say he is still a Swiss one. Neither country recognizes that the citizenship in the other is real; but Toni might suspect that there was some reality in both if he were jailed by one country for evading military service, and later extradited and hanged by the other for treason.

We may summarize the whole business of classification by the two following statements:

1. **When a thing is classified in any given way, it presumably has some similarities to other things in the same classification. When we call it by a class name we *emphasize these similarities.***

2. **But since no two members of a class are exactly alike (unless we are dealing with pure abstractions), there must also be some differences. And when we call a thing by its class name we *neglect these differences.***

In other words, to call anything by a class name tells only *half the story.* Our laziness, our vanity, and our emotions all tend to obscure this fact. We find it convenient and agreeable to say, "All those Micks are alike," or "A German is a German—I don't care what you say." But all Irishmen are not alike, and the statement that a German is a German, conclusive as it sounds, doesn't really tell us anything.

Alfred Korzybski devised a convenient technique for indicating the *other half* of the story. He says, in effect: "There is no such thing in nature as *the German*—there are only German$_1$, German$_2$, German$_3$, and so forth. The fact that they have some things in common is indicated by the word *German;* but we need the index numbers 1, 2, 3, and so forth to remind us that there are also differences between them. Moreover, even German$_1$ does not stay the same. We should learn to distinguish between German$_{1939}$ and German$_{1970}$."

It is not likely that you will add much to your popularity if you go around talking about "German$_{1970}$" on every possible occasion. But if you get into the habit of thinking in terms of dates and index numbers, you may avoid not only some unsound conclusions but some unfortunate events. It is all very well to say that "a cow is a gentle animal" if you realize that you are merely talking in terms of probabilities, based on a limited experience. And your statement may seem satisfactory enough as applied to the next seven cows that you happen to meet. But if cow_8 gores you, you can't stop the bleeding by explaining that she is not a real cow.

GENERALIZATIONS

The fact that generalizations often have exceptions is, of course, widely realized. In fact, many of us have been specifically taught to avoid generalizations completely. It is quite impossible to do this, and we should be of no use to ourselves or anybody else if we seriously tried to. $Tiger_8$, for instance, may be as gentle as cow_8 is rough; but until you are perfectly sure of this you had better act on the firm generalization that tigers are dangerous. But we should try to understand the nature of generalizations so that we won't be completely at their mercy.

All generalizations are based on the *assumption of regularity*, and we need such an assumption to guide our lives. If we could not take it for granted that water is usually wet, the year about twelve months long, and our mothers' meals reasonably free from poison, living would be something of a strain. But in order to act efficiently, we have to know when we can assume that the regularity is complete and certain, and when we must assume that it is only approximate and probable.

It is only when we are dealing with such concepts as triangles and circles that we have complete and certain regularity. What is true of one circle must be true of all, because they are all alike by the definition which created them. Consequently, if we have learned anything about circles by studying a few of them, we can generalize confidently about all the others. If the ratio between diameter and circumference of even one circle is *pi,* the same ratio must hold for all others.

But when we deal with physical things we are in a much more complicated situation. Physicists assume that the "forces of nature" operate regularly—or at least that they "tend" to. For instance, the speed of light is said to be a constant, with a value of approximately 186,000 miles per second. They therefore use this figure in all sorts of equations and it works out very well, but two things must be noted.

One is that the figure is not quite exact. We can measure accurately enough to determine that the figure is a little over 186,000 miles, which is close enough for most practical purposes, but we cannot find the exact number of odd feet—our instruments are not fine enough. Consequently there is always a little margin of error in our calculations.

The other is that the exact figure would represent not the actual speed of light, but the speed at which light would travel in a perfect vacuum if such a thing existed. The actual speed of a given ray of light, even in outer space, is always at least a tiny bit slower.

Any generalization about physical things is therefore at best a matter of approximation and probability. All our observations show that light *tends* to travel at about a certain speed. Since we assume regularity, we expect that light will always *tend* to travel at this speed. When we can figure the interfering factors—glass, mist, or cosmic dust—we can correct the theoretical speed and come very close to the actual speed. But we can never be sure we have recognized all the interfering factors, or figured them correctly.

When we have to generalize about a more complex situation, such as the chemical effects of apples or the habits of a group of people, we have many more variables to consider, and the chance of making mistakes about some of them is much greater.

A child who has one apple tree in his back yard may come to the conclusion that red apples taste sweet and are safe to eat, while green apples taste sour and sometimes lead to cramps. He reaches these conclusions by approved scientific processes; but his generalizations have a rather small base. When he encounters other apple trees he may find out that some green apples are sweet and some red ones are sour. He will have to revise his original idea that color is a reliable index of taste. It is still evidence, but it must be considered along with other things.

Perhaps he will find that the color of the seeds is a more reliable guide than the color of the skin, but he won't find this or anything else a perfect guide. Apples vary enormously, and so do the people who eat them. This is not because the forces that make up an apple or a person are more erratic than those that make up a beam of light. It is because there are more of them, and they are more likely to modify each other's behavior. If we want to make a generalization about apples that will be useful and reasonably reliable, we'd better limit it.

This limitation on the usefulness of generalizations as applied to physical things was not understood in the Middle Ages. It was assumed, for instance, that iron was "essentially" iron, and "naturally" uniform. If something that seemed to be iron happened to act in a peculiar way, it simply wasn't "really" pure iron, and there you were—a little flustered, perhaps, but with your definitions and generalizations "essentially" undisturbed. It was therefore quite generally assumed that mathematical or logical statements about physical things could be exact and rigorous. Since the complete and exact truth could apparently be expressed in words, it seemed that the correct definitions would hold good for all members of a class, and that universal generalizations could be perfectly sound.

Such ideas are not respectable today. Almost any scientist will now tell you that his "knowledge" is only tentative. It consists only of what he has learned from observation and experiment (his own or others'); and it is subject to correction or revision whenever new or more accurate observation suggests the necessity. But the old habits persist, and a good many people who follow the "scientific method" very carefully in their own special fields forget about it when they move into others.

PREJUDICES

One of the most harmful kinds of generalization is the kind that results in a prejudice against a group—racial, religious, occupational, or of some other kind. The fact that such prejudices are harmful is now widely recognized, and a good deal of progress has been made in overcoming them; but we might move even faster if we supported our humanitarian efforts with an analysis of the mechanics of the situation.

In the first place, we should recognize that not all generalized disapprovals are prejudices. Some of them might be called "postjudices," because the judgment is reached *after* a reasonable examination of the evidence. If you happen to know a gang of fifty Corsican thugs who spend their time robbing stores, setting fire to hospitals, and cutting up passing citizens with pocket knives, there is no prejudice involved in disliking them for what you know they have done. But if you assume that all other Corsicans are naturally inclined to act in the same way because they are Corsicans, then **you are prejudging people before they have acted. That is a prejudice. A reasonable (though not entirely accurate) opinion of a small group has been unreasonably extended to cover a much larger group.**

THE PURPLE-EYED CORSICANS

The next thing to notice is that a prejudice usually involves the assumption that there is an invariable relation between two characteristics —one readily perceptible, but not in itself significant; the other difficult to perceive, but definitely vicious. Suppose we notice that all Corsicans have purple eyes. We should not at first dislike them for that; purple eyes in themselves can do no harm. But they make it easy to recognize Corsicans—so whenever we see a man with purple eyes we know that he is certain to be handy with a match box and a pocket knife. You can't tell us that Corsicans aren't different from other people—look at their eyes.

This would be very sound reasoning if there were really an invariable association between knife-wielding and any kind of pigmentation. Nobody has yet proved that there is. However, it is easy to understand why some people think they have.

Let's assume that there actually is a town called Eastport where all the thugs are purple-eyed Corsicans, and where practically all the Corsicans are highly undesirable citizens. It is natural enough for the other inhabitants of this town to react to purple eyes as they would to a rattle on a snake's tail—not dangerous in itself, but a fair warning of poison in the fangs. The association is there, and only a fool would disregard it. But the assumption that the association is one of cause and effect requires investigation. All the evidence we have shows that people—regardless of the color of their eyes—can be badly warped by the pressures of an unfavorable environment. If it happens that the Corsicans in this town live under especially severe pressures, there may be some reason other than their nationality that makes them so unpleasant.

Possibly they came to the town late, when blue-eyed and brown-eyed citizens had already taken up the available land, opened the necessary stores, and so forth. The Corsicans could find jobs only as day laborers, at low pay; and they could find shelter only in run-down houses and shacks. Even these places were expensive, considering the wages they earned, and they crowded together to save rent. It is hard to heat enough water on one stove to bathe three families, and the shacks began to take on a characteristic odor. The rather limited diet that they could afford helped the odor along, and the word began to get around that Corsicans smelled. These Corsicans certainly did.

Those of the children that went to school did not have a very happy time. Naturally, their language was something of a handicap. Moreover, the other children made fun of them—of their accent, of their "stupidity," of their shabby clothes, of their unpleasant odor, and of their purple eyes. The other children would have done most of this by themselves; but they were encouraged by their parents to be even more unkind. They were warned not to sit next to the Corsicans, who were dirty and probably diseased, and not to play with them too much. Pretty soon the Corsicans learned to keep to themselves—whereupon they were accused of being clannish and un-American.

All of the young Corsicans were made to feel inferior. Some of them accepted their status despondently. Others made rather pathetic efforts to improve it. Still others grew bitterly resentful and tried to fight back. They couldn't do much at school, where they were outnumbered; but if three or four of them happened to find a brown-eyed boy alone in an alley, they would beat him up. This was not at all sportsmanlike of them, but then they were not very nice people by now. In fact, practically all of the things that the older inhabitants said of them were beginning to be true. It was rather too bad that their parents had chosen to move to Eastport rather than Westport; for in Westport many of the earliest settlers had been Corsicans. Many of their descendants now owned businesses and fine homes and belonged to the country club. Nobody thought there was anything funny about their purple eyes. Curiously enough, they didn't even smell bad. But in Westport you must learn to be wary of the Maltese. They were brought in as construction hands, and it was a great mistake. . . . You can't trust a yellow-eyed man. They use knives. There is even an odor about them.

REVISING PREJUDICED GENERALIZATIONS

Naturally, we have to make generalizations based on our experience. A man who has lived all his life in Eastport shouldn't be blamed if he thinks he "knows Corsicans." But if he says, "You can't tell me anything about Corsicans," we may suspect that he is afraid to examine new evidence because it might shake his confidence in his own wisdom. If he moved to Westport with a fairly open mind, he might discover that the Maltese there were surprisingly like the Corsicans in Eastport, once you looked past the purple and yellow eyes. He might even come to the conclusion that what made both groups so unpleasant was a combination of slum conditions and social disapproval, rather than national origin. But the chances of his having an open mind might be rather small. So many of us give more weight to one early impression than to a dozen later ones.

I once had a student who cherished a very strong prejudice against Texans, about which we talked at some length. It developed that he had known four loud-mouthed, narrow-minded, arrogant Texans, whom he disliked for what seemed to me very good reasons. He came to consider them as "typical Texans"—a rather small base for a generalization. He then met one or two "nontypical" Texans, and was broad-minded enough to like them as exceptions. Later he met a number of other likable Texans. Since his "nontypical" Texans now outnumbered his "typical" ones, you might think that he would now revise his generalization, but it apparently never occurred to him to do so. It wasn't that he couldn't count, but he thought of "typical" Texans as Texans, and of agreeable Texans simply as people, so that the comparison never suggested itself. Moreover, he had meanwhile met a number of other arrogant and loud-mouthed people; and since they fitted in with his picture of Texans, he thought of them as Texans, too—

although he didn't really know whether they came from Texas, Oklahoma, or Missouri. He had never given the matter any thought. When he put all his facts together, he found that they added up as follows: (1) 4 unpleasant people known to be from Texas; (2) 17 pleasant people known to be from Texas but never counted as Texans; (3) about 30 unpleasant people *assumed* to be from Texas with no real evidence. The student managed to revise his generalization.

This is not an incident invented to prove a point. The conversation actually occurred, and I have no reason to believe that the student was not telling the truth—he looked sheepish enough. Probably most prejudices do not involve as wild a distortion of the evidence as this one; but there is a general tendency: (1) not to count the Corsicans who don't fit the picture; (2) to count everybody who does fit the picture as a Corsican, whether or not he really is one.

It is perhaps worth mentioning that a prejudice may be harmful to the holder as well as to the object. If you move to Westport and insist on hiring a "nice" Maltese girl instead of a "nasty" Corsican as a baby sitter, you may come home early some day and find your little darling smoking marijuana.

EXERCISES

    I. In which of the following does the definition control the class, and in which does the class control the definition?

    1. Adolf Hitler: A Jew is anyone whose grandmother, paternal or maternal, had Jewish blood.

    2. The State of Israel: A Jew is anyone whose mother was a Jew, or who declares himself a Jew.

    3. Four children to four others in a backyard: "You be cops and we'll be robbers."

    4. Senator Bilbo: A Negro is anyone who has one drop of Negro blood in his veins.

    II. $E = MC^2$ is said to be a formula. Is it a definition, a classification, or a generalization?

Suggestions for Discussion or Theme Writing

    I. If Bilbo could give the definition above, why could not a senatorial candidate opposing him successfully argue that a white was "anyone with one drop of white blood in his veins"?

    II. What is the interrelationship of definition, generalization, and classification?

    III. What is the value of "defining your terms" in writing?

THE USES
AND
LIMITATIONS
OF
LOGIC

INDUCTION AND DEDUCTION

The kind of reasoning used in the formation of generalizations, discussed in Chapter Five, is called *inductive*. **Properly used, it begins with careful observation of physical phenomena and works up to a systematic explanation of them. This explanation is called a hypothesis.** It may be anything from a bare guess to a firm and well-tested belief, but it is always subject to reexamination and possible revision when new evidence comes in. For example, many of the hypotheses of Isaac Newton, which for centuries seemed to be absolutely solid, have had to be modified in the light of Einstein's theory of relativity. Newton's system has not been destroyed, it has been refined. For most purposes it still works well enough, but when we are dealing with the great distances found in outer space or the tiny distances found within the atom we find that Einstein's system works better. And of course the time may come when we know enough to modify that.

The inductive method is the one primarily used in the experimental approach to knowledge. The mathematical or logical approach begins from the other end. Whether logic is a branch of mathematics or mathematics is a branch of logic is a question I do not feel competent to settle. **At any rate, both mathematicians and logicians proceed by *deductive reasoning.*** That is, they begin with general statements assumed to be true and work down from these to more particular statements which must be true if the general ones are.

It is silly to argue about which of these methods is better. They are appropriate for different purposes. A scientist usually forms his hypotheses by a combination of induction and hunches, and he may test them the same way (if he doesn't have any hunches, he may be a good technician, but he'll never get very far except by pure luck). But once he is satisfied with a hypothesis he will say, "All right, let's assume this is true. Now what follows?" It is now time for a stage of deductive reasoning, to open new possibilities. Of course his conclusions must again be checked by observation, and then—and so forth, and so forth. Science moves forward by steps, and it takes two legs to walk.

Anybody can reason inductively up to a point; but the ability to do it well seems to depend rather on mental makeup than on a special method. *Deductive reasoning*, on the other hand, follows a method that can be usefully explained. It is often called *formal logic*, or simply *logic*, the term which will be used for the rest of this chapter.

COMPARING STATEMENTS

Logic may be defined roughly as a systematic method of *comparing statements* in such a way that they will produce reliable additional statements. Suppose, for instance, that somebody asks you whether a German-born friend of yours has become a naturalized citizen of the United States. Since you have never heard the matter discussed, you do not immediately know; but you decide to see whether anything you do know will lead you to the correct answer. Is there anything about him that is *characteristic* of either citizens or noncitizens? Among other things, you know that he is employed as an engineer in the State Highway Department, and you remember that in your state only citizens are eligible to hold such jobs. You therefore conclude that he *must be* a citizen. Two bits of information which apparently had nothing to do with each other when you picked them up have been made to produce a third bit of information.

Everybody of even moderate intelligence compares statements in some such way as this; but a good many people do not know how to *test the connections* to see whether the results they get are reliable. Suppose we compare two attempts to prove the same thing:

1. All Communists read Marx.
   Jones reads Marx.
   Therefore Jones is a Communist.
2. Only Communists read Marx.
   Jones reads Marx.
   Therefore Jones is a Communist.

Perhaps you see at a glance that the first argument proves nothing at all, while the second is quite sound. However, if you read the newspapers you must realize that millions of people are actually convinced by arguments like the first, so it may be just as well to study the structure of both arguments. The easiest way to do this is to change the form of the statements so that they can be readily diagramed.

1. All Communists are readers of Marx.

This can be diagramed as follows, with the circle marked C standing for Communists, and the circle marked R standing for readers of Marx:

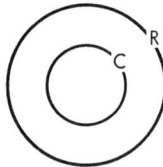

Jones is a reader of Marx.

If we want to add the information in this statement to the diagram we already have, we must put a little circle J for Jones somewhere within the circle marked R for readers. But there is nothing to tell us *where* in the circle it goes—whether it should be within or without the circle marked C for Communists.

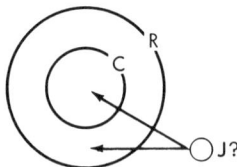

We therefore have no basis for deciding whether Jones is a Communist or not.

2. Only Communists are readers of Marx.

This has to be diagramed with the circles in a different relation:

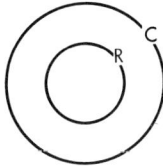

Jones is a reader of Marx.

If we add the information in this statement to the diagram we have just drawn, we must put the little circle for Jones in the medium-sized circle marked R; and if we do this we *inevitably* put it also within the larger circle marked C.

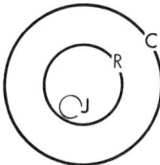

We are therefore justified in drawing the conclusion that Jones is a Communist. If the first two statements are true, the conclusion *must* be true.

SYLLOGISMS

The kind of argument we have been considering is called a *syllogism*. It is the principal device of traditional logic, and very useful if you know how to handle it. There are various types of syllogisms, which can be discussed at great length and in highly technical terms. But the basic principles are simple, and by using our three circles we can get at these principles rapidly and directly.

A syllogism consists of two statements *assumed to be true*, from which a third statement would follow inevitably. The first two statements are usually called the *premises,* and the third the *conclusion.* Thus if we say (1) that all college students are intelligent and (2) that Dick is a college student, we can draw the conclusion that Dick is intelligent. Of course if the statements are not true, the conclusion may not be true either; but it is *logically sound.*

THE FIRST STATEMENT

The first statement must show the relation between *two classes.* Typical statements of this kind are:

All Frenchmen are Europeans.
Some Irishmen are policemen.
No Bolivians are Europeans.
Some Irishmen are not policemen.
Casey is an Irishman.
Casey is not a policeman.
The Spartans were Greeks.

Notice three things about these statements: (1) we may talk of all or part of a class; (2) an individual (Casey) is considered a class by himself; (3) the verb in the statement is always some form of the verb *to be.*

If you have a statement like "John *eats* pie," you have to change it to "John *is* a pie eater" before you can use it in a syllogism. It is then easy to show the relation between the two classes by drawing two circles. There are only a limited number of possible relations. The most obvious are these three:

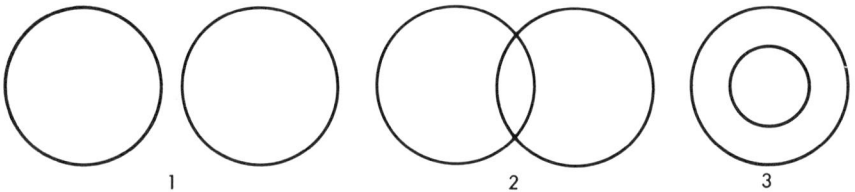

The first of these is simple, reliable, and reversible. It indicates definitely that the two classes do not coincide at all. If the two circles stand for Bolivians and Europeans, this diagram shows not only that no Bolivians are Europeans, but that no Europeans are Bolivians.

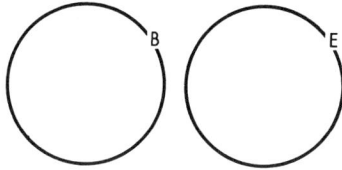

The second is also reversible, but it is not as simple as the first. Suppose we use it to diagram the statement that some Irishmen are policemen. Does it also indicate that some policemen are Irishmen? A glance shows

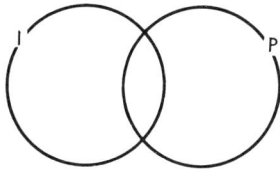

that it does. Since the two classes overlap, some members of each must also be in the other. But this diagram fails to give us any reliable information about the parts of the two circles that do *not* overlap. If we want to be really careful, we had better draw it this way:

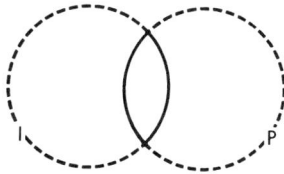

The solid parts of the two circles indicate our definite information; the dotted parts indicate mere possibilities. Thus the diagram indicates that certainly some *and possibly all* Irishmen are policemen; and that certainly some *and possibly all* policemen are Irishmen. We cannot be sure *from our premise* that either circle actually extends beyond the overlap. Of course we may know as a matter of general information that there are Irishmen who are not policemen and policemen who are not Irishmen; but neither fact follows logically from the statement that some Irishmen are policemen.

We might also draw overlapping circles to indicate that some Irishmen are *not* policemen. To do this accurately we would need a diagram like this:

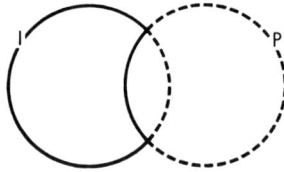

The area within the solid curves indicates the Irishmen who are not police-men (in the overlapping area) or policemen who are not Irishmen. In other words, a really accurate diagram might show the circles overlapping, separate, or with the P inside the I. But on the basis of our statement, the only diagram we can draw is one that shows that *at least some* Irishmen are not included in the class of policemen.

The third diagram also has to be considered with care. Suppose we use it to indicate that all Frenchmen are Europeans:

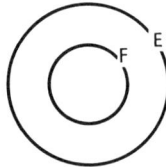

This seems to indicate that there are some Europeans who are *not* French-men. This is true enough, but it is not contained in the statement which our diagram is supposed to illustrate. Therefore we might draw a more careful diagram this way:

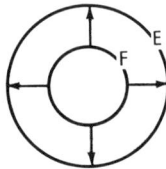

This shows that the inner circle *cannot* extend beyond the outer circle; but, as the arrows indicate, it may completely fill the larger one.

For most ordinary purposes we do not have to be as careful as all this; we can draw our circles with solid lines and without arrows. But we should remember to be very careful not to make any assumptions from the parts of circles that could be drawn differently.

There is another thing about the third diagram that deserves special emphasis, because failure to realize it is the most common cause of faulty logic. It can represent either of the following statements.

All Frenchmen are Europeans.

Only Europeans are Frenchmen.

But it does not imply the statement that all Europeans are Frenchmen or that only Frenchmen are Europeans. Remember: (1) the class described by *all* must be represented by the *smaller* circle; (2) the class described by *only* must be represented by the *larger* circle.

THE SECOND STATEMENT

The second statement in a syllogism must show the relation between *one* of the classes in the first statement and a *third* class. The information contained in this statement may then be added to the diagram representing the first statement. We gave examples of this in the two syllogisms, one valid and one invalid, that attempted to show that Jones was a Communist. Other examples will be found in the next paragraph.

THE CONCLUSION

If the diagram representing the first two statements now shows definitely the relation between the third class and the class *not* mentioned in the second statement, a valid conclusion may be drawn. Otherwise the syllogism proves nothing at all.

1. All Norwegians are blonds.
   John is a blond.
   No conclusion possible.

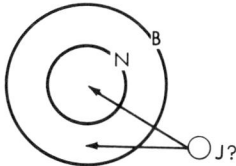

2. All blonds are Norwegians.
   John is a blond.
   Conclusion: John is a Norwegian.

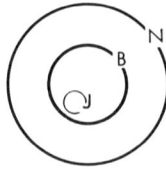

3. No marines are cowards.
   Dave is a marine.
   Conclusion: Dave is not a coward.

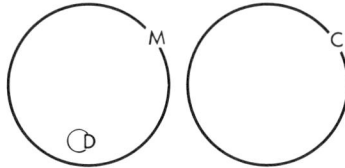

4. Some of his friends are sailors.
   All of his friends are clever people.
   Conclusion: Some sailors are clever people.

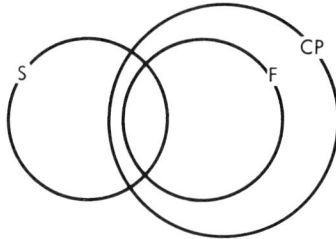

5. Only big men are tackles.
   Dick is a big man.
   No conclusion possible.

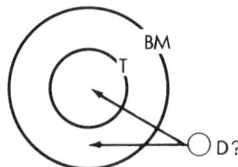

Of course you may be quite capable of testing a syllogism for validity without drawing a picture of it; but if you have to check one it is much easier to do it with the three circles than by learning a large number of rules about *universal negatives, particular affirmatives,* the *laws of conversion,* and the *fallacy of unwarranted distribution.* All you have to do is to draw the first two circles in such a way as to indicate the information contained in the first statement, add the information contained in the second statement, and see whether the combined diagram proves anything or not.

There is, of course, a good deal more to logic than the study of syllogisms; and we hope we have not given the impression that the whole subject can be condensed into one neat little capsule for handy absorption. But the basic principles of the logical method are illustrated in the material we have examined, and the importance of this method should be obvious. A man who thinks illogically is like one who pays no attention to the difference between the signs for multiplication and division. When he attempts to work out a problem for himself, he is completely unreliable. And when he receives information, he is likely to be at the mercy of the man who hands it out.

TRUTH AND VALIDITY

If you learn the method shown in the preceding pages you can avoid *illogical conclusions,* because you will have found out a reliable way of tracing the connections between *statements assumed to be true.* **But you must resist the temptation to believe that when a conclusion is logically sound or "valid" it is inevitably true.** The conclusion is certainly true *only* if the basic statements are certainly true. And this is *never* possible when the statements deal with physical things. This does not mean that logic is useless in dealing with physical things, but only that it must be used with appropriate caution.

A TRUE SYLLOGISM

Examine the following syllogism:

All squares are rectangles.
ABCD is a square.
Therefore ABCD is a rectangle.

This is not only a sound syllogism but a perfectly true one, because both squares and rectangles are *pure abstractions created by definition,* and the definition of a rectangle includes the definition of a square. All squares have the same properties *by definition*. It is therefore unnecessary to examine every square that has been conceived or that may be conceived in the future to see if its sides and angles are equal; if they are not equal, it is not a square. The same is true of "all rectangles." Remember, *no square has ever been drawn*. The *figure* ABCD that you see on a blackboard or in a book is not a square, but merely the representation of a square. If you should measure it with very accurate instruments and find that two of the angles were 89 degrees and the other two 91 degrees, you would not have found an exceptional square that violated the rule. You would merely have found a slightly inaccurate *representation* of a square, which is nothing to get excited about.

AN APPROXIMATELY TRUE SYLLOGISM

On the other hand, let us consider the following syllogism:

All Englishmen are tea-drinkers.
Derek is an Englishman.
Therefore Derek is a tea-drinker.

This follows the same form as the syllogism about squares and rectangles, and is equally sound from a logical point of view. We may therefore say that *if* the first two statements are true, the conclusion is equally true. But if we examine the argument closely we notice an important difference. Englishmen are *not* created by definition, but by cohabitation. We cannot, therefore, be certain in advance that they are all alike. We are not justified in making a statement about all Englishmen until we have examined them all. If Derek is an Englishman, we have to find out that he is a tea-drinker before we are justified in making the statement that all Englishmen are tea-drinkers. In other words, we have to know that he is a tea-drinker before we can prove that he is a tea-drinker. Our logic does not seem to be getting us very far.

This does not mean that logic is useless when applied to physical things, but only that it never produces hundred percent certainties in this field as it does when applied to mathematical abstractions. With physical things, logic can give us only probabilities and approximations—but so can measurements. Let us rephrase our syllogism about Derek in such a way as to make it useful.

A very high proportion of Englishmen are known to be tea-drinkers.
It is very nearly certain that Derek is an Englishman.
Therefore it is extremely probable that Derek is a tea-drinker.

If we are expecting to have Derek as a guest, this more elastic syllogism will be useful. In the first place it suggests that we have some tea on hand when Derek comes. It also suggests that we ask him about his taste before we start forcing tea down his possibly unwilling throat. If it turns out that he is an unusual Englishman, we are spared a shock—and maybe we can get a refund on the unopened tea.

THE LIMITATIONS OF LOGIC

The reason that logic cannot be used rigidly with physical things may be explained quite simply. In a class of abstractions *created* by definition, all members are exactly alike, and some characteristics are *inevitably* associated with others. If you prove that something is a circle, you know that the relation of its diameter to its circumference is exactly *pi*, because that's the way circles are. But when we turn to the physical world we find:

1. That the members of a class are never exactly alike. Even if the class has only one member, that one is constantly changing.

2. That the association of characterisics is merely a matter of probability.

Consequently, when a man says, "All Syrians (or women or college professors or Fords) are alike," he is not telling the truth, though he may be perfectly sincere. And when he says, "Anybody that would do that would steal sheep," he is treating a probability (possibly a pretty good one) as if it were a fact.

There are two obvious temptations to say (and think) things like these. First, it is flattering to the ego to pretend that we know "all about" something. Second, it saves a lot of trouble. If you "know" in advance that all Mexicans are lazy, all Scotsmen stingy, and all politicians dishonest, you are spared the task of finding out about them one by one. Before yielding to these temptations, however, it might be a good idea to consider whether you can afford to yield to them.

It is often said that many fanatics and certain types of lunatics are among the most logical people in the world. You can't find fault with their chains of reasoning, and even their facts are often approximately right. But because they treat approximations and probabilities as absolute certainties, their conclusions are wildly wrong.

LOGIC—HANDLE WITH CARE

Using sound logic on any practical problem is like using sound mathematics on an engineering problem—if you don't do it, you may go hopelessly astray. But when a good engineer has made his exact calculations, he always allows a reasonable margin of safety, because he realizes two things. There *may* be a factor or so he has not allowed for; and a part that should stand a thousand pounds of strain *may* break at five hundred. When we are dealing with the physical universe we never know *all* about anything. And no matter how carefully we define our classes, we can't make their members exactly alike.

IMITATION LOGIC

It is possible to make honest mistakes in our reasoning, just as it is possible to make honest mistakes in arithmetic. But it is also possible to shortchange people logically. In fact it is a very widespread habit indeed, and it gets far more toleration than it deserves. Pillars of society who wouldn't think of sneaking a quarter out of the change for a ten dollar bill seem to feel no guilt at all as they talk their customers out of millions—of dollars or votes or whatever it is that they happen to need. The general attitude seems to be that outright and provable lies are bad, but that tricking people into reaching the wrong conclusions is quite legitimate.

Consider advertisements, for instance. Some of them give real evidence in favor of their products. When you read that a big trucking company has saved 20 percent on its tire bill by switching to Rollright Tires, you may well be looking at a sound argument. If you have trucks of your own you'll want to check further before buying. Maybe the company switched from an off brand that's only half as good as some of the others, in which case a 20 percent improvement isn't enough. Maybe there are other concealed tricks. But when a manufacturer uses advertisements of this sort, which invite factual checking, and which would boomerang if the facts weren't accurate, there is a pretty good chance that the facts will stand up.

A second kind of advertisement doesn't bother with evidence at all, but simply tries to get you to react without thinking. If you have heard about Sticko Gum often enough and long enough, you may come to feel (not think) that Sticko *means* gum, and that it would be rather farfetched to ask for any other kind. The gum may or may not be good, but there's no use arguing with this kind of advertising, because there is nothing to argue about.

It is a third kind of advertising with which we are concerned—a kind that pretends to appeal to your reasoning powers, but actually tries to short-circuit them. There are various subtypes, but they all have one thing in common: they try to tempt you to accept some sort of loose association as a substitute for an accurate connection. Are you worried about your waistline, your skin tone, or your gas mileage? Okay, do something about them—but is there any real reason to think that the product that brought them to your attention is the best cure? The people in the picture certainly look happy with their Butterfly motorboat. But (even if they are not paid for doing so) are there enough of them to make a convincing sample? The Purple Streak may well be the only car that has all seven of those features —but are they the most important features? And do you really know for sure that twisty-bar suspension is any better than curly-spring?

Of course advertisers aren't the only ones that try to make you accept their arguments rather than examine them. Politicians, charitable organizations, governments, even religious bodies, may do the same. The motives are often excellent, and there are times when it may pay you to yield without a struggle. But when you act emotionally you might as well know what you're doing and not pretend that you are guided by pure reason.

There have been various analyses of the kinds of tricks used to make you think you're thinking. Thirty-odd years ago the Institute for Propaganda Analysis gave a good deal of publicity to "the seven" common propaganda devices.

1. The Name-Calling Device.
2. The Glittering Generalities Device.
3. The Transfer Device.
4. The Testimonial Device.
5. The Plain Folks Device.
6. The Card-Stacking Device.
7. The Bandwagon Device.

It became a popular classroom game, complete with objective tests and statistical analyses, to classify all suspicious statements under these headings.

We are not going to try to play the whole game here because it has a tendency to shift the emphasis from "Is this statement sound?" to "What shall we call this unsound statement?" and often winds up in hairsplitting arguments. But we must take time for a few words about one of them, because The Testimonial Device seems to have become a national disease.

Under appropriate circumstances testimony is perfectly reasonable grounds for belief. We don't have time to study everything, and the obvious way to get a sound opinion on a subject about which we don't know much is to ask a man who does. But if the answer is important to us, we ought to make sure of at least three things:

1. That the man's expert knowledge really covers the question. Maybe a low earned-run average qualifies a man to judge razor blades, but the connection seems remote.

2. That the opinion is really unbiased. The fact that endorsements have a cash value, and that "celebrities" often switch, for a consideration, from one brand to another, is well known—but it doesn't seem to interfere with advertising effectiveness.

3. That most other experts would accept his opinion. This doesn't mean that the majority of experts is always right. But if you believe a man *against* most other experts, you shouldn't do it simply on the grounds that he *is* an expert. You ought to understand his reasoning, or have some other sound grounds.

This third point deserves special attention. It is amazing how many people will seriously argue that spiritualism, for instance, simply must be true because three well-known scientists have said that they believed in it. "And if men like that, with trained minds and international reputations, believe in it there simply *must* be something in it." The fact that hundreds of equally well-known scientists have said they don't believe in it is left out of account.

EXERCISES

I. Examine the appeals that are *apparently* being made in the statements below; note the presence or absence of techniques or devices described in the chapter. Accordingly, label the statements R (reasonable), or U (unreasonable), and among the former indicate those you happen to believe (perhaps intuitively) are true as well as reasonable. Where appropriate, construct syllogisms to analyze the situations, but notice that in almost every case you will have to complete the syllogism by drawing upon *unstated assumptions* which *you* see underlying the situation. Another person may draw upon other underlying assumptions, producing other syllogisms with other conclusions.

1. Cousin Bill, a veteran of the Vietnam War, can certainly qualify for aid under the G.I. Bill to help him finish school.

2. Sue must be a member of that sorority. I saw her at the last meeting they had.

3. Of course he just returned from a winter vacation down South—look at his tan!

4. If we don't keep our young people from smoking pot, they will all be heroin addicts before they are 30.

5. Of course Mr. Anthony won't support this ecology measure—he's president of the General Pesticides Corporation.

6. Bill must be dumb if he flunked a quiz as easy as that one.

7. With an accent like that, he must be from Canada.

8. Karen's roommate has to be an English major. She's always typing.

9. Philip must be smart. Did you hear about all the honors he has won?

10. Of course he's a good boy. I've known that family through three generations.

II. In each of the situations below, list as many as you can of the underlying as-sumptions that may be implicit in the point of view expressed. Indicate, where applicable, if an assumption involves one of the propaganda devices listed in this chapter. Finally, construct at least two syllogisms out of each situation—both valid (but not necessarily having true conclusions). Try for contradiction (opposite conclusions in the two syllogisms), or sequence (conclusions of one syllogism becoming a premise of the next syllogism).

1. Why not get the Handi-Dandi study notes for *Ivanhoe*? I read the notes for *Romeo and Juliet* and got an "A" on my paper.

2. Of course she knows what she's doing. She's in charge, isn't she?

3. Jim must be angry. I haven't seen him all day.

4. Your rose bush is so big! You must use expensive fertilizer.

5. All the history majors I know wear glasses. Do you think I'm going to major in history and ruin my eyes?

6. She must have cheated. She said she didn't study much but she got a 93% on the test.

7. Your mathematics teachers must have been very poor, Mr. Jones. There is a mistake on your income tax return.

8. Since you oppose building a swimming pool at Main Street and Crosstown Boulevard, it is apparent that you dislike children and don't care about their welfare.

9. According to what I heard, Bob and Ed had a big fight yesterday. Poor Bob has a terrible black eye from that bully Ed.

10. Of course I had a fair deal. The dealer was a Republican, wasn't he?

Suggestions for Discussion or Theme Writing

Test your skill with logic and imitation logic by supporting a proposition that is almost certain to be disagreed with. Among other techniques, try introducing some fallacious premises on which to base further argument (you might have to cloud the issue to cover the false premises). Wherever possible, use logical processes or those that appear to be logical. Accept the statements in their most literal or traditional sense, without semantic dodges. Write a theme in support of one of the following:

1. The earth is flat.

2. All left-handed people are superior.

3. An evil spirit secretly controls your car.

4. Rain is caused by angels having water-balloon fights.

5. Crabgrass is conspiring to take over the world.

6. The cook in the student cafeteria has discovered a strange new animal whose meat is totally tasteless.

7. Brown shoelaces are bad luck.

8. Singing in the shower is hazardous to your health.

9. There are actually little people living inside your television set.

10. Baseball is derived from an ancient spring fertility rite.

11. Leaves turn colors and fall so that the ground can absorb the colors for next spring's flowers.

12. Toasted marshmallows are addictive and should be prohibited by law.

13. Rumors are started by sparrows who sit on telephone wires and listen to the conversations.

14. Dream of a death and there will be a wedding.

15. America was discovered not by Columbus but by my ancestor "_____."

REPORTS,
INFERENCES,
AND
VALUE
JUDGMENTS

THREE DESCRIPTIONS OF AN ACTION

Two boys were talking. There was a blow, and one of the boys fell to the ground. Three girls standing nearby were asked to describe what had happened.

Irene said: "Tom and Max were talking. Then Tom hit Max in the face and Max fell down."

This is a report. Irene's words tell nothing that she hadn't seen and heard. She draws no conclusions and offers no opinions—simply recounts the facts that she has observed.

Jane said: "Tom and Max were arguing about something. Then Tom got mad and knocked Max down."

This is not a pure report, because Jane's words go beyond what she had seen and heard. She tries to guess at the reason. We could easily make several other guesses. "Getting mad" is a complicated chemical process not visible to the naked eye. Maybe the boys were putting on an act. Tom might have been trying to kill a mosquito—a big, dangerous one. Or maybe he knocked Max down rather sorrowfully, to prevent him from committing a crime. All these explanations are unlikely. Jane's guess is probably quite right; but it is still a guess, and the chances are she doesn't know it. Very few people have been trained to separate their inferences from what they have actually observed.

If you think that the moral of all this is that reports are better than inferences, you are wrong. They are simply different. We really need a flourish of trumpets here to emphasize the point. There are times when you should simply report the facts and let somebody else decide what they mean. There are times when you should decide yourself. But you should *always* know which you are doing. People who can't distinguish between observable facts and their inferences from those facts cause a lot of trouble —particularly for themselves. However, before we go into this any further we'd better listen to the third girl.

Ann said: "Max and Tom were talking, and without any warning at all that big bully Tom hit poor Max when he wasn't looking and knocked him down."

This is a judgment. Ann has gone a step further than Jane. Not only has she guessed about things she couldn't see, but she has weighed the whole incident (including the part she has guessed) on her scale of values.

Here again we must emphasize that there is nothing wrong about what she has done. True, she would probably not go unchallenged if she talked that way as a witness in a lawsuit. There the jury is supposed to do the evaluating, and the witness is supposed to give a report as nearly factual as is humanly possible. But if she told her friends the simple, observed facts and made no comment at all on the values, they would probably think she was either cold-blooded or feeble-minded. A person who has no values, or who is unwilling to bring them out, is not of much use to society (and that is *our* value judgment). But even when we are sure enough of our judgments to fight for them, we shouldn't mistake them for observable facts.

WHEN IS EACH KIND APPROPRIATE?

Let's consider the matter from the other side for a moment. What do *you* want when you ask a question? If you ask a friend about a movie or a new restaurant, you probably want a value judgment. You want to decide whether or not to go, and you have some respect for his judgment or you wouldn't bother to ask him. You may want him to report a few details— is it a mystery or a romance, or do they specialize in chicken or steaks— but your main question is simply, is it good enough to be worth your while?

If he gives you a 40-minute report on the details and then tells you to form your own opinion, you'll probably never ask him again. Or suppose your car is making funny noises and you call in the drag-race expert from next door to listen to it. He can observe only the same noises that you can, but he has learned to draw better inferences from them. Maybe he can tell you what's making the noise and how important it is. You want his inferences, his value judgments, and perhaps a little free labor to boot.

On the other hand, suppose your little sister and brother have been squabbling and you are trying to bring peace back into the family. The more you hear about who was mean and who was unfair and who really started it the more confused you get. Their inferences and judgments don't help you a bit. What you'd like to get is a simple report on what happened. Then you could do your own inferring and judging, and decide what action to take.

We cannot draw an absolute and permanent line between observations and inferences, or between inferences and judgments. Ordinarily we will accept the statement that a man saw a deer as a simple report of his observations. But if he shoots the deer, and it then turns out to have been a cow, we have to revise our estimate. We may then say that he saw a shape, inferred that it was a deer, and will now have to pay two hundred dollars for confusing an inference with an observation. Perhaps the difference between inferences and value judgments is even harder to define rigorously. However, we can make reasonably reliable distinctions. We might define an inference as the result of examining observed facts in the light of past experience. We may have to hurry over "observed facts" a little, but so does everybody else. Then we can define a judgment as an evaluation of either facts or inferences. And finally (to turn to the title of our chapter) we can insist that a report must confine itself to a record of observations, with no inferences and no judgments—or at least with no statements that can be proved to be either of these things. However we define them, we will certainly find that many people firmly believe that *their* inferences and *their* judgments are reports of observable facts. Let's assume that a student has written the following paragraph:

> Mrs. Smith is one of the most disagreeable women I have ever met. She is completely selfish, has very bad manners, and flies into a temper at the slightest excuse. She is mean to all her family, and I pity anybody who has to associate with her.

Now suppose the instructor says, "That is all right for a judgment, but I would like you to write a report to back the judgment up. Tell me some of the things that you have seen Mrs. Smith do that led you to make this judgment." He is likely to get another paragraph that looks something like this:

> I have frequently seen Mrs. Smith do very selfish things. She insists on monopolizing the family car, even when her husband and children need it much more than she does, and she spends more on clothes than she can afford, while her husband goes around practically in rags. I have seen her get perfectly furious just because her husband suggested going to a different movie from the one she wanted to see. She expects him to wait on her all the time, but she doesn't even thank him when he holds her chair or gets up to bring her a book which she could have easily reached. She scolds her children in a very unpleasant voice, and doesn't take the slightest interest in their plans or even in their welfare.

This paragraph contains a good deal more information than the first one, but it is *not* a report of observable fact. Such words and phrases as the following indicate inferences or judgments or both: *very selfish; insists on monopolizing; even when her husband and children need it more than she does; practically in rags; perfectly furious; just; expects; doesn't even thank.*

It is possible that some of these inferences and judgments are wrong. She may, for instance, be devoted to her children but afraid of spoiling them. But let us assume that Mrs. Smith *is* a thoroughly unpleasant woman, and that all the inferences and judgments are quite sound. They are still inferences and judgments, and they have no place in a factual report. They would not, for instance, be admitted as testimony in a lawsuit. Let us see if we can write a clean report on what the student had actually observed. It might go something like this:

> One rainy morning I heard Mr. Smith ask his wife if he could take the car that day. She said that that was ridiculous, since she had a lot of shopping to do. Mr. Smith then walked to the bus station, four blocks away. About an hour later, after the rain had stopped, I saw Mrs. Smith drive to the grocery store, two blocks away. She was gone about ten minutes. The car stayed in the garage for the rest of the day. I have never seen Mr. Smith drive to work.

> Mrs. Smith has a new fur coat every two years, and more hats and shoes than any woman I know. In the last four years I have seen Mr. Smith wear only two suits. Both are now very shiny at the elbows.

> One evening they stopped at our house and borrowed the paper to see what movies were showing. Mrs. Smith said, "There is nothing much good —I suppose we might as well see Doris Day." Mr. Smith said, "I hear *The Pawnbroker* is very good—why don't we see that?" Mrs. Smith threw the

paper down on the table and said, in a much louder voice than she had been using, "I should think a man who can't afford to take his wife to a night club would at least let her choose the movie." She then walked out of the house without saying another word to anybody. Mr. Smith thanked us, said goodnight, and followed.

Another evening when they visited us Mrs. Smith sat down, then reached over and put her cigarettes and matches on a table about two feet away. A few minutes later she interrupted her own conversation to say, "Cigarette, Harry." Mr. Smith got up, crossed the room, took a cigarette from her package, handed it to her, and lit it. She did not thank him.

Although her house is two doors away from ours, I often hear her telling her children that they are lazy, stupid, clumsy, and selfish. I cannot hear their answers. Late one afternoon she was sitting on our porch when her boy came over and asked if they could have dinner early that night so he could get to scout meeting on time. She told him that they would have dinner when she was ready. She continued to sit and look at a magazine for half an hour after my mother had excused herself and gone in to prepare our dinner. Both of her children have a great many colds. My mother once suggested that she give them vitamin pills. Mrs. Smith said that they were too expensive and that she had no faith in them.

There are several things to notice about this report. It may or may not be unbiased. We simply can't tell whether the writer has left out all the nice things that he has seen Mrs. Smith do, or whether he has never seen her do anything nice. But as far as it goes the report does tell what Mrs. Smith did, without making any guesses, no matter how reasonable, about why she did it. In the second place it leaves out all words that indicate judgment. There is a difference between saying "She did not thank him," which is a simple observation, and "She did not *even* thank him," which would certainly suggest that she should have. Maybe she should, but a report is no place to say so. And in the third place, since the reader is allowed to form his own reactions, they will probably be much stronger than if we had tried to force ours on him. Anybody reading the judgment is likely to think, "The writer certainly has got it in for Mrs. Smith. I wonder how much of that is true and how much is prejudice." But anybody reading the report is almost certain to feel that Mrs. Smith is a thoroughly unpleasant woman. Even if he suspects that some evidence on her side has been left out—that she can't really be quite *that* bad—she will seem bad enough.

The technique works just as well in the other direction. If you want to describe your favorite character you will probably arouse more enthusiasm by showing him in action at his best than by telling how good you think he is.

REPORTING LEADS TO EXPANSION

Now if you will just glance back at the various accounts of Mrs. Smith you will notice that the report is very much longer than the judgment. This is not an accident. **You simply cannot give the evidence on which a judgment is based in as few words as you can give the judgment itself.** It takes only three words to say "Mary is wonderful," but it takes a good many more to report things about Mary that lead reasonably to such a conclusion. This is something that may be worth remembering the next time you discover, after writing fifty or a hundred words, that "there is nothing more to say." There is at least a strong possibility that what you have said is a judgment—your own brief summary of a lot of evidence. If so, the best way to expand your material is to get back to the facts or events on which the judgment is based.

Naturally a good many papers call for opinions—inferences and judgments—as well as facts. But even in such papers **it is usually a good idea to give a reasonable selection of the facts first.** Your reader is much more likely to be interested in your opinions if he can see some of the evidence on which they are based.

That is the polite way to put the point of this chapter. There is a less pleasant way. We said earlier that it is impossible to draw absolute lines between reports, inferences, and judgments. **But we can safely say that a writer who cannot report will likely be weak in inferring and unreliable in value judgments.** The reason is obvious: if he cannot observe clearly and accurately and report what he has observed, it is unlikely that he has whatever it was solidly enough in mind to make reasonable inferences and value judgments regarding it.

There is one skill a competent writer cannot do without: to be able to describe what he sees without leaping to judgment. Most prose judges; it is impossible to keep some kind of value frame out of almost all writing. The mere fact that one chooses to write about one thing and not about another is some kind of judgment.

But most of us leap to judgment. Behind that leap lies the assumption of our own keenness of vision, our vast powers of analysis, our unshakable fairness, our steely logic and common sense. That looks like a job for Superman, and we are forever leaping out of mental telephone booths into judgments.

One midwestern university, hoping to cope with this problem, has turned its entire first-year English program into a report-rehabilitation center. Each class is split into groups of four. In the beginning, one person from each group is given an object—a roll of Life Savers, a pencil, a dime—

and is told to go out of the building, give the object to a stranger, and say, "I want you to have this." Then he is to return and write down what he saw when he offered the object. His audience is the other three students; his purpose is to make them see what he saw—and that is not a bad definition of the purpose of all writing.

Perhaps you can guess what the first reports say. "He got mad." "He looked at me in a funny way." "He stared at me in contempt and walked away." "He was completely unreasonable: wouldn't take the dime, wouldn't listen to an explanation, and walked away angrily." All those reports are inferences or value judgments or both. They do not report, and the group tells the writer so.

Another member is sent out. And another and another until the group can report that in one instance it saw what happened, not how the writer reacted to what happened.

The advantage of the system is that the writer actually gets to talk to his audience, to receive their criticism directly, something not many writers can manage.

We are not sponsoring the system. If you, however, find yourself leaping to judgment, why don't you buy a roll of Life Savers. . . .

EXERCISES

I. In each of the sentences below, an attempt has been made to emphasize only one of the three processes: reporting, inferring, or judging. Mark each sentence R (report), I (inference), or J (judgment) to indicate which process seems to predominate in the sentence or the situation underlying it.

Where more than one process is evident, mark more than one letter, and add a comment to clarify your answer.

1. My brother goes to bed regularly at 2 A.M., and that's much too late.

2. There are 28 desks in the average classroom in the Waldenmier Building.

3. Mr. Andrews is unhappy—he must have lost that contract bid he was making.

4. She came into class late and was very embarrassed.

5. Philip irresponsibly left his car unlocked, and he was properly chagrined when his camera was stolen from the front seat.

6. The cat is hungry.

7. German chocolate cake is absolutely fantastic.

8. The baby is playing happily in the backyard.

9. Did you see that no-good Sue cheating on the last test?

10. Coffee is bad for children.

11. Milly is so disorganized and irresponsible that she is always overtired.

12. Bill is in love.

13. They are out together every weekend, and that's too often.

14. He stupidly forgot to mark down the due-date of the paper, and was very unhappy when the teacher refused to accept his lame excuses.

15. Vacation starts June 15.

16. Humphrey must be on the varsity this year, because I saw him leaving the varsity locker room with his grip.

17. Cars like that should not be allowed on the street.

18. Of course he is from Kentucky. I saw him driving a car with Kentucky license plates.

19. He drinks a lot and stays out late and is always in trouble—in short, he's not acceptable to the Nominating Committee.

20. Hyacinth changed her major from math to economics.

21. Hyacinth didn't like math.

22. Hyacinth was too lazy to be a math major.

23. Fred doesn't like to water ski because he's too cowardly for such a dangerous sport.

24. Paul dubiously agreed on the outlandish plan, and was not a bit surprised when it failed.

25. Jeremy got a low mark on his last theme; the instructor must not like him.

II. Sometimes even a report consisting of verifiable information may, by its choice and arrangement of the facts it uses, make certain inferences and/or judgments appear unavoidable. Study the hypothetical news story below, and list the inferences that the newsman might be inviting you to make. Finally, indicate after each inference which judgment (approval or disapproval) might follow along naturally, once the inference has been accepted.

THE STATE CAPITAL The State Legislature today passed Representative Chauncy Smugbluff's anti-pollution bill. Stiff opposition to the bill by the Outts Party had kept the legislature deadlocked for several weeks. Last-minute support for the measure by three major industrial lobbies swung the balance in favor of the bill. The governor is expected to sign the bill into law sometime tomorrow.

Opponents of the bill claimed that it was unenforceable and perhaps unconstitutional, but in an impassioned speech before the upper house, Representative Smugbluff replied, "The enormity of the ecology problem can no longer be neglected by the agencies of democratic government. This bill is desperately needed, today, if our children are to breathe clean air and drink clean water tomorrow."

The bill calls for new controls over industrial sewage and air pollution. It includes new regulations for smokestack filters, repurification of water, and waste-product dumpage. Details of the enforcement of these measures will be settled shortly, according to the bill's supporters. The State Ecology Commission is already preparing for the court challenge it feels is inevitable.

When questioned about the bill at his morning press conference, Governor Morely said, "I promised the people of this fine state that something would be done during my administration to end pollution. My thanks go to Mr. Smugbluff and the industry of this state for their grand and noble efforts in seeing this bill through."

DEVELOPMENT
OF
THE
LANGUAGE

8

If you looked at the French and Italian words for *hundred—cent* and *cento* respectively—you would easily guess that they are related. They both developed from the Latin word *centum*. And if you looked at the German word *hundert* you could recognize it as a close relative of the English word. You would be right, but you could not prove it quite so easily, because we do not have any written records of the early form of Germanic from which modern English and German developed. We have to prove the relationship by other methods, which are too complicated to go into here.

You would probably not guess that *hundred* and *centum* are also related; but if you happened to think of these two words along with *horn* and *corno, house* and *casa,* and various other pairs that begin with *h* in English and *c* in Italian, you might suspect that these resemblances were systematic, and that English is also related to Italian, although not nearly as closely as French is. Your suspicions would be justified. Experts can trace the relations among all four of these languages and a good many others. We can say roughly that French and Italian are sister languages, both born of Latin; that English and modern German are approximately second cousins; and that English and Italian are something like third cousins twice removed.

Nobody knows for sure how language began, or even whether it began just once or at a number of different times and places. What we do know is that some languages, as we have just seen, show evidence of a common origin, while others do not. If our written records went back a few thousand years further than they do, it is possible that we might find signs of resemblance between the languages that we have just mentioned and Chinese or Arabic or Navajo. But if such resemblances ever existed, they disappeared a long time ago, and it seems most unlikely that we will ever find any evidence to prove them. We must therefore study them as separate families, though they may have had a common ancestor.

ORIGIN OF ENGLISH

English belongs, in a rather complicated way, to the Indo-European family, which includes most of the European languages and a few Asiatic ones. We do not know where the original speakers of the parent Indo-European language lived. Guesses about their homeland range all the way from northwestern Europe to central Asia. According to all the early records they were a tall, blond, and warlike people, with a good deal of energy and intelligence. In their native land they had developed neither writing nor cities, so there is not much evidence about how they lived when they were at home. But when they went out in search of new lands—which they did in various waves from about 2500 B.C. to about 1000 B.C.—the Indo-Europeans seem to have been generally successful in conquering other countries.

When a wave of them settled in a territory already crowded, they mixed with the original population. In time they lost their distinctive appearance by intermarrying with the earlier inhabitants, and sometimes they also gave up most of the features of their language. When a wave went to a more thinly settled territory, they naturally preserved their physical characteristics comparatively unchanged for a much longer time; and they were likely to preserve the distinctive features of their language also, though the two things did not always go together.

The Slavic and Celtic languages, as well as Indian, Persian, and some others, are of Indo-European origin, but the three branches with which English is most concerned are the Greek, Latin, and Germanic, particularly the last. All languages are changing to some extent all the time; and before the invention of writing they seem to have changed faster. Since the various waves of conquerors left their homeland at different times, they were speaking noticeably different varieties of Indo-European at the times of their departures; and the further changes that took place after they left made their languages more and more unlike. As they split up and settled in different regions, the differences became so great that the Greeks, for instance, could not possibly understand the Germans; and a little later some of the Germans could not understand other Germans.

Old Germanic split into North, East, and West Germanic. West Germanic split into High and Low German. And Low German split into further dialects, including those of the Angles, Saxons, and Jutes. There were differences in pronunciation, and even in word endings, between these last three; but most of the root words were enough alike to be recognizable, and the three tribes seem to have had no great difficulty in understanding each other. About 450 A.D. members of all three tribes moved into what is now called England (from Angle-land), and began to take it over. It is at this time that we usually say the English language, as such, began.

It is worth noticing that even at the very beginning of English as a separate language there was no one simple standard. The Jutes undoubtedly thought that the Angles "talked funny," and vice versa. Efforts have been made for centuries to develop a set of standard practices, and there is much to be said in their favor; but they have never been quite successful, and they probably never will be. There is just no way to make millions of people talk exactly alike.

These early English settlers do not seem to have made much of an effort to understand the language of the Britons who were living in England (then called Britain). The Britons also spoke an Indo-European language, but it belonged to the Celtic rather than the Germanic branch, and was by now completely unrecognizable to the newcomers. The English added only a handful of Celtic words to their language—not nearly as many as the Americans later picked up from the Indians.

We can only guess about how the language would have developed if the descendants of these three tribes had been left to themselves. The fact is that two great invasions and a missionary movement changed the language enormously. The total result of these and other influences was that the English vocabulary became the largest and most complex in the world, and the grammar changed its emphasis from inflections (changes in the forms of words) to word order.

THE SCANDINAVIAN INFLUENCE

Some three hundred years after the West Germanic tribes had settled in England, there was another wave of invasions, this time by Scandinavians. In the history books these people are usually referred to as "Danes," but there were Swedes and Norwegians among them, and their speech was probably no more uniform than that of the first wave. The dialects they spoke belonged to the Northern rather than the Western division of Germanic. They differed rather more from the dialects of the Angles, Saxons, and Jutes than these differed from each other—roughly, about as much as Spanish differs from Italian. In spite of different habits of pronunciation, most of the root words were enough alike to be recognizable. The difficulty caused by differences in inflection was partly solved by dropping some of the inflections altogether and being broad-minded about the others. Spelling was not much of a problem, because most people could not read or write, and those who could, spelled as they pleased. There were no dictionaries to prove them wrong.

Although these Danes moved in on the English, and for a time dominated them politically, their conquest was nothing like as thorough as that of the English over the Britons. After the early fighting the two peoples settled down together without much attention to their separate origins, and the languages mingled. On the whole, English rather than Danish characteristics won out; but many of the words were so much alike that it is impossible to say whether we owe our present forms to English or Danish origins. Sometimes both forms remained, usually with a somewhat different meaning. Thus we have *shirt* and *skirt,* both of which originally meant a long, smock-like garment, although the English form has come to mean the upper part, and the Danish form the lower. Old English *rear* and Danish *raise* are another pair—sometimes interchangeable, sometimes not.

THE NORMAN CONQUEST

In 1066 the Normans conquered England. They, like the Danes, had originally come from Scandinavia. But they had settled in northern France, and for some undiscoverable reason had given up their own language and learned to speak a dialect of French. For several centuries Normans, and other Frenchmen that they invited in later, held most of the important positions in England, and it seemed quite possible that French would become the standard language of the country. But the bulk of the population were still English, and they were stubborner than their rulers. Most of them never learned French, and eventually—though only after several centuries —all the nobles and officials were using English.

It was not, however, the English of the days before the conquest. A good many French words had gotten into the language; and most of the inflections that had survived the Danish pressure had dropped out, with a standard word order making up for their loss. We need not go into the argument about whether the new word order had to develop because the endings dropped out, or the endings disappeared because the new word order made them unnecessary. The two changes took place together, and by the time of Chaucer (died 1400) the language had become enough like modern English to be recognizable. The pronunciation was quite different and the spelling was still catch-as-catch-can; but a modern student can get at least a general idea of Chaucer's meaning without special training, while he can no more read Old English than he can German or Latin, unless he has made a special study of it. Compare the two following passages:

1. Hwaet! We gardena   in geardagum
    Theodcyningas   thrym gefrunon
2. Whan that Aprille with his shoures soote
    The droghte of March hath perced to the roote

In the first two lines from *Beowulf* (about 700 A.D.), only *we* and *in* are readily recognizable; while in the first two from Chaucer's *Canterbury Tales*, only *soote* (sweet) offers much of a problem.

From Chaucer's time to our own the language has developed with no outside pressure comparable to that of the Danish and Norman invasions. Still more endings have disappeared, and there have been other changes; but the greatest development has been in the vocabulary. A considerable number of Chaucer's words have dropped out of use, and a much greater number of new words have been added. Some of these new words have been made by compounding or otherwise modifying old ones, but most of them have been borrowed from other languages, particularly Latin.

THE LATIN INFLUENCE

Even before they came to England, our ancestors had picked up a few Latin words, and they learned others from the Christian missionaries who began to convert them in the sixth century. These early borrowings were taken directly into the spoken language, and most of them have now changed so that their Latin origins are not easy to recognize. *Street, wine, bishop, priest,* and *church* (the last three originally borrowed from Greek by the Romans) are examples.

After the Norman Conquest, borrowings from Latin were enormously increased. French itself is directly descended from Latin, and we cannot always tell whether an English word came directly from Latin or through French. *Suspicion,* for instance, could have come into English by either route. But we do know that many words must have come straight from Latin, either because they don't occur in French or because their French forms are different. Scholars often could not find an English word for an idea they wished to express; and even if they could, they might think that a Latin word was more exact or more impressive.

English has also borrowed words from many other languages, particularly Greek, and is continuing to do so at present; but ever since the late Middle English period it has been a matter of helping ourselves, rather than yielding to pressure.

DEVELOPMENT OF A LITERARY STANDARD

The changes that took place in the language throughout the Old and Middle English periods were a natural development, unguided by any theory. Men talked more or less as their neighbors did, and anybody who wrote tried to indicate the sound of his speech on paper. There were no dictionaries, no grammars, and no printed books of any kind. As far as we know, very few people thought about the language at all; and most of those who did think about it seem to have considered it a crude and rather hopeless affair, unworthy of serious study. There were exceptions, of course, but they did not have much influence. Local differences were so great that a man trained in northern England would have serious difficulty reading a manuscript written in the southern part. However, the dialect of London had a certain prestige throughout the country; and although this dialect itself was by no means uniform, changing with shifts in city population, it gradually came to be accepted as the standard. By the latter half of the fifteenth century it was quite generally used in writing throughout the country except in the extreme north. The introduction of printing in 1476, with London as the publishing center, greatly strengthened the influence of the London dialect. Strong local differences in spoken English remain to this day, especially among the less educated classes. But throughout the modern period written (or at least published) English has been surprisingly uniform.

EIGHTEENTH-CENTURY MOVEMENT TO REGULARIZE THE LANGUAGE

Until the eighteenth century the uniformity was the result of social pressure rather than of educational theory. Early English grammars (the first appeared in 1586) had been written either to help foreigners learn English or to prepare English students for the study of Latin grammar. On the whole these books neither had nor were intended to have any influence on the use of English by native speakers. It was not until about 1750 that there was any general attempt to teach Englishmen systematically how to use their own language.

This development was inevitable, and on the whole valuable, since it worked to prevent further splintering of the language. But if it had been postponed for a few more generations our grammar today would be considerably simpler than it is. By 1750 most of the Old English irregular verbs had either dropped out of use or become regular: *help, holp* had become *help, helped; wash, wesh* had become *wash, washed,* etc. A number of others were in the process of making the same change; authors of unquestionable education and standing were writing *blowed* instead of *blew, throwed* instead of *threw,* etc. Most of us probably have a very strong feeling that such forms as *blowed* and *throwed* are just naturally wrong; but our equally strong feeling that *helped* and *washed* are right shows that our reaction is based simply on habit rather than any fixed principle.

At the same time many of those troublesome verbs like *sing* and *take,* which have a separate form for the past participle, were simplifying to a single past form. The fact that only about forty of our verbs now require these separate forms proves conclusively that we don't need them, and most of them would probably have disappeared by now if they had been allowed to depart in peace. But after two centuries of insistence on the importance of these unfortunate survivals, we may never get rid of them.

We should probably still have some irregular verbs even if eighteenth-century grammarians had not deliberately resisted the tendency to regularize, but there would certainly not be so many. We might even (like the Scandinavians) have lost the distinctive third person singular—and with it the whole problem of agreement of subject and predicate.

It is easy to curse these early grammarians for the trouble they have handed down to us; but it is more interesting to try to understand why they thought and acted as they did. **Linguists today are divided about whether there are any universal principles underlying all languages; but they all recognize that known languages show remarkable differences in their structures, and agree that these differences are perfectly legitimate. They also agree that all languages are continually and inevitably changing.** Two centuries ago many grammarians believed that the "true" structure of language was as international as that of arithmetic, and that any change in a language—particularly if it involved the loss of an inflection—was decay rather than progress.

As a simple example of structural difference, consider the Latin sentence, *Virgines amat Marcus*. This means that Marcus loves the (nice) girls—not, as an American student might suspect, that those girls love Marcus. Moreover, it will have the same meaning no matter in what order the three words are put, provided the endings remain the same. If we wanted to say that the girls love Marcus, we would have to change *amat* to *amant* to show that it was plural, and *Marcus* to *Marcum* to show that he was receiving rather than giving out all that affection; and again the order of the words would make no difference.

Old English had the same sort of structure, but **in Modern English the order of words has become critical; and though the inflections that remain still have some importance, they are decidedly secondary.** Suppose you saw the sentence, "The girls loves Marcus." There is nothing in the form of either noun to tell which is the subject; and though the singular verb indicates that *Marcus* is the subject, you simply would not believe it. On the basis of the word order you would assume that the girls did the loving, and that the writer had simply made a mistake in the verb form— and you would almost certainly be right.

Most of us are delighted that many inflections have disappeared and we don't have to learn them; but we are likely to cherish those that we already know. Thus we are quite happy about such expressions as *one sheep grazed* and *three sheep grazed*, where neither the noun nor the verb gives any indication of number; but we would object to *one cow graze* and *three cow graze*, though there is no logical reason why a change of either animal or tense should make distinctive inflections more necessary. The authors of eighteenth-century textbooks, having been trained thoroughly in the grammar of Latin and not at all in that of English, felt even more strongly. To them the small number of inflections was "the greatest defect in our language." They could not actually restore the ones that had already completely disappeared, but they did make a deliberate and fairly successful effort to preserve those that were disappearing, and they often talked about the lost ones as if they were still there. We must remember that they lived a century before the theory of evolution began to color all our thinking, in a period that is often called "The Age of Reason." They could therefore not be satisfied with a description of how people—even "the best authors"— actually did use the language. They wanted to lay down rational rules about how they *should* use it; and they saw no reason why the rules should not be permanent, "fixing" the language for all future time.

AFTER-EFFECTS OF EIGHTEENTH-CENTURY GRAMMATICAL THEORIES

Of course the language continued to change in spite of all objections; and if the grammarians had done no more than slow up the rate of change it could be argued (although not proved) that their efforts had on the whole been useful. But they did something much worse than this. By insisting on rules which often had no foundation in the speech habits of the people, they converted "grammar" into an artificial and generally distasteful subject. When a Frenchman studies French grammar, he is learning how educated Frenchmen actually talk and write; and in his later life he can practice what he has learned in school with a comfortable assurance. But a good deal of what an Englishman or an American learns under the name of grammar has nothing to do with the use of our language; and a good deal more is in direct conflict with the actual practices of most educated people.

The result is that many Americans go through life feeling inadequate, even guilty, about their language habits. Even if they actually speak English very well, they seldom have the comfort of realizing it. They have been taught to believe in a mysterious "perfect English" which does not exist, and to regard it as highly important; but they have never had the structure of the language explained to them.

AMERICAN ENGLISH

In the early part of the seventeenth century English settlers began to bring their language to America, and another series of changes began to take place. The settlers borrowed words from Indian languages for such strange trees as the hickory and persimmon, such unfamiliar animals as raccoons and woodchucks. Later they borrowed other words from settlers from other countries—for instance, *chowder* and *prairie* from the French, *scow* and *sleigh* from the Dutch. They made new combinations of English words, such as *backwoods* and *bullfrog*, or gave old English words entirely new meanings, such as *lumber* (which in British English means approximately *junk*) and *corn* (which in British means any grain, especially wheat). Some of the new terms were needed, because there were new and un-English things to talk about. Others can be explained only on the general theory that languages are always changing, and American English is no exception.

Aside from the new vocabulary, differences in pronunciation, in grammatical construction, and especially in intonation developed. If the colonization had taken place a few centuries earlier, American might have become as different from English as French is from Italian. But the settlement occurred after the invention of printing, and continued through a period when the idea of educating everybody was making rapid progress. For a long time most of the books read in America came from England, and a surprising number of Americans read those books, in or out of school.

Moreover, most of the colonists seem to have felt strong ties with England. In this they were unlike their Anglo-Saxon ancestors, who apparently made a clean break with their continental homes.

A good many Englishmen and some Americans used to condemn every difference that did develop, and as recently as a generation ago it was not unusual to hear all "Americanisms" condemned, even in America. It is now generally recognized in this country that we are not bound to the Queen's English, but have a full right to work out our own habits. Even a good many of the English now concede this, though some of them object strongly to the fact that Americanisms are now having an influence on British usage.

There are thousands of differences in detail between British and American English, and occasionally they crowd together enough to make some difficulty. If you read that a man, having trouble with his *lorry,* got out his *spanner* and lifted the *bonnet* to see what was the matter, you might not realize that the driver of the *truck* had taken out his *wrench* and lifted the *hood.* It is amusing to play with such differences, but the theory that the American language is now essentially different from English does not hold up. It is often very difficult to decide whether a book was written by an American or an Englishman. Even in speech it would be hard to prove that national differences are greater than some local differences in either country. On the whole, it now seems probable that the language habits of the two countries will grow more, rather than less, alike, although some differences will undoubtedly remain and others may develop.

It also seems probable that there will be narrow-minded and snobbish people in both countries for some time to come. But generally speaking, anybody who learns to speak and write the standard English of his own country, and to regard that of the other country as a legitimate variety with certain interesting differences, will have little trouble wherever he goes.

EXERCISES

The facts of this chapter may be important in themselves, but more important are the implications. Try to determine what is true and what is false in each of the following statements.

1. English changes continually, and the changes always lead to diversity.

2. English was once an inflected language; now it is a distributive language. (If you have trouble with this one, learn the principle involved now, because you will never understand the rhetoric, syntax, or grammar of English until you grasp this principle.)

3. Speakers of English have always borrowed their vocabulary from foreign languages.

Suggestions for Discussion or Theme Writing

Grammatical changes in a language necessarily cause changes in rhetoric. For example, classical rhetoric, which speaks of "loose" and "periodic" sentences, is built on the practices of two inflected languages: Latin and Greek. It is impossible to say, because there is no precedent for it, what classical rhetoric would make of sentences like these from the chapter you just read:

"As they split up and settled in different regions, the differences became so great that the Greeks, for instance, could not possibly understand the Germans; and a little later some of the Germans could not understand other Germans."

"There were differences in pronunciation, and even in word endings, between these last three; but most of the root words were enough alike to be recognizable, and the three tribes seem to have had no great difficulty in understanding each other."

There is no category, no definition of sentences like that in classical rhetoric. Those sentences are not loose or periodic; they are cumulative.

Rewrite those sentences into periodic sentences, that is, into sentences in which the grammatical form and essential meaning are not completed until the end is reached. Then say which version you find more effective and why.

THE PATTERNS
OF
GRAMMAR

THE GRAMMAR WE ALL KNOW

The very popular statement that "grammar is a lot of nonsense" contains a great deal of truth, though not quite in the way that is usually intended. Let's look at some nonsense and see what we can learn from it:

The floog sirily mirlated naxes with a sool pern.

Since most of the words are strange we don't know exactly what this statement means, but we do know the following things:

		CLUE
1.	Whatever happened, the *floog* did it.	position
2.	There was probably one *floog*.	no -*s* ending

3. It was done to the *naxes*.	position
4. There was more than one *nax*.	*-es* ending
5. The action of *mirlating* is over.	*-ed* ending
6. *Sirily* tells something about how it was done.	*-ly* ending
7. *With a pern* tells more about how it was done.	word *with*
8. There was only one *pern*.	word *a*
9. *Sool* tells what kind of a pern it was.	position

We know these things because our language contains a system of patterns which convey what is sometimes called "structural meaning" almost without regard to the dictionary meanings of the particular words used. As the clues above indicate, the main elements in the patterns of written English are:

Word order, or relative *position*

Word form (usually, but not always, a matter of endings)

Function words like *a, the,* and *with,* which are more important for what they tell us about how other words are used than for exact meanings of their own.

In spoken English at least three other elements, called *pitch, stress,* and *juncture,* must be recognized. These are to some extent implied in writing, but are not indicated as explicitly as the first three. We will therefore postpone discussing them until we have seen how the more obvious elements work.

Most students assume that a language is made up simply of words, which have only to be arranged according to logical rules in order to make good sentences. Actually, each language—in fact, each dialect—has its own patterns as well as its own words, and these patterns are matters of habit rather than logic. We have been exposed to our own particular patterns of word form, word order, and function words for so long that we now react to them automatically even when they are filled with nonsense words. If there were just one dialect of English, we could use them automatically, too—at least in short sentences—and not have to think about them. But most of us have grown up in such a confusing mixture of dialects that simple imitation is not enough. In order to speak and write with accuracy and confidence we have to learn to choose between equally familiar short patterns, and to find some way of combining these into longer structures. If we approach these tasks with some sort of system,

we'll have a better chance of knowing when we have covered the ground—
or at least that part of it that concerns us most.

COMPETING APPROACHES TO GRAMMAR

Only a few years ago it was commonly believed that the scope and
content of English grammar had been definitely settled by unquestionable
though generally anonymous authorities, and that all a student had to do
was to learn what they had set down. Today the situation is quite different.
The whole question of how the language is organized is being restudied
from at least three distinct approaches—traditional, structural, and trans-
formational—each of which proves to be far from uniform when closely
examined.

It would take a good many pages to give even a reasonably clear indication of the differences between these three approaches; and it would
take a great many more—plus a sizable helping of arrogance—to pretend
to give a fair evaluation of their possibilities, or to predict the kind of syn-
thesis which may eventually develop. The study of grammatical theory is
now much more interesting than it used to be, but it is too complicated
to be handled incidentally in a course devoted to composition. The description of language patterns in this and the next few chapters is therefore as free from technicalities, and as impartial in its assumptions, as we
can make it.

GRAMMATICAL POSITION

In analyzing our nonsense sentence we gave only one clue for each
bit of information, as if the three elements of position, word form, and
function words could be completely separated. Actually they cannot. For
instance, grammatical position is not merely numerical position in a sentence but relative position; and we recognize it by considering word form
and function words as well as word order. Take another look at the first
four words of our sentence:

The floog sirily mirlated

We know that the *floog* did the *mirlating*—that it is what we call the subject—not by the fact that it is the second word in the sentence, but by
taking all the following facts together:

1. When we see a pattern like "The _____ _____ _____ed"
we assume that the word ending in -*ed* is the verb, and that one of the
two words between *the* and_____*ed* is the subject.

2. Since the word just before the verb ends in -*ly* it almost certainly tells something about the verb and therefore cannot be the subject.

3. Therefore the other possible word—*floog*—is the subject. (Notice that if the sentence had begun "The floog *siliry*" instead of "The floog *sirily*" we would take *siliry* to be the subject and *floog* to be an adjective modifying it.)

It is obvious that the study of grammatical position could become a pretty complicated subject, but we don't have to go into it very deeply. To begin with we are interested only in the way it can help us to classify four important kinds of words.

THE KINDS OF WORDS

We have to classify words in order to discuss them in groups. Even in the last section we had to use the terms *verb* and *adjective,* though we have not yet had time to define these; and if we couldn't say things like "the possessive form of a noun is always written with an apostrophe," it would take quite a while to cover the language. Unfortunately, nobody has ever found a perfect way to classify words in English. The two most obvious ways are by form and by meaning. If we base our classes on either one of these we run into trouble with the other; if we try to use both at once we get a complicated mess; and if we decide to have two separate classifications we find that they overlap so much that it is very difficult to keep them separate.

As a compromise, not perfect but reasonably workable, we will use in this book a system based on three main principles:

1. **We will use such familiar** *single* **terms as** *noun* **and** *adjective* **to designate the ways words and word groups function in sentence patterns.**

2. **We will use such** *double* **terms as** *inflected noun* **or** *regular noun* **(which means "noun inflected in a certain way") to discuss forms and form changes.**

3. **We will not bother to classify a word at all unless we have a definite reason for doing so.** And if a word happens to be both a noun (by use) and an inflected noun (by form) we will use whichever designation seems to be handiest at the time.

CLASSIFICATION BY POSITION

We began this chapter by analyzing a sentence composed of three familiar words, *a, the,* and *with,* and six nonsense words, *floog, sirily, mir-*

lated, naxes, sool, and *pern.* We could of course make up any number of similar sentences; and if we made up, say, ten pages of them, we should discover the curious fact that **all the nonsense words could be reasonably put into just four classes:**

1. Words that pattern like *floog, naxes,* and *pern,* which can be called *nouns.*
2. Words that pattern like *mirlated,* which can be called verbs.
3. Words that pattern like *sool,* which can be called *adjectives.*
4. Words that pattern like *sirily,* which can be called *adverbs.*

The nucleus of an English sentence is a combination like *man is* or *girls sang* or *floog mirlated,* in which one word seems to name something and the other seems to say something about it—even if both words are nonsense or completely unknown. In such combinations we call the naming word the subject—and the kind of word that is or could easily be the subject we call a *noun.* The saying word we call the *verb.* Words that seem to describe nouns we call adjectives—*big* man, *young* girls, *sool* pern. And words that seem to describe verbs we call *adverbs—probably* was, *merrily* sang, *sirily* mirlated.

More than 99 percent of all the words in English fall into these four classes, and more are being added to them every year. They are therefore called open or unlimited classes. There is nothing surprising about seeing an unfamiliar word in a position that seems to indicate any one of these classes; and even if we are quite sure that the word has no real meaning we somehow feel that we know how it acts.

All the other kinds of words (which we will not classify just now) total only a few hundred altogether, and no new ones are being added. We have to know these words individually to react to the patterns of our sentences; and if we replace them by nonsense words the patterns disappear. Let's try it:

Pra floog sirily mirlated naxes tran oc sool pern.

Possibly the successive endings *-ly, -ed,* and *-es* still suggest some meaning, but there is no longer a firm pattern for the sentence as a whole. Nonsense substitutes for *a, the,* and *with* won't work.

At first glance classification by position may seem a very roundabout way of getting at such familiar definitions as "a noun is a word used to name a person, place, thing, or idea," but it has its advantages. These familiar definitions work beautifully in selected sentences, but simply do not apply to the language as a whole unless we stretch them until they are practically meaningless. The reason is that we do not always use the same grammatical patterns to express the same ideas, and it is silly to pretend that we do. Look at the following sentences:

Sometimes he works and sometimes he loafs.

His industry and laziness alternate.

He is alternately industrious and lazy.

He acts industriously and lazily by spells.

Each of these conveys the same basic information; but the contrast between his working and his loafing is shown in the first sentence by verbs, in the second by nouns, in the third by adjectives, and in the fourth by adverbs. There just is no fixed relation between the meaning conveyed and the grammatical pattern used to convey it; and since we are discussing grammar, not philosophy, we'd better depend on the perceptible patterns.

THE FORMS OF WORDS

The second element in our grammatical patterns is word form. Some words, like *always, into, must,* and *which,* have only one form; **but most words have from two to five different forms called *inflections*.** Inflected words fall into four groups, three of which may be divided into *regular* and *irregular* subgroups.

Inflected nouns
  Regular: boy, boy's, boys, boys'
  Irregular: man, man's, men, men's
Inflected pronouns
  All *irregular:* I, me, my, mine, myself
Inflected verbs
  Regular: save, saves, saved, saving
  Irregular: take, takes, took, taken, taking
Inflected adjectives
  Regular: big, bigger, biggest
  Irregular: good, better, best

These are the only kinds of inflection in English. Such endings as *-al, -dom, -hood, -ic -ish, -ize, -ly, -ment,* and *-ness* are considered to make different words rather than different forms of the same word. (It is much simpler to accept the fact that this is so than to try to decide whether it should be.) They are called derivational suffixes, and will not be discussed here.

There are many thousands of regular nouns and regular verbs, and both groups are still growing. Whenever we adopt a new noun, like *sputnik*, everybody seems to assume at once that the only reasonable plural is *sputniks*, not *sputnak* or *sputniki*. In other words, we automatically treat it as a regular noun. And if we adopt a new verb, or make a new verb out of an old noun, we treat *it* as regular. As soon as we read that sputniks *orbit* we know that we can also say that they *orbited* or have *orbited*, not that they *orbat* or have *orbiten*. It is therefore only the regular nouns and verbs that are "open." There are about six hundred regular adjectives, and this class might be called "open at one end." Nobody knows why, but whenever we adopt a new two-syllable adjective ending in -*y*, such as *newsy* or *corny*, we give it the regular -*er* and -*est* endings. All other new adjectives are unchanging, and show degrees by *more* and *most*.

Nobody has much trouble with the spoken forms of these three regular groups, and the spelling of the written forms follows rather simple rules which will be given later. The four irregular groups are more difficult, since each word has to be learned individually. Fortunately these groups are much smaller than the regular ones, and are shrinking rather than growing. They will be discussed in more detail later.

Along with the four inflected groups we must consider one group of words that never change form but do have a characteristic form of their own—the -*ly* adverbs like *badly* and *wonderfully*. This is another open class; we feel free to add -*ly* to almost any adjective and thus make a new adverb, if we can find a use for it.

FUNCTION WORDS

Function words are words which are used to form grammatical patterns, and which cannot be changed without changing the patterns. Look at the following sentence:

The old man *had* cheerfully started *the* job *with* a sharp knife.

The words in ordinary type could be varied indefinitely without changing the pattern. We could find dozens of substitutes for *started* or *job*, and hundreds for each of the others. But if we change *the* to *an* or *had* to *has* or *with* to *on* we get a different pattern at once. *The* implies that you know which old man the sentence is about; *an* implies that you don't. *Has* puts the statement in a different time relation from *had*. And the things that you can reasonably do *on* a knife are quite different from those that you can do *with* it.

The difference between function words and others (sometimes called *content words*) is not absolutely sharp or reliable, and you can argue with the statements in the preceding paragraph if you care to. But if we consider the distinction as a matter of convenience rather than of desperate doctrine, we will find it useful. Function words are used principally to make up grammatical patterns; content words are used to fill those patterns and give them specific meanings. You have to know the meanings of the content words in a particular sentence to understand that sentence; but you have to know the ways most function words are used to understand English at all.

It is reasonably easy to divide content words into four classes—nouns, verbs, adjectives, and adverbs. A satisfactory classification of function words is a good deal more difficult. For the moment we will merely indicate three principal types:

1. **Auxiliary verbs,** like those italicized in the following verb phrases: *will* go, *could* eat, *has* been, *is* going, *must have* seen.

2. **Connectives,** including all prepositions (*to, from, with*, etc.), conjunctions (*and, because,* etc.), and many words often called adverbs and pronouns (*there, when, which*, etc.).

3. **Certain special modifiers of the kinds sometimes called determiners** (*a, the, those*, etc.) **and qualifiers** (*very, quite*, etc.).

THE PARTS OF SPEECH?

It may seem curious that we have discussed two different kinds of classification of words, one by function and one by form, without even mentioning the "parts of speech." **But the fact is that the whole concept of parts of speech depends on a stable relation between form and function which has almost disappeared in our language.** The concept can, of course, still be applied to modern English, but it no longer seems to be really useful; and those people who insist most strongly that there *are* parts of speech disagree about whether it is the function classes or the form classes that deserve this name. And those who take form as the basis disagree about whether it is simply the form of the words or the form of the patterns in which the words are used that must be considered.

Since there is no discoverable way of settling this argument (or of stopping it, either), we will simply disregard it. Anybody can call anything he wants to the parts of speech. Meanwhile we will try to make it clear whenever we are talking about either form or function. When the two overlap (as they often do) we can use either set of terms safely as long as we don't overgeneralize. Thus in the sentence "The best cost no more" we can say that *best* is an irregular adjective in form but a noun by function in this sentence; and we can call *cost* either an irregular verb or simply the verb without much danger of misleading anybody.

CONVERSION BY SUFFIX

Earlier in the chapter we mentioned that endings other than inflections are called suffixes—for instance, *-dom, -ize, -ly,* and *-ment.* Suffixes are sometimes used to give words different meanings without changing their functional classification. Thus we have *gray* and *grayish*, both normally adjectives, and *man* and *manhood*, both normally nouns. More often suffixes convert words from one classification to another, as in the following examples:

> *Verbs to nouns* appease—appeasement, serve—service
>
> *Adjectives to nouns:* free—freedom, happy—happiness
>
> *Nouns to verbs:* atom—atomize, gas—gasify
>
> *Adjectives to verbs:* dark—darken, tranquil—tranquilize
>
> *Nouns to adjectives:* child—childish, man—manly
>
> *Adjectives to adverbs:* glad—gladly, frantic—frantically

This kind of conversion is common in many languages, including Greek, Latin, and French, from which a great many English words come. It explains many of the related words in the language.

FUNCTIONAL SHIFT

Conversion of a word to a new function *without* the use of a suffix occurs much more often in English than in most other languages. This is known as **functional shift,** and it has gone so far as to make a single classification of words into parts of speech almost meaningless, as we have already suggested. The general tendency is to use any word in any way that is convenient and makes sense, without regard to its original classification. Thus we may use *work* as a noun (a *work* of art), a verb (they *work* hard), or an adjective (his *work* clothes). We cannot use it as a connective, not because of any grammatical rule, but simply because there is no way to do it. And nobody but a historian of the language has any reason to care about what its original part of speech may have been.

If a word shifts its function to that of a noun or a verb, it takes on the regular inflections of its new class. Thus the irregular noun *man* gives us the regular verb *to man*, with the forms *man, mans, manned, manning*. Likewise the irregular verb *to drink* gives us the regular noun *drink, drinks*. In other shifts of function no new inflections are needed.

REASON FOR FUNCTIONAL SHIFT

Quite obviously the underlying reason for functional shift is economy —either the use of a shorter word for a longer one or the use of a word instead of a phrase. Use of the plain form of a verb as a noun eliminates either the *-ing* inflectional ending (*talk* for *talking*) or a suffix (a *serve* for a *service* in tennis); and use of a noun as an adjective eliminates a suffix (*wool* clothes for *woolen* clothes, *atom* bomb for *atomic* bomb). On the other hand, use of an adjective as a noun often saves a word or more (*the poor* for *the poor people, the beautiful* for *that which is beautiful*). Verbs converted from nouns are particularly economical, though not always graceful. Thus *to requisition* stands for *to put in a requisition for, to contact* for *to get in touch with*.

When the two kinds of economy conflict, the one that makes the greater overall saving generally wins out—at least in circles where efficiency is more prized than grace. Thus *to certificate* is longer than *to certify*, but shorter than *to furnish with a certificate*. It is therefore often used when the certification consists of supplying a document rather than guaranteeing a statement.

LIMITS TO FUNCTIONAL SHIFT

The fact remains that many functional shifts that might well have taken place have not done so. Sometimes this is because a familiar word that makes a shift unnecessary is already available. Thus the verb *to man* made it unnecessary to convert *boy, girl,* or *woman* into verbs. Juveniles or females can *man* a boat. Sixty years ago, when automobiles were still competing with carriages, we used *to auto* down to the beach, since *to drive* was not sufficiently specific, and any other available expression would have been longer. Now that carriages have practically disappeared the one-syllable verb *drive* clearly means to go by automobile. *To auto* is no longer economical, and there would not be enough saving in *to car* to make it worthwhile.

At other times we have simply failed to make a shift for no discoverable reason. Thus we say *to reward* and *a reward, to punish* but *a punishment.* A noun *punish* may develop in the future, but it has not yet done so. Moreover, some shifts that certainly have developed are often condemned. That is, although the general principle of functional shift is universally accepted, a few individual shifts have become shibboleths. We often hear that *like* must never be used as a conjunction, that *than* and *as* must never be used as prepositions, and that *loan* and *contract* must never be used as verbs.

To object to these uses on the basis of any grammatical theory is simply silly. Thousands of other words have extended their functions in exactly comparable ways, and there is not the slightest reason why this handful should not do the same. If we must condemn such expressions we should do so by making the honest statement that there is a certain amount of prejudice against them—just as there is now a prejudice against calling a man "a certain party" or a woman "an elegant female"—though there is no doubt whatever that *party* and *female* are, in other expressions, acceptable as nouns.

INTONATION PATTERNS

So far we have dealt only with those elements of our grammatical patterns which are visible as well as audible. In spoken English at least three other elements would be perceptible (though not necessarily recognizable by people without some training). These can sometimes be suggested in writing, but cannot be indicated as explicitly as the first three. Compare the two following sentences:

Jack put salt in his coffee.

Jack put salt in his *coffee?*

Since these are identical in all three of the elements so far discussed, many people would call them "the same sentence punctuated in two different ways." But, intelligently read, they sound different and they mean different things—which should be enough to make them different sentences. The fact that the differences do not appear as clearly in writing as they do in speech proves only that our system of writing is imperfect—it indicates some differences less clearly than others. If you read both sentences aloud carefully and naturally you will see that they vary in three ways:

1. The first syllable of *coffee* is pronounced more strongly in the second sentence than in the first. This is a difference in *stress.*

2. This syllable is also pronounced on a lower musical tone, and the next one on a higher tone. These are differences in *pitch*.

3. At the end of the first sentence the voice comes down in pitch as it fades into silence. At the end of the second it does not. This is a difference in *juncture*. In order to make the comparison as simple as possible we have discussed the difference in stress, pitch, and juncture only at the ends of the two sentences, but they occur throughout. Every syllable that is pronounced at all must be pronounced with some degree of stress and at some pitch; and whenever two successive words are not completely run together the transition between them can be called juncture. Thus *white house* has a kind of juncture not found in *White House;* the sort of pause often shown by a comma is a second kind; and the rising and falling tones as your voice fades off after different kinds of sentences are two others.

It is possible to indicate all these things consistently by a special system of writing—the stress by accent marks, the pitch by numbers, and the juncture by special symbols. Thus the second sentence might be written as follows:

$$^2\text{Jâck}+\text{pùt}+\text{sâlt}+\text{in}+\text{his}+{}^1\text{cóffee}^3 \uparrow$$

(It might also be indicated in several other ways.) This more complete system of writing is very useful for experts who wish to make a detailed analysis of our sound patterns, but it is a little cumbersome for ordinary use. Most of us would rather get along with just a few hints, such as the italicizing of *coffee* and the question mark at the end. Moreover, experts are still disagreeing about such questions as how many degrees of stress and pitch are significant and how regular and dependable are our uses of these elements. We are not therefore going into these matters in much detail. But we should realize that the experts are right in principle—these elements are quite as real as the first three, and at least some of the time they are quite as important. We shall see this when we come to consider the structure of sentences.

Stress, pitch, and juncture together make up *intonation*. Every spoken sentence must have its pattern of intonation; and every good written sentence at least suggests one. If you don't believe intonation is as real or as important as the other sounds, perhaps you can remember a time when you were seriously misquoted by somebody who claimed to be repeating exactly what you had said, and who did repeat the same words in the same order—but who changed the intonation pattern so as to give an entirely different meaning.

INFLECTIONS

Earlier we pointed out that words may be classified by either form or use, and that form and use overlap but do not perfectly coincide. For instance, *boy* has the written forms *boy, boy's, boys,* and *boys'*, which are typical of regular nouns; and most of the time it is used as a noun—that is, to name something being talked about. But it may also be used as an adjective, as in the expression *boy baby.* On the other hand, *poor* has the forms of a regular adjective, *poor, poorer,* and *poorest,* and is generally used as an adjective; but it may also be used as a noun in such sentences as "The *poor* are suffering." There are times when the classification by use is important, but for the rest of this chapter we shall consider only the classification by form, since this is the only way we can lay out all the inflected words of the language in an arrangement that is both systematic and reasonably simple.

INFLECTED NOUNS

Nouns may have as many as four forms, plain and possessive in the singular and plain and possessive in the plural:

	SINGULAR	PLURAL
Plain	A *boy* is here.	Three *boys* came.
	A *man* is here.	Three *men* came.
Possessive	A *boy's* dog.	The two *boys'* dogs.
	A *man's* dog.	The two *men's* dogs.

Many nouns do not have the possessive forms, and are thus inflected only for number. A few (mostly kinds of fish and game) do not have separate forms for their plurals (*salmon, trout, deer, elk.*) Nouns which have neither a possessive nor a separate plural form are of course uninflected and will not be considered here.

Notice that the plain plural form *boys* has no apostrophe, but that all the possessive forms have one. If you are confused by possessive forms it is probably because there are several different systems in use. The following system, which is the simplest and most consistent, is at least as good as any of the others:

1. Write the appropriate plain form, singular or plural.

2. Add an apostrophe to indicate the possessive form.

3. Then add an -s unless you have already added one to form the plural.

REGULAR NOUN PLURALS

All nouns which add an /s/, /z/, or /iz/ sound (spelled -s or -es) to form the plural are considered *regular,* in spite of minor variations. Since most students can choose correctly between the three plural sounds more easily than they can learn rules about them, the following rules will deal only with the spelling of the written forms:

1. Most words form their plurals by adding simple -s: *bat-bats, place-places,* etc.

2. When -s alone would make an unpronounceable combination, -es is added: *box-boxes, match-matches, loss-losses,* etc.

3. Six common words ending in -o form their plurals in -es: *echoes, heroes, Negroes, potatoes, tomatoes,* and *torpedoes.* (So do eleven others which are much less common, at least in the plural, if you want to know: *bilboes, buboes, dadoes, dingoes, embargoes, goes, innuendoes, jingoes, mulattoes, noes,* and *vetoes.*) All other words ending in -o either may or must be written with -s plurals.

4. Words ending in -y preceded by a consonant take a plural in -ies: *copy-copies, lady-ladies,* etc.

When the -y is preceded by a vowel there is no such change: *boy-boys, monkey-monkeys,* etc.

5. Words ending in -f or -fe take a plural in -ves if the sound changes: *half-halves, wife-wives;* but *belief-beliefs, safe-safes.*

IRREGULAR ENGLISH PLURALS

A few common native English words form their plurals in some other manner than by adding -s or -es. Fortunately, they are all so well known that they give little trouble. They are:

child–children	louse–lice	ox–oxen
foot–feet	man–men	tooth–teeth
goose–geese	mouse–mice	woman–women

FOREIGN PLURALS

The English language has borrowed thousands of nouns from other languages, particularly Greek and Latin. It used to be the general practice to borrow both the singular and plural forms. Since the result was bewildering to those who knew only English, many people took a great deal of pride in their ability to handle such pairs as the following:

alumna–alumnae	dogma–dogmata
cactus–cacti	corpus–corpora

In the last fifty years or so, however, there have been two important changes:

1. New words have been introduced only in the singular, and have formed their plurals in the normal English way. Even the most learned people say *electrons* and *protons* instead of *electra and prota*.

2. Regular English plurals in -*s* or -*es* have developed alongside of the foreign plurals for most foreign words that are in reasonably common use, as the following list indicates:

SINGULAR	FOREIGN PLURAL	REGULAR PLURAL
appendix	appendices	appendixes
bureau	bureaux	bureaus
curriculum	curricula	curriculums
enema	enemata	enemas
focus	foci	focuses
ganglion	ganglia	ganglions

There are still some people who think the foreign plurals are better just because they are older; and there are others who apparently use them just to prove that they can. But the prevailing tendency is certainly in favor of regularity and simplicity. Foreign plurals tend to remain in use only under the following conditions:

a. The words are learned technical terms not in common use: *homunculus–homunculi; phylum–phyla*.

b. The plural forms occur more frequently than the singular: *datum–data; bacterium–bacteria*.

c. An -*s* would cause three *s* sounds in a row: *crisis–crises*, not *crisises*.

So much progress in this direction has been made, that the following rules are now quite safe:

1. If you are used to hearing an -*s* plural, use it confidently.

2. If you are pretty sure that an -*s* plural is not correct, use the table below:

NOUNS ENDING IN		TAKE A PLURAL IN	
-a	(alumna)	-ae	(alumnae—pronounced -*ay* or -*ee*)
-us	(alumnus)	-i	(alumni—pronounced -*eye*)
-on	(phenomenon)	-a	(phenomena)
-um	(bacterium)	-a	(bacteria)
-sis	(thesis)	-ses	(theses—pronounced -*eez*)

COMPOUND NOUNS

Most compound nouns now regularly take the plural -*s* on the end, even if it did not originally belong there: *cupfuls, jack-in-the-boxes.* There are a few exceptions when the first part of the compound is the main word and is described by what follows:

brothers-in-law   commanders-in-chief

courts-martial   passers-by

Even these words show a tendency to shift the -*s* to the end. All our good dictionaries now list *attorney generals* along with *attorneys general,* and the newest ones list *court-martials* as well as *courts-martial.* If you are in doubt and can't look it up, it is advisable to put the -*s* on the end, on the theory that natural ignorance is better than affectation.

To indicate possession, all compound nouns and groups of words that form a unit put the 's on the end: my *brother-in-law's* car, the *King of England's* doctor, *anybody else's* opinion.

INFLECTED PRONOUNS

There are eight simple inflected pronouns, listed below with all their forms.

SUBJECT FORMS	OBJECT FORMS	POSSESSIVE FORMS
I	me	my, mine
he	him	his
she	her	her, hers
it	it	its
we	us	our, ours
you	you	your, yours
they	them	their, theirs
who	whom	whose

Notice that:

1. Most of them have separate "subject" and "object" forms, whereas nouns have one plain form.

2. Their possessive forms do *not* have an apostrophe, and some of them do not have an *-s*.

3. Most of them have two different possessive forms, one used when they are followed by the noun they modify (that is *my* book), the other when they stand alone (that book is *mine*).

The first seven pronouns are often called *personal pronouns*. The easiest thing to call the other one is simply *who*.

THE COMPOUND PERSONAL PRONOUNS

The personal pronouns are combined with *self* and *selves* to form the following compound pronouns:

SINGULAR	PLURAL
myself	ourselves
yourself	yourselves
himself	themselves
herself	
itself	
ourself (reserved for kings, queens, and editors)	

Notice that some of these are based on the object forms of the simple pronouns, others on the possessive forms. It is important to get these straight, because such forms as "hisself" and "theirselves" are generally considered to be signs of great ignorance.

These words are used both to show "reflexive action" (he cut *himself*) and to show special emphasis (he did it *himself*). They are sometimes called "reflexive pronouns" in the first use and "intensive pronouns" or "intensive adjectives" in the second, but except in comparing English with a foreign language these terms are quite useless.

COMPOUND FORMS OF WHO

The compound pronoun *whoever* has the natural object form *whomever*, but the possessive form varies, appearing as *whosever, whose-ever, whose ever,* and even *whoever's*. With so much choice, it is hard to go definitely wrong.

INFLECTED VERBS

There are at most ten uninflected verbs in the standard language. *Must* and *ought* have only one form apiece, and on the whole it seems better to consider *could, might, should,* and *would* as now separate from *can, may, shall,* and *will* rather than as the past tenses of these verbs, though there are arguments for the opposite opinion. All other verbs except *to be* (see page 127) have from three to five inflected forms, and one phrase form that occurs so frequently it needs a name. These are:

	REGULAR	IRREGULAR
The plain form	walk	write
The singular form	walks	writes
The past tense	walked	wrote
The past participle	(walked)	written
The present participle	walking	writing
The infinitive	to walk	to write

Only about 45 verbs have a separate form for the past participle. The rest extend the use of the past tense form. However, it is convenient to call *walked* a past participle whenever it is used in a way parallel to *written.* Some grammarians call the plain form an infinitive whenever it comes directly after another verb (will *walk,* must *write*), but in this book the term infinitive always means the plain form preceded by *to.* Since the singular form and present participle are always (except in the verb *to be*) formed regularly from the plain form, the only difficulties are the past tenses of about 140 irregular verbs and the separate past participles of about 45 of these.

STRONG AND WEAK VERBS

The division of English verbs into "strong" and "weak" classes, each containing subclasses, is useful in studying the earlier stages of the language and is worth a few words of explanation here. The strong verbs originally formed their past tenses by a vowel change (*sing, sang*), while the weak verbs formed theirs by the addition of *-ede, -ode,* or *-de,* which later developed into *-d, -ed,* or *-t.* A thorough study of the laws of sound change shows that even such curious pairs as *bring—brought* have developed according to a regular process.

However, comparatively few people have time to make such a study, and a superficial approach to it merely causes unnecessary confusion (for instance, *bleed—bled* and *feed—fed*, which seem to meet the definition of strong verbs, are historically weak). Fortunately, this difficult subject is not in the least necessary in mastering the contemporary language. The important questions for a student of Modern English are simply whether a verb is regular or irregular, and if it is irregular, how?

REGULAR VERBS

Most English verbs are now completely regular, so that if we see any one form we can be sure of what the others will be, even if we have never seen the verb before and have not the slightest idea what it means. The only things we have to watch in these verbs are certain general spelling principles discussed on pages 124–26.

IRREGULAR VERBS

About 140 English verbs, most of them in very common use, are in some degree irregular. All but two of them (*begin* and *forsake*) are monosyllables, though some of them have compounds which follow the same pattern as the simple verbs (*get, forget; take, overtake*). There are a few other verbs which have both regular and irregular forms in good use, such as *thrive—thrived* (or *throve*). These are not included in the lists below unless the irregular forms are decidedly more usual.

Some optional irregular forms are as acceptable as the regular forms, but they are omitted here to simplify the picture. Anyone who finds that he uses an irregular form not listed here can easily check it in a dictionary to see whether it is in good standing. But if he masters the following lists he can be confident that he knows all the irregular forms *required* by standard usage. Even those verbs which are irregular only in spelling (*pay, paid*) are included.

VERBS WITH NO SEPARATE PAST TENSE

The following verbs ordinarily use the plain form for the past tense and past participle as well as for the present. The forms *betted, quitted, ridded, wedded,* and *wetted* are common in British usage, but rare in American.

bet	hurt	shut
bid	let	slit
burst	put	split
cast	quit	spread
cost	rid	thrust
cut	set	wed
hit	shed	wet

VERBS THAT ADD -D IRREGULARLY

The following verbs form their past tenses with -*d*, but not in the regular way:

flee	fled	pay	paid
have	had	say	said
hear	heard	sell	sold
lay	laid	shoe	shod (also *shoed*)
make	made	tell	told

VERBS THAT CHANGE -D TO -T

The following verbs form their past tenses by changing -*d* to -*t*:

bend	bent	rend	rent
build	built	send	sent
lend	lent	spend	spent

VERBS THAT ADD -T

The following verbs form their past tenses by adding -*t* and making some other change, at least in sound:

bring	brought	leave	left
buy	bought	lose	lost
catch	caught	mean	meant
creep	crept	seek	sought
deal	dealt	sleep	slept
dwell	dwelt (also *dwelled*)	sweep	swept
feel	felt	teach	taught
keep	kept	think	thought
kneel	knelt (also *kneeled*)	weep	wept

VOWEL-CHANGE VERBS WITH NO SEPARATE PAST PARTICIPLE

The following verbs form their past tenses by a change in the vowel, at least in sound. They do not add *-d* or *-t*, although some of them end with these letters in both present and past:

bind	bound	meet	met
bleed	bled	read	read (pronounced
breed	bred		*red*)
dig	dug	shine	shone (also *shined*) [2]
feed	fed	shoot	shot
fight	fought	sit	sat
find	found	slide	slid
grind	ground	spit	spat (also *spit*)
hang	hung (also *hanged*) [1]	stand	stood
hold	held	stick	stuck
lead	led	strike	struck
light	lit (also *lighted*)	win	won
		wind	wound

THE *-IN-, -UN-,* AND *-IN-, -AN-, -UN-* VERBS

All the following verbs have *-u* in the past participle, and all but five may unquestionably have it in the past tense as well. The simplest procedure is to learn to say *I began, I drank, I rang, I sang,* and *I swam,* and use the *u* form everywhere else. You can even find dictionary support for *I begun, I rung,* and *I sung,* but these three forms are now generally considered wrong.

begin	I began	I have begun
drink	I drank	I have drunk
ring	I rang	I have rung
sing	I sang	I have sung
swim	I swam	I have swum
shrink	I shrank *or* shrunk	I have shrunk
sink	I sank *or* sunk	I have sunk
spring	I sprang *or* sprung	I have sprung
stink	It stank *or* stunk	It has stunk

[1] *Hanged* is used only in reference to death by hanging.

[2] "The sun *shone*," but "He *shined* the shoes."

cling	I clung	I have clung
fling	I flung	I have flung
sling	I slung	I have slung
slink	I slunk	I have slunk
spin	I spun	I have spun
sting	I stung	I have stung
string	I strung	I have strung
swing	I swung	I have swung
wring	I wrung	I have wrung

VERBS HAVING N IN THE PAST PARTICIPLE

The following verbs have separate past participles containing *n*, sometimes preceded or followed by *e*. In standard English the forms with the *n* are never used in the simple past tense, but only in verb phrases or as modifiers.

bear	I bore	I have borne
beat	I beat	I have beaten
bite	I bit	I have bitten (sometimes *bit*)
blow	I blew	I have blown
break	I broke	I have broken
choose	I chose	I have chosen
do	I did	I have done
draw	I drew	I have drawn
drive	I drove	I have driven
eat	I ate	I have eaten
fall	I fell	I have fallen
fly	I flew	I have flown
forsake	I forsook	I have forsaken
freeze	I froze	I have frozen
get	I got	I have gotten, got
give	I gave	I have given
go	I went	I have gone
grow	I grew	I have grown
hide	I hid	I have hidden (sometimes *hid*)
know	I knew	I have known
lie	I lay	I have lain
ride	I rode	I have ridden
rise	I rose	I have risen

see	I saw	I have seen
shake	I shook	I have shaken
slay	I slew	I have slain
smite	I smote	I have smitten
speak	I spoke	I have spoken
steal	I stole	I have stolen
stride	I strode	I have stridden
swear	I swore	I have sworn
take	I took	I have taken
tear	I tore	I have torn
throw	I threw	I have thrown
tread	I trod	I have trodden (sometimes *trod*)
wear	I wore	I have worn
weave	I wove	I have woven (sometimes *weaved*) [3]
write	I wrote	I have written

COME AND *RUN*

These two verbs are exceptional in that their plain forms rather than their past tenses are used as past participles:

| come | I came | I have come |
| run | I ran | I have run |

THE VERB *TO BE*

The verb *to be* is a mixture of three old verbs (*aren, beon,* and *wesan*), which accounts for the wide differences in its forms. It is unique in having three present-tense forms (*am, are,* and *is*), none of which is identical with the plain form; and separate singular and plural forms (*was* and *were*) in the past tense. It also has the plain form (*be*), the present participle (*being*), and the past participle (*been*), for a total of eight forms, or three more than any other verb in the language.

INFLECTED ADJECTIVES

Most adjectives of one syllable and many of two syllables (especially those ending in *-y*) are inflected to show degree: *hot, hotter, hottest; pretty,*

[3] Especially in such a use as "He *weaved* his way through the *crowd*."

prettier, prettiest. Hot is called the positive form, *hotter* the comparative, and *hottest* the superlative. This type of inflection is called comparison.

Adjectives of more than two syllables are not inflected in standard usage, but show degrees by *more* and *most* (*more beautiful, most beautiful,* etc.). Some adjectives of one and two syllables are treated in the same way, particularly those ending in -*ful* and -*ish*. There is no logical reason for this difference in treatment—it is simply a habit that has developed. When in doubt, it is safer to use *more* and *most*.

Some people have argued that such adjectives as *black, straight,* and *perfect* should not be compared in either way, because their meaning is absolute and not a matter of degree. According to this theory we should say "more nearly black," etc. However, *blacker, straightest, more perfect,* etc. are quite understandable, and are certainly in standard use.

IRREGULAR COMPARISON

A few adjectives have irregular comparative and superlative forms. The most common of these are:

PLAIN FORM	COMPARATIVE FORM	SUPERLATIVE FORM
bad	worse	worst
far	farther	farthest
	further	furthest
good	better	best
little	less	least
	littler	littlest
	lesser	
many	more	most
much	more	most
old	older	oldest
	elder	eldest

Elder, eldest, and *lesser* are not used much now except in a few set phrases, such as *elder statesman, eldest son,* and *lesser of two evils. Farther-farthest* and *further-furthest* are interchangeable as adjectives, though only *further* is used as a verb ("He *furthered* his brother's career"). *Littler* and *littlest* are generally used for physical size, *less* and *least* for all other purposes ("He found the *littlest* boy without the *least* trouble").

Such words as *utmost, topmost,* and *northmost* are often called irregular superlative forms, but it is simpler to consider them as separate words.

Most of our adverbs are formed from adjectives by adding *-ly* (or *-ally* if the adjective ends in *-ic*). The fact that some adjectives, such as *friendly* and *manly*, also end in *-ly* causes some confusion. This can be avoided by remembering that *uninflected* words ending in *-ly* are all adverbs; *inflected* words with this ending may be adjectives, nouns (*jelly, tally*), or verbs (*to rely, to tally*).

Since the *-ly* ending is not considered an inflection, mention of adverbs may seem out of place here; but it is convenient to indicate that most of them are derived from and paired with adjectives.

EXERCISES

1. A few nouns, notably some denoting kinds of fish and game, follow a pattern of inflection that is interestingly different from that of most nouns. Describe and illustrate this difference.

2. In writing the plural possessive of nouns, when might the apostrophe end the construction and when not?

3. Most English nouns appear in how many forms? What are the distinguishing marks?

4. When adding *-s* alone would produce an unpronounceable combination, how do you write the plural of noun forms?

5. What signal helps determine that we write the plural of *baby* as *babies* but the plural of *donkey* as *donkeys*?

6. Nouns ending in *-o* may be written with *-s* plurals, with just a few (but important) exceptions. List some of these exceptions.

7. How can one's ear help him decide how to write the plural form of words ending in *-f* or *fe*?

8. List three common words which form their plural irregularly (that is, with other than *-s* or *-es*).

9. When we form the plurals of *electron* and *proton* by writing *electrons* and *protons,* what earlier practice are we breaking away from?

10. Indicate the foreign plural of the words whose Anglicized plurals are *appendixes* and *curriculums.*

11. Give three fairly sensible reasons why some foreign plurals have remained in English.

12. Check your dictionary for its handling of the plural form of the word *spoonful*. What seems to be the general tendency with such compounds?

13. How would you indicate possessive form with the compound *commander-in-chief*?

14. How many simple inflected pronouns are listed in the chapter? How many of these are called "personal" pronouns?

15. List some of the most notable characteristics of the way personal pronouns are inflected.

16. When a simple inflected pronoun has two possessive forms, when do you use which?

17. Pretend that there is a regular English verb whose infinitive form is to *grimp*. Indicate its other forms.

18. We may spend much time studying the forms of irregular verbs because (a) most of them are in common use and (b) they provide convenient shibboleths for linguistic snobs. Fortunately, however, the number of them is very small. About how many are there?

19. What handy reference book (besides this text) can usually tell you if a particular verb form is in good standing?

20. Write three sentences whose verbs are in the past tense although they have no separate past tense form.

21. *Send* and *spend* form their past tenses by changing -d to -t; suggest two more verbs that fall in this category.

22. List five verbs whose past tenses involve a vowel change from the plain form.

23. Your ear might tell you that "have ran" and "had came" are not standard inflections of these two verbs, yet what is unusual about the way these two form the past participle?

24. What three verbs does our verb *to be* reflect? How many more different forms does this verb have than any other verb in the English language?

SIX KINDS OF SENTENCES

There is a widespread superstition that (a) every legitimate unit of utterance is a sentence; and (b) every sentence must somehow have a subject and predicate, even though one or both of these may not be discoverable by ordinary ears or eyes, but must be "understood." If we want to get away from mind reading and talk ordinary sense, we must give up either (a) or (b). We can say that such utterances as "Who?" and "Heads up!" and "Please pass the salt," which are certainly all right in their places, are legitimate nonsentences; or we can say that there are several kinds of sentences, only one of which must have a subject and predicate. One method would work about as well as the other, but since "legitimate non-sentences" seems to many people like a contradiction in terms, we will take the second choice.

We use at least six kinds of sentences, which may be called *questions*,

answers, commands (including **requests**), *exclamations, comments,* and
statements. Only the last of these must contain a *clause;* and it is the
clause, not the sentence, which *must* have a subject and predicate. The first
five have no structural requirements except that their intonation should
be in keeping with their meaning. They may contain as little as a single
word.

> *Question:* Where?
> *Answer:* Beyond that rosebush.
> *Command:* Forceps.
> *Exclamation:* Cheers!
> *Comment:* Not bad.

These are all completely standard in conversation, or in writing that is intended to give the flavor of conversation. We could of course expand each
one to include a subject and predicate, but we would not necessarily improve them by doing so; and there is certainly no sound reason to pretend
that they are abbreviations of longer expressions. The surgeon who says
"Forceps" is not thinking "Please pass the forceps" or "Nurse, I need the
forceps next." He thinks "Forceps" and he says "Forceps" and he gets forceps, which is language at its most efficient.

It is only the sixth kind of sentence, the *statement,* that must contain
a subject and predicate—a noun-verb combination like *Alice says* or
everybody was or *Finnegan pitched.* Except in plays, stories, and directions for do-it-yourself projects, the great majority of all written sentences
are, or are intended to be, statements; and sentence fragments—generally
regarded as the number one sin in student writing—are almost always un-
successful attempts at statements.

The difference between statements and the other five types may be
explained in this way: the other five types depend heavily on intonation
patterns to indicate not only their specific meanings but the fact that
they are intended as complete utterances. For instance, if somebody asked
you what your brother was doing, you might answer, "Working in the
garden." If you did, you would use the same intonation pattern that you
would use to finish the longer sentence "He is working in the garden."
Your sentence would therefore *sound* complete; and since the words "He
is" would not be in the least needed, it would *be* complete. But if you
began a conversation with the same four words, you would probably say,
"Working in the garden—" leaving your voice hanging in a way that indicated that you planned to add other words—as you probably would.
Therefore the four words would neither sound like nor be a sentence. And
in writing, the four words will be a satisfactory sentence only if they are
put in a setting that clearly indicates that they are to be pronounced with
a final intonation pattern.

If you ask what *is* a final intonation pattern, you won't find the answer here. There are many of them, and the details are complicated. But you probably know the difference between the way your voice sounds when you finish saying something definite, and the way it sounds when you simply break off in the middle of something.

Of course, statements also have intonation patterns, but they depend less on these and more on the readily visible elements of word order, word form, and function words. Our habit of writing largely in statements is therefore very sensible, for it leaves a reader less to guess at. Since it is the clause structure of statements that causes writers most trouble, we shall discuss this at some length before returning to a briefer consideration of the other kinds of sentences.

THE SUBJECT-VERB COMBINATION

Any group of related words that contains a subject-verb combination is a clause, and every statement must contain at least one clause. Examples:

SUBJECT	VERB
It	is
I	have
My wristwatch	says

It doesn't do much good to memorize the definitions of these elements. The important thing is to learn to recognize them. For instance, a subject is often defined as "a noun about which the verb says something." But in the sentence "Stan gave Dick the money," the verb says something about three different nouns. Only one of them, *Stan*, is the subject; and it is recognizable simply by the way it is combined with *gave*, not by its meaning. If we reported the same transaction by saying, "Dick was given the money by Stan," we'd have a different subject, *Dick;* and if we said, "The money was given to Dick by Stan," we'd have still a third one.

The subject may be either a single word or a group of words, and it is not always next to the verb:

SUBJECT	VERB
The *man* in the service station	*told* me so.
One of the players	*was* too anxious.
To drive a car like that	*takes* real nerve.

In each of these sentences we could call everything before the verb the *complete subject* and the italicized word or words the *simple subject.* Sometimes it is hard to decide just how much of the subject is *simple,* and it often makes no particular difference. But in such a sentence as the second it is important to notice that the simple subject is *one,* not *players,* and the verb is therefore *was* rather than *were.*

The verb may be either a single word like those in the sentences above or a verb phrase such as *will go, must have been, ought to do,* or *might have been driving.* But it cannot be simply a participle or an infinitive, or a combination of these such as *having been* or *wanting to go.* Such phrases are useful in expanding clauses, but they do not take the place of the definite combinations *have been* or *wants to go.* A verb phrase may be interrupted by negative words or other modifiers:

He *has gone.* He *has* not *gone.* He *has* already *gone.*

In each of these sentences the verb phrase is simply *has gone.*

INDEPENDENT AND SUBORDINATE CLAUSES

There is one other requirement for a statement. Its clause, or at least one of its clauses, must be independent. That is, it must not be introduced by a connective which shows that it is subordinate to something else. Any group of related words containing a subject-verb combination is a clause, but only an independent clause can stand alone as a statement:

INDEPENDENT CLAUSES	SUBORDINATE CLAUSES
He went there	because she went
They will do it	if you want them to
We can leave it	when Andy comes

Each of the independent clauses could be used as a complete statement, or it could be joined to the subordinate clause at its right to make a longer one. But the subordinate clauses would not be complete statements if they were used alone. Other kinds of subordinate clauses, less likely to be mistaken for statements, will be illustrated later.

COMPLEMENTS

Aside from the subject and verb, a clause may contain one or two *complements.* A complement is a noun whose relation to the subject is shown simply by the verb. Thus in the sentence "Stan gave Dick the money," both *Dick* and *money* are complements. But in the sentence "Stan gave the money to Dick," only *money* is a complement, since *to* is used to connect *Dick* with the rest of the clause. In the sentence "He saw Dave, Al, Peter, and Charlie," there is only one complement, in four parts.

In highly inflected languages like Latin, it is important to distinguish between various kinds of complements, because different ones require that the nouns be in different forms—or nouns in different forms indicate different relations when used as complements. Even in English people often talk about *direct objects, indirect objects, retained objects, objective complements, subjective complements,* and so forth, but on the whole this seems to be a waste of energy. Certainly complements show a number of different relations. But unless you understand exactly what relations are shown in a given sentence you can't classify the complements; and if you do understand them you don't learn anything further by making the classification except some technical terms—and they won't last from one book to another because grammarians have disagreed so widely on what are the proper terms that one kind of complement has fourteen different names and another has eighteen. But it *is* useful to see how complements function in clause patterns, because their functioning is one of our most important ways of indicating the connection of ideas.

THE BASIC CLAUSE PATTERNS

Whether or not a clause is a complete sentence, it must contain a subject and verb, and it may also contain either one or two complements—not more. These are its only possible major elements; anything else it may contain must be a modifier of one of these or a connective.

The three basic clause patterns are illustrated by the three statements:

1. The *subject* is something.
2. The *subject* does something.
3. The *subject* is affected by something.

The first two are called *active,* the third *passive.*

"THE SUBJECT IS . . ."

In Pattern 1 the verb acts rather like an equal sign, connecting two names for the same person or thing. It is usually some form of the verb *to be,* though a few other verbs are possible:

The man   is   a mechanic.
                     was
                     used to be
                     ought to have been
                     became
                     seemed to be

These vary in detail, but in all of them the identity between the subject (*man*) and the complement (*mechanic*) could be symbolized (though of course not fully represented) by the formula:

The man = a mechanic

In this pattern there cannot be more than one complement, and there may be none. In such a sentence as "The man is busy," *busy* is not another noun renaming the subject, but an adjective modifying it; and in the sentence "The man is *in the next room*," the whole phrase *in the next room* is a modifier. In neither sentence could *is* be replaced by an equal sign without a considerable distortion of the meaning. On the other hand, "The man from the new garage on Fremont Street seems a much better mechanic than the one usually sent over by the Sloan garage" is just the simple *man = mechanic* pattern with a few trimmings.

"THE SUBJECT DOES . . ."

In Pattern 2 the subject and complement are different people or things, and the verb can be symbolized by an arrow rather than an equals sign, to show that the subject acts on the complement:

The man   needs   a mechanic.
                     hired
                     will have to get
                     had seen
                     might have injured

All of these and a great many more could be symbolized by the formula:

The man → a mechanic

Like Pattern 1, Pattern 2 can occur with no complement, as in "The man works hard" or "The man hunts a good deal." *Works* and *hunts* could be symbolized by arrows rather than equal signs, but there is nothing for the arrows to point to in these sentences. Unlike Pattern 1, Pattern 2 can also occur with two complements (see page 137).

IS OR DOES?

Unfortunately, Patterns 1 and 2, as patterns, look exactly alike. If you saw a sentence full of unfamiliar words, such as "The kleef plunned a veddle," you could not be sure whether to represent *plunned* by an equal sign or an arrow—though the arrow would be a much better bet on percentages. Sometimes even one unknown word could cause uncertainty:

A tyro became the star.

A tiara became the star.

The first requires an equal sign, because *tyro* means a beginner, and *became* must therefore mean "developed into." But the second requires an arrow, because *tiara* means a sort of crown, and therefore *became* must mean "looked well on."

This ambiguity of patterns actually causes very little trouble—much less than ambiguity of words does. We mention it only to show that it doesn't pay to be too dogmatic about the meaning of grammatical constructions. Both words and patterns convey meaning, but they do it simultaneously. Unless you are struggling with a particularly difficult passage, you don't think first of the words and then of the patterns, or vice versa. You react to the words *in* the pattern. But if you have written a rather complicated sentence and are wondering whether it hangs together or not, some knowledge of the patterns may help you decide.

Verbs that can be represented by equal signs may be called *linking verbs,* and the complements that follow them *subjective complements.* Verbs that can be represented by arrows may be called *transitive verbs,* and their complements *direct objects.* Unfortunately, a good many other names are also used for the same things. Rather than get into an argument about which names are better, we will try to avoid them all as far as possible. The two patterns can generally be recognized and understood even if you don't know what to call them.

CLAUSES WITH TWO COMPLEMENTS

Verbs of the arrow kind may be followed by two complements, but not more. Look at the following sentences:

The man gave the boy a dollar.

The man called the boy a liar.

In the first, the two complements refer to different things, and you may call *boy* the *indirect object* and *dollar* the *direct object*. In the second, both complements refer to the same thing, and you may call *boy* the *direct object* and *liar* the *objective complement,* unless you happen to have been brought up under a different terminology. But the chances are pretty strong that you know what both sentences mean, and can make up other sentences on the same patterns, without calling any of the complements anything.

Once again the patterns are theoretically ambiguous. If you saw such a sentence as "The moof drissed the nule a flid" you could not tell which way to analyze it. Once in a great while even a sentence composed of familiar words, but without context, might be taken either way. Thus "He made the boy a soldier" might mean either that he turned the boy into a soldier or that he may a toy soldier for the boy to play with. But the chance of misinterpreting the patterns is again much smaller than that of misinterpreting the words. If we assume that the sentence deals with training, not toy making, there is still room for a good deal of difference of opinion about what qualities would have to be developed to justify the statement.

"THE SUBJECT IS AFFECTED . . ."

The third basic clause pattern is the passive one. Here are three variations:

The speaker was cheered by the large audience.

The speaker was given a round of applause.

The speaker was made the butt of many jokes.

The last two have a complement apiece—the limit for passive clauses. By a peculiar sort of perverted logic, *round* and *butt* may be called "retained objects." Rather than explain why, we call them simply complements.

WHY TALK ABOUT COMPLEMENTS?

Since we are not going to insist on calling the various kinds of complements anything in particular, or have any exercises in distinguishing one from another, you may very reasonably wonder if there is any good reason for talking about them at all. The answer is that they, along with subjects and verbs, are the major elements in clauses—they serve to form the framework. And it is sometimes very useful to be able to separate the skeleton from the padding in order to see how a sentence works. Actually, if there were any set of terms in general use it would be worthwhile to go a little further in the analysis of complements; but with so many conflicting ones current it seems better to treat the whole subject as simply as possible.

THE IMPORTANCE OF PATTERNS

Before we go any further into the details of sentence structure, we should consider why it is that certain arrangements of words affect us as they do. We listen before we talk, just as later we read before we write. Long before we ever think about grammar or logic we come to realize that certain arrangements of words have fairly reliable meanings—quite as reliable as the words themselves. When we get to the point of making sentences of our own, we naturally imitate the arrangement of sentences that we have already heard. Unless we imitate pretty accurately, we are likely to be misunderstood and even more likely to be laughed at. Therefore we soon learn to be very accurate, at least with the simplest and most familiar patterns. Just how far we get with this automatic development depends on a number of things, which pure ignorance keeps me from analyzing here. Some children manage to make surprisingly complicated sentences quite young. Others, to put it mildly, don't.

By the time we get to school and begin to study language formally, we are already so used to the commonest patterns that we may feel they are based on the laws of nature. Actually they are simply group habits that happened to develop. We might as well have developed a very different set of habits; but we had to develop *some* set and use it fairly uniformly or we could not communicate with much success. The proof of this statement is not hard to establish. Beyond the simplest patterns our habits are not nearly as uniform as they well might be—and a great many people have extreme difficulty in understanding what they hear or read, and in making their own ideas clear to others.

However, almost all of us get far enough so that when we read a sentence we automatically expect to find certain elements and to find them in a certain order. The first thing we look for is the subject; and we assume that the first word that can be the subject *is* the subject unless there is definite evidence that it is not. Thus if a sentence begins with *John*, our first expectation is that it is going to tell us something about what John was or did, and we are usually right. But if it begins "John, Dick is . . ." the comma after *John* corrects the first impression. We now assume that the sentence is addressed to John but will tell about Dick. Or if the sentence begins "When John . . ." we can see at once that although some statement is going to be made about John, the main statement will be made about somebody or something else. We then keep our minds alert for the main subject.

Once we have found the subject, we expect a verb that combines with it to make a statement, and perhaps a complement to complete the statement. If these elements appear in their expected order, we accept the sentence as natural and "understand" its structure—whether or not we know what the writer had in mind when he wrote the words. For instance, suppose you read that "The Calonians cultivated shaners." You can't possibly know who the Calonians were or what shaners look like, but you are likely to have a feeling that something definite has been said, just because the sentence follows a familiar pattern.

It is extremely useful to have a pattern so reliable that it automatically indicates the relation of words to each other, so that we don't have to guess about it or take the time to figure it out. Sometimes we could get along without it. For instance, we might understand such a sentence as "John pie ate" by realizing that very few pies are man-eaters. But we could only guess about the meaning of "John Tom hit." There are two obvious possibilities, and there is no pattern to help us decide which one is intended. For this reason we normally use a word order that gives a clear indication of how the words are related to one another *no matter what words are used;* and we follow this order when the particular words used are such that we do not actually need it.

Suppose we list five words in alphabetical order: *book, gave, Lucy, Pete, the.* These five words could be arranged in 120 different ways, but only *two* of the ways would make clear, normal statements:

Lucy gave Pete the book.
Pete gave Lucy the book.

A few other combinations would be possible if we used commas, such as:

Pete, Lucy gave the book.

Still others would be possible as parts of sentences, but would not make complete statements:

The book Lucy gave Pete *is interesting.*

Most of the combinations, however, would be mere jumbles that would convey no information at all.

What we have to consider now is the area between those patterns that are learned automatically and those that have no meaning at all. Within this area there are a great many arrangements of words that skilled people can handle and respond to but that unskilled people can find difficult to understand and even more difficult to use. Of course word order is not the only element in grammatical patterns, as we saw earlier; but it is probably the one that causes most trouble, and it is certainly the one with which we shall be most concerned in the rest of this chapter.

CLASSIFICATION OF SENTENCES

Sentences (i.e., statements) are classified according to their clause structure as follows:

1. *Simple* (containing a single independent clause):

One of his younger brothers works at the new cotton mill in Davis.

2. *Compound* (containing two or more independent clauses):

Eloise still lives in New York, but Pasquale has been in Oregon for years.

3. *Complex* (containing both independent and subordinate clauses):

When he has time, Milton likes to go fishing.

(If a complex sentence contains more than one independent clause, it may be called compound-complex.)

There is no particular value in merely learning to label the various types of sentences, but it is convenient to consider them separately to avoid having to face too many problems at once.

EXPANSION OF SIMPLE SENTENCES

The major elements of a clause are *formally* the most important ones, but they are not necessarily the ones that contribute the most information. You might describe a dog by saying, "It is a dangerous and vicious animal, likely to bite anybody." You can guess which words would probably make the greatest impression on your audience. But in the structure of the clause *it—is—animal* are the major elements, and all the rest are secondary.

We may expand a simple sentence by adding modifying words or phrases to any or all of its major elements, or to the sentence as a whole. There is no theoretical limit to this expansion—it is quite easy to compose a technically simple sentence hundreds of words long and containing an indefinite number of related ideas. There is, however, a flexible practical limit. A sentence should not be so long or so complicated that the reader or listener will have trouble grasping it as a whole.

1. Perkins saw Eddie.
2. Yesterday afternoon old *Perkins,* the barber, definitely *saw* little *Eddie* getting on the bus.
3. Looking out the window yesterday afternoon during the rainstorm, old *Perkins,* the barber with the reputation of knowing everything about everybody in town, definitely *saw* little *Eddie,* the son of the new owner of the Elite Cafe, getting on the ancient bus driven by . . . etc.

All three sentences have the same three major elements in the same order. The first contains nothing else. The second contains a reasonable number of modifying elements which give it additional meaning. But the third is too much for one bite. There are so many modifying elements that the direct line of the statement is buried.

Modifiers are considered more thoroughly later in the chapter. Here we need notice only that while a simple sentence contains only one *formally complete statement,* a number of *implied statements* may be worked in by the addition of words and phrases. This use of implied statements (if not carried too far) greatly increases the efficiency and economy of our communication, as the following comparison shows:

Perkins is old.
Perkins is a barber.
Perkins saw Eddie.
Eddie is little.
Eddie was getting on the bus.
This definitely happened.
It happened yesterday afternoon.

Yesterday afternoon old Perkins, the barber, definitely saw little Eddie getting on the bus.

It is also possible to split any or all the elements in a simple sentence:

S	V	C¹	C²
The *man*	*gave*	the *boy*	a *dollar*
The *man*	*promised*	the *boy*	a *dollar*
and	and	and	and
the *woman*	*gave*	the *girl*	a *doughnut*

Each element of the clause is compound, but there is still only one clause.

COMPOUND SENTENCES

A compound sentence consists of two or more independent clauses, each of which could be a simple sentence. It therefore offers no new problems in the internal structure of its clauses. In spoken English it is often quite impossible to tell whether a series of independent clauses is intended as one compound sentence or several simple ones. Except in prepared speeches, the speaker himself has usually given the matter no thought, and the listeners can only guess. In written English the distinction is made simply by punctuation. If the writer wants his independent clauses to be considered separately, he puts a period after each. If he wants to show that two or more statements are so closely connected that they should be taken as a single unit, he can do so by writing them as a single sentence. Frequently it makes little difference which he does.

We played tennis for a while, and then we went swimming.

I like Morris, but Doris bores me.

She went one way, he went the other.

The company was good; the food was awful.

We could split each of these sentences in two by substituting a period for the comma or semicolon. Whether or not this would be an improvement is a matter of individual judgment. If we split the sentences, we could drop the connectives *but* and *and* or keep them.

The clauses of a compound sentence should always be separated by punctuation, by some such connective as *and, but, or,* or *nor,* or by both. The reason is simply that the clauses *are* independent, and should not be allowed to run together. We need some indication of where one statement ends and the next begins. Elaborate rules stating when each of these separating devices should be used are not of much value. The writer should choose his means according to the effect he wishes to produce.

A comma indicates a slight break in the thought, and should be used alone only when the clauses are both very short and very closely related; otherwise it will result in a run-on sentence. A semicolon indicates a stronger break, and can be used with clauses of any length. A connective clearly indicates the intended relation between the two ideas; to omit the connective challenges the reader to find out the relation for himself, and this challenge is sometimes more effective than the ready-made indication. Further discussion of this problem will be found on pages 360–61.

There is no fixed limit to the number of clauses a compound sentence may contain; but it should not be so long that it is difficult to grasp as a unit.

COMPLEX SENTENCES

A complex sentence contains at least one subordinate clause as well as at least one independent clause. So far we have mentioned only one kind of subordinate clause—the kind of adverbial clause which modifies the whole independent clause (see page 133). Subordinate clauses may also be used as subjects, complements, or modifiers of any of the elements in larger clauses. This interlocking makes it possible:

1. To split one clause by another:

1—	2	—1
The man	who discovered that	was a genius.

2. To run two clauses together, with no separation by punctuation or connective:

Mrs. Trimble said the train would be late.

Here the clause *the train would be late* is the complement in the main clause. It fits in directly after *said* exactly as *a few words* would.

The possible variations in the structure of complex sentences are almost infinite. We can write modifiers of modifiers of modifiers and clauses within clauses within clauses as long as our ingenuity holds out—at the risk, of course, of losing our readers—not to mention ourselves. Some of the most troublesome problems in the use and structure of subordinate clauses are discussed later in the chapter.

THE BORDERLINE BETWEEN COMPOUND AND COMPLEX SENTENCES

By definition, a compound sentence contains only independent clauses; a complex sentence contains at least one subordinate clause. This brings up three questions:

1. Can independent and subordinate clauses be reliably distinguished by their own structure?

Not always. Many clauses beginning with such words as *after, if, because, what, whom,* and *when* can immediately be recognized as performing a subordinate function; but a great many clauses cannot be classified without considering the sentences in which they appear. For example, almost any independent clause may be turned into a subordinate one by prefixing some such clause as "I know . . ."

2. Can independent and subordinate clauses be reliably distinguished by their functions in sentences?

The line between the two is so fine that it sometimes depends on the arbitrary classification of certain connectives as "coordinating conjunctions" and others as "subordinating conjunctions":

Independent: Clem was interested, *but Dick was bored.*
Subordinate: Clem was interested, *while Dick was bored.*

Independent: He was tired, *for he had been up since dawn.*
Subordinate: He was tired, *because he had been up since dawn.*

3. Is there any practical advantage in distinguishing between independent and subordinate clauses?

Not in borderline cases, such as those shown just above. However, *some* subordinate clauses bring up special problems that do not occur in independent clauses. If we don't push it too far, the classification can be useful in organizing these problems for study.

EXERCISES

Classify the sentences below as follows: S (one independent clause), Cp (two or more independent clauses), or Cx (one or more independent clauses and one or more subordinate clauses).

If any of the sentences seem to you to be particularly bad, explain why.

1. The balding construction worker wondered who had sent him leather sandals.
2. We wanted to fly to Utah for some skiing, but the strike of airline mechanics and engineers ruined the plans.

3. The experimental rat that escaped into the storeroom was, after all, the least valuable of the animals.

4. The nicely dressed young man smiled at the children sailing boats and tossed a nickel into the fountain.

5. Walking calmly along the gutter, the squirrel showed no fear of falling.

6. Whoever bought your old desk showed excellent taste in cabinetry.

7. I believe Mr. Ratham ordered the tape recorder.

8. We had cocktails before leaving the house, and George ordered wine for us with the dinner, and we all had after-dinner drinks, and later Emma fixed coffee when we arrived at her apartment.

9. Morton could, since he was chairman, have called the meeting to order before now.

10. Only seventeen and already a college graduate, Bart was at that time a very self-conscious individual.

11. I think that anyone would want to win a new car.

12. The axle he designed will soon be ready for testing.

13. The driver of the car is my Uncle Henry, who, as you know, owns four restaurants in Cleveland.

14. He told us that someone had made the drive in four hours, and we wondered if such a thing were possible.

15. He did what you told him.

16. The demonstrator holding the sign and the policeman wearing the helmet glared at each other in passing.

17. What you are attempting is against regulations.

18. Inside the trunk, the policeman found fifteen unmatched tennis shoes and a bathing suit wrapped in a red towel.

19. The man who spoke was the representative from Kansas who used to own a dry cleaning store.

20. The Easter Bunny brought me what I asked for.

21. The first cars were ingenious devices but often overheated, so they were not reliable for long trips in summer.

22. He will probably attempt to murder anyone who interrupts him at this point.

23. The old dog, confused by the long drive, snapped at the daughter of the storekeeper.

24. She said she warned him not to go.

25. Why anyone would go to Florida in August is a mystery to me.

HOW MODIFIERS WORK

A modifier may be defined roughly as a word, phrase, or clause that supplies any kind of additional information (even negative information)

about the element with which it is associated. A verb is not considered as modifying its subject. Thus in the sentence, "*Young* Lorenz worked *hard,* but made *no* progress," only the italicized words are called modifiers. If the modifier is a phrase or clause, it may itself contain secondary modifiers:

He saw *a tall* man *in black* clothes.

Here the words *a* and *tall* and the phrase *in black clothes* modify *man;* and within the phrase, *black* modifies *clothes.* In discussing the structure of sentences we shall not usually have to bother about the internal structure of phrases.

We can avoid a good deal of trouble if we realize from the beginning that it is in human minds, not on printed pages, that modification takes place. No word automatically does anything at all to another word; but the relative positions of words stimulate us to make certain associations. When we see a combination like *tall man* we can be quite sure that the writer meant *tall* to refer to *man,* and that any normal reader will take it as he meant it. It is a convenient short cut to express all this by saying "*tall* modifies *man.*" In dealing with this particular pattern—adjective plus noun—the statement is safe because our habits are so uniform that there is very little chance of either a misunderstanding or an argument.

But suppose we encounter a sentence like "He sent the man from Texas." The writer might mean "He sent the Texas man (somewhere or other);" while a reader might take it to mean "He sent the (unidentified) man out of Texas." Are we justified in taking sides and saying what the phrase *from Texas* "really" modifies?

We could, of course, "make a rule" that in such sentences the final phrase must always be considered as referring to the word immediately before it, or a different rule that it must always be considered as referring back to the verb; but neither one of these rules would be an accurate description of good usage. The simple fact is that our habits of association are not as regular in this type of construction as in the *tall man* pattern, largely because there is less need for them to be. Let us look at some other examples, and illustrate the natural associations by simple diagrams:

1. He met a man from New York.

He	met	a man
		from New York

Here the phrase clearly refers to the complement.

2. He knocked the glass from the table.

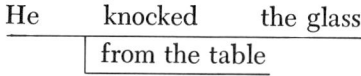

He	knocked	the glass
	from the table	

Here the phrase clearly refers to the verb.

3. He sent a present from Paris.

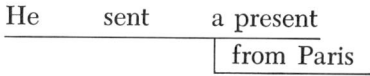

He	sent	a present
		from Paris

or

He	sent	a present
	from Paris	

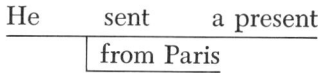

This might mean that he sent a present-from-London from Paris, or a present-from-Paris from New York; but the most probable guess is that both the present and the sending were from Paris. If this is true, one diagram would be as good as the other.

4. He shot the man from the bank.

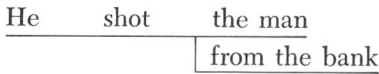

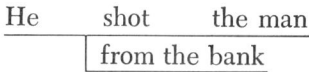

He	shot	the man
		from the bank
He	shot	the man
	from the bank	

Here the two diagrams represent entirely different situations. Was the shooting done from the bank, or was the man shot an employee of the bank?

In the first two of the four sentences above the particular words used help the grammatical pattern to indicate clearly the intended association. The third sentence is technically ambiguous, but there is not much chance of a serious misunderstanding. The fourth sentence, however, when printed alone, could mean either of two quite different things. It would probably be clear if spoken, because the speaker could show by his intonation pattern whether the man or the shooting was from the bank, and a listener would probably follow him. And it might be clear in writing if the context made one interpretation or the other automatic. But as a single written sentence it is completely ambiguous.

Thus we have four sentences containing the same grammatical pattern (as far as a reader can tell without knowing the exact meanings of the words) but indicating quite different relations of ideas. If we try to make a general rule to cover all four we may arrive at something like this:

The reader's natural tendency is to make the easiest association possible. Since the final phrase comes right next to the complement, the obvious first guess is that it refers to the complement. But if this association seems unreasonable, he will carry the phrase one position further back and try it with the verb. A writer should bear this tendency in mind, and arrange his sentence so that no misleading or ridiculous association is easily possible.

Of course we usually make our associations rapidly and subconsciously. It is only when we are puzzled by sentences, or when we deliberately analyze or diagram one, that we consciously consider such problems. We may do this quite informally by saying something like, "Oh yes, I see—*from the bank* goes with *shot,* not with *man.*" Or we may do it (usually at a teacher's request) formally and according to rule.

When we do attempt to analyze formally by rules, we have good reason to ask how sound the rules are. Let us look at another sentence that can be diagramed in two ways:

John waved a greeting to the man.

```
John        waved       a greeting
                        | to the man
John        waved       a greeting
            | to the man
```

Here there is not the slightest doubt as to what the whole sentence means; yet we can make diagrams to indicate two quite different theories as to what the phrase modifies. And if we look for comparisons, we can find evidence on both sides:

John's greeting to the man was cordial.

```
John's      greeting     was        cordial
            | to the man
```

John threw the ball to the man.

```
John        threw       the ball
            | to the man
```

We may, of course, argue about which comparison is closer, and perhaps feel we have proved that one or the other of the diagrams is right.

But this is merely playing a game with definitions. Association of *to the man* with *any* element in the sentence is neither as close nor as uniform as associations of the *tall man* type; and we can't make it so by drawing a picture.

Sometimes the question that arises is not which element a word modifies, but whether it modifies any one element or a combination of several:

Yesterday my brother went to town.

Here we could explain *yesterday* as modifying either the verb *went* or the whole clause *my brother went to town*. It makes a simpler diagram to relate the modifier to a single word, but the more natural thing to say is that it seems to modify the whole clause. Incidentally, this interpretation helps to explain why some modifiers can be put almost anywhere in a sentence, while others have a fixed position.

If there is any moral in all this, it is that a diagram may be a useful way of indicating a connection of ideas, but offers no convincing proof, since people who disagree about what the relations are will naturally draw different diagrams.

POSITION OF MODIFIERS WITH NOUNS

The obvious place to put a modifier is close to the word it modifies, and the two closest positions are immediately before and immediately after. Normally we put a single-word modifier of a noun before, and a phrase or clause modifier after. Thus we should say, "A tall man," "The man in the street," and "The man who was here yesterday."

The habit of putting a phrase afterward is so strong that if for any reason we put it first we usually convert it into a single word by the use of hyphens. Thus we write *well-behaved children* and *off-the-cuff speeches*. The habit of putting a single word first is not quite so strong. Nobody would say *a man tall*, but we might say either *the only available man* or *the only man available*. The modifier comes first at least nine times out of ten. When it comes after the noun, it is usually because it introduces, or easily could introduce, a phrase. Thus we should say:

A broken bough	A bough broken by the wind
An appropriate sum	A sum appropriate for the purpose

The reason that such words as *appropriate, available,* and *possible* may be used after the noun even when they do not introduce a phrase is that they tend to suggest a phrase in a way that words like *tall* and *beautiful* do not. We should say "He is a possible winner," and not "He is a winner possible." But we might say either "The only possible explanation" or "The only explanation possible," because we are used to such expressions as "The only explanation possible under the circumstances."

MODIFIERS IN SERIES

When two modifiers come before a noun, there are four possible relations:

1. Both may modify the noun independently. If so, the modifiers are usually "leveled" by *and, but, or,* or a comma:

Old, tired men	*Long* and *boring* books	*Air* or *sea* travel

2. The first may modify the second, while the second modifies the noun:

Dark green water   *Very old* men

3. The second may modify the noun, while the first modifies the combination:

A *long comic* book   The *old hired* man   A *new dollar* bill

4. The two may be taken as a unit modifying the noun:

A *high school* boy   The *land conservation* program
The *Great Society* program

It is often a hair-splitting process to decide exactly which kind of these relations is intended (for instance, in *dark oak table*), and therefore unnecessary to indicate which one you have selected. When there is a chance of misunderstanding, the two more closely related words may be joined by a hyphen:

A *comic-book* salesman   *High-school* expenses
A *comic* book-salesman   *High* school-expenses

Many writers regularly use hyphens to indicate combinations of *modifiers* even when there is no danger of ambiguity:

A *high-school* team	but	The *high school* is new.
The *Great-Society* program		The *Great Society* is an expansion of the New Deal.

Such combinations are not usually included in dictionaries as hyphenated words, but they are clearly established as such in standard usage. If a combination comes into very frequent use it is often written as a single word. Thus we may read *high school* texts, *high-school* texts, or *highschool* texts.

The series of modifiers preceding a noun may be considerably longer than two, whether they all modify the noun or some of them modify others:

A long, interesting, well-documented, and highly important book

The present Scottsdale High School athletic program committee

These longer series involve no further theoretical problems, but anybody with a sensitive ear will probably decide that the second one is at least a word too long.

ADVERBIAL MODIFIERS

Modifiers of verbs can be placed more freely than modifiers of nouns. This is partly because there is usually only one verb in a clause, while there are likely to be several nouns, and partly because it often makes little difference whether we associate an adverbial modifier specifically with the verb or more generally with the clause as a whole. For instance we might find any of the following orders:

Slowly Emmett walked down the street.
Emmett *slowly* walked down the street.
Emmett walked *slowly* down the street.
Emmett walked down the street *slowly*.

Some readers might prefer one of these sentences to the others, or feel that they all showed some differences in emphasis. But there is no question that the same general information is conveyed by all four, and that a great many readers would consider them completely interchangeable.

Some modifiers are less flexible than others. If we substituted *fast* for *slowly*, we could not use the order "Fast Emmett walked," because a reader would probably think *fast* described Emmett, rather than the way he walked down the street. We should also be unlikely to say "Emmett fast walked," though we might have some trouble in explaining why. Other modifiers might have different numbers of possibilities, and it might make a definite difference where some of them were put.

The fact that there is no satisfactory general rule for such constructions need not trouble us. "Modification" is merely a matter of habitual association, and a position that seems natural to the writer will usually be satisfactory to the reader. There are, however, a few words about which an arbitrary theory has been developed. It is often said that the following pairs of sentences have different "real meanings," approximately as indicated:

I *only* want ten cents. (I don't expect to get it)
I want *only* ten cents. (That is all I want)
I'll *just* see him for a minute. (Not talk to him)
I'll see him for *just* a minute. (It won't take longer)
He doesn't *even* have a dollar. (So he can't spend it)
He doesn't have *even* a dollar. (He has less than a dollar)

The theory is that words like *only, just,* and *even* necessarily modify the words that immediately follow them. But the theory simply isn't true. It describes a habit that we might have developed, not one that we actually have developed. When we hear such sentences, the sensible thing to do is to try to figure out what the speaker actually means. If we want to express such ideas, and have any fear of being misunderstood, we can always say something like "All I want is ten cents" or "My desire for ten cents is merely a wish."

SUCCESSIVE MODIFYING PHRASES

A phrase is usually placed immediately after the word it modifies. This ordinarily causes no trouble; but when two phrases are used, one of them must come first. There is then a possibility that the second may be taken as modifying the last word in the first phrase, instead of the word with which the writer associated it. This may result in an actual misunderstanding or in a ludicrous suggestion.

There is a man *from Kansas   in the car.*

Both phrases clearly refer to *man.*

There is a man *in the car   from Kansas.*

Either the man or the car may be from Kansas.

The car was identified *as the one stolen   by Jim Dodd.*

If Dodd merely identified the car, he might bring a libel suit on the basis of this sentence.

No general rule can be given on which type of phrase should be put first. A writer must remember that the reader will probably associate the second phrase with the nearest word to which it can reasonably apply, which is often the last word in the first phrase. If such an association would lead to misunderstanding, the writer may reverse the phrases. If the result is still unclear, he should completely rewrite the sentence.

GENERAL PRINCIPLES OF MODIFICATION

A comprehensive treatment of the problems of modification would require far more space than we can afford in this book; but careful attention to a few general principles will solve most of them:

1. Modification depends on association of ideas.

2. It's not enough for a writer to prove that his association is possible. Unless he makes it automatic for his readers, his sentence is ambiguous.

3. A written sentence gets no help from intonation. Word order is therefore doubly important.

Two common difficulties are discussed in the INDEX TO USAGE under the headings *Dangling Modifiers* and *Squinting Modifiers.*

EXERCISES

I. Each of the following sentences is accompanied by a word or phrase to be used as a modifier. Insert the word or phrase in such a way that a reader will have no reasonable doubt about what association is intended. (There may be many satisfactory arrangements, of course, so restate in a second sentence the idea you intended in the original.)

1. I inadvertently broke my cup and spilled coffee on the carpet. (brightly patterned)

2. I watched the ballplayers. (cold and miserable)

3. Gregory commented that the food was cold. (frequently)

4. This morning the committee met to plan the ceremony. (in the Student Union)

5. John spoke to Mike, who stormed out of the room. (angrily)

6. The old lady frowned at the young woman. (in the low-cut dress)

7. The officer called to the young boys. (from the local army base)

8. The burly halfback shook hands with the aged fan who had climbed down onto the field. (gingerly)

9. We wondered if the new supervisor would be on the morning flight. (from New York)

10. I told him he should leave that afternoon. (quietly)

11. At exam time I study late into the night and drink a lot of coffee. (usually)

12. He carried the child out of the candy store. (screaming and crying)

13. The delivery truck stopped, and a man carried a package up to the corner house. (old and battered)

14. A friend of mine came to visit me when my roommate was out. (for the weekend)

15. We were asked to hand in our answer sheets. (immediately)

II. Resolve the ambiguity or confusion in the following sentences by overhauling the present modification.

1. Coated with rust and seaweed, they could not read the name on the anchor.

2. The group enjoyed feeding the dolphins with raw fish, including Elmer.

3. Upon first taking off from the airport, the seat backs must be in an upright position.

4. Jeremy always boasted that he once weighed 5 lbs. 14 ounces as an all-state offensive tackle.

5. State officials insist that no one should drive a car or a truck less than sixteen years old.

6. Calling to us to follow her, the horse with Genevieve on top galloped out of the barnyard.

7. Because she was trained to jump, my sister paid a handsome price for the mare.

8. Completing the north wall just as the whistle blew, the tools were cleaned and put away in just a few minutes.

9. Despite his heavy harness and blinders, the groom had trouble controlling the startled horse.

10. Having picked his rib clean, Leroy asked if there was any more meat.

11. We spent the morning catching the escaped chickens, with Warren in command.

12. Potted and bright pink, Uncle Charlie brought us an azalea plant.

13. Leaving the expressway at Main Street, the traffic delayed the wedding party.

14. After drinking most of the wine himself, the stairwell looked like a mountain to David.

15. We always like gathering to watch the youngsters in the family hunt for Easter eggs, but not grandfather.

THE FUNCTION OF SUBORDINATE CLAUSES

We mentioned that subordinate clauses could be used as subjects, complements, or modifiers of any of the elements in larger clauses. Here are some examples:

SUBJECT
His decision   is all right with me.
Whatever he decides

                                    COMPLEMENT
He knows   my opinion.
                                    what I think of him.

                                    MODIFIER (adverbial)
He comes   often.
                                    whenever he can.

                                    MODIFIER (adjectival)
He hates   troublesome   people.
                          people   who cause trouble.

Another way of expressing approximately the same idea is to say that all subordinate clauses function as nouns, adjectives, or adverbs. There is no rule against using a clause as a preposition or a verb—but if you can think of a way to do it you will become famous (in a very limited circle, of course).

In classifying clauses by function we sometimes come across borderline cases, just as we do in classifying single words. We are not going to bother about such cases in this chapter, nor are we going to attempt a complete inventory. We are simply going to discuss those kinds which seem to cause trouble and confusion most often.

RELATIVE MODIFYING CLAUSES

Adjective clauses are also called *relative clauses*. Some examples are given below:

He is the man *who was here yesterday*.
Her singing, *which was really beautiful,* drew a cheer from the crowd.
This is the one *that I like best.*

That is the house *where Jim used to live.*

A boy *we know* has three horses of his own.

Notice that three of these clauses begin with *wh-* words, and the other two could be made to begin with such words; we could change the clause in the third sentence to "*which* I like best," and the one in the fifth sentence to "*whom* we know," though these changes would not necessarily improve the sentences.

These *wh-* words are called *relatives* because they are said to relate the clauses in which they occur to the words that these clauses modify. When *that* is used in place of a *wh-* word (as in the third sentence) it is called a relative, too. Clauses like "we know" in the fifth sentence are sometimes called "relative clauses with the relative omitted," but if you want to be really fancy you can call them "asyndetic parataxis." It is all right to use them without calling them anything if the meaning is clear.

IDENTIFYING AND AMPLIFYING CLAUSES

Compare the two following sentences:

The man *who was here yesterday* left that package for you.

George Akers, *who was here yesterday,* left that package for you.

In the first sentence the italicized clause is called *identifying* because it is needed to tell you what man left the book. It is not set off by commas because it is so closely connected with the main statement that no commas are needed. But in the second sentence you already know who the man is—his name is George Akers. The clause is not used to identify him but to give you some additional information about him. It amplifies the statement and is therefore called an *amplifying* clause. And since this additional information interrupts the main statement (George Akers left that packge for you), you set it off by commas. If you read the two sentences aloud naturally, you will probably find that your voice pattern tells you which one needs the commas.

Identifying clauses are often called *restrictive* or *essential*, and amplifying clauses *nonrestrictive, descriptive,* or *nonessential*. Any of these terms will do, but students seem to find *identifying* and *amplifying* easier to remember and keep straight.

When a relative clause comes at the end of a sentence instead of in the middle, it cannot be set off by two commas; but the choice between one and none follows the same principles as those explained above:

Identifying: There's the motel where we stayed last year.
Amplifying: There is the Vista Motel, where we stayed last year.

VARIATIONS IN IDENTIFYING CLAUSES

In identifying clauses, *that* may always be substituted for *who, whom,* or *which;* and unless the relative word is the subect of the clause, it may be omitted entirely. Look at the following examples. You may have heard some of them called wrong by people who are sure there can be only one right way to do anything, but all are certainly in standard use.

1. A man *who* could help you with that is the ranger at McNary.
    A man *that* could help you with that is the ranger at McNary.
2. He is the one to *whom* you should send it.
    He is the one *that* you should send it to.
    He is the one you should send it to.
3. Here is a book *which* you might find interesting.
    Here is a book *that* you might find interesting.
    Here is a book you might find interesting.

The ideas that the relative should always be expressed, that *who* and *that* or *which* and *that* are never interchangeable, and that sentences should never end in prepositions may all be summed up in Churchill's famous note to an over-fussy editor: "This is the sort of nonsense up with which I will not for an instant put."

RESTRICTIONS ON AMPLIFYING CLAUSES

In amplifying clauses the relative word cannot be omitted, and *that* should not be substituted for a *wh-* relative word. These restrictions cause no trouble with sentences like "Sally, *who* knows her best, says she isn't really sick at all." Few of us would be tempted to put the clause in any other form. But such sentences as the following do cause some confusion:

Len Fogle, *whom* we met at the beach, is sending us some peaches.
Silas Marner, which we read in high school, bores me to tears.

We can't simply leave out the *whom* and *which,* and neither *who* nor *that* is generally accepted here as standard. If *whom* and *which* do not seem natural, the best substitutes are *a man* and *a book.*

RELATIVE NOUN CLAUSES

Relative clauses may also be used in any construction in which a noun is possible. When so used, they begin with either the simple *wh-* relatives or with *whatever, whichever,* or *whoever.*

> He knows *who did it.*
> They will give it to *whoever comes first.*
> *Why he wants it* is a mystery.
> We don't know *when it happened.*
> This is *where they used to live.*

Only two troublesome questions arise:

1. There is a widespread prejudice against introducing *definitions* with *when* or *where,* as in:

> A debate is *when you argue a question.*
> A dead end is *where you can't go any farther.*

The objection may not be logically sound (compare the standard "This is *where they used to live*"), but it is strong enough to be worth considering.

2. In choosing between *who* or *whoever* and *whom* or *whomever,* there is a theory that "the form of the relative pronoun is determined by its function in the clause in which it occurs, regardless of the function of this clause in the sentence." According to this theory the following uses are obligatory:

> I know *who did it.* (*Who* is the subject.)
> I know *who it was.* (*Who* is the "subjective complement.")
> I know *whom you saw.* (*Whom* is the "direct object.")
> Tell me to *whom you gave it.* (*Whom* is the "object of a preposition.")
> Give it to *whoever comes first.* (*Whoever* is the subject.)
> Give it to *whomever you see first.* (*Whomever* is the "direct object.")

If we take this theory seriously we shall have to recall a number of the concepts of Latin grammar which we have dismissed as inappropriate to English, simply to justify rules about one pronoun in its simple and compound forms. Luckily, all the available evidence indicates that, in spite of the objections of purists, the following sentences are in good standard usage:

I know *who* you saw.

Tell me *who* you gave it to.

Give it to *whoever* you see first.

SOME PRACTICAL RULES FOR USING *WHO* AND *WHOM*

If you have learned to use *whom* naturally wherever the Latin-based theories call for it, you might as well continue to do so. If you find the choice between *who* and *whom* troublesome, follow these rules:

1. Use *whom* in such set phrases as "to *whom* it may concern" and "for *whom* the bell tolls."

2. Say "the man it belongs to" and "the boy we were talking about" rather than "the man to *who(m)* it belongs" and "the boy about *who(m)* we were talking."

3. Remember that *who(m)* can often be omitted or replaced by *that* or an explanatory noun.

4. Whenever you are in the slightest doubt, use *who.* "I don't know *who* it belongs to" is standard English, no matter what the rules say, simply because it fits in with the natural patterns of the language, and most standard speakers use it. But "John Dawson, *whom* I consider is a fine man" is slightly ridiculous as well as "incorrect." We get the impression that the speaker is trying awfully hard and still not making it.

5. Don't give *whomever* a thought. *Whoever* is unquestionably in standard use in all constructions.

NONRELATIVE *THAT* CLAUSES

Earlier we considered clauses in which *that* could be used as an alternate for *who, whom,* or *which.* In such clauses *that* serves as a structural part of the clause, either the subject or the complement. There are other subordinate clauses for which *that* serves simply as an introductory connective:

1. I know *that* he is coming.

Here *that* could be omitted. "I know he is coming" is also standard.

2. The idea *that* he is coming cheers me up.

When the *that* clause serves to explain a preceding noun, the *that* cannot be omitted.

3. *That he had worked hard* was proved by the results.

The use of *that* clauses as subjects is much less common than it used to be, and seems to many people rather stilted. However, the popular habit of simply leaving out the *that* ("He is tired is the whole trouble") is definitely not standard. This sentence could be revised in either of the following ways:

The fact that he is tired is the whole trouble.
The whole trouble is that he is tired.

IF AND WHETHER CLAUSES

Clauses beginning with *if* and *whether* cause no trouble when they are used as modifiers, since *if* and *whether or not* have quite different meanings, and *whether* alone is never used in a modifying clause.

We are going at seven *if* you are here.
We are going at seven *whether or not* you are here.

We simply would not say, "We are going at seven *whether* you are here" without adding "or not," either after *whether* or at the end of the sentence.

There is no good reason why these clauses should cause any more trouble when they are used as complements, but a number of arbitrary rules have been made by people who like to make distinctions even when they can prove no difference. All of the following variations are acceptable:

I don't know *if he is coming.*
            if he is coming or not.
            whether he is coming.
            whether he is coming or not.
            whether or not he is coming.

If we used the clause as a subject rather than a complement, we should probably use one of the forms beginning with *whether.*

Whether (or not) he is coming hasn't been decided yet.

SEQUENCE OF TENSES

There are certain clauses in which the tense of the verb does not indicate actual time, but simply shows a grammatical relation to the main verb. Take such a sentence as "If I saw any, I would show you some." Here *saw* does not indicate past time, but rather implies that I *see* none now. This kind of adjustment is called *sequence of tenses,* and occurs in three types of clauses: (1) after verbs of saying, thinking, etc. (sometimes called "indirect discourse"); (2) in purpose clauses; (3) in certain conditional clauses.

In all three types the verb (or the first form in a verb phrase) is *shifted from the present to the past.* There are some differences between the types, however, and these differences will be discussed in the next three sections.

INDIRECT DISCOURSE

When a subordinate clause is introduced by a verb of saying or thinking in the *past tense,* the subordinate verb (or first auxiliary) is put in the past tense, regardless of the time indicated. This tendency is best illustrated by showing direct statements shifted to indirect discourse.

He *knows* you.	He said he *knew* you.
He *has* done it.	He told me he *had* done it.
He *will* come tomorrow.	He promised he *would* come tomorrow.
He *can* do it.	He thought he *could* do it.

This convention of sequence is almost invariably observed after verbs of *thinking.* We can hardly say "I *thought* I *have*" or "He *knew* we *are* there." But there is now a strong tendency to drop the convention after verbs of *saying.* Such sentences as the following are becoming very common, especially in newspapers:

He *said* he *believes* that it will work.
He *promised* he *will* take action tomorrow.

Such sentences amount to direct quotations in content, although they are indirect in form. They are sometimes distinctly clearer than the older type;

for when sequence is observed, both "I *am* there" and "I *was* there" may appear in indirect discourse as "He *said* he *was* there." Theoretically, this ambiguity could be avoided by always shifting a direct *was* to an indirect *had been;* but actually this is seldom done.

PURPOSE CLAUSES

When the verbs *may, can, will,* and *shall* are used in subordinate clauses to indicate *purpose,* sequence of tenses is regularly observed:

> He *is* resting so he *can* play tomorrow.
> He *was* resting so he *could* play the next day.
> He *works* in order that he *may* be secure.
> He *worked* in order that he *might* be secure.
> He *has* been saving so he *will* have some spending money.
> He *had* been saving so he *would* have some spending money.

Sequence is not used in clauses indicating *result:*

> He worked Sunday so he *could* (purpose) rest today.
> He worked Sunday, so he *can* (result) rest today.

CONDITIONAL SENTENCES

Such sentences as the following, in which one statement depends on another introduced by *if,* are known as conditional sentences:

> If he *had* any money yesterday, he *will* still *have* it tomorrow.
> If he *had* any money, he *would* give you some.

Notice the difference between the two. In the first, the *condition* is an open question—we don't know whether he had any money or not. In such sentences the verbs are used independently, and any tense may be used in either clause. But in the second there is a clear indication that he does not have any money. *If* clauses of this type are called *contrary-to-fact* clauses. Sentences containing contrary-to-fact clauses follow a rather curious pattern. Fortunately, most of us use it automatically.

1. The main clause must have a verb phrase beginning with *could, might, would,* or *should.* Present and future time are indicated by *would go, might help,* etc. Past time is indicated by *would have gone, might have helped,* etc.

2. In the *if* clause, present and future time are indicated by the past tense, and past time by the past perfect.

If we *had* the money, we *might buy* it.
If you *tried* tomorrow, you *could* probably *find* one.
If he *had known* the truth, he *would have acted* at once.

A special difficulty in conditional sentences is the choice between *was* and *were* when the *if* clause has a singular subject. The rule is that *was* is required to express actual doubt, and *were* to express a contrary-to-fact condition.

If it *was* there yesterday, it must still be there.
If I *was* rude, it was unintentional.
If Morgan *were* here, he could tell us.
If I *were* you, I wouldn't do that.

This leftover bit of the subjunctive mood is certainly unnecessary, since no other verb has preserved a special form; and recent studies indicate that even in standard usage *was* now appears about half the time in contrary-to-fact clauses. However, a good many speakers of standard still consider the use of *were* in such clauses a matter of great importance. Since people are actually losing chances for good jobs by saying "If I *was* you," *were* is obviously of much greater practical importance than, for instance, *whom*.

There are some clauses that lie between the extremes of contrary-to-fact conditions and definitely open questions:

If anything *were* to happen to him, she would collapse.
He looks as if he *were* unhappy.

In such clauses the usual alternative is not to substitute *was* for *were*, but to say "If anything should happen" or "If anything happened," and, in the second sentence, "He looks unhappy."

INVERTED CONTRARY-TO-FACT CLAUSES

It used to be fairly common to indicate that a condition was contrary to fact, or that a wish was unlikely to be fulfilled, by inverted clauses without the *if*.

Had it not been for the rain, they would have gone.
Were he only to come, we should be saved.

Such clauses are now going out of use.

ADVERBIAL CLAUSES

Most subordinate clauses other than those discussed are adverbial.

He came *when she called.*
Frank finally got the car started, *after all the rest of us had failed.*
Warner and Betty, *although they were both tired,* kept on working.
He got up early *so he could see the eclipse.*
He has practiced regularly, *so he may have a chance.*

There is often an argument over whether such clauses modify only the main verb or the whole independent clause—and another argument about whether they are "temporal," "concessive," or whatnot. Neither argument seems to serve any useful purpose, since there is seldom any question of structure involved.

The "proper use" of connectives introducing such clauses has also received a great deal of attention, but most of the rules evolved are highly unreliable. For the most part we must simply depend on our ears to pick up the standard patterns of speech. When we are in serious doubt about the appropriateness of a particular connective, the specific information in a dictionary is usually more helpful than any general treatment in a grammar.

EXERCISES

I. Mark the italicized clauses in the following sentences A (amplifying) or I (identifying). Set off the amplifying clauses with commas. Read the sentences aloud, with and without pauses for the commas, and see if you think the punctuation has any value.

1. Philip's gray overcoat *which was the only coat he had* was lost by the dry cleaner.

2. The old man *who operates the elevator* directed me to the proper office.

3. A young man *whom I met at Gloria's party* called me on the phone last night.

4. The florist delivered the flowers *you sent for.*

5. Sally knew everyone there but Charlie Mixan *who was new in town.*

6. Jeremy Halloran *the local mechanic* has opened a new garage.

7. This is Mr. Smith *who owns the film company.*

8. Anyone *who can drive* should contact the Transportation Committee.

9. The only copy *that was not already in use* was incomplete.

10. Uncle John was particularly fond of Woody Greer, *who worked for Grandfather many years ago.*

II. In some sentences below, the italicized word is unnecessary. Cross out the ones you think could be omitted.

1. Harvey, *who* dislikes cold weather, has been transferred to Alaska.

2. No one expected *that* David would be appointed.

3. Even his coach was not sure *what* his chances were.

4. He was never really sure *which* form was correct.

5. Belinda was always fond of Bartholomew Crumbler, *who* threw snowballs at her in grade school.

6. The elegant clothes *that* Nick wears are paid for by his father.

7. The foreman *whom* Leo had known was quick to offer him a summer job.

8. If he still claims *that* he is loyal to Pat, I don't know who will believe him.

9. The suit coat *that* he ordered was altered to his measurements.

10. Groughtonville, *where* the hero was born, scheduled a parade in his honor.

III. Insert an acceptable relative word in each of the blanks below, unless you decide (that) none is needed to complete the meaning.

1. Sue's puppy, _____ escapes from her room regularly, met up with the Hall Advisor yesterday.

2. The incident spoiled the record _____ Sue was sure to set for hiding forbidden animals in the dorm.

3. The Advisor confiscated the dog and put it in her bathtub, _____ she thought was the safest place.

4. The puppy, _____ is noted for its ingenious escapes, got out of the bathtub and found the Advisor's new slippers.

5. The furry slippers were a gift _____ her aunt had given her.

6. Sue made an unexpected trip home, _____ she left the animal for safekeeping.

7. Regulations about pets _____ the handbook had contained are today posted on the bulletin board.

8. The students _____ still have pets keep them carefully out of sight.

9. Sue, _____ offered to replace the slippers, thinks the Advisor is overreacting.

10. The Advisor, _____ is not noted for her sense of humor, glares every time Sue walks by.

Earlier, we listed six kinds of sentences—statements, questions, answers, commands and requests, comments, and exclamations. Up to now we have been considering statements, which are the only kind with a definite structural requirement. It is now time to pay some attention to the other kinds.

NONINFORMATIVE "STATEMENTS"

Sentences with the clause structure of statements may be used as questions, commands, or exclamations (if they are used as answers or comments, they remain statements):

> *Question:* He will be here tomorrow?
> *Exclamation:* That's a shame!
> *Command:* All members of the team will report here at four o'clock.

Questions and exclamations in such form should be short enough for the reader to see the end punctuation at the first glance. Otherwise he must either start to read them as statements and then reconsider or (as often happens) simply disregard the final punctuation and so miss the point. Many people will pay some attention to punctuation if it strikes their attention before they have made up their minds about a sentence, but not afterward.

QUESTIONS

The question is the only kind of sentence in which clauses of different form from those used in statements appear. Such reversals as the following are typical:

STATEMENT	QUESTION
He is going there.	Is he going there?
They have finished.	Have they finished?
You could have done it.	Could you have done it?
He lives there.	Does he live there?
He finished it yesterday.	Did he finish it yesterday?

Since most students find it very much easier to use such sentences acceptably than to learn rules about them, no rules will be given.

It is also possible to convert statements into questions by adding such tags as *is he? didn't they?* and *won't you?* at the end. For sentences of more than a very few words these tags work much better than simple question marks, since they do not affect the normal intonation pattern of the main part of the sentence. Take such a sentence as "He'll be driving over from Los Angeles tomorrow if he can get away from the office in time, won't he?" If you leave out the *won't he* and depend entirely upon the question mark, the intonation becomes much more difficult.

These tags cause little trouble unless the verb is *am* and the pronoun *I*. Neither the Irish *Amn't I?* nor the British *Aren't I?* is generally accepted in this country; and *Am I not?* is at least as far astray on one side as *Ain't I?* is on the other. We don't have any handy general tag like the French *n'est-ce pas?* or the German *nicht wahr?*, and *Huh?* doesn't really sound elegant. Perhaps the best thing to do is to revise the whole sentence so that no tag will be needed.

INDIRECT QUESTIONS

When one speaker's question is quoted exactly by another, it remains a direct question and requires a question mark.

John asked, "How many quarts of oil do you need for the boat?"

But if it is merely reported by another speaker it becomes part of a statement and needs no question mark.

John asked how many quarts of oil you will need for the boat.

ANSWERS

Answers may be in the form of statements, or they may be simply the words or phrases needed to supply the information requested. It is rather silly to supply a subject and verb just to make an answer conform to an over-generalized definition of a sentence. However, very short answers sometimes seem curt to the point of rudeness, especially if there are several of them in a row. Adding a subject and verb (not necessarily the most obvious ones) is one way to pad them out to a more pleasing figure.

Q.   What time is it?
A.   It is ten.

Q. How do you know?
A. I know by the kitchen clock.
Q. Is the clock right?
A. Yes, the clock is right.

This sounds like either sarcasm or a quotation from a primer.

Q. What time is it?
A. Ten.
Q. How do you know?
A. Kitchen clock.
Q. Is the clock right?
A. Yes.

This sounds like a strong, silent man—of about ten years.

Q. What time is it?
A. Ten o'clock exactly.
Q. How do you know?
A. I can see the kitchen clock.
Q. Is the clock right?
A. It was by the radio at noon.

This sounds much more courteous—but notice that adding *exactly* is just as helpful as adding *I can see the.*

EXCLAMATIONS

Exclamations, even more than questions, must be short to be effective. Don't write: "Isn't it wonderful that Molly gets a three-week vacation this year and is going to spend all but two days of it here with us!" Break it in two and say: "Molly gets a three-week vacation this year and is going to spend all but two days of it here with us. Isn't that wonderful!" The purpose of an exclamation point is to make a reader react with some excitement. He may do it for a few words but not for too many at once—and he certainly is unlikely to go back several lines to get excited about what he has already taken in with complete calm.

COMMANDS AND REQUESTS

Commands and requests may be in the form of statements, questions, "imperative sentences," or (when the situation makes them clear and courtesy does not forbid them) phrases or single words:

> *Statements:* You will report to the mess sergeant.
> I wish you'd get Mr. Adams on the phone.
> *Questions:* Will you kindly stop that noise?
> Would you pass the cream, please?
> *"Imperative sentences":* Don't drive so fast.
> Please wait just five minutes more.
> *Words and phrases:* Not so fast.
> Tickets, please.
> Careful.

In speech the intonation of commands and requests is particularly important. Polite phrasing makes an impatient or domineering tone sound worse rather than better. In writing there are no particular structural problems.

COMMENTS

If you must know, "Comments" is an entirely new classification for sentences, invented in this book to supply a defense for the instructor who criticizes sentence fragments by writing in the margin, "Not a sentence." However, it is a very useful type of sentence in its place (which is usually *not* in the middle of a student paper) and has been in use for a long time, even if it has lacked a name.

CLAUSELESS SENTENCES IN WRITING

The five types of sentences we have just discussed may or may not have a clause (subject-predicate) structure. Even without clauses they are completely standard in conversation. Obviously they are needed in plays and fiction, where the only structural requirement is that the language should seem appropriate to the characters. They may also be used to give a conversational flavor to other types of writing. There is nothing wrong with addressing a reader directly—telling him to do this and asking him about that—if you think he'll stand for it. But on the whole, clauseless sentences require a little more skill and judgment than statements; and if they are not successful they fall very flat indeed.

SENTENCE FRAGMENTS

Such expressions as those italicized below are called *sentence fragments.*

I looked out. *John running down the street.* I called him.
Suddenly I heard a noise. *Under the oak tree.*
It must be a dismal life. *To have no friends at all.*
We'll probably do it tomorrow. *If he comes.*

The first three lack complete verbs, and the fourth is a typical subordinate clause. All of them might be satisfactory in some settings, but when they occur in places where our training has led us to expect full sentences, they jar on many readers, and a teacher is almost certain to mark them wrong.

A student may argue quite correctly that the sentence fragments shown above are perfectly clear, and that many successful writers make very free use of similar fragments.

If we answer him honestly, we must admit that the sentence is not always the most effective unit. Compare the two following paragraphs, one written in sentences, the other in fragments:

> In summer the desert is blazing hot. The merciless heat of the sun is intensified by reflections from the bare, red rock of the hills. There seems to be no animal life, and even the few gaunt saguaros look as if they were at the end of their endurance.

> Blazing summer on the desert. Merciless heat of the sun. Heat pounded back by the bare red rock of the hills. Not an animal in sight. Only scattered, gaunt saguaros, waiting for the end.

The omission of any part of a familiar pattern naturally throws emphasis on what is left; and if we read without prejudice, we may well decide that the second treatment is more effective, because it presents the impression more vividly and leaves it up to the reader's imagination to supply the connections. But this very fact makes it more of a strain on the reader. Too much of it is tiring; and unless the material is unusually interesting, we are likely to turn to a writer who gives us ready-made connections that are easy to follow.

Anybody who has read much English has come to expect sentences as the normal units of expression. Consciously or subconsciously, he looks for a subject and predicate in each one. Any departure from the pattern jars his attention. If the departure is deliberate and skillful, it can be very effective. If it is merely careless, it is usually irritating and sometimes bewildering. A man who is confident of his writing and unconcerned about criticism may do as he pleases. Anybody who wants to avoid conventional criticism will do well to write in full statements except when he is clearly imitating conversation.

EXERCISES

I. Indicate which of the following could be completed by (a) supplying a complete verb, (b) supplying a subject, (c) omitting a subordinate connective, (d) adding an independent clause, or (e) none of the above. (In some cases both c and d may apply.) After marking the entries, go back and make the appropriate adjustments.

1. The blond basketball player wearing knee pads.
2. Unlocking the battered old doors every morning.
3. Similarly, all of the physics majors.
4. But such glib answers to the problem.
5. Repairs you learn to make yourself which are often economical.
6. Using primitive irrigation methods to provide water for their crops.
7. Why one person would ever attempt such a project.
8. Despite her peacemaking efforts, always squabbling.
9. The rest of the team ready to intervene at a moment's notice.
10. At the library, behind the reference desk.
11. The instructor, nervous and insecure, gone into the classroom.
12. Never would ask for help from Harvey, ever again.
13. The Thanksgiving dinner in their small apartment to be a crowded, boisterous event.
14. That anyone would want to read the entire "Faerie Queene."
15. Although she worked for them for ten years.
16. Wherever he might have been sitting when the announcement was made.
17. Whether we will ever be recognized for our contribution.
18. Thereby expecting to save himself writing the extra paper.
19. Missing the train, but he was not badly delayed.
20. The end-of-term party, to end sometime near daybreak.

II.

1. Change the meaning of the following sentences by changing the intonation pattern as you read them aloud:

   Ken is ill. (Try to arrive at six different patterns.)
   Bert refused to furnish his car for transporting the high school signs.

2. If the word *scridge* made its way into English as a verb, what would be its inflected forms?

3. In which of the examples below does adding a suffix cause funtcional shift and in which does it not? When it **does**, indicate what the shift consists of.

green—greenish
dark—darken
girl—girlhood
atom—atomize
free—freedom
black—blacken

Suggestions for Discussion or Theme Writing

I. If a statement such as "The pood poog pirlated pirely" can be analyzed as an English sentence although none of the words are English words, and the statement is therefore meaningless, **what** is the connection between grammar and meaning?

II. If I can say, grammatically:

The pood poog pirlated pirely.
Pirily the pood poog pirlated.
The pirlating poog was pood.
The pirely pirlating pood poog died.
The pood poog has pirlated.

why cannot I say, given the original **sentence**:

The pirely pirlated poog pood?

III. Grammar has several elements (relative position, word form, function words) and if any of the elements is missing, **the** grammatical structure breaks down. When it does, meaning also breaks **down**. Take, for example, these newspaper headlines:

1. CUT OFF EDGES OUT MIX
2. GAY COPS MANZY FEATURE EVENT
3. BOYS LIFE NUDGES FIRE

Yet to some readers those statements have instant meaning. Write a theme in which you point out what gives them meaning, after we tell you that they are all sports headlines dealing with

1. a favorite losing in a greyhound race
2. the result of the main race at Mananita Raceway
3. one horse beating another by a nose.

OUTLINING
AND
PARAGRAPHING

THE REASON FOR OUTLINING

Earlier we discussed the use of a very simple type of outline as a way of organizing the material for a paper. Most students seem to feel that to require a more systematic and elaborate outline is utterly unreasonable—the sort of thing that might be expected from an English instructor, but certainly *not* the sort of thing that a sensible student should take seriously, or learn any more about than he can help. But the fact is that a really sound outline, written in complete sentences and carefully checked for consistency, is one of the best labor-saving devices ever devised. Very few students can afford to neglect it.

THE THESIS SENTENCE

Before the word *thesis* meant a long paper with lots of quotations and footnotes, it meant the argument or intellectual position that such a paper sets forth. **In other words, if you write a paper involving any thought, your thesis is the main idea that you develop, and you should be able to express it in a *thesis sentence*.** Some people write mostly by accident, and can construct such a sentence only after they find out what they have said; but it really saves a good deal of trouble to write it first.

Suppose you decide to write a paper about required as against elective courses. There is obviously a good deal that could be said on this subject, and you might wander around indefinitely if you just plunged in with no particular plan. Just writing *about* a subject isn't enough. You have to decide definitely the main things you are going to say; and about the best way to decide whether these things add up and stick together is to put them into one sentence and examine it for direction, consistency, and completeness. Then work the sentence over until it satisfies you. Not until you feel that it is a satisfactory summary of your whole argument can you really call it a thesis sentence.

Here are three possible *preliminary* thesis sentences for a paper on required courses, indicating the three most probable general attitudes:

1. There are three reasons why required courses are almost worthless to most students.
2. Although many students object, a well-rounded set of required courses provides a much better framework for an education than a patchwork of electives.
3. The arguments for electives and required courses are so nearly even that I can't make up my mind which I prefer.

Each one of these at least indicates a direction, and might pass for a thesis sentence in a pinch; but not one of them is detailed enough to give you much help in the next step. Remember, an outline, intelligently used, is not an extra task to be skimped as far as possible; it is a preliminary step designed to make the whole job easier and more efficient. A good outline is worth two rough drafts; and if yours is good enough you won't have to do much more than copy to get your final paper. Suppose you decide that the first of the three preliminary thesis sentences expresses your attitude. You have three reasons in mind now; an hour from now you don't want to be scratching your head and saying desperately, "Now what in the world was that third reason?" Moreover, now is as good a time as any to decide the order in which you are going to consider the reasons. You might therefore expand the sentence to something like this:

> Required courses are almost worthless because of (1) student resentment and resistance; (2) unstimulating class attitude; and (3) no real challenge to instructors.

Possibly there is something to be said on the other side, but at least you have a thesis that can be developed. Question: do you want to develop it and present it in just that form to the instructor in a required course? Tact never hurt anybody; and besides, whatever else may be wrong with an English course, it is not likely to be one of those passive ones where you just sit. Maybe you'd better start that sentence with "required *lecture* courses."

THE MAIN HEADINGS

In its revised form this thesis sentence indicates pretty clearly both the line you are going to take and the main divisions of your paper. Let's assume that the length is supposed to be from three to five hundred words. Then three paragraphs will be about right, and the three numbered divisions can be used as a basis for the three main sentences in your outline. Of course you might have an introductory paragraph and a closing paragraph, or one of your main divisions might turn out long enough to break into parts; but the obvious division is into three, and you might as well start out with that in mind.

You may be tempted to put down topic headings instead of sentences, perhaps something like this:

I. Student resentment

II. Class attitude

III. Instructors not interesting

All right, you have put them down, and thereby saved a few minutes, but what is the next step? These headings don't seem very helpful. Maybe it would be better to take a little longer and write definite sentences. Your developing outline might then look something like Figure 1.

DOWN WITH REQUIRED COURSES

lecture

Thesis sentence. Required ⌄ courses are almost worthless because of (1) student resentment and resistance; (2) unstimulating class attitude; and (3) no real challenge to instructors.

I. The first objection to required courses is that students resent them and won't do their best work.

II. You are not stimulated when the other students are obviously bored.

III. Since we are automatic victims, the instructors don't even have to try to be interesting.

Figure 1

These sentences are more likely to suggest further subdivisions than the mere headings have; but before you go any further you had better see how they fit with each other. If you have any experience with outlines, it will take you only a glance to see that they do *not* fit. The first sentence talks about "students," the second talks about "you," and the third talks about "we." The viewpoint is shifting around for no apparent reason, and your instructor won't stand for it. Writing your actual paragraphs this way would mean either a complete revision or a poor grade. But if you can catch the shifting viewpoint in the outline you can straighten it out in a couple of minutes. This is the first great advantage of efficient outlining.

Suppose you decide to eliminate the "you" and "we," and stick to the third person throughout. And while you are at it, it might be a good idea to pick up "the first objection" with "the second" and "the third." Your outline might now look like Figure 2.

DOWN WITH REQUIRED COURSES

lecture

Thesis sentence. Required ∧ courses are almost worthless because of
(1) student resentment and resistance; (2) unstimulating class
attitude; and (3) no real challenge to instructors.

I. The first objection to required courses is that students resent them and
won't do their best work.

II. ~~You are not stimulated when the other students are obviously bored.~~
The second is that the general boredom makes the classes far from
stimulating.

The third is that

III. ~~Since we are automatic victims, the instructors don't even have to try to~~
be interesting.

Figure 2

DEVELOPING THE OUTLINE

You are now ready to put in the subdivisions—still in sentence form. You might come up with something like Figure 3.

DOWN WITH REQUIRED COURSES

lecture

Thesis sentence. Required͜ courses are almost worthless because of (1) student resentment and resistance; (2) unstimulating class attitude; and (3) no real challenge to instructors.

  I. The first objection to required courses is that students resent them and won't do their best work.

     A. Students must take courses in fields in which they have no interest.
       1. Agriculture majors must take a course in art or music.
       2. English majors must take introduction to Physical Sciences.

     B. Even if a student has a potential interest in a required course, he is likely to loaf just because it was forced on him.

     C. The instructors are often dull in required courses.

  II. ~~You are not stimulated when the other students are obviously bored.~~ The second is that the general boredom makes the classes far from stimulating.

     A. In a good class you learn as much from the other students as from the instructor.

     B. Students in a required course are too bored to contribute very much.

     C. The two dullest classes I have are the required ones in economics and psychology.

     The third is that
  III. ~~Since we are automatic victims,~~ the instructors don't have to try to be stimulating.

     A. The best classes are those that offer a challenge to the instructor as well as the students.

     B. The instructor in an elective course knows that he has to be interesting enough to attract students.

     C. Instructors in required courses have no such challenge, and often become quite dull.
       1. Dr. Tanner hasn't changed his lecture notes in 23 years.
       2. Nobody knows whether Dr. Schoonmaker has changed his notes or not, because his voice puts everybody to sleep.

Figure 3

CHECKING THE OUTLINE

By now your outline has grown to the point where you could use it to write a paper of the required length—but you'd better not. It is just at this point that its real value is available. The ideas are now set down in skeleton form, where they can easily be checked for possible omissions, repetitions, or inconsistencies. Moreover, there is still some blank space between the lines. Changes in the content and organization can be made without recopying, and additional points can be inserted where they clearly belong. Your outline is actually better than a solidly written first draft—but only because it is written in complete sentences. Phrase headings simply wouldn't show those inconsistencies and shifts in viewpoint that ruin so many papers. Let's check it over and see what we find.

Sentence I,C has nothing to do with the main heading for I; it would fit better under III. In fact it is included in III,C. Leave it there, and cross it out under I. Sentence II,C has to be considered carefully. The shift to an "I" subject may be justified if you simply give an illustration and remember to get back on the main track; but why are these two classes dull—because of the other students or because of the instructors? If the trouble is with the instructors, this item belongs under III, especially if you are thinking of the two classes taught by Tanner and Schoonmaker; you don't want to discuss them twice. But if the trouble is with the students, make it clear right in the outline—otherwise you might go off the track later. Take another look at II. Do you really need three subheads under it? Maybe two, with a comparison of typical attitudes, would be better. If you make that change, your final outline might look like Figure 4.

DOWN WITH REQUIRED COURSES

lecture

Thesis sentence. Required∧courses are almost worthless because of (1) student resentment and resistance; (2) unstimulating class attitude; and (3) no real challenge to instructors.

I. The first objection to required courses is that students resent them and won't do their best work.

    A. Students must take courses in fields in which they have no interest.
        1. Agriculture majors must take a course in art or music.
        2. English majors must take introduction to Physical Sciences.

    B. Even if a student has a potential interest in a required course, he is likely to loaf just because it was forced on him.

    C. ~~The instructors are often dull in required courses.~~

II. ~~You are not stimulated when the other students are obviously bored.~~
The second is that the general boredom makes the classes far from
stimulating.

   A. In a good class you learn as much from the other students as from
   the instructor.

   B. Students in a required course are too bored to contribute very much.
   ex. In economics there is no discussion even in class.

   C. ~~The two dullest classes I have are the required ones in~~
   ~~economics and psychology.~~

The third is that
III. ~~Since we are automatic victims,~~ the instructors don't have to try to
be interesting.

   A. The best classes are those that offer a challenge to the instructor
   as well as the students.

   B. The instructor in an elective course knows that he has to be
   interesting enough to attract students.

   C. Instructors in required courses have no such challenge, and often
   become quite dull.
      1. Dr. Tanner hasn't changed his lecture notes in 23 years.
      2. Nobody knows whether Dr. Schoonmaker has changed his notes
      or not, because his voice puts everybody to sleep.

Figure 4

Once you have made these changes, you might be ready to go ahead
and write your paper; or you might decide to make the outline even more
complete. Some students find it wise to put practically every detail in the
outline, because the skeleton form makes it easy to check. By writing one
good outline they can save themselves a couple of drafts. Others find they
can get along with no more than what is shown above. You will have to
find your own level. But remember that complete sentences give you both
a check on the general structure and a guide to the final form that is much
more reliable than you would get from words or phrases that might be
pointed in any of several directions.

WHAT IS A PARAGRAPH?

No paragraph necessarily correlates exactly with a I or A or 1 of an outline, but paragraphs do grow out of outlines.

Because the sign of a paragraph is visual—a dent in the margin—those who discuss paragraphing often search for a visual metaphor to approximate the structure of a paragraph. Thus we read of paragraphs as:

1. chains of sentences, or

2. boxes of sentences, or

3. sentence pyramids.

All of those things are true and yet not true. A paragraph is a chain of sentences because each sentence must link in some way with the one before it, but it is not a chain because all the links are not and cannot be equally strong and equally important. A paragraph is a box of sentences in that it holds inside it sentences that could not appear in any other box, but it is not a box because it is linear in development (like a chain?). To speak of a paragraph as a pyramid is simply confusing because (a) a pyramid is built upward from a base, a paragraph downward on the page, and (b) the pyramid (as a paragraph) will sometimes stand on its base, sometimes on its apex, depending on where one puts the topic sentence.

Visual metaphors are ultimately self-defeating when one talks of paragraphing, because it is just as valid to speak of a bad paragraph as a chain, a box, or a pyramid, as to speak of a good paragraph in those terms.

A paragraph is simply a series of statements that have a common topic, arranged so as to appear logical to the reader. "Logical" here means "as in rational thought." Rational thought does not have just one possible shape. It follows that nobody can talk sensibly about paragraphing if he must talk about it in terms of an infinite number of possibilities—any more than he can talk sensibly about it in terms of a chain, a box, or a pyramid. Inevitably, we settle for a few common, useful, and familiar patterns, all of them having the appearance of rational thought. That is not to say that people really think this way; instead, this is the way rational people write down their thoughts after considering them carefully. The paragraph is a relay system: not a way of thinking but a way of relaying thought from one unique mind to another.

Thought is movement—from one idea to another. A paragraph is a record of considered thought in which not only the ideas but the movement must be made clear to the reader. That movement can be shown most easily in two different patterns. Which pattern the writer uses depends upon his purpose.

1. **A writer may propose to give information.** In that event, he wants first to tell the reader what kind of information he is about to give and to forecast the order in which he will give it.

2. **A writer may propose to draw a conclusion from information.** In that event, he wants first to present the reader with the information and then draw the conclusion. It follows that he must present the information in the order that will lead to the conclusion he is going to draw.

Any body of material can be worked into either of the patterns. Here is an example of the first pattern:

> Over the centuries the word *ballad* has been used in four senses. The *folk ballad* is a narrative, a product of an anonymous poet, designed for oral presentation, impersonal in its treatment of events. The *literary ballad* is a narrative, a product of one identifiable poet, printed and forever fixed in form, and imitative in its verse form of the folk ballad. The *lyrical ballad* is not narrative but reflective, the printed product of one identifiable poet, highly personal in its treatment of events. In our own day, *ballad*, when the word is used by disk jockeys or song promoters, means simply "a love song."

The paragraph is designed to give information. It is an extended definition, almost a list. No conclusions are drawn, no insight proposed. The pattern is:

Topic Sentence and Definitions

The pattern could just as well have been:

Topic Sentence and Examples

or

Topic Sentence and Illustrations

It is a simple pattern, but not quite so simple as this discussion may imply, because the writer of this pattern has to decide on the *order* of his Definitions, Examples, Illustrations. The order in this paragraph is chronological: the folk ballad is the oldest form and the pop ballad most recent.

That order is forecast in the topic sentence: "Over the centuries . . ."
Here is an example of the second pattern:

> Early summer of 1967 came on unusually hot and muggy in Detroit. The
> inner city, four square miles of dirt and squalor, was a sauna bath. People
> crowded the streets, trying to escape the heat and stench. Too many people;
> jobs were scarce in a supposed time of plenty; federal grant money wasn't
> trickling down to the people who needed it. Detroit's black newspaper was
> asking for justice and honesty. People squatted and sweated; the police
> roamed and sweated. Tempers thinned and broke. The *News* and the *Free
> Press* reported a series of minor clashes between police and citizens, mostly
> in the black communities. Then, after midnight one hot June morning,
> police raided an after-hours "blind pig" on the East side, in full view of
> a neighborhood that couldn't sleep because of the heat. A rock was thrown,
> a shot fired, a window broken, and the most costly and deadly riot in the
> history of the United States had begun. The only way to stop it was to
> turn off the sun.

The most important sentence in this paragraph is the final one—but
note that its content is hinted at in the first sentence.

The pattern of the paragraph is the reverse of the previous one. This
one is:

Details and Topic Sentence

It could just as easily have been:

Illustrations and Topic Sentence
or
Facts and Topic Sentence

The pattern is intended to lead the reader to an inevitable happening or
conclusion.

The order of the paragraph is quite different from that of the preceding one. The order is not chronological; the heat does not occur before or
after the lack of jobs or the failure of federal funding, but rather alongside them. The chronology, except for the account of the raid, is vague.
The order might be said to be climactic, i.e., rising to a high point. But
that is an effect of something else.

The movement is from the general to the particular—from the early
summer heat in Detroit to the hot inner city of Detroit to the hot, roaming
occupants of the inner city to their reasons for being hot and roaming to

the general results of that to one specific incident that exploded the inner city at that moment. And it draws a conclusion; it implies a hypothesis.

We are dealing then with two patterns and several orders. The first pattern is *closed*. You announce what you are going to say and then say it. The second pattern is *open*. You do not announce what you are going to say but simply hint at where you are going.

Obviously some purposes are better served by the first pattern than by the second. **Pattern 1 is preferable if:**

1. you are offering information that is generally accepted,
2. you are offering information that is easily proved, supported, documented,
3. you are offering information that is quite personal or impressionistic,

always supposing that in 1, 2, and 3 you are not drawing conclusions, inferences, or judgments from the material.

Some purposes are better served by Pattern 2. **This pattern is preferable if:**

1. you are offering a series of impressions from which you want to draw a conclusion that you want the reader to accept,
2. you are offering a series of random facts from which you want to draw a conclusion that you want the reader to accept,
3. you are offering a series of personal experiences from which you want to draw a conclusion that you want the reader to accept.

Inside each pattern various orders are possible. We have looked at two only: the chronological, and the general to the particular. There are others: cause to effect, effect to cause, particular to general, along with a reversal of chronology. It is not very helpful just to list alternatives, however. Some principles do apply:

1. **The easiest and most clearly understood order is chronological.**
2. **The general to particular is easily understood and accepted by the reader, since he is able to set limits to the material under consideration and concentrate on development.**
3. **The particular to general is the most suspect to the average reader, since he can supply particulars that you can't and may infer that you are carefully selecting your evidence to lead him to a suspect conclusion.**

4. Cause to effect is more easily understood and accepted than effect to cause.

5. Any manipulation of strict chronology is less easily understood and more suspect than the obvious alternative.

EXERCISES

Assume that you listed the topics below as possible subjects of discussion in a paper on spy thrillers. Realizing the topics cover too wide a range for your purpose, you decided to divide the original subject and make three separate papers: I The Character of the Spy; II The Typical Adventure of a Spy; III Television's Espionage Agent: The Western Hero Updated.

    a. Mark each of the topics below I, II, or III, according to the division in which you think it most appropriate. (Some may be marked for more than one paper, others not at all. Or you may wish to fill in with topics missing from this list but necessary for the development of the paper as you envision it.)

    b. Develop a thesis sentence for each of the three papers. Add or delete topics to accommodate the more precise focus which the thesis sentence produced in each case.

    c. Select *main headings* for one of the three papers, rewriting the designated *topics* as *complete sentences,* incorporating your particular slant on the subject and the use you wish to make of each topic.

    d. Check *main heading* sentences against each other and against the *thesis sentence* for consistency of point of view, parallelism of structure, aptness, balance, etc.

    e. Add subdivisions in *sentence form* and check these against each other, against *main headings,* and against the *thesis sentence.*

    f. Compose two or more of the actual paragraphs as directed by your instructor; do not overlook an opportunity to employ some transition words or sentences to offset the paragraph break.

1. women in spy thrillers
2. the typical enemy agent
3. violence
4. security measures
5. gadgets and electronic devices
6. spy spoofs
7. the suave and sophisticated spy and the rough-and-ready Western hero—types of ideals
8. "good" spy's tactics and "bad" spy's tactics
9. issues in spy thrillers

10. "cliff-hangers" just before commercial breaks

11. sex in spy shows

12. spy as invulnerable

13. role of the government

14. chronological development of spy-thriller form

15. value of spy thrillers

16. kinds of people who watch spy thrillers

17. stereotyped reactions against spy thrillers

18. settings for spy thrillers

19. spy thrillers are dramatizing the tensions of modern life

20. typical false identities for the spy

or

  I. The "On the Road" theme, the "Discovery of America" myth
 II. The Youth of America as Social Critics
III. Hippies, Dropouts, Revolutionaries, the Drug Culture

acid rock music
speed
psychedelic artifacts
peace movement
draft resisters
protest songs
demonstrations
SDS
stereotype characters
rejection of an older generation's values
basic conflicts
rejection of God
mysticism and drugs
long-haired hippie freaks
communal versus nuclear families
motorcycles
groupies
the universities
dropouts
the police ("pigs")
marijuana laws
Hell's Angels
the West Coast
Black Power
Eastern and Western religions
easy answers to complex problems

identity crisis
the flag
blue-collar workers
flower power
make love not war

Suggestions for Discussion or Theme Writing

There are three thoroughly practical applications for this chapter.

I. Analyze your last theme by the outlining and paragraphing standards set up in this chapter, and then write another theme discussing your strengths and weaknesses in these areas.

II. Write your next theme. Then append to it a discussion of how your theme conforms to the outlining and paragraphing standards set up in this chapter.

III. Write a theme in which you review the outlining and paragraphing standards set up in this chapter and analyze their strengths and weaknesses.

CHECKING
SENTENCE
STRUCTURE

TWO KINDS OF ERRORS

The most obvious errors in grammar are those that involve incorrect word forms; but the errors that interfere most seriously with communication are those that have to do with the structure of sentences. Unless you can make your clauses fit together and put your modifiers where they belong, your readers are likely to be either completely bewildered or so contemptuous that they won't care what you are trying to say. Some instructors will flunk an otherwise-A paper if they find a single sentence fragment or run-on sentence. They are also likely to feel very strongly about ambiguous modifiers and shifted constructions. There are some things you are supposed to know for sure.

The basic patterns of English sentences were discussed in Chapter Nine—complete with enough exercises for most tastes. Unfortunately, many students do such exercises as guessing games, without really trying to master the principles involved. This is natural enough: exercises are usually aimed at a few specific points, and the sentences in them can often be analyzed or corrected almost mechanically. But when it comes to checking over your own sentences the problem is more complicated. Similar mistakes are not conveniently grouped together; you have to check every sentence for everything. The following sections contain suggestions for a reasonably systematic examination.

EXAMINING A FIRST DRAFT

Take the first draft of a paper you have not yet turned in. If you don't have one ready, write it before going any further.

Now examine your sentences one at a time. Make sure that each one contains a subject-verb combination that makes a definite statement. If it does, and if the whole sentence strikes you as clear and sensible, put a check mark after it. If it doesn't, and you can see what is wrong with it, make the necessary change and then put the check mark. But if you have any doubt that the sentence hangs together effectively, put an X after it; it needs revising. We are not concerned just now with the fine points of style or even of grammar, but simply with the basic structure of your statements. If they are not completely clear to you, you can't expect them to satisfy your reader.

SENTENCE FRAGMENTS

There is no clear line between some clauseless sentences and sentence fragments. The same group of words may be a sentence in one place and a fragment in another. In fact, the same group of words may be admired in a book by Hemingway and marked wrong in a paper by you, even when it is used in the same kind of situation. This is very sad, but life is like that. However, most instructors will let you use clauseless sentences if they are sure you are doing it consciously. The usual arrangement is for the student to put an asterisk (*) before each intentional clauseless sentence. The instructor may still criticize it, but he won't be as likely to mark your paper down for it. You might ask him if he is willing to accept such an arrangement.

Here we will consider only unintentional sentence fragments.

There are two requirements for a full sentence. It must have both a subject and a verb, and the main statement made must not be overshadowed by a connective such as *although, before, if, since,* or *when.* A simple example is:

John has gone away.

If we omit *John,* or *has gone,* or even *has,* there is not enough left to be a full sentence. And if we substitute *having* for *has,* the sentence is still defective. Even a compound participle like *having gone* does not make the kind of definite statement that *has gone, goes,* or *went* makes. If you have been getting marked down for fragments, check every sentence and see if the necessary parts are all there.

In a sentence as short as the example, you are not likely to have any trouble if you actually *look at what you have written.* This seems simple enough, but some students find it very hard to do. They focus their eyes on the sentence, but instead of seeing what they *have* written, they remember what they *meant to* write. They look, for instance, at "John gone away" and pronounce with complete sincerity, "John *has* gone away." If you have any trouble of this kind, it will help to leave a considerable time between the writing and the checking—you are less likely to be misled by echoes. And when you do check, read aloud if possible, or at least with a complete consciousness of the *sound* of the words. Next, try to find the right pace to get your eyes and ears working together. If you read too fast you may insert words without noticing that they are not actually there. If you read too slowly you will simply repeat the words individually and not notice if any are missing, because you will lose all feeling for the sentence. Some students find that beginning with the last sentence and reading up makes it easier to see the words that are actually there.

If a fragmentary sentence is fairly long, it may be a little more difficult to find a missing element, but the approach is the same. Look at the following example:

> Under the influence of Senator Roberson, Chairman of the Armed Services Committee, and for years an advocate of greater air power, voted to increase the appropriation.

Here there is a satisfactory verb, *voted,* and several nouns, any of which could be used as a subject; but none of them is used as a subject here. Unless you can find a clear-cut *subject-verb nucleus,* you have no sentence.

If you can see at a glance that the sentence about Senator Roberson is incomplete, you can easily change it so that it means something definite; there are a number of ways to do this. But if you have to puzzle over it, you had better break it into at least two parts. You might come up with something like this:

Senator Roberson, Chairman of the Armed Services Committee, has for years been an advocate of greater air power. Under his influence *the Senate* (or *the committee*) voted to increase the appropriation.

Of course you don't want to carry this process too far. Look at the next version:

Senator Roberson is Chairman of the Armed Services Committee. For years he has been an advocate of greater air power. He influenced the Senate. The Senate voted to increase the appropriation.

This (especially the last two sentences) is almost childish. But it is at least better than the long fragment.

In the other type of sentence fragment, there *is* a subject-verb nucleus, but the statement it makes is overshadowed by a connective.

When he was living in New Jersey.
Although they were very tired.
Because Mr. Jones asked me to.

We could make sentences of each of these either by omitting the first word or by adding an independent clause; or we could use two of them as legitimate nonsentences in answers to questions. But as they stand they do not make definite statements, and if you use them as sentences you are almost certain to be marked wrong.

RUN-ON SENTENCES

You are expected not only to write complete sentences, but to write them one at a time. Two sentences that would stand separately may often be joined by a connective or a semicolon, but it isn't safe to use anything less. If you do, you will have written a *run-on sentence*. If you use only a comma to join the two independent clauses (which could be separate sentences) your instructor may call the result a *comma fault* or *comma splice*. If you use nothing at all to join them, he may call it a *fused sentence*. The term *run-on sentence* covers both types. Almost anybody can see that a fused sentence is unsatisfactory, but many people do not understand the objection to comma splices. It may therefore be worthwhile to study the construction rather carefully.

Let's start off with two independent statements:

You wouldn't have much chance of making the team at State. There are too many lettermen coming back.

This is satisfactory. Although there is nothing but position to tie the two statements together, most readers would have no trouble making the connection. You might, however, emphasize the connection by using a semicolon instead of a period:

> You wouldn't have much chance of making the team at State; there are too many lettermen coming back.

This punctuation makes it a little clearer that the two ideas are to be taken together as parts of a larger whole. If you want to make the relation even more obvious, you could substitute a connective (with or without a comma) for the semicolon:

> You wouldn't have much chance of making the team at State (,) *because* there are too many lettermen coming back.

Since all three versions are equally correct, you may choose whichever you happen to prefer. In this particular example it certainly makes little difference. But notice the following points:

1. A connective indicates the relation between the two ideas most definitely. It is therefore a trifle easier for the reader, and probably a little more natural for most writers.

2. A semicolon indicates that the two ideas should be considered together, but leaves the reader to find the exact connection. It is thus half visual aid and half mild challenge. Semicolons are becoming comparatively rare except in rather academic writing.

3. A period is the most distinct indication of separation. It is therefore the normal way of separating two independent clauses unless you want to indicate that they are closely related.

You might say that you don't see what's wrong with putting just a comma between the two clauses and writing it this way:

> You wouldn't have much chance of making the team at State, there are too many lettermen coming back.

A really satisfactory answer to this objection is not easy to make. The sentence is as clear with a comma as with a semicolon, and some capable writers would punctuate it that way. But most English instructors would mark it wrong, and they would have a sound reason, which we can best show by making the sentence a little longer:

> In spite of your size, speed, and ferocious determination, you wouldn't

have much chance of making the team, according to Davis in the *Morning Post,* there are too many lettermen coming back.

In this version there are commas in both the clauses, and we need something stronger than a comma to set the clauses apart and show where the principal break should be. We might put a semicolon either after *team* or after *Post,* depending on what we wanted "according to Davis in the *Morning Post*" to modify (did he say that you couldn't make the team, or that many lettermen were returning?).

Since a comma splice is often ambiguous, most instructors feel that it should never be used—or at least that it should be used only by experts under special circumstances. The following examples might pass without criticism:

He took one side, she took the other.
He was cold, he was tired, he was hungry.

The sentences are short, they don't need connectives, and semicolons would only slow them up. However, using comma splices even in such sentences as these is rather like swinging on a three-and-nothing count— you'd better get a sign from the coach before you try it.

If you are not yet convinced, consider the two following sentences:

When he was in New York last year he stayed with his brother.
He was in the East last year he stayed with his brother.

The first contains only one independent statement, "he stayed with his brother." The subordinate statement "When he was in New York last year" is obviously a mere qualifying remark that is closely related to the main statement. Since the nature of the relation is shown by the word *when,* there is no need for a connective between the two clauses. And since the relation is close, there is no need for strong punctuation between the clauses. You could put a comma after *year* if you felt that a pause was appropriate, or you could leave it out; but a period or a semicolon would be worse than useless.

The second sentence, however, contains two independent statements. Since that is enough for two sentences, you should either punctuate it as two sentences or show that the two statements are so closely related that they can reasonably be considered as parts of a larger whole. One way to do this would be to insert a connective. Another way would be to use a semicolon, which would indicate that the two statements are separate but are to be considered together. Suppose, for instance, that somebody has asked why "he" seemed to be annoyed with his family. You might write (with that dry wit that makes you so popular) "He was in New York last year; he stayed with his brother." If you don't have that dry wit, or fear that your reader won't appreciate it, maybe you'd better be more explicit.

With this comparison in mind, you might consider the following statements:

1. The relation between two independent clauses is not usually as close or as obvious as the relation between an independent and a subordinate clause.

2. The relation between two independent clauses should therefore be either explained by a connective or suggested by a semicolon. A comma is usually not enough.

3. Since the relation between an independent and a subordinate clause is close, there is often no need for any punctuation between them. If you would naturally pause between the two, insert a comma.

SHIFTED CONSTRUCTIONS

Another type of serious structural error is the *shifted construction*—a sentence started in one way and finished in another. For instance:

> He had spent his vacations for nearly twenty years along the trout streams of the eastern slope of the Rockies were his favorite fishing waters.

We could improve this attempt at a sentence by inserting a comma and a *which* after *Rockies*; but it would probably be inaccurate to say that the writer forgot to put these items in. More probably he started out with the intention of stopping the sentence at *Rockies*; but by the time he had written that much, he had forgotten that he had written *streams* as part of a modifying phrase, "along the trout streams. . . ." He therefore went on as if *streams* were the subject. The result is a fusing of two possible sentences. The words, "the trout streams of the eastern slope of the Rockies" could be the end of one of the sentences or the beginning of the other; but the writer should have made up his mind which sentence he was writing.

Here are some other examples:

> He came here because of *the reputation of the Law School* was what attracted him.

> She is a great admirer of *Richard Burton, Laurence Olivier, and Rex Harrison* are among her favorite actors.

FAULTY PARALLELISM

A special type of shift is illustrated in the following sentence:

I thought I would go up to Roosevelt Lake and trying to get some bass.

When the writer started on this one, he had two reasonable possibilities:

1. I thought I would   go
                                  try

2. I thought of   going
                                  trying

Both of these are what are called *parallel constructions,* as the diagrams indicate. They are obviously economical and effective, since they eliminate useless repetition. Without them we would have to say, "I thought of going and I thought of trying," or "I thought I would go and I thought I would try." But they have to be consistent to be effective. This writer apparently forgot which way he had chosen to start. The intention of the writer is still clear, but the effect is definitely clumsy. Here are some additional examples:

It's really easier to do the work yourself than if you have to supervise somebody else.

They called just when the phone was ringing and somebody at the back door.

It is possible to be too particular about parallel structure, but the following principle is a good one to keep in mind:

Whenever a statement *branches into parts,* keep the parts parallel. Balance a clause by a clause, a phrase by a phrase, a participle by a participle, an infinitive by an infinitive, and so forth. If you do this, your reader can follow your ideas readily. If you don't, he may have to go back over your sentence and guess about the connections you intended. Even if he guesses right, he won't admire the construction.

There are so many possible ways of shifting constructions, that it would only be confusing to try to list them all. But there is one great underlying commandment that is worth remembering: *Make sure that you have finished your sentence the same way you started it.*

AMBIGUOUS MODIFIERS

If a reader doesn't associate your modifiers with the words you meant them to modify, the result may be anything from a laugh at your expense to complete misunderstanding. The main thing to bear in mind is that a reader cannot hear the writer's intonation pattern, which often is enough to show a listener which words go with which. A writer must therefore be careful to use relative position and punctuation as helpfully as possible. The general theory of effective modification has been discussed earlier. Two particularly troublesome errors are *dangling* and *squinting modifiers* (discussed under those headings in the INDEX TO USAGE). A modifier dangles when it can be attached only to the wrong word: Drifting along in a balloon, the earth looked like a toyland. A modifier squints when it can be attached to either of two words so that two different meanings appear: In *David Copperfield* the hero is forced to tell the story of his marriage to a close friend.

EXERCISES

Mark OK those sentences below which you think are satisfactory. Mark the others F (fragment), R (run-on), S (shifted construction), P (faulty parallelism), A (ambiguous modifier), and O (other—for any that don't seem to fit any of the categories). Correct all but the ones marked OK by punctuation or by rewriting.

1. Some schools will not grant doctoral degrees in English until the student has learned an ancient language, such as the University of Michigan.

2. Lazy young people unwilling to stay home and work, and would like to fool around and make trouble, ask their parents to send them away to college.

3. Being serious about studies does not necessarily mean being stodgy, on the contrary, it means recognizing certain goals and working to attain them.

4. If people were only aware of all that art museums have to offer and then through these offerings put to their utmost use.

5. Repairing car engines is difficult without training because you have to teach yourself there's no one around to help you if you have a problem.

6. Since I believe the issues and history of the Vietnam War and our foreign policy in general are massively complex that I will limit myself here to three major considerations.

7. Although too much emphasis may be placed on athletics, they are certainly not the only students to benefit from sports.

8. A big roan stallion 17½ hands high, with matched black sox and a white streak half-covered by his forelock.

9. As students we used to ice skate or ride cafeteria trays down hills and of course skiing for those who could afford it.

10. The research is done by the attorneys which is usually quite extensive and then the brief is written and typed.

11. Although we all loved Rosalind very dearly we felt that a chicken—even a little chicken—should live on a farm.

12. That he won the election by such a landslide this was what his opponent could never understand.

13. How to read critically write clearly and learn, if it is possible to recognize major authors by their style.

14. Twelve of the 60 people surveyed had beards or 5 percent of the group, according to my calculations.

15. Miss Pindur raises African violets, works crossword puzzles, and will practice the harp for hours on end.

16. After the snow started, we crawled along the highway, seeming to be heading into a wall of white.

17. A student had 81% on one test, while on another he had 89%, thus improving by 8 points.

18. The chapter should be skimmed completely first to know approximately what the material to be covered will consist of.

19. When the semester ended all the students could think of was getting some sleep and to eat a few decent meals, not to mention the freedom of semester break.

20. Seymour Franklin, the big redhead and the fellow who always wore his high school letterman's jacket.

21. For at least twenty years an usher for the Christmas service, the old gentleman looked forward keenly to his annual participation in the celebration.

22. In the spring the grass turns green and the tulips and peonies sprout small and brave in the local gardens.

23. Whether a suit coat or a sports coat will be proper for the occasion is a matter with which I am not willing to cope.

24. We finished finals on the second Friday in May was very cold that year.

25. When I get some free time I'm going to work on my hobbies: knitting a sweater for my boyfriend, work on my backhand in tennis, and to play the guitar.

Suggestions for Discussion or Theme Writing

I. On the basis of your own experience and whatever inferences you can make from this chapter, write a theme in which you discuss the causes of the following errors:

sentence fragments
run-on sentences
shifted constructions
faulty parallelism
ambiguous modifiers

II. In a paragraph that avoids all the errors listed in I, state which errors you tend to make most frequently and say why.

EXPLAINING

12

TELLING WHAT YOU KNOW

In earlier chapters we discussed ways of organizing material for a paper. The emphasis was on developing the writer's personal ideas about a subject—an emphasis which is often entirely appropriate. But there are many occasions when it is reasonable to assume that the reader does not particularly care what the writer *thinks*; he wants an explanation of what the writer *knows*, so that he can use the material for his own purposes. And since the ability to explain clearly is important in any job that involves working with other people, most instructors give it a good deal of attention.

YOU KNOW MORE THAN YOU REALIZE

Modesty is an admirable virtue, but it can easily be carried too far. When you are writing about a subject with which you have had little direct experience, it is appropriate to find authorities to support your statements. But there are many subjects on which even a modest freshman can reasonably consider himself an authority, at least when addressing an audience with a different background. We are likely to think that the things we know best are so obvious that they are hardly worth talking about—especially when we have just changed our environment and are trying to learn an entirely new set of things. If you have grown up on a Western ranch you have a lot to tell—and a lot to learn from—a boy from a New England fishing town or a big Southern city. Don't laugh if he asks what seem to you silly questions about things that "everybody knows"—it will be too easy for him to get back at you. And if he asks you questions that you can't answer for sure, don't be sidetracked into analyzing complications and possibilities that he can't possibly understand. You can assume that he wants an answer, not a debate. Qualify it if necessary, but keep it as simple as possible. After all, you have the best information *available* at the time.

WHERE DO YOU BEGIN?

When you do your explaining by writing a paper there is no one to ask you direct questions, so you have to anticipate the questions a curious-but-unknowing person might ask about your subject. It is a good idea to begin with the most basic ones, since it is much easier for a reader to skim over what he already knows than to have to guess about things you have mistakenly assumed that he knows.

Considering the wild variety of human curiosity, it may seem presumptuous to contend that we know in advance what questions a reader might ask about subjects an instructor has not yet assigned. Of course we do not know all the possible questions, still less the form in which they will be put—we have at least ten common patterns for asking one another the time of day. But there are a few questions which, in one form or another, will be asked by almost anybody in search of information. One of these naturally comes first; until it is answered we are not likely to ask any others, because our curiosity cannot be brought to bear. If, for example, a curious child found you working on a wheelbarrow, a precision timepiece, or an atomic reactor, his inquiry would probably be the same: **"What is it?"**

Adults ask this question, too, when they come across something that arouses their interest or grabs at their curiosity.

What is an *alexandrine*?

What's a *Texas leaguer*?

What is a *quasar*?

What's a *powder monkey*?

If you are setting out to explain a subject on which there is not wide general familiarity, you may wish to begin by anticipating in your intended reader the basic question: "What is it?

> A powder monkey is a man whose occupational duties include the handling of explosives and the placing and detonating of those explosives where their use is required. In logging, for instance, it is often necessary to blast an opening under a log so that a line can pass through to be fastened around the log. In this situation, the powder monkey. . . .

The appropriate length of an answer to the question, "What is it?" is a matter of speculation, since it depends upon the strength of the questioner's interest or the depth of his curiosity. If, in answer to a question, you say, "the *frug* is a *modern dance*," you may satisfy one person while leaving another desiring further information. Sometimes a questioner nods and walks away before you've told him all you intended, but if his curiosity goes deep, he will stay to hear you out. Thus, in anticipating "What is it?" you'll have to trust intuition, the assigned theme length, or your own limitations to tell you when you've said enough.

> *Question:* What's a *basenji?*

> *First Answer:* Dog.

> *Second Answer:* A basenji is a small African dog having a smooth, usually brown coat and a curly tail. He is well muscled and energetic, and he keeps himself very clean. He rarely barks, but may make another sound which resembles a chortle or a yodel.

> *Third Answer:* A basenji is a small dog whose breed originated in Africa but was transported to the United States about thirty years ago. The basenji has a pointed muzzle and pointed ears, a curly tail, and forelegs that are slender and straight.

> Stanley, my basenji, is sort of tan, with white markings, but I understand that others may vary from light brown to black in their basic color. Although Stanley was the runt of his litter, he stands about fifteen inches at the shoulder, and weighs close to twenty pounds. This proportion of weight to size will give some indication of how solid and well-muscled he is. His grace of movement is remarked about by many who see him. But, in tall weeds, he springs up and down like a person on a pogo stick, appearing and disappearing, yet apparently getting his bearings in that instant his vision is unobscured. He is also unusual in the way he keeps his short-haired coat so clean, by grooming himself, somewhat in the manner of a cat cleaning itself. Furthermore, I am continually fascinated by the wry expression he can put on. But what other people find most unusual is that he never barks. I won't say he *can't* bark, but only that I have never heard

him, and I'm told that basenjis rarely do. He makes many other sounds, however; some of them are so like human sounds that to hear him you might think you are hearing a person laugh, or cry.

You will notice that all three answers to the question explain (on different levels of abstraction) how an unknown word or thing fits into the general context of known words or things.

OTHER QUESTIONS YOU CAN ANTICIPATE

The person who receives an answer to "What is it?" may find his curiosity whetted, and the way now open for new inquiries. These further inquiries will vary with the subject. As soon as a curious child has learned all he can about a watch from handling it and listening to it, he may decide he must take it apart to find out, literally, what makes it tick. Curious adults often experience a similar impulse. Give them something good to eat, and they are apt to ask, **"What's in it?"** Show them some complicated system, and they may want to know what it consists of. The subjects you wish to explain may be such that you can anticipate questions about the interrelation of basic constituents.

What components are essential in a stereo system?

What constitutes a naval task force nowadays?

What goes into a dry martini?

Since it is not common for people to ask what a powder monkey or a basenji is made of, except perhaps in a zoology class, there must be some other follow-up questions after "What is it?" It seems reasonable that inquiries into *purpose* or *function* might also arise at this point.

What is the purpose of a cyclotron?

What is the function a thermostat performs?

What is the basenji used for?

Possible response: I must admit that Stanley, my basenji, does little more than to keep me company, but that is all I ask of him, and that is enough for me. Basenjis have been called the "Companions of the Pharaohs," so I suppose dogs of his breed have been serving this purpose for quite some time; ancient works of Egyptian art picture them at it.

Several important characteristics make Stanley (and, I presume, the basenji in general) an ideal house pet. His intelligence made it a cinch to train him to the rules of indoor living; I was repeatedly amazed at his eagerness to please me and be praised. His even temperament and playful disposition make him a desirable companion, and his remarkable changes of expression (noteworthy among basenjis) assure me of being entertained by him in my loneliest hours. Moreover, his short smooth coat is very clean, kept that way by his repeated washings; his grooming habits are much like a cat's. Above all others, the characteristic my fellow apartment dwellers appreciate in Stanley is his unwillingness or inability to bark. Never a bark have they heard from him.

While Stanley has only to enjoy his ease in my quarters, other basenjis have been trained to work at an interesting variety of tasks. From my reading I'm convinced that the basenji can be trained as a bird dog, both for pointing the birds and retrieving the kill. His outstanding senses of sight and smell aid him as a hunting dog in these and other tasks. In his native Africa it is said that he is sometimes used in hunts where silence is desired —and what better than a "barkless" dog for such work? Yet other tribes are said to hang noisemakers around his neck and use him to "beat" the bush, to drive game into the open. Thus this little-known canine demonstrates his usefulness—as companion or worker.

So far we have anticipated only the questions of those whose knowledge on the subject at hand is such that they can profit from considering the thing or class of things (basenjis, for instance) in isolation. As we presume wider knowledge in the inquirer, however, we may also presume his increasing ability to view the subject in the context of related things, so that at least three closely related questions seem to follow naturally:

How is it like_____?

How is it different_____?

How does it fit in the overall picture?

WHAT IS IT LIKE?

After a person begins to get a grasp of a subject, it seems reasonable to assume that he may begin to associate his newly acquired knowledge of that subject with what he already knows about other subjects. A confrontation of the *known* with the *partly known* or *newly acquired* may provoke new curiosities—new inquiries.

How does the game of chess resemble the game of checkers?

Does spelunking involve any of the skills of mountain climbing?

What are the shared characteristics of motor scooters and motor bikes?

What similarities, if any, exist between the basenji and the dachshund?

Possible response: Although they are both assigned to the "hound" breed, there are few points of similarity in the basenji and the dachshund. They may on occasion be close to the same weight, and both have the hound's keen sense of smell. But at about that point, physical similarity ends—unless you wish to add that both are clean and relatively free from the "doggy odor" that some people find unpleasant. Regarding disposition, however, there may be further similarities. . . .

When you develop a theme by anticipating "How is it like_____?" you should bear in mind that the usual procedure is to link the unknown (your subject) with the known (the reader's prior knowledge). Therefore, the dachshund, a widely known type, is chosen for comparison with the little-known basenji. Actually, the Rhodesian ridgeback may have as much in common with the basenji (at least their African heritage), but such a comparison would involve comparison of two relatively unknown subjects. Above all, remember that you are presupposing a natural connection in peoples' minds, so some basic similarity is taken for granted; rather than compare anvils with honeysuckles, or ostriches with parallelograms, you are expected to compare cars A and B, poems (a) and (b), dogs 1 and 2, and so forth.

HOW IS IT DIFFERENT?

This question seems to follow so naturally on the heels of the previous one that the two are often asked in the same breath and answered in the same presentation. It is conceivable, however, that occasions, might arise wherein similarities would be so widely known that only differences need be explained.

How do collegiate and professional baseball differ?

What accessories does Car A have that Car B does not have?

How does decaffeinated coffee differ from ordinary coffee?

How does oleomargarine differ from butter?

How does the basenji differ from the general run of dogs?

Possible response: The basenji is larger than the "toy" dogs and "miniatures," but he's smaller than most of the other breeds. His line goes back thousands of years, so I suppose his breed is older than many. He is probably cleaner than most other dogs, and more diligent about keeping himself that way; thus he is said to be "odorless." But what sets him conspicuously apart in the dog world is his disinclination toward barking. While other dogs may howl, bay, and bawl, the basenji is said to murmur, chortle, and yodel. Furthermore, . . .

Obviously, some compatible relationship must be evident before comparison or contrast becomes useful to an explainer, or before either becomes apparent to a curious questioner. It is possible, of course, for two quite dissimilar things to be compared in terms of a single likeness or a limited alignment of characteristics, such as a flatiron and a boat (because of their similar shapes), but the result is an *analogy*, a device as common to argument as to explanation.

When comparison and contrast are combined, there are two common ways of organizing the explanation. Suppose you wish to consider likenesses or differences in Items A and B, on points 1, 2, 3, 4, and 5. The first method involves discussing Item A, on all five points, then moving over to Item B, points 1, 2, 3, 4, and 5. The alternate method focuses attention on the points, one at a time, considering first A, then B, at each juncture. Both methods are effective in the hands of professionals. The particular situation may help you determine which to use.

HOW DOES IT FIT IN?

When a person has a satisfactory grasp of a subject by itself or within limited relationships with other subjects, he may become curious about the more complicated interrelationships which will clarify an overall view. A graphic response to such a curiosity can be found in the *tables of organization* which the U.S. Armed Services and some large corporations display. In neat rectangular boxes joined by interconnecting lines, these tables show how each office fits into the grand design, subordinate to the office marked in the box above while directing the office(s) marked in the box(es) below, and roughly equivalent to those on the same horizontal line.

Sometimes people ask for explanations which seem to seek a similar bird's eye view.

How does the World Bank fit into the picture of national and international financial institutions?

Where does a semi-professional baseball team fit into the picture of organized baseball in the United States?

How does the American Kennel Club classify the basenji?

Possible response: According to American Kennel Club classification, the basenji belongs to the "hound" breed. As such, he is thereby associated with such dogs as the tall, swift Afghan hound, the sad-faced basset, and the perky dachshund. These and the other *hounds* constitute one group of what are called *sporting dogs.* In the other group are what we often call "bird" dogs: setters, retrievers, and spaniels.

The two groups of *sporting dogs* share the AKC's attention with four other groups. One of these is classified *working dogs* (boxers, collies, St. Bernards, and so forth). Another large group includes the *terriers* (fox terriers, Skye terriers, etc.). The remaining two groups are the *toys* (Chihuahua, Pekingese, etc.) and the *nonsporting* dogs, a group including the Dalmations, bulldogs, and poodles.

The process involved here, as you have probably noticed, is one of discovering, identifying, or inventing major divisions and their subdivisions. In the sample, we used classification labels that are quite standardized, since they are those recognized by a very prestigious body, the American Kennel Club. You may invent your own classifications and class labels, if the occasion calls for it.

> My Fellow Students: Drudges, Dreadnaughts, and Dropouts
>
> Football Spectators: The Interested, the Uninterested, and the Disinterested
>
> Library Users: Loungers, Gossipers, Studiers, and Handholders

By the time you have divided and then subdivided a number of subjects, it will occur to you that this is the process of making *formal outlines* —although from a slightly different angle of approach. Nevertheless, this process of developing an explanation will probably work best when you are committed to a fairly broad subject yet one on which there is general, though perhaps not thorough, familiarity. If, for instance, you must explain as best you can how the U.N. is set up, how the Executive Branch of the U.S. Government is organized, how the books are arranged in the nearest library, or how you would classify the undergraduates of your acquaintance according to personality types, your best bet may be to look for a few logical major divisions, subdivide them, and go on from there.

QUESTIONS ONLY CERTAIN SUBJECTS MAY INVITE

The questions we have anticipated so far are those which curiosity on any subject might provoke. Let's now consider three more that are appropriate to only certain subjects. The first two may follow naturally when the subject is a memorable and significant event:

What caused it?
What were (or will be) its effects?

The third is to be expected when the subject involves a process:

How do you do it?

WHAT CAUSED IT?

Assignment of cause is usually, if not always, a matter of interpretive judgment, so it is speculative at best. It fits into the process of explaining only when judgments are accepted at face value and confined to generally accepted and agreed-upon relationships between events. When the relationship becomes controversial—in other words, when one's assignment of causes is challenged—*explanation* ceases and *argument* begins. This may produce a more interesting paper, but it will be of another kind, developed in another way. You are not likely to be qualified to write a purely explanatory paper on such subjects as "What caused the Depression of the 1930's?" or "What factors contributed to the defeat of Germany in WWI?" But if you are writing a paper on your favorite baseball team you might want to put in a paragraph or two on "What caused their almost disastrous slump in June?"

WHAT EFFECTS?

This question is subject to some of the same limitations as the one discussed just above. But if the effects have already happened you may be able to offer an interesting explanation. Thus a paper on transistors might have a section on how they influenced the development of electronic equipment. And one on a new freeway might contain some reasonable guesses on how it will change the life of a certain area.

If the questioner wants an answer rather than a controversy, you offer him your best explanation.

What effects did a successful manned landing on the Moon produce in the U.S. space program?

What resulted from the development of the transistor?

What effects on mobilization in the U.S. were attributed to the attack on Pearl Harbor, December 7, 1941?

HOW DO YOU DO IT?

When your subject consists of a process, you can expect to be asked to explain that process, step by step.

How is registration accomplished at your school?

How do you prepare lobster Newburgh?

How is a parachute landing performed?

How do you make a blouse?

How do you go about launching a boat?

Some writers like to generalize about the complete process—its purpose, expected results, and so forth, while they get warmed up. Others advocate the cookbook approach, wherein they catalog their equipment, describe the work area, and so forth. But such preliminaries need not obscure the fact that at the heart of a presentation like this is a *series of steps.* These correspond somewhat to the *sequence of events* in a narrative, but in the latter you are involved with what happens or happened *once.* In the how-to-do-it, the process is abstracted out of any particular performance; we presume the instructions have been and could be followed repeatedly with comparable consequences.

Essential to explaining a process is the realization that you are arbitrarily dividing a vast and complicated series of movements, judgments, decisions, and so forth, into seemingly positive, manageable parts. For one person, launching a boat may involve three major divisions of activity: (a) getting the boat *to* the water, (b) getting the boat *into* the water, and (c) getting people and equipment into the boat. (Each of these major divisions easily breaks down into minor steps.) Another writer may assume the explanation begins when the boat is at the water's edge; but he may arbitrarily decide that *mounting the engine* on the boat is a separate phase of the operation. This is a matter of interpretation, so do not fret about it. It is more important that you be able to envision the process in terms of major and minor steps. And remember, you have a *sequence.* Order is essential; *when* to do it is just as vital to your explanation as *what* to do.

Sometimes the order of steps is so vital that you may use formalized expressions such as "First. . . . Second. . . ." or "Step One. . . . Step Two." Such a presentation can be deadly dull, however, unless the process is vital enough to provide its own motivation.

Some teachers advise the use of imperative sentences throughout.

Back the trailer down the ramp.
Ease the boat off the trailer by. . . .

This is not wholly satisfying; it may be difficult to sustain. "I" and "you"
are equally troublesome, but usable with practice. Some teachers expect
a completely impersonal approach.

After the boat is brought to the water's edge, it is then eased into the
water by. . . .

However, if the emphasis is on the *how-it-is-done*, the process may be described in the third person, present tense.

After backing his trailer down the ramp to the water, the driver sets
his brakes and prepares to launch the boat. First, he. . . .

None of these is clearly superior. Follow your teacher's instructions, or use
the one that seems most natural to you, but at least avoid mixing the patterns conspicuously.

SELECTING AND ORDERING THE QUESTIONS YOU ANSWER

If you tried to answer every possible question, any paper would become interminable. You may have noticed that in our discussion of basenjis
there was nothing on "What causes basenjis to be unable or unwilling to
bark?"—"What effects have other dog breeders felt from competition by
basenji breeders?"—or "How do you train a basenji?" Moreover, there are
a number of reasonable questions we have not considered anywhere in this
chapter, including "How do you know?" (inviting supporting detail) and
"Who said so?" (inviting research). We didn't want the chapter to be interminable, either. But perhaps a few generalizations may be helpful.

First, both the questions you select and the amount of space you give
to their answers are likely to vary with (a) how much you know about
a subject, and (b) how much you think the reader wants to find out. Second, you may get some guidance from the natural sequence that operates
when a person is trying to find out something. We have already mentioned
that he is likely to wonder "What is it?" before "What is it made
of?" or "What does it do?" And until these last two are answered he will
not be ready for comparisons and contrasts of the unknown and the known,
or how the particular unknown fits into some broader scheme. The sequence is not, of course, absolutely fixed; you *could* wonder *why* your

Aunt's ten-room beach house has disappeared before you wondered what happened to it, but that hardly seems likely. If you are really trying to communicate, it is useful to look for a sequence of questions whose answers will give your reader information *in an order* that will be easy for him to manage. Keeping that reader in mind is one of the most important—and one of the most often neglected—techniques in effective writing.

Suggestions for Discussion or Theme Writing

A subject that you have special information on may be a process, a place, a thing, or perhaps even a feeling. To have special information is not necessarily to be the resident expert, but it does mean that you have extensive or intensive personal insight.

Choose a process, a place, a thing, or a feeling that you judge you have special insight into, and write a theme about it. Before you write the theme, state on a separate piece of paper the audience you are writing for and what you assume they already know of the subject. Attach that piece of paper to the theme when you hand it in.

LETTERS

LETTERS

PERSONAL LETTERS

Most people like to get letters, but a great many people dislike writing them, not only because of the time and effort they take, but because the writers (or potential writers) feel embarrassed and uncertain about how to go about the job. The suggestions below are not guaranteed to eliminate such feelings, but they may help. We can begin by analyzing the form in a very simple example.

> 327 N.W. Davison St.
> Portland, Oregon 97209
> July 20, 1971

Dear Bob,

We have been here two weeks now, and it looks like a good summer. There are some tennis courts only about five minutes away, and

211

next weekend two of the boys at the plant and I are going to try the trout fishing on the McKenzie. The job is fairly tough, but interesting, and I'm off at four thirty. Can't complain.

I ordered a lumberjack shirt for you. They were out of your size, but said they could get it to you in about two weeks.

How do you like your job with Fenner? Can't say I envy you, but maybe I'm wrong. Drop me a line some time if you're not too exhausted.

Yours,
Dick

THE FORM

No detail of the form used above is sacred, but here are a few things to notice:

1. *The address.* If you want an answer, you'd better put the address on every letter. Not everybody keeps an address book, and some people throw envelopes away as soon as they have opened them (possibly so they'll have an excuse for not answering). You could put it at the end of the letter; but if you put it down first you won't forget it, or leave it out because you have come to the end of the page.

2. *The date.* You could use "Tuesday" instead of "July 20," or leave out the date entirely. But if your letter refers to any event that your friend might want to pin down later, a point of reference might be helpful. If he begins to worry about whether his shirt has gone astray, "Tuesday" won't help him much.

3. *The salutation.* You can say just "Bob" if you want to; but there is nothing either effeminate or presumptuous about addressing anybody as "Dear" in a letter, even if you wouldn't do it in person. Also, it saves time and effort to do it automatically, instead of carefully weighing details that don't matter. You can substitute either a dash or a colon for the comma, if you prefer, or use no punctuation here at all.

4. *The ending.* Don't worry about endings being trite; they are unimportant, and usually unnoticed, formalities. If you happen to think of a more original ending, use it cheerfully; but don't strain for it. "Yours very truly" will do for slight acquaintances. "Sincerely yours," "Cordially yours," and "Yours" are successively warmer.

5. *No apologies.* About the only other thing worth noticing is that Dick did not apologize either for writing the letter or for ending it. It seldom adds anything to a letter to begin with "I bet you are surprised to be hearing from me," and end with "Well, I guess I'd better stop now. This

isn't much of a letter but. . . ." Dick assumes that Bob will be pleased to hear from him, begins with what he has to say, and stops when he has finished. It is an admirable practice.

Even if your only purpose in writing a letter is to ask a favor, an apology is seldom necessary. If what you ask is burdensome, you might say you are sorry to put him to so much trouble. But it is better to begin directly with "Could you do me a favor?" than to pretend that you would be writing him anyway and that the favor is merely incidental. He probably will not be deceived.

"SOCIAL" LETTERS

Dick apparently didn't find it much of a strain to write to Bob, but he might feel oppressed at the idea of composing a letter to Bob's mother to express his thanks for a pleasant weekend or a birthday present. Perhaps the best advice we can give him is not to make too much of a production of it, and to be as nearly natural as he thinks she can stand. Something like the following might do:

Tuesday

Dear Mrs. Cartwright,

I want to tell you what a good time I had at your house last weekend. It was nice of you to have me, and everything we did was fun. The only drawback is that now I'll have to start all over again, getting adjusted to the dining hall food.

Please give my best to Mr. Cartwright. I'm still enjoying that story he told about the Model-T Ford. And tell Nancy I haven't either got more freckles than she has. I just counted.

Thanks again—I don't know when I've had a better time.

Sincerely yours,
Dick Burton

This certainly is not a model of grace and charm, and if you can do better nobody would be less surprised than the author. But Mrs. Cartwright will be pleased to get it. Dick *has* taken the trouble to write, and it sounds as if he'd had a good time and liked the whole family. Also, he hasn't tangled himself up with unnecessary superlatives about "your gracious hospitality" and "your lovely home." He seems to think the weekend was natural as well as pleasant. He is a nice boy, and will probably be asked again.

No return address is given, because no reply is expected. "Tuesday" is at least as good as "November 14," because it will probably mean more at the first glance, and Mrs. Cartwright is not likely to file the letter for reference. The tone is still informal, but not quite as free and easy as in the letter to Bob, except for the message to little sister. **This letter should be in longhand, and preferably on reasonably good, but not fancy, stationery.**

Bob will probably never have any occasion for anything much more complicated than this in the way of social correspondence. His sister may— and she may feel that a few "perfect's" and "lovely's" are necessary. The only advice I feel competent to offer is, to keep it as simple as you can.

ROUTINE BUSINESS LETTERS

A business letter may be headed in one of the following ways:

> 219 Tyler Avenue North
> Seattle, Washington 98109
> August 3, 1971

Mutual Insurance Company
64 Fifth Avenue
New York, N. Y. 10011

Dear Sirs:

Mr. James A. Whiting
Mutual Insurance Company

Dear Mr. Whiting:

Director of Personnel
Mutual Insurance Company
64 Fifth Avenue
New York, N. Y. 10011

Dear Sir:

The street address serves no particular purpose, unless you are corresponding with a number of companies with similar names and want an extra check to make sure the right letter gets into the right envelope. However, many people feel it looks more businesslike.

The chief thing to remember about a routine business letter is that it will presumably be read by busy people who usually have no interest in either your personality or your problems. There is nothing to be gained by trying to impress them, and you waste everybody's time if you go into unnecessary detail about matters that they will handle by strict routine. You may feel that "Please suspend my subscription to your magazine until further notice" sounds a little curt; but if that is all you have to say, don't pad it. The clerk who handles such requests doesn't care why.

Don't try to write in a special "Business English." Just be as clear as possible, as brief as you can be without sacrificing clarity, and sign yourself "Yours very truly."

IMPORTANT BUSINESS LETTERS

Of course there are some business letters that are far from routine. If you are trying to get a job or a contract, to make a sale, or to ask for special consideration of any kind, you will want to make a definite impression. Possibly you can do it by "pouring on the old personality." It is well to remember, however, that your reader probably won't be much concerned about your personality unless he can think of a way to use it, and that he is much more likely to be interested in his problems than in yours. You may have sold magazine subscriptions by explaining that you are working your way through college, but you won't sell many tractors that way.

If you are starting a business correspondence on an important matter, the most important thing is to consider the whole matter carefully from the other man's probable point of view, and proceed accordingly. To give your point of view and be prepared to deal with his objections is not enough. He may answer simply that he is not interested, and leave you nothing to argue about. You have nothing to gain by starting out as opponents, and the best way to be on the same side is to find out where he is and work from there.

LETTERS OF APPLICATION

One very important kind of business letter is an application for a job, but the number of people who have no idea how to write such a letter is amazing. Of course there is no one pattern that will please everybody, but there are a number of common types that will please nobody. It may therefore be worth your while to consider a few general points about how to write to a prospective employer (hereafter called "he" or "him") before developing your individual variations.

1. **Start your letter simply and directly by saying what job or what kind of job you are applying for.** Don't apologize for bothering him, or tell him you know how busy he must be—you'll just be wasting a little more of his time. And unless you are quite sure either that you are a genius or that he isn't quite bright, don't try to bowl him over with a fancy opening. Here are two beginnings which, with minor variations, have been closing doors on their writers for years:

Are you looking for a man who . . . ?" In brief, no.

"Currently working in the research department of Western State Electric Co., I am anxious to locate in a community in the congenial climate of.. . ." You are, are you?

Not nearly so bad, but still clumsy, is, "I am interested in applying for a position as a technician in your department. I should like to know whether there is an opening. I am etc." Never mind the interest—say "I am applying" or "I wish to apply." And never mind asking whether there is an opening. You are writing the letter on the chance that there is.

2. **Even if it means a little extra work for you, give him all the information you think he might want in the first letter.** Some applications say in effect: "I'm male, 26 years old, and would like a job. If you have any further questions I'll be glad to answer them." He won't have any further questions—why should he? Unless you tell him enough to interest him, you won't get more than a form letter in reply.

3. **Don't ask him any questions in the first letter, or put any other burden on him.** If he gets a number of letters that seem about equally promising, he'll probably answer those that take least effort. Wait until he shows an interest in you before bothering him.

4. **If you enclose a picture, choose one that is appropriate for the job you are seeking, not merely one that flatters your vanity.**

5. **Don't enclose a stamped, self-addressed envelope.** If he can't or won't answer without one, you don't want the job anyway.

THE DATA SHEET

Most important of all, *enclose a data sheet.* This device has at least three advantages. First, it puts the essential facts together in convenient form, where they can be scanned almost at a glance—to see if the rest of the letter is worth reading. Second, it provides some protection against leaving out essential information. Third, it allows you to do your boasting impersonally. After all, the main purpose of a letter of application is to tell how good the applicant is; but since some of us feel uncomfortable about bragging, and most of us are easily irritated by other people's bragging, the problem of how to do this effectively is a delicate one. The best general solution is the *data sheet* (also known by various other names ranging from *poop sheet* to *curriculum vitae*). There is no one form for these, but the example below would be reasonable for a college freshman applying for a summer job with a possible future.

DATA SHEET

Ronald F. Sebring

Home address: 317 South Pima Avenue, Chandler, Arizona 85224

Year of birth: 1953   *Height:* 5'11"   *Weight:* 175   *Health:* excellent

Marital status: single   *Draft status:* 2–S   *Rel. Pref.:* Methodist

Education: Graduated from Chandler High School, 1971
Now Freshman at Prescott College
Grade average, first semester: B+

High school activities:
Basketball: three letters, Captain senior year
Tennis: one letter
Organizations: Hi-Y, International Relations Club (vice-president),
Lettermen's Club (president), several class offices

College activities:
Basketball: freshman numerals
Tennis: squad member
Organizations: International Relations Club, Wesleyan Foundation

Working Experience:
Paper route, 2 years. Yard work etc., 3 years. Carry-out boy, Bayliss
Market, summer of 1966. Checker, same store, summer of 1967. Now
earning over half my college expenses with job on college grounds.

References:
The following people have offered to write references:

James F. Finton, Assistant Manager, Bayliss Market, 746 North Morton
Avenue, Chandler, Arizona, 85224
Homer Mattux, Supervisor of Grounds and Buildings, Prescott College,
Prescott, Arizona, 86301
Professor J. T. Simmons (my adviser), Department of Economics, Prescott
College

Ronald could have this duplicated and send a copy with every letter
of application. Some employers won't care whether he is a Methodist or a
Buddhist, and they might count a point against him if he wrote a sentence
about his religion in his letter; but they are used to seeing this entry on
data sheets, and can simply skip over it if they are not interested. And for
some jobs, such as counseling at a boy's camp, the information may be
required. Not every employer will care if he is an athlete, but his record
in basketball and tennis support his statement that his health is excellent.

His activities and offices indicate that he gets along well with people and has some ability as a leader, and he seems to be both responsible and hard-working, though possibly a trifle serious-minded for some tastes. The fact that he worked the second summer for the same store, but at a better job, is especially significant. Altogether, he has given a fairly attractive picture of himself without sounding in the least conceited.

Your own qualifications will of course be different. If you are the same height as Ronald but weigh only 115 pounds and have asthma, you can't put your health down as excellent. But you may be able to put down something like this:

> *Health:* Good, except for uncomfortable but not disabling asthma. Have missed only nine days of work or school in last five years, and quality of work has not suffered.

You are not supposed to lie, but you are entitled to present the facts in a favorable light.

USING THE DATA SHEET

Important as the data sheet is, it needs a little help from the letter. If the sheet is impressive in itself and the job is purely technical, the letter can be brief and colorless. But usually an employer will want to know what you are like as well as what you can do, and most employers have a firm (though often unjustified) belief that they can read character from a letter. In general the best method is to be simple and direct. You may wish to call his attention to one or two items in the data sheet that you think are especially important for his job, and perhaps to explain them a little more fully. It is also reasonable to explain why you want this particular job; but do it in a way that shows your preference is to his advantage as well as yours.

For instance, if you apply for a job in Southern California on the grounds that you "have always wanted to see the West Coast," why should he care? But if you explain that the doctors have told your dependent sister that she needs a warmer climate, there are two small points in your favor. First, you sound like somebody who might stay long enough to be worth hiring. Second, you apparently have some sense of responsibility. It is even possible that he might be moved by a third, or humanitarian, reason. But you shouldn't count on that one, and you certainly shouldn't emphasize it. He wouldn't hold *his* job long if he hired people mainly out of charity or benevolence.

No model letter of application will be given here, mostly because experience shows that students tend to follow such a model far too closely.

But remember at least the following three points: use a data sheet, keep the letter simple and direct, and concentrate on what *he* will want to know.

EXERCISES

Suggestions for Discussion or Theme Writing

    I. Gezelda Fooberdink is convinced that three-sentence business letters are unpardonably rude if not absolutely immoral. In one paragraph, argue with her.

    II. Now hold true to your arguments and write one concise letter from each of the following two categories. Include photostats of bills, checks, or whatever seems necessary—it makes the explanation much easier.

Complaints

1. Your weekly magazine hasn't come in three weeks, and your subscription runs until next August.

2. The book club sent you the wrong selection. (Send it back.)

3. The bursar claims you owe tuition you already paid—three months ago.

4. Traffic court sent you a warning about an unpaid ticket—the traffic court of New Jersey, and you've never been to New Jersey.

5. You were guaranteed delivery of a Captain Marvel Secret Code Ring and Spy Kit within three weeks, and, a month later, nothing has come.

Requests

1. You want a transfer application to Cheaperthanhere University.

2. You want information about getting a driver's license in this state. You already have one from your home state.

3. You want any literature the American Kennel Club has to offer for your paper on basenjis.

4. You want information on room rates at the Beachside Motel in Miami.

5. You want to order tickets to a concert. Include a check.

    III. Prepare a data sheet now for next summer's job hunt. Put it away someplace safe.

    IV. Pick your dream job, claim to have whatever qualifications you want, and write both data sheet and letter of application.

THE RESEARCH PAPER

14

The bane of many college freshmen is the research paper, often with good reason. Some are turned away from research because of the sour aftertaste.

Too many research papers assigned and written for first-year English are nothing of the sort. They are instead exercises designed to acquaint the student with methods of retrieving information, taking notes, selecting proper data, organizing unfamiliar material, and documenting fact and opinion.

Important as those skills are, they don't necessarily add up to research writing. Research involves as a first step searching the world's knowledge on a given question, but its ultimate purpose is either to advance the world's knowledge or to demonstrate to the world where one writer's unique understanding fits into the world's knowledge.

Research writing adds to knowledge. It is *not* a rehash of known facts

directed to known conclusions. The only way to avoid its being that is to find a question that needs answering.

FIVE STEPS IN RESEARCH

The general aim of research is to answer questions by giving fair consideration to the best available evidence. Research may be conducted in a laboratory, by a field of investigation, or in many other ways; but the research for a freshman paper is usually confined to printed material, either collected in a source book or waiting to be discovered in the college library. **The job may be broken down into the following five steps: (1) finding a good question; (2) locating the best printed evidence on this question; (3) considering this evidence until you reach a reasonable conclusion; (4) organizing your findings; (5) presenting these findings in such a way that a reader can easily check their accuracy and completeness.**

A good many students concentrate too much and too early on the fifth step. The mechanics of a term paper—physical organization, footnotes, bibliography, and so forth—are certainly important, and will be explained in this chapter at some length. But these things are only means to an end. If you understand how and why they work you should be able to get them straight and use them reasonably and accurately. If you don't you may well blunder along, trying to get two footnotes on a page (whether it needs ten or none), oppressed by a sense of futility and feeling extremely vague about what you are trying to do. We shall therefore examine the general principles of research writing first, and then try to show how sound mechanics fit in with these principles.

STEP ONE: FINDING A GOOD QUESTION

There are at least three requirements for a good question:

1. **It should interest you.** It will take you a good many hours to write a respectable term paper, and there is no use being bored when you might be finding out something that you want to know.

2. **It should lead to a fairly definite answer.** If you ask "Is jazz better than classical music?" you can wander around indefinitely, and you may develop an interesting essay, but you'll never have a satisfactory term paper. You would do much better to ask (a) "What are the technical con-

tributions of jazz?" or (b) "What proportion of music critics now consider jazz a serious and important form of music?"

3. **It should be limited enough to be handled adequately within the assigned length.**

LIMITING THE QUESTION

Most students begin by asking a much bigger question than they can answer satisfactorily in a paper of perhaps 2,500 words. This is natural, and nothing to worry about. You are not committed to answering all of the original question. When you learn enough to realize that it is too big, narrow it down; and when you learn still more, narrow it down again. It does not matter how small the eventual question is, as long as you treat it adequately. For instance, if you began by asking "What kind of man was Abraham Lincoln?" you would find thousands of pages on the subject, and you could not compress all the information into a term paper. But if you finally narrowed it down to something like "What kind of a soldier was Lincoln in the Black Hawk war?" you would find comparatively little material scattered through your various sources. By getting all this material together, and comparing it carefully, you might construct an interesting paper.

Here are some other examples of topics narrowed down to a reasonable scope:

1. *General topic:* Winter Sports
   First reduction: Skiing
   Second reduction: Skiing Techniques
   Final question: How Have Skiing Techniques Changed Since 1940?

2. *General topic:* Poetry
   First reduction: Ballads
   Second reduction: American Ballads
   Third reduction: Cowboy Ballads
   Final question: How Is the Dying Cowboy Theme Treated in American Ballads?

3. *General topic:* Furniture
   First reduction: Antique Furniture
   Second reduction: American Antique Furniture
   Final question: Why Are Duncan Phyfe Chairs So Highly Prized?

The sooner you narrow down your question, the sooner you will know what sort of material to look for and what you can afford to disregard; but you can expect to lose some time exploring the area before you have selected your particular subject. This lost time is not entirely wasted; you need some general background in order to treat your subject with some sense of proportion.

STEP TWO: GATHERING THE EVIDENCE

If you are writing a "controlled" research paper the evidence you are to use has already been collected for you. If you are writing a "library" paper you must try to gather the *best* available evidence that bears on your question. A freshman is not expected to be completely successful, for it takes some experience to find out what the "best available evidence" is and how to locate it. But your instructor will certainly expect you to do more than pick up the first few books and articles that seem to pertain to your subject and leave yourself at their mercy, regardless of their value. So will instructors in other courses; and so should you, if you want a college education to go along with your degree. Some of the things which should be considered are listed below:

1. **What are the author's qualifications?** Anything that you can find out about his position, training, and experience is worth considering.

2. **What evidence does he give that he has done his work carefully?** Footnotes indicate that he is willing for a reader to check his sources. A bibliography gives some idea of the extent of his study. A good index shows that he expects readers to look up specific points, and not merely read through once.

3. **Who published the work?** An article in a scientific journal is more likely to be accurate than one in a popular magazine. A book put out by a university press or by a well-established publishing house that does a good deal of business with colleges has something in its favor—so many faces would be red if the critics made fun of it.

4. **How is the work regarded by competent critics?** You may be able to find book reviews or references to it in other works on the same subject.

5. **Does the author impress you as writing carefully and impartially,** or does he show a definite bias? Does he seem to be more interested in dramatic effect than in accuracy?

The next few sections contain some suggestions on how to find not only material but good material. There are several ways to begin, and no one of them is always best. You will have to work out one for yourself—and probably modify it next time.

THE CARD CATALOG

Before deciding which books to use, you must find some books to examine. One place to begin looking is in the card catalog of your library. There should be at least three cards for every nonfiction book—one for the author, one for the title, and one for the subject. The listings by author and title are simple and very reliable, but no library has ever devised a completely satisfactory listing by subject. Some books deal with dozens of different subjects, and it would not be practicable to have a separate card for each one. Accordingly, a card is made out for the most obvious subject, and perhaps additional cards are made out for one or two others, but there are a good many gaps. If you don't find enough under what seems to you the obvious heading, try to think of other headings that might be applied to the same subject, or to a broader field including that subject. Thus you might find useful material on skiing in books listed under "Winter Sports," "Outdoor Sports," or "Athletics."

It is therefore not advisable to try to get too much from the card catalog at the first attempt. It is better to draw two or three books pertaining to your subject whose cards indicate that they contain *bibliographies* (lists of books in the same field or in closely related ones). These bibliographies will give you the authors and titles of other books, which you can then look up in the card catalog with much less effort. Moreover, the bibliographies often give information about the contents and value of the books listed, and are therefore useful in helping you to find the "best evidence."

INDEXES TO PERIODICAL LITERATURE

Some of the material that you need has probably been published in periodicals rather than in book form. Such material may be located through various periodical indexes:

The Reader's Guide to Periodical Literature is either the index students will find most useful or the one that will prove the most dangerous. *The Reader's Guide* indexes about 200 popular or semi-popular magazines. If the purpose of your paper is merely formal—that is, to demonstrate that you can retrieve information, put it in proper, usable form on cards or sheets, reduce it to an outline, and write a literate paper—*The Reader's Guide* is useful and adequate. If the purpose is, in addition, to acquaint you with the research tools available to those in specialized fields, *The Reader's Guide* is inadequate. If your purpose is to investigate thoroughly a specialized, perhaps technical question and deliver a paper that is precise and informative, *The Reader's Guide* can be downright dangerous.

Every specialized field has its own index, which often includes not only periodicals but books, reviews, and pamphlets. Students who want specialized information should consult, for example:

Agricultural Index
Applied Science and Technology Index
Art Index
Biography Index
Book Review Digest
Business Periodicals Index
Chemical Index
Education Index
Engineering Index
Essay and General Literature Index
International Index to Periodicals
Poole's Index to Periodical Literature (Predecessor to the *Reader's Guide*—covers the years before 1907)
Public Affairs Information Service
Short Story Index
Social Science and Humanities Index
Writings on American History

These vary considerably in both the quality of the editing and the periods covered; and your library may not have them all. But since any one of them may save you hours of looking for needles in haystacks, it is worthwhile looking for any that seem appropriate.

The *New York Times Index* will help you locate immediate accounts of news events. Even if the *Times* itself is not available, the dates will probably enable you to find stories in other papers or news magazines.

GENERAL REFERENCE WORKS

The indexes listed in the preceding section merely tell you where to go for information. In this section are listed a few of the more important general works which can be used as direct sources. Some of them (particularly the encyclopedias) also indicate further sources. It will be worth your while to examine each of these, even if you have no immediate need for them. There are other things that you will want to know later, and it is useful to have an idea of the sorts of information that are available.

1. General encyclopedias
   Collier's Encyclopedia

  Columbia Encyclopedia
  Encyclopedia Americana
  Encyclopaedia Britannica (for material before the first World War,
   the 11th edition as well as the latest should be examined)
  New International Encyclopaedia

2. Special encyclopedias
  Catholic Encyclopedia
  Encyclopaedia of the Social Sciences
  Hasting's *Encyclopaedia of Religion and Ethics*
  Jewish Encyclopedia
  New Schaff-Herzog Encyclopedia of Religious Knowledge

3. Annual compilations of facts and figures
  Annual supplements to the *Britannica*, the *Americana*, and the *New*
   International
  Facts on File
  Statesman's Yearbook
  Statistical Abstract of the United States
  World Almanac

4. Collections of biographical information
  American Men of Science
  Current Biography: Who's News and Why
  Dictionary of American Biography
  Dictionary of National Biography (British)
  Living Authors
  Webster's Biographical Dictionary
  Who's Who (British)
  Who's Who in America

There are, of course, a great many other important and useful reference works. These are listed merely as a hint. They are not discussed, because there is very little value in knowing facts about them. The important thing is to get used to handling a good many of them.

BIBLIOGRAPHY CARDS

Whenever you find a title that looks really promising, you will do well to make out a bibliography card at once. You may eventually decide not to use the source, but it is less trouble to make out a number of unnecessary cards than to search again for the exact material needed for one. Use a 3 x 5 inch card and follow the basic form indicated in the accompanying illustration.

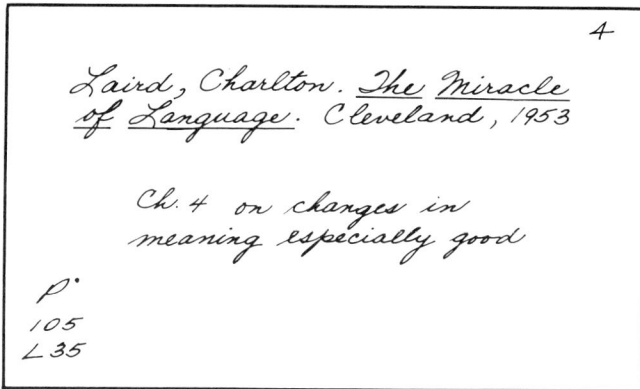

4

Laird, Charlton. *The Miracle of Language*. Cleveland, 1953

Ch. 4 on changes in meaning especially good

P.
105
L 35

Notice:

1. The last name of the author is given first, so it is easy to arrange the cards in alphabetical order. If you can find them, use the full forms of the given names, rather than initials. There are a surprising number of John C. Smiths (not to mention J. C. Smiths) in the card catalog of a big library, and the second principle of documentation is to make it as easy as possible for a reader to find your references. (The first, of course, is accuracy.)

2. The title is underlined. It is very unwise to use abbreviations here. You might expand them incorrectly when you refer to the work in your paper.

3. The city of publication and the date are given in that order, and punctuated as illustrated. If no date is given, put "n.d." in place of date. (In modern books the date usually appears on the back of the title page. In older books it is often on the title page itself).

4. The library call number is noted in the lower left-hand corner, so that you won't have to look it up again if you have to use the book a second time.

5. The number 4 in the upper right-hand corner is an arbitrary code number. You can save trouble by using such a number instead of a fuller reference on your note cards (to be discussed later) and in the first draft of your paper.

6. Any comment that you think may be helpful to you may be written in the remaining space.

The example just given shows the simplest kind of source and is in the form used in the MLA (Modern Language Association) style sheet, which most English instructors prefer. Unfortunately, some very different methods are used in some fields of study, and even in English a number of minor variations occur. If you are writing on a biological subject your English instructor may permit you to follow the form ordinarily used in that discipline; but since no one man can keep all the possible variations straight in his head, he is much more likely to insist that in his class you do it his way. He may require you to include the name of the publisher—a useful variation that makes it easier for a reader to order a book in which he is interested. If so, put a colon after the city, and then write the name of the publisher exactly as it appears on the title page, followed by a comma and the date.

VARIATIONS NEEDED FOR DIFFERENT KINDS OF SOURCES

Since you will have to include a bibliography in your paper, it is important to make out your cards in such a way that you can simply copy from them without further adjustment. All entries follow the same general principles, but various kinds of sources require different bits of information; and it is essential to present this consistently so that a reader can use it without unnecessary effort or uncertainty. Examples follow:

1. Basic form:

Laird, Charlton. *The Miracle of Language.* Cleveland, 1953.

Putting the last name first and reversing the indentation make the entry easy to find in an alphabetical list. The title is italicized in print, underlined in typescript or longhand. Remember, if the date is not indicated, write "n.d." to show that the omission is not your fault.

2. Two authors:

Smith, James Harry, and Edd Winfield Parks. *The Great Critics.* 3rd ed. New York, 1951.

Since only the first author's name is alphabetized, the second is given in normal order.

3. More than two authors:

Bernbaum, Ernest, and others. *The English Romantic Poets: A Review of Research.* New York, 1950.

Since this book has five authors, "and others" saves a good deal of space. The Latin abbreviation "*et al.*" saves even more, but is passing out of use.

4. Anonymous works:

Manual of Style. 10th ed. Chicago, 1937. (University of Chicago Press.)

If no author is shown, alphabetize under the title—and that may be all you can do. But if the title page contains any other information that might make the book easier to locate, or give some indication of its value, put that at the end of the entry in parentheses.

5. Indication of a particular edition:

See number 2 above for the position. Since editions may vary in both contents and page numbering, any edition except the first should always be indicated. The date should be of the first printing of the edition cited.

6. Books in a series:

Furnival, Frederick J., ed. *Political, Religious, and Love Poems.* Early Eng- lish Text Society, Original Series, N. 15. London, 1866.

The title of the series and the volume number are given to make it easier to find the book in a library, since such series are normally shelved together rather than under the individual authors or titles. The abbre- viation "EETS, O.S." may be used if you have reason to believe your readers will be familiar with it, or if your bibliography is so extensive that you list frequently used abbreviations to save space.

7. Book compiled from various sources:

See number 6 above.

8. Edited or translated volume of a single author:

Tennyson, Alfred Lord. *Representative Poems,* selected and ed. by Samuel Chew, New York, 1941.

Chew, Samuel, ed. *Representative Poems,* by Alfred Lord Tennyson. New York, 1941.

If your main interest is in the original author, the entry should appear under his name. If your main interest is in the editorial comment or the quality of the translation, this should be reflected in the entry. (A trans- lation would of course have "trans." rather than "ed.")

9. A work of several volumes:

Baker, Ernest A. *The History of the English Novel.* 10 vols. London, 1924–39.

The separate volumes of scholarly works are often printed at different dates. If you use only the seventh volume of Baker's work, your entry should read:

Baker, Ernest A. *The History of the English Novel*, VII. London, 1936.

10. Subtitles:
A reasonably short subtitle that gives some information about the book should be included and separated from the main title by a colon as in number 3 above. A long or uninformative one may be omitted. If you are in doubt, give as much as seems useful, followed by three periods to indicate omission.

11. Pamphlets and bulletins:

The Constitution of the United States: Literal Print. Washington, 1934. (U.S. Department of State, U.S. Government Printing Office.)

The Short Ballot. Constitutional Convention Bulletin No. 5. Springfield, Illinois, 1919. (Legislative Reference Bureau.)

The only reason for treating pamphlets and bulletins (the exact line between the two is indeterminate) differently from books is that they are likely to be harder to locate. Such publications appear with a bewildering variety of information on their title pages. The best principle to follow is to take only what seems useful, either to help a reader find the publication or to convince him that it is significant. If the actual author is shown, the entry should be under his name.

All the references above are to complete publications. Those that follow are to articles, essays, stories, and so forth included in books or periodicals. Notice that the title of the part referred to is in quotation marks; it is the name of the *publication* that is italicized. The one important exception is that the title of a work which could reasonably be published separately is italicized even if it happens to be published as part of a larger work. Thus we italicize *The Tempest* even if we find it in *The Complete Works of Shakespeare*.

12. Selection from book by one author:

MacLeish, Archibald. "Actfive," *Collected Poems: 1917–1952*. Boston, 1952.

13. Selection from a compiled volume:

Weinrich, Uriel. "On the Semantic Structure of Language," *Universals of Language*, ed. by Joseph H. Greenberg. 2nd ed. Cambridge, Mass., 1965, pp. 142–216.

14. Article in a journal:

Halle, Morris, and Samuel Jay Keyser. "Chaucer and the Study of Prosody,"
College English, XXVIII (Dec. 1966), 186–219.

Notice that here, as in a selection from a book, the title of the article
is in quotation marks, and the name of the publication is in italics. The
number of the volume is given because bound periodicals often have the
number rather than the date on the back. Roman numerals are used to prevent any possible confusion with page numbers. Since the paging of learned
journals runs throughout the year, the month may be omitted if the issue
is so old that it is likely to be found only in bound volumes.

15. Article in popular magazine:

"The New Melting Pot," *Time,* LXXXVIII (Dec. 2, 1966), 30–31.

In magazines which have separate paging for each issue the month
(and the exact date for those which appear more than once a month)
should always be given. (If the author is known, the entry is of course
under his name.)

16. Newspapers:

Buchwald, Art. "Capitol Punishment," *The Washington Post,* Dec. 29,
1966, A, 16.

Phoenix *Arizona Republic,* Jan. 14, 1968, p. 31.

Author and title should be indicated for columns and other special features, but not for ordinary news stories. If the sections are numbered
separately, they should be indicated by letter or capital Roman numeral.
The date is not parenthesized because it does not repeat information indicated by the volume number. The name of the city is italicized only if it
appears in the masthead.

17. Encyclopedias:

"Leonardo da Vinci," *Encyclopaedia Britannica* (1966), XIII, 963–72.

This form of reference is usually considered sufficient for undergradu-
ate papers. However, important articles in encyclopedias are usually signed,
either with the full name of the author or with his initials. If initials are
used, an identifying list will be found somewhere—whether in each volume,
the first volume, or the index volume. If you take the trouble (voluntarily
or otherwise) to identify the author, put the entry under his name.

STEP THREE: CONSIDERING THE EVIDENCE

One way to compose a term paper is to read a few books and articles, write from memory, and then put in as many footnotes as seem reasonably impressive, either by desperately trying to find the actual sources again or by making guesses that you think will get by. This method is not likely to earn you a good grade, and will most certainly cheat you of an opportunity for valuable training. A more systematic approach is therefore desirable.

MAKING A TENTATIVE OUTLINE

Your first few hours of reading will be largely exploratory. You will want to get a general picture of the subject and some idea about how much of it you can reasonably cover. You began by asking a question, but your paper is to be a statement of what you have found. As soon as you have done enough exploring to have some idea of what you are going to cover, you can save yourself a good deal of time by making a tentative outline. This should be in the form of topics and subtopics rather than sentences, because you should not decide exactly what you are going to say until you have seen the evidence. There should be plenty of space between the lines to permit the insertion of new subtopics as you discover them. The growing outline will serve several purposes:

1. It will help you to look for the material that you need—and to avoid wasting many hours on material that is not pertinent to your purpose.

2. It will help in the narrowing-down process. If you find that the job is bigger than you thought, and you are now most interested in Section III, you can throw out Sections I and II and concentrate on III. This is much better than pretending to cover the larger subject but actually skimping two-thirds of it.

3. It may suggest gaps that you should fill in.

USING NOTE CARDS

Once you have made your tentative outline, do all the rest of your reading with a pencil in hand and a stack of cards available. You are now looking for specific information, and you are responsible both for getting it exactly right and for telling your reader exactly where you got it. You will save yourself time and agony if you make your notes clear enough and full enough so that you can use them without going back to the source, which another student may have borrowed by the time you want it again—

leaving you completely helpless. Take your notes on cards or card-sized slips of paper (either 3 x 5 or 4 x 6 inches), and follow three invariable rules:

1. Never put more than one item on a card—this is the main reason for using cards rather than sheets of paper. You will have to rearrange the information you gather in the order demanded by *your* organization of material, which may be quite different from that of your source; and you will have to bring together material on the same point from different sources. The easiest way to do this is to arrange your cards to fit your outline. If you have several items on one card you will have to choose between cutting it into unmanageable scraps and doing extra copying.

2. Be sure that your notes are full and clear enough to be usable a a month later. An abbreviation that seems obvious now may be meaningless then. If you use your cards as a piecemeal first draft rather than as an extra step, you can save a great deal of trouble.

3. Be sure that each card contains an exact reference to the source, and an indication of the place in your paper where you expect to use the information.

Below are two examples of cards that follow these principles. The first indicates the place in the paper by a reference to the outline, and the source by a code number. The second indicates the place by a subject heading and the source by a shortened form of the bibliographic entry. Either method will do.

SEVERAL KINDS OF NOTES

You cannot take notes successfully unless you have a fairly definite idea of what you are looking for. You should use your tentative outline as a rough guide—remembering that it may be wise to revise it somewhat as you go along. Your paper will probably contain at least three kinds of material, listed below. It is wise to take clear and full notes for each of the three kinds. **Since the first two should be indicated by footnotes when you put them into your paper, make sure your cards show the exact page references.** The third kind may not require footnotes, but it is wise to make your notes as soon as they occur to you, and to put them on cards that can be fitted in with the others.

1. **Facts found in various sources and organized to suit your own purpose.** You do not need a footnote for any statement that is original with you or for any matter of really general knowledge; but you do need one for *every fact* that you have found in your research. Don't fail to put one in just because you have seen the fact mentioned in several different books and *now* think you can take it for granted. Show your reader where you got

II A   5,158

"It is faily [*sic*] clear that
no language represents such
operations with maximum
economy."

Propositions   Weinreich, 158

"It is faily [*sic*] clear that
no language represents such
operations with maximum
economy."

it. If you find a dozen facts on the same page you may put them all into one paragraph, with a single footnote for the whole paragraph. The thing to remember is that a reader who wants to check the authority for any one fact should be able to turn directly to the page on which it occurs. Make a note of every fact that you expect to use. Then you will have no trouble putting in a footnote.

2. **The opinions of your sources about the significance of these facts.** If you say that the Sioux Indians were better fighters than the Blackfeet, your readers are going to wonder how you know. It is much better to say that "Major Langham, who had fought against both, considered the Sioux Indians better fighters than the Blackfeet." This is not proof, but it is evidence worth considering.

3. **Your own conclusions,** based on a study of both the facts and the opinions of your sources. Remember that, although you get your raw material from other people, the final paper is your own. You are not supposed

to accept evidence unless it convinces you. It is particularly unfortunate to cite contradictory evidence as if you believed both sides, but a good many students do exactly this. Suppose you have not only Langham's statement that the Sioux were better fighters, but Colonel Hamill's statement that the Blackfeet were better. What are you going to do about them?

There are any number of possibilities. Perhaps the statements were made fifty years apart. Then there is no real contradiction, merely evidence of a shift. Perhaps you can find evidence that one man was prejudiced, or that one had much more experience than the other. In any case, it is your job to evaluate both statements and to indicate your own conclusion. If you find that you can reach no conclusion, say so definitely. It is much better to say "The evidence is conflicting and I can't decide" than to write as if you didn't notice the conflict.

QUOTATIONS

Sometimes you may want to use the exact words of one of your sources, particularly when they indicate opinions. When you do, be sure that you enclose them in quotation marks on your cards, so that you can identify them as quotations when you see them in your paper. **Remember also that you should not make any change whatever without indicating it clearly.** Use the following devices:

1. Indicate omissions by three dots.

> *Original:* Smith, who had been ill for weeks, died November 23.
> *Quotation:* "Smith . . . died November 23."

2. Enclose corrections or clarifications in brackets.

> *Original:* He knew that Brown had lived there since 1863.
> *Quotation:* "He knew that [Charles A.] Brown had lived there since 1863 [actually 1861]."

3. If you want to leave a mistake uncorrected, indicate that you are doing so intentionally by putting *sic,* underlined or italicized and in brackets, immediately after the mistake. *Sic* is Latin for "thus." In this use it means "That is the way he wrote it."

> *Original:* He left New Orlins in 1926.
> *Quotation:* "He left New Orlins [*sic*] in 1926."

In the finished paper a quotation of more than four lines should be indicated by single spacing and indenting rather than by quotation marks.

PARAPHRASES AND SUMMARIES

You should use quotations only when the exact words of the source are important for your purpose. Ordinarly you should simply take the material and find words of your own. Two rather common tendencies are particularly unfortunate:

1. Quoting without acknowledgment. Your instructor will be *so* surprised to find that you are suddenly writing like Walter Pater. The fact that you change an occasional word does not justify this kind of copying.

2. Deliberately changing the words while slavishly following the ideas. This is perhaps a little better than (1), but not much. When you copy from a writer, do it exactly and give him credit. When you merely use his facts and opinions, you should still acknowledge whatever you have taken (and there is nothing shameful in taking a great deal). But remember that your purpose is different from his. Take what you need in as few words as possible. Then write your own paragraphs in your own way.

Sometimes you will want to expand a statement found in a source. More frequently you will have reason to condense it. Everything he says may be important, interesting, and concisely expressed; but if you take only what is useful for your immediate purpose, you can usually save a good many words.

STEP FOUR: ORGANIZING YOUR FINDINGS

When you have finished taking your notes you are ready to begin putting the paper together; and if you have done a good job so far, you should have practically all the material available except for some fairly obvious expansions. The first step is to rearrange your notes according to the headings of your outline. You will probably find that some of the notes should now be discarded—for instance a card made from one book may have been superseded by a better card taken from a second book. You may also find that there are some obvious gaps. You will then have to consider the notes and outline together, and decide either that you can afford to eliminate part of the outline or that you should take additional notes. When your notes and outline match you will probably find it advisable to rewrite the outline in the full sentence form discussed in Chapter Ten before going any further. Your tentative topic outline shows only what you are going to talk about. A sentence outline will help you to decide and clarify exactly what you are going to say.

The process of transferring material from good notes to sheets of paper is mostly mechanical, but you will probably need an intermediate draft before the final copy. Be extremely careful to copy accurately, and to *document* as you go along—that is, to indicate where you got each piece of information that is not either original with you or a matter of common knowledge.

FOOTNOTES

You indicate a footnote by placing its number at the end of the information to which it refers, and slightly above the line. At the bottom of the page you indent five spaces and repeat the same number, again slightly above the level of the line you are going to write. Follow this number with an indication of the exact page where you found the information. In your draft you may give simply the code number of your source, thus:

Smith left Springfield on April 2, 1837.[1] He went first to . . .

[1] 6, 323.

In your final copy you will replace the code number 6 with the exact information from your bibliography card. Be sure to indicate all your footnotes on your draft. If you wait until the final copy, the task of putting them in correctly will be much more difficult.

STEP FIVE: PUTTING YOUR PAPER IN FINAL FORM

Before typing the final version of your paper it is well to go over your draft with the idea of making it as useful as possible. The primary aim of research writing is neither to impress nor to charm the reader, but to give him reliable information as directly and economically as possible. The cardinal virtues are accuracy, clarity, and brevity, in that order. If you are writing about Lincoln, for instance, it is usually better to call him *Lincoln* eight times on one page than to try to "avoid monotony" by referring to him under eight different disguises which may confuse and will certainly delay a reader. Above all, make sure that you haven't tried to smooth over any weak spots by being vague. If you don't know something, say so.

When you actually type the final version follow the directions in the next two sections unless your instructor directs you otherwise.

FOOTNOTE FORM

The first footnote reference to a source is taken from the bibliography card with four slight changes:

1. The author's name is given in normal order instead of with the last name first. Since footnotes are not arranged alphabetically, there is no reason for reversing the order.

2. The reverse indentation is abandoned for the same reason.

3. The city and date are enclosed in parentheses.

4. Commas are substituted for periods except after abbreviations and at the end. (I can think of no compelling reason for the last two changes, but they are established, and it is easier to follow them than to get into a a losing argument with your instructor.) Compare the two following entries:

BIBLIOGRAPHY

Laird, Charlton. *The Miracle of Language.* Cleveland, 1953.

FOOTNOTE

[1]Charlton Laird, *The Miracle of Language* (Cleveland, 1953), p. 63.

Later references to the same source should be abbreviated:

[4]Laird, p. 71.

If you refer to several works by the same author, his name alone will be ambiguous. You should therefore add either the date or a shortened form of the title:

[4]Laird (1953), p. 71.

or

[4]Laird, *Miracle,* p. 71.

When a footnote refers to the same source as the immediately preceding one, it may be abbreviated still further by using *Ibid.* (from Latin *ibidem,* "in the same place"). This is not worth doing unless it effects a real economy. Thus:

[7]Ernest Bernbaum and others, p. 153.
[8]*Ibid.,* p. 169.

but

¹¹Laird, p. 117.
¹²Laird, p. 148.

Notice that *Ibid.* is capitalized and followed by both a period and a comma. There is disagreement about whether it should be underlined.

The use of such other Latin abbreviations as *op. cit.* (in the work cited) and *loc. cit.* (in the place cited) is fortunately decreasing. You may have to learn some of these terms in order to understand your sources, but you are hereby advised against using them yourself.

Footnotes referring to all kinds of sources are modified from the bibliography cards in exactly the same way. Here is a possible series:

¹Archibald A. Hill, *Introduction to Linguistic Structures* (New York, 1958), p. 89.

²Paul Roberts, *Patterns of English* (New York, 1956), pp. 3–4.

³Karl Dykema, "Progress in Grammar," *College English*, XIV (1952), 95.

⁴Jerrold A. Katz and Paul M. Postal, *An Integrated Theory of Linguistic Descriptions* (Cambridge, Mass., 1964), p. 47.

⁵*Ibid.*, p. 53.

> or

⁵Katz and Postal, p. 53.

⁶Archibald A. Hill, "A Postulate for Linguistics in the Sixties," *Language*, XXXVIII (1962), 347.

⁷Charles C. Fries, *The Structure of English* (New York, 1952), pp. 18–19.

⁸Fries, p. 148.

⁹Hill (1958), p. 237.

Number the footnotes consecutively throughout the paper. Single-space the lines in each footnote, and double-space between them.

MECHANICS OF FINAL COPY

In its final form the paper should have the following parts:
1. Title page.

SOME NEW IDEAS ABOUT ENGLISH GRAMMAR

By

David A. Ferguson

Term Paper Prepared for English 102, Section 49

May 4, 1971

2. Outline or table of contents (instructor's choice).

3. The body of the paper (complete with footnotes).

4. Bibliography (an alphabetical list of the sources referred to in the footnotes). Use the exact form on your bibliography cards—assuming that you have followed instructions in making them out. The bibliography for the works referred to in the preceding section would then appear as follows:

> Dykema, Karl. "Progress in Grammar," *College English*, XIV (1952), 93–100.
> Fries, Charles C. *The Structure of English*, New York, 1952.
> Hill, Archibald A. *Introduction to Linguistics Structures.* New York, 1958.
> ———. "A Postulate for Linguistics in the Sixties," *Language*, XXXVIII (1962), 345–51.

(Notice two things: the author's name is not repeated, but is replaced by a dash, and his works are listed in chronological rather than alphabetical order.)

> Katz, Jerrold A., and Paul M. Postal. *An Integrated Theory of Linguistic Descriptions.* Cambridge, Mass., 1964.
> Roberts, Paul. *Patterns of English.* New York, 1956.

Listed below are acceptable rules for preparing the final copy of your paper:

1. Type your paper double-spaced on 8½ x 11 inch unlined paper. Single-space long quotations (five lines or more) and indent them five spaces. Single-space bibliographical entries and footnotes. Leave a double space between footnotes and between the items in the bibliography.

2. Margins: left, 15 spaces; right, 10 spaces; top, 10 spaces; bottom, 6 spaces.

3. Number your pages (except the first page). Place the number even with the right margin, 8 spaces from the top.

4. Indent the first line of each paragraph 5 spaces.

5. If you are going to use graphs, tables, or illustrations, consult your instructor about their placement and form of acknowledgment.

6. Do not fold your paper. Fasten it with a paper clip, staple it along the left side, or bind it in a folder.

7. Make a carbon copy just in case of calamity.

POSSIBLE VARIATIONS

The rules just given are distinctly arbitrary; the sky will not fall if you follow a slightly different model. You may find some variation, also, in the exact form of the footnotes and bibliographical entries in different sources. If your instructor suggests some departure from the form suggested here, you will do well to follow him. But you had better follow some one definite form throughout. If you waver between several, the result is likely to be ambiguous, and is almost certain to draw criticism.

SHORTCUTS

Finally, here are some suggested shortcuts:

1. A healthy proportion of all research writing is done on university campuses by university professors. A live source is often a better starting point than a printed source because the printed source was to some extent out-of-date by the time it got printed. Why students who want to explore questions in anthropology talk only to their English instructors about the projects when anthropologists are available is an open question for research in psychology.

2. The most important research tool in a library isn't a book, but the reference librarian. He carries in his head an astonishing list of guides, bibliographies, indexes, handbooks, and directories. Pick his brains before you begin plodding through catalogs and indexes. He also knows the short-cuts. Research can be exhausting; there is no point in making it even more debilitating.

3. Much information on current topics is available by mail or telephone. Take the easiest route to the most reliable source. Especially if you live in a large urban area, one of your reference books ought to be the telephone directory.

4. Use bibliographies of bibliography to save time. Look, for example, at Theodore Besterman's *A World Bibliography of Bibliography*.

5. Let technology work for you. Instead of copying out of sources long passages that deserve study, make a Xerox copy. Spend a dime, save half an hour, and avoid a dozen errors in transcription.

EXERCISES

Answer the following questions briefly and simply:

1. What is the difference between research and information retrieval?

2. What do you see as the role of information retrieval in research itself?

3. What do you feel is the benefit of information retrieval to the student? If you don't see a benefit, why not?

4. What are the advantages of carefully organized note cards?

5. You are writing a paper on the history of your city. Name at least two sources besides the library.

6. What three things should you look for in evaluating an author?

7. Why have a bibliography?

8. Which of the suggested shortcuts impressed you as most valuable, and why?

9. Where do you find the reference librarian?

10. What is the purpose of a tentative outline? Does making a tentative outline mean you can skip a sentence outline? Defend your answer.

11. What kinds of things should be footnoted, and why?

12. When is a direct quotation placed within quotation marks and when is it single-spaced and indented?

13. How should the form of bibliography information on a note card relate to the form of bibliography information in the final draft of your paper?

14. What are the uses and hazards of the *Reader's Guide to Periodical Literature?*

15. What happens when you find generally qualified people disagreeing with each other on a given subject?

Suggestions for Discussion or Theme Writing

I. Take one of the general subjects below and, in a cooperative class effort, draw forth a number of topics which effect a reduction of the original. If it is then possible and reasonable to make further reductions of the result of the first operation, do so. Finally, develop one or more usable research questions for each final reduction.

Student demonstrations in the 60's
The Indochina War
Water pollution
Federal aid to private schools
Sonnet sequences
The use of technology in education
Black music
History of education in the United States
Relationship between language forms and culture
Political influence of minority groups

II. Discuss the "answerability" of the following questions:

1. What was Jefferson's boyhood like?

2. Were all of John Donne's religious poems written after he was ordained?

3. Do blonds have more fun?

4. What was the effect of the Korean War on the United Nations?

5. How did the draft system develop?

6. What have been the effects of slavery on this country?

III. Discuss the relative merits of the following as sources for a paper on the question: How important is milk in the diet of an adult? (a) the American Medical Association, (b) a cardiologist, (c) the Association of American Dairy Farmers, (d) the editor of a national newsmagazine, (e) the director of a recent study on the effects of drinking milk.

IV. Which of the following might best provide information on what happened at that accident at Sutpen's Corner last night? (a) the driver of the car, (b) an eyewitness, (c) the reporting police officer, (d) the newspaper man who wrote the feature story on it, (e) a passenger in the car, (f) Henry Sutpen, who owns the land.

THE CRITICAL
REVIEW

An astonishing number of people make good livings writing critical reviews of books, articles, presidential speeches, plays, congressional actions, movies, or television programs. College instructors assign critical reviews not so much because they want you to make a good living as because a review forces you to get a firm grip on somebody else's ideas and technique and then wrestle with them, in public and at length. The review trains and tests your ability to read, summarize, analyze, organize, and evaluate.

Whether the thing to be reviewed is a book, article, film, filmstrip, short story, or play, reviewing it generally proceeds by these assumptions:

1. **Assume that the audience you are writing for is the same audience that the author of the work is writing for.** (Do not review the book *War and Peace* as if it were written for high school juniors.)

2. **Assume that your audience has not seen or read the work you are reviewing, yet assume that they have already formed an opinion on it.**

The principle is logically contradictory, like so many realities. Your audience is composed of people who have seen or read it and others who haven't. More practically, your instructor may or may not have seen or read it. You just can't tell; hence the necessary assumption.

3. **Assume that your task is two-part:**

    a. **to summarize the significant content (review)**

    b. **to evaluate the content (criticize)**

Then tell yourself immediately that this doesn't mean that the paper will have two parts. If the thing is simple and short, a short summary and a short evaluation probably will do. If the thing is long or complicated or both, you will do better to divide the material and use short pieces of summary followed by short pieces of evaluation. This plan naturally requires a short introductory summary and a short concluding evaluation.

4. **Assume that a good review is an accounting of both the strengths and weaknesses of the work.** Presumably, if there weren't some strengths, it would never have been published or filmed or acted, and if it didn't have weaknesses, the author wouldn't be human.

5. **Assume that you have to show why something is good, bad, or indifferent before you say finally or out of hand that it is so.**

6. **Assume that a good summary states clearly the purpose or thesis of the original, confines itself to important points, and avoids rearranging the proportion and emphasis of the original.** The assumption here is that the ultimate dishonesty in writing is to paraphrase unfairly someone else's work and then evaluate the paraphrase instead of what the author really said.

7. **Assume that the primary purpose of evaluation is not to say *good* or *bad* but to supply what the author lacks.** It is reasonably certain that a review that says, "This thing is awful" is not so valuable as one that says, "This thing might not have been so awful if the author had. . . ." That may be a negative way of saying, "This thing is good, but. . . ."

That point raises the question of what the author can lack. He can lack exactly what you can in writing a theme. His assumptions may be perverse, his evidence weak, his conclusions irrelevant or illogical. His style may be illiterate, his material unorganized, his tone insipid.

If the list sounds viciously negative, remember that your audience is not the author but the reader. Your summaries will include the valuable parts of the material. By supplying what the author lacks, you don't destroy it; you add to its value for the reader.

8. **Assume that a critical review reveals as much about the reviewer as it does about the thing under review.**

Intuitive geniuses may ignore all these assumptions, since the assumptions are based on history, experience, and common sense. Intuitive geniuses are those fortunate people who say things like, "I don't know much about _____, but I know what I like," and then expect other people to take them seriously.

Suggestions for Discussion or Theme Writing

I. Choose an article from a technical journal in your major field and review it.
II. Choose a short story or filmstrip and review it.
III. Review a popular film—by seeing the film and determining what statement the film makes about the world.
IV. Compare a book with the film that was made from it by indicating the difference between the statements made by each.

INDEX
TO
USAGE

a, an

The two forms *a* and *an* are called the *indefinite articles. A* is used before a consonant sound (*a* book, *a* union). *An* is used before a vowel sound (*an* error, *an* honor). Since initial *h* is pronounced more lightly in British usage than in American, you may find *an* printed before some words where you would expect *a* (*an* hotel, *an* historical novel). *A* is the normal American form in such places.

Abbreviations

1. *For economy.* Abbreviations may be used freely whenever economy of effort, space, or printing cost is more important than appearance. They are therefore common in footnotes, concise reference books, catalogs, merchandise orders, etc. The writer should avoid any abbreviations that will not be immediately clear to his expected readers unless (a) he pro-

vides a list of the abbreviations he uses; and (b) he uses each abbreviation often enough to effect a real economy. For instance, if he refers twenty times to the *Journal of English and Germanic Philology*, it is worthwhile to use *JEGP*; but if he refers only twice to the *Journal of Modern Philology*, he would do better to write it out both times instead of using *JMP*.

2. *Titles. Dr., Mr., Mrs.,* and *Messrs.* are regularly abbreviated when used with names. Such other titles as *Captain, Colonel, President, Professor,* and *Reverend* may be abbreviated when used with initials or given names, but not when used with last names only. Thus: *Capt.* (or *Captain*) *Henry Wade*, but always *Captain Wade; Prof. E. H. Walker*, but *Professor Walker*.

3. *Months.* In dates (except in footnotes and bibliographical entries), the months may be abbreviated as follows:

Jan.	Apr.	Oct.
Feb.	Aug.	Nov.
Mar.	Sept.	Dec.

Notice that the three shortest names (*May, June,* and *July*) are not abbreviated, and that *Sept.* is the only abbreviation containing four letters.

Abbreviations are used only for exact dates:

Dec. 17, 1967, but *January*, 1968

4. *The pronunciation test.* In ordinary writing, you should use abbreviations other than titles *only if you would pronounce them as written.* Thus *10 a.m.* and an *FHA loan* are satisfactory, but a *ten ft. pole* and *govt. bonds* are not. When a pronounceable abbreviation is a shorter form of a standard word, its use is definitely informal, but not necessarily objectionable. "I have three *exams* next week" is appropriate in a friendly letter (even from one *prof* to another), though we should probably tell a prospective employer that they were *examinations*.

5. *Periods with abbreviations.* It used to be the general rule to put a period after every abbreviation, and after every letter in an abbreviation consisting of a series of initials. There is now a growing tendency to omit many of these periods. Practice varies so much that it is impossible to give absolute rules, but those that follow are reasonably reliable:

a. In series of initials, periods are required after small letters, but are optional after capitals. Thus *a.m., f.o.b.,* and *i.e.;* but *FHA* or *F.H.A, RAF* or *R.A.F.* The reason for this is that abbreviations written in small letters without periods might be mistaken for ordinary words (such as *am* and *fob*). There is less danger of this with series of capitals.

b. Other abbreviations which represent actual pronunciation are not followed by periods. Compare "one *prof* to another" with *Prof.* (pronounced *Professor*) E. H. Walker.

(at) about

Theoretically, *at ten o'clock* means one thing, *about ten o'clock* means another, and *at about ten o'clock* is an illogical construction that should never be used. Actually, *at about ten o'clock* is in standard usage; people start out to set a definite time, then decide to leave themselves a margin. However, *at* adds nothing to *about*.

above

"The paragraph *above*" is safe from criticism. Such expressions as "the *above* paragraph" and "as the *above* indicates" are, on the evidence, established in standard use; but they annoy many people. When *above* is used to refer to anything more than a page or two back, it should be accompanied by a page reference.

accent

The noun *accent* always has the stress on the first syllable. The verb may have it on either syllable. The noun may mean (among other things): (a) stress ("The *accent* is on the first syllable"); (b) an accent mark ("'Negligée' is written with an *accent*"); (c) a characteristic way of speaking ("a Brooklyn *accent*"). The verb usually means to stress.

accept

Accept (to receive willingly) is often confused with *except* (to leave out). The easiest way to keep the words straight is to remember that *ex-* usually means "out."

We will *except* that case from consideration.
I will *accept* all the papers *except* the ones written in pencil.

acknowledgment, acknowledgement

See **judgment, judgement.**

Active Constructions

See **Passive Constructions.**

ad

When *ad* is used informally for *advertisement,* it should be written without a period.

A.D. and B.C.

A.D. (from *anno domini,* "in the year of our Lord") was originally placed before the date (A.D. 236). It is now more often placed after the date, as B.C. (before Christ) regularly is.

B.C. is used regularly for dates before the Christian era. A.D. is used only for dates so early that there might be some doubt about which era was meant, or to give a touch of formality.

Adapt

See **Adopt.**

Adjectives and Adverbs

There is a clear difference between the uses of the modifiers in the following pairs of sentences:

He is a *happy* man.	He sang *happily.*
She was a *beautiful* girl.	It was *beautifully* clear.
He is *glad* you came in.	He will *gladly* do it.
That is an *extreme* case.	He drove *extremely* well.
He has a *bad* foot.	He has a *badly* injured foot.
A *certain* truth is rare.	*Certainly,* it is true.

In the left-hand sentences the adjectives are used to modify only nouns and pronouns. In the right-hand sentences the adverbs are used to modify anything else, such as verbs, participles, adjectives, other adverbs, and even (as in the last example) the whole sentence.

Not all uses are as clear-cut as those shown above, but for most pairs of modifiers the following rules work reasonably well, though practice is so divided that you can't please everybody.

1. When the modifier *clearly* refers to the action of the verb, use the adverb.

2. When the modifier refers to the subject, *or when it could be taken either way,* use the adjective.

Thus we say "Ann looks beautiful," even though an argument that the modifier tells how she *looks* is at least as logical as one that says *looks* is more nearly parallel to *is* in "Ann is beautiful" than it is to *sings* in "Ann sings beautifully." In borderline cases both adjective and adverb may be in standard use, but there is a better chance that the adjective will be. We can say "They lived *happy*" as well as "They lived *happily*"; but if we say "The roses smelled *sweetly*" we give the impression that we are trying too hard and still missing.

The adverbial uses of *quick* and *slow, loud* and *soft,* and a few other "flat adverbs" have been established as standard for centuries, though not in all positions. Most native speakers can afford to trust their ears and not worry. Thus "He works *quick*" is entirely defensible, even though some critics will object to it. "He *quick* finished the job" is not—but who would be tempted to say it?

For *good, bad, fine, mighty,* and *real* see the specific entries in this Index.

In Old English the genitive cases of certain nouns and pronouns, usually ending in *-es,* were often used adverbially, and this use has often continued. Thus in "He works *nights,*" *nights* is not plural, but equivalent to *at night.* Such forms as *backwards* and *since* (earlier *sinnes,* and still earlier *sithenes*) have the same origin.

adopt, adapt

To *adopt* is to take as your own. To *adapt* is to change to meet a special purpose.

adviser, advisor

Either spelling will do.

affect, effect

These two words give little trouble as nouns, since *affect* is only used as a technical psychological term; but they cause much trouble as verbs, since they are pronounced alike and have rather closely related meanings. To *affect* means to influence; to *effect* means to bring about a result. In informal English, *effect* is more likely to be a noun and *affect* a verb.

agenda

In Latin, *agenda* is the plural of *agendum,* something to be done. In English it means a list of things to be done (or at least considered), and is normally treated as singular.

aggravate

Originally this meant only "to make more serious," as in "The long trip aggravated his injury." Many people still object rather strongly to the meaning "to irritate or annoy," but this usage is probably now more common than the original one.

Agreement of Pronoun with Antecedent

See **Pronouns, Antecedents, and Referents.**

Agreement of Verb with Subject

Grammatical agreement is a matching of inflections to indicate which words go together. English verbs have lost so many of their inflections that agreement is often impossible (*did* agrees, or rather fails to disagree, with any subject) and almost never important to the meaning of a sentence. Nevertheless, clear-cut violations of simple agreement are generally regarded as very serious mistakes. In complicated situations both theory and practice are so divided that nobody can please everybody, and only a very smug character can be sure he is always right.

1. *Simple agreement.* The following combinations are standard:

I	am
he, she, it, the man	is
we, you, they, the men	are
I, he, she, it, the man	was
we, you, they, the men	were
he, she, it, the man	sings
I, we, you, they, the men	sing

Anybody who does not find these completely natural had better practice them. Some dialects have very different patterns, but the only common departures among people whose general usage is standard are *you was* for *you were* and *he don't* for *he doesn't.* Both of these combinations can be justified on historical grounds, but they have a very low standing today.

2. *Singular subjects with plural meanings and plural subjects with singular meanings.* When a singular subject has a plural meaning or vice versa, the general tendency is to make the verb agree with the idea instead of the form, unless a strong sound pattern is involved.

The *jury is* making its decision. (jury considered as unit)
The *jury are* eating their dinners. (jury considered as individuals)
My *family like* (or *likes*) you. (either will do)
Everybody is coming. (*-body are* would sound wrong)
None of them *are* (or *is*) coming. (although *none* is actually a negative

compound ending in *one*, most people do not think of it in this way. Also, *none* does not usually come immediately before the verb)
Neither of his parents *is* (or *are*) still living. (both are dead)
Ten thousand *dollars is* a lot of money. (*are* would be possible, but we generally consider the money as one sum rather than as many dollars)
Her *patience and understanding is* (or *are*) amazing. (depending on whether we consider that she has two separate virtues or one compound one)

3. *Verb separated from subject by intervening noun of different number.*

The *collector* of all these objects *was* a Frenchman.
This *kind* of mushrooms *is* (or *are*) good to eat.

In the first of these, the verb refers not only to a singular subject but to a single person, and there can be no reason except carelessness for using a plural form. But in the second, while the formal subject (*kind*) is singular, it is actually the plural *mushrooms* that are good to eat; and the verb may agree with either. The tendency is to use the form appropriate to the *idea in mind at the time*, rather than to the particular word by which that idea has been previously indicated.

Since a faulty agreement seldom interferes with meaning, it doesn't always pay to be too particular.

I hope the *box gets* here in good condition.
I hope the *box of apples* gets here in good condition.
I hope the *box* of those delicious Hood River apples *gets* here in good condition.

We could not say *box get*, but *box* of *apples get* would be likely to pass unnoticed; and *box of those delicious Hood River apples get* would probably sound to most people more normal than *box . . . gets*. Since the only importance of the form is the impression it makes on the audience, there is not much advantage in being too correct to be appreciated.

4. *Agreement after* who. Another type of agreement that causes more trouble than it is worth occurs when the form of the verb is supposed to be determined by whether *who* refers to a singular or plural noun—a matter to which the speaker has often given no thought.

a. He is one of those *men who* always *know* what to do.

It is often said that *knows* would be wrong here, because there are a number of men who know. However, the meaning of the statement is that he, among others, *knows* what to do; and the temptation to use the singular form is hardly worth resisting.

    b. He is the only *one* of those men *who* always *knows* what to do.

Here theory and natural practice agree on the singular form. Only one man *knows*.

    c. He is the only one of those *men who* always *know* what to do that I like.

This is the kind of sentence that is devised by writers of textbooks to prove that theoretical agreement is important. It is not recommended for any other purpose.

    5. *Agreement after* it *and* there.

    a. *It* is always followed by a singular verb.
       It *is* the Browns.
    b. After *there* the verb normally agrees with the following subject:
       There *is* a man.
       There *are* three men.
    c. When *there* is followed by a compound subject of which the first member is singular, the verb may be either singular or plural:
       There *is* (or *are*) a man and a couple of boys over there.

    6. *Subjects of different number or person joined by* either . . . or *or* neither . . . nor. The problem presented by such sentences as the following has never been satisfactorily solved:

Neither John nor I (go, goes) there very often.
Either his parents or his brother usually (help, helps) him out.

Many grammars give a rule that in such sentences the verb should agree with the nearer subject. Actually, practice is hopelessly divided. Use whichever verb form seems natural, and don't worry about it.

    ain't

    Originally a contraction of *am not*, then used as a substitute for *aren't* and *isn't*, and finally for *hasn't* and *haven't*. Most people (including many who are sure they don't) use it in some or all of these meanings in informal speech, though often only in a supposedly humorous way. However, since it is quite generally regarded as the very battle flag of "bad grammar," it is well to avoid it if you are concerned about the impression you are making. It should not be used in writing except in dialog or as a mild attempt at humor.

Many linguists now say that *ain't* has a much better standing as a contraction for *am not* than in any of its other uses, partly because of its origin, and partly because there is no satisfactory standard equivalent, especially in questions. The Irish *amn't I?* and the British *aren't I?* have never been generally accepted in this country, and *am I not?* sounds inhumanly formal.

This sounds very logical, but the fact is that most people either accept *ain't* freely or don't accept it at all.

alibi

In Latin, *alibi* means "elsewhere." In legal English an alibi is a defense that the accused was somewhere else at the time of the crime, and therefore could not have committed it. The word is now often used for any kind of excuse, frequently with the implication that the excuse is not a very sound one: "What's your *alibi* this time?"

all (of)

We say *some of it, some of them, all of it, all of them*. If we replace the pronouns with nouns, we still say *some of the money, some of the boys;* but in such expressions as *all (of) the money, all (of) the boys*, the *of* somehow seems unnecessary. It is therefore better to leave it out, at least in writing.

all ready, already

The two separate words preserve their original meaning. The compound word has the entirely different meaning, "by now" or "by that time." "They are *all ready* there" means "All of them are ready there." "They are *already* there" means "They are there by now."

all right, alright

The form *alright* is patterned after *already* but developed much later. It will probably be accepted without question in a few years, but today many people regard it as a serious mistake and nobody seems to praise it particularly, so you might as well avoid it.

all the farther, all the harder, etc.

Phrases of this type are standard in such sentences as "He worked *all the harder* because he had been advised to take it easy." As substitutes for such expressions as *as far as*, they are not generally accepted as standard, though they are used by educated people in some areas ("Is that *all the farther* you can go?").

all together, altogether

The two separate words preserve their original meanings. The compound means "completely," "in all," or "on the whole."

They are *all together*. (all of them are together)
They are *altogether* trustworthy. (completely)
He has five cars *altogether*. (in all, but not necessarily in one place)
Altogether, I don't think much of him. (on the whole)

almost

Almost is often shortened to *most* in conversation. If you use the shorter form in informal writing, use it firmly, and don't write '*most*, which looks cute.

although

See *though, although*.

alumna—alumni

A woman graduate is an *alumna*, plural *alumnae* (pronounced *alumnee* or *alumnay*). A male graduate is an *alumnus*, plural *alumni* (pronounced *alumneye*).

A.M. and P.M.

Abbreviations for *ante meridiem* and *post meridiem*, meaning "before noon" and "afternoon." Midnight is 12 P.M., noon 12 A.M. Often the context makes A.M. or P.M. superfluous: "Class begins at 12:05." Either small or capital letters may be used. These abbreviations are not in good standing except for specific times. "From 3 to 5 p.m." is standard, but "This a.m." is not. Such redundant expressions as "10 A.M. in the morning" are never justified.

Ambiguity

A statement that can reasonably be understood in two ways is said to be *ambiguous*. Intentional *ambiguity* is sometimes convenient (so is lying). Unintentional ambiguity is one of the most serious errors in communication. It doesn't do much good to prove that a sentence *could* be read the way you intended it. If it is not completely clear at first reading, don't try to justify it—rearrange it so that a reader will automatically get the meaning that you intend. Two of the commonest causes of ambiguity are carelessly placed modifiers (see pages 196, 283, 364) and pronouns that might refer to more than one thing.

among, between

Among always implies more than two. *Between* originally implied only two, but is now generally recognized as acceptable with larger numbers.

amount, number

Amount is used of things considered in bulk; *number*, of things that can be counted.

A large *amount* of money.
A large *number* of nickels.

Analytic and Synthetic

An *analytic* language (such as English) indicates the relation of ideas principally by word order, connectives, and auxiliary verbs. A *synthetic* language (such as Latin) indicates the relation of ideas primarily by changes in the forms of the words.

and

There is nothing ungrammatical about beginning a sentence with *and*, though a more specific conjunction is often preferable.

and etc.

Since the *et* in *etc.* is the Latin word for *and*, an extra *and* before it is quite useless, and to many readers distinctly annoying.

and/or

And/or is a recent and useful invention, and is already widely used in business and legal language (though there are many people who object to it even in these fields). It is not firmly established as standard in general writing, and the small economy achieved by writing "pie and/or ice cream" instead of "pie or ice cream or both" is hardly worth the criticism it is likely to arouse.

and which

And which should be used only after an earlier *which*.

> This plan, *which* was proposed by Mr. Moore, *and which* certainly seems promising. . . .

but

> The plan proposed by Mr. Moore, *which* (no *and*) certainly seems promising. . . .

ante-, anti-

Ante- means before, as in *antecedent* (going before). *Anti-* means against.

Anti- (pronounced *antee* or *anteye*) is much the more common of the two. It is followed by a hyphen only when the word to which it is prefixed begins with *i* or with a capital letter (anti-intellectual, anti-American, but antiaircraft).

Antecedent

An *antecedent* is the word to which a pronoun refers. In the sentence "Bathgate did his best, but he couldn't manage it," *Bathgate* is the antecedent of both *his* and *he*. *It* has no antecedent in this sentence. Consequently, we cannot tell from this sentence alone what *it* stands for. Unless the reference is perfectly clear from an earlier sentence, some change should be made.

Antonym

When two words have opposite meanings, each is called the *antonym* of the other. Thus *good* and *bad, long* and *short, wet* and *dry* are pairs of antonyms.

any and its compounds

1. Such expressions as "This is the best of any hotel in town" and "She is younger than any girl in her class" are not only theoretically illogical, but generally criticized by careful speakers. It is therefore advisable to leave out the *of any* in the first sentence, and to expand *than any* to *than any other* in the second.

2. The following compounds should be written as single words whenever the only stress is on the first syllable: *anybody, anyhow, anyone, anything, anyway, anywhere, anywise.* Some of them may be written as two separate words when the stress is divided (*any body* of water, *any one* thing).

Anyways is sometimes used as a variant form of both *anyway* and *anywise,* but is often criticized. *Anywheres* is even more generally condemned.

Any place and *anyplace* as substitutes for *anywhere* are not exactly wrong, but they won't get you any extra points.

3. Compounds with *every, some,* and *no* follow the same principles.

any more

In the sense of *nowadays, any more,* or *anymore* is in general use in questions and negative statements. In positive statements, such as "Everybody seems to be going to college any more," it is normal only in limited areas, and is likely to strike people from other parts of the country as most peculiar.

Apologies

One of the best ways to get a paper marked down is to begin it with an apology. The instructor ought to be able to find something wrong with it without your telling him—but if you insist on helping him you should be prepared to take the consequences. Moreover, if he has demanded 500 words, he means 500 words on the subject, and probably won't count those used to excuse it—though of course he will notice any errors in this part.

Apostrophe (')

The principal uses of the *apostrophe* are:

1. To indicate the possessive forms of nouns (the *boy's* hat, the *girls'* faces) but not of pronouns (*its* head; that is *yours*).

2. To show the omission of one or more letters in a contraction (*it's* true; they *can't* do it).

3. To indicate the plural of figures, letters, and words considered as

words (three 2's; two t's; too many and's). It is permissible to omit this apostrophe unless the result would be confusing. We could write 2s, ts, and ands; but if we wrote is instead of i's it would probably be mistaken for the verb.

4. In representing conversation, apostrophes may be used to indicate the omission of certain sounds: "He an' John were drivin' on one o' the back roads." It is advisable to use apostrophes rather sparingly for this purpose. Too many of them interfere with comfort in reading. Moreover, they may be quite unfair. Are you sure that *you* always pronounce *and* and *of* in a sentence exactly as you would if you were reading them from a list? And would it really be an improvement if you did?

Apposition, Appositive

When a noun is placed immediately after another noun or pronoun to explain it, it may be called an *appositive,* and the construction is called *apposition.* The second term may or may not be set off by commas or parentheses, and it may be either a single word or a phrase.

My brother *Everett* is in California.
Everett, *my oldest brother,* is in California.
His sister (*the youngest one*) will be here tomorrow.
That is Ernest Hemingway, *the famous novelist.*

This construction usually gives little trouble, although overelaborate theories of punctuation sometimes cause confusion. It is sometimes said, for instance, that the sentence "My brother John is here" implies that I have several brothers, while the sentence "My brother, John, is here" implies that I have only one. This is putting more strain on the commas than they can be depended on to bear. If we wish to indicate that we have only one brother, or more than one, we had better say so in definite words and depend on our ears, rather than rules, for the decision whether or not to use commas. "My brother John is here" and "My brother, John, is here" are both acceptable sentences, regardless of the size of the family.

apt to, liable to, likely to

The traditional distinction between these phrases is that *apt to* indicates a natural tendency (he is *apt to* work too fast); *liable to* indicates exposure to consequences, particularly legal ones (he is *liable to* be sued); and *likely to* indicates simple probability (it is *likely to* rain tomorrow).

However, anybody who attempts to follow these distinctions exactly runs into a good many hairsplitting decisions, and most people have given up the attempt. Both *apt to* and *likely to* are now in standard use for all three purposes. *Liable to* is more likely to be criticized except in its original meaning.

archaic, current, obsolete

Current means still in normal use.

Archaic means still in use, but having a distinctly antique flavor. *Smitten* is current, especially when it refers to being hit by Cupid's arrows, but *smote* is archaic.

Obsolete means no longer in use. *Obsolescent* means disappearing from use. *Eke* in the sense of "also" is completely obsolete. *Vaudeville* now seems to be obsolescent because there is practically none left to talk about.

around, round

Only *round* can be used as an adjective (a *round* table). In most other uses the two are interchangeable. Those people who make distinctions between the two do not agree on what the distinctions are. However, only *around* is generally used as a synonym for *about*. In the sense of "approximately" (they have *around* fifty cows) this is definitely informal. In the sense of "in the neighborhood" *around* has pretty well replaced *about* in American, though not in British, usage.

as

As a synonym for *since* or *because, as* is always rather weak, and often ambiguous. The reader may think it means *while*. As a synonym for *while* it is less likely to be misunderstood, and is often preferable. See also **Comparisons** and **like, as.**

as to

As to is certainly standard, but not always graceful, and many readers have a strong prejudice against it. The following recommendations are therefore offered:

1. When it adds nothing to a sentence, leave it out.

I am doubtful (*as to*) whether he can come.

2. If *about* or *as for* will do as well, choose one of them.

He is very optimistic (*as to*) *about* your chance for the scholarship. *As* (*to*) *for* your other suggestions, I really have no opinion.

I don't know why *as for* should be superior to *as to*, but nobody seems to object to it.

Auxiliary Verbs

The last form in a verb phrase normally indicates the principal idea involved and is called the *main verb*. The other forms indicate such shadings as time, definiteness, obligation, and direction of action, and are called *auxiliary verbs* or *helping verbs*.

Occasional Auxiliaries. A number of verbs may be used in either main or auxiliary functions:

MAIN	AUXILIARY
He *is* a man.	He *is* working.
He *has* a boat.	He *has* built a boat.
He *got* the money.	He has *got* to be there.
He is *going* there.	He is *going* to be there.
Let us alone.	*Let* us consider the facts.
He *used* the books.	He *used* to read in bed.

There is often a difference of opinion on whether a combination of verb forms should be considered as one verb phrase or as two or more successive verbs. It makes little difference—the combinations exist, whatever we call them.

The "Pure" or "Model" Auxiliaries. The verbs *can, may, must, ought, will,* and *shall*, sometimes called "pure" or "model" auxiliaries, form a curious group. The historical reasons for their peculiarities are too complicated to go into here, but the net result is that all of them have lost both some of their forms and some of their uses.

1. None of them has an *-s* form, a participle, or an infinitive.

2. When used in verb phrases, they can only stand first. Such combinations as *may can, used to could,* and *hadn't ought* are not in standard use. The first two have some standing in parts of the South, and would be useful everywhere to avoid the "be able to" construction, but they have not been generally accepted.

3. They have nearly lost their independent functions. Even when they are used alone, they almost always invite attention to verbs previously used

Who can finish this?	I *can* (*finish*).
Are you going to work?	I *ought to* (*work*).

awake, awaken

See **wake, waken.**

awful, awfully

A generation ago schoolteachers were making a determined effort to stop the use of *awful* and *awfully* in any sense not connected with "awe-inspiring." Now most of them are willing to settle for a careful distinction between the adjective (it was simply *awful*) and the adverb (I had an *awfully* nice time). However, you might as well avoid both forms in formal writing.

Back Formation

Sometimes a noun like *beggar* is mistakenly thought to have come from a shorter verb plus a suffix; then the verb *beg* is accidentally invented in the belief that it already exists. (*Beggar* actually came from *Beghard*, not from *beg* + *-er*.) This process is called *back formation. Opine* from *opinion* and *enthuse* from *enthusiasm* are other examples—not universally admired.

backward, backwards

When an adverb is required, *backward* and *backwards* are interchangeable.

The boy seems to enjoy walking *backward* (or *backwards*).

When an adjective is required, the word is *backward*:

He was a *backward* boy.

bad, badly

"I felt bad" was standard English long before "I felt badly" developed in a mistaken attempt to be "correct." However, the mistake became so common that both expressions must now be accepted, on the evidence, as standard.

With other verbs indicating sensation (*taste, smell*, etc.) only *bad* is standard.

balance

Balance is a standard bookkeeping term, but is not generally considered an improvement over *rest* in such sentences as "They kept the rest of them for themselves."

because

The first syllable is often dropped in conversation, but it isn't wise to indicate this in writing. It looks too cute for anything.

being as

Being as and *being as how* are not standard. Use *since* or *because*.

beside, besides

Beside means "by the side of" or "not included in" (*beside* the question).
Besides means "in addition to."

between

Between originally implied only two, but the numeral sense has been largely lost, and *among* is not always a satisfactory substitute. We could hardly say "She was torn *among* three possible decisions." Such an expression as "five acts, with an intermission *between each*" may be illogical, but it is clear, and there is no convenient alternative. "*Between* each pair" would be inaccurate, and "with an intermission after each of the first four" would be pedantic. Let nature take its course.

blame

"He *blamed* John *for* it" is often said to be better usage than "He *blamed* it *on* John." Both expressions are standard.

blond, blonde

In French, *blond* is masculine and *blonde* is feminine. Some people preserve the distinction in English, speaking of a man as a *blond* and of a woman as a *blonde;* but the general tendency now is to use *blond* for all purposes.

born, borne

We say that a child was *born* except in a phrase that explains who bore it.

He had *two* children *borne* by his first wife.
He had two children *born* of a former marriage.
She had *borne* him a son.
In any sense not involving birth, the form is always *borne.*

boy friend, girl friend

A few years ago these expressions were generally considered, by people who did not themselves use them, to be somewhere between comic and pathetic. They continue to be widely used, probably because there are no entirely satisfactory standard equivalents. However, when *boy*, *girl*, or *friend* is sufficiently clear, is it just as well to avoid the combination. For *girl* friend, a man can always substitute *girl*, and a woman can use either *friend* or *another girl*. A man is not supposed to have a *boy friend*, but a woman is, and we suppose she can call him that if she wants to.

Brackets ([])

The principal use of *brackets* is to insert in quoted material something that was not in the original. Since it is a scholarly principle that quoted material may never be changed, even when it is unclear or actually wrong, brackets are a very useful device, and may often be used to avoid cumbersome footnotes. For instance:

He was born in 1853 [actually 1855] in Springfield, Illinois.

Brackets may be made on a typewriter by combining underlining and slant marks.

broadcast

Past tense either *broadcast* or *broadcasted*.

broke

Broke may be slang, but it's better than "financially embarrassed" or —well, what else would you say?

bunch

Bunch is unquestionable in such expressions as *bunch* of grapes, *bunch* of keys. To designate a group of animals, *bunch* is rather informal, but apparently growing more popular. Such expressions as *bunch of people* and *bunch of money* are decidedly free-and-easy.

burst, bust

Burst (past tense also *burst*) is an old verb meaning to break because of an expanding force from within. Pipes, fruits, and blood vessels can *burst*, and orators can *burst out* or *forth*, and so can prisoners.

Bust was originally a corrupted form of *burst*, but is rapidly becoming recognized as a legitimate and different word meaning *break* in any sense, especially figurative ones.

To *bust* a bronco or a trust is now standard.
To *bust* a leg is decidedly informal.
To go *busted* is slang.
Bust has the regular past form, *busted*.

bus

Plural usually *buses*, sometimes *busses*. Formerly often written *'bus* to indicate that it was originally a shortened form of *omnibus*.

but

A number of very peculiar rules about *but* have been invented. Actually, it is very hard to misuse. Both "Nobody came *but I*" and "Nobody came *but me*" are standard. So is "There aren't *but* two of them," even though some writers criticize this as a double negative. It is also permissible to begin a sentence with *but*. But it gets monotonous if you do it often.

but that, but what

Such sentences as "I don't doubt *but that* it will rain tomorrow" would be at least as good without the *but*. The use of *but what* for *but that* in such sentences is not standard.

calculate, guess, reckon

A generation ago *calculate*, *guess*, and *reckon* were quite generally condemned in schoolrooms as inferior regional expressions for *think* or *suppose*. Now *guess* is firmly established throughout most of the country, though it is still sometimes considered a "Yankee word" in the South. The Southern *reckon* now seems to be generally accepted but seldom used by Northerners. *Calculate* was always confined to a much smaller area than either of the others, and seems to be losing ground.

can, may, could, might

Schoolteachers have been battling against the use of *can* to indicate permission for generations, and have achieved some success. A good many people are careful to use *may* in this sense, and some of them are quite critical about those who say, "*Can* I go now?" But the general tendency is now to reserve *may* for possibility (He *may* go tomorrow), and to use *can* to indicate either permission or ability.

Could and *might* are sometimes used simply as the past tenses of *can* and *may*. They are also sometimes used to indicate a small probability. "I could do it tomorrow" is much less promising than "I *can* do it tomorrow." "I *might* go next week" often implies doubt, while "I *may* go next week" leaves the question completely open.

cannot, can not

Usage is divided but *cannot* is becoming more frequent than *can not*.

can't

Like all contractions, this is somewhat less formal than the uncontracted form. Otherwise there is nothing wrong with it.

can't help (but)

The competing constructions *can't help* (liking) and *can't help but* (like) are now both established as standard. The first is more frequent with personal subjects, the second with an implication of general inevitability: "The emphasis on grades *can't help but* encourage students to choose easy courses." However, both constructions can be used both ways.

Capitalization

Capital letters are used for:

1. *Proper nouns.* See page 276.
2. *Proper adjectives.* See page 350.
3. The pronoun *I*, both alone and in such contractions as *I'll, I'm,* and *I've.*
4. *Sentence capitals.* The first word of a sentence is normally capitalized, though advertisers and experimental writers sometimes use lower case to get a special effect. The first word of a quotation is capitalized only if it is also the first word of a sentence.

A cynic once remarked, "Virtue is its only reward."
"Virtue," a cynic once remarked, "is its only reward."
He called the new law "a fantastically silly piece of legislation."

5. *Lines of verse.* The first word in each line of verse is usually capi-

talized. If you are writing original verse you can suit yourself. If you are copying somebody else's verse, follow his practice.

6. *Titles of books, poems, articles, etc.* The most usual practice is to capitalize all words in a title except unimportant words of three letters or less that stand neither first nor last.

For Whom the Bell Tolls	*A Bell for Adano*
"The Man With the Hoe"	*The Rise and Fall of the Third Reich*

Cardinal Numerals

The numerals *one, two, three,* etc. are called *cardinal,* as opposed to the *ordinal* numerals, *first, second, third,* etc.

Caret

An inverted v used to indicate an omission.

daughter
She was the youngest∧of John Davies.

The word *caret* is Latin for "(something) is lacking."

Case

A *case* is a form of a noun or pronoun which originally indicated its grammatical relation to the rest of the sentence. Modern English nouns may have two cases, plain (or *common*) and possessive (or *genitive*). Pronouns may have three, nominative (*he*), possessive (*his*), and objective (*him*). In this book these are called the subject, possessive, and object forms.

1. *Uses of the subject forms.* The forms *I, he, she, we,* and *they* are always required as the subjects of verbs. This causes little trouble with single subjects, but double subjects and subjects followed by explanatory nouns need special attention:

STANDARD	POPULAR
He and *I* did it.	*Me* and *him* did it.
We girls had a picnic.	*Us girls* had a picnic.

The rule is simply to use the same form of the pronoun that you would use if it stood alone.

In distinctly formal English the subject form is also required when the pronoun is joined to the subject by any form of the verb *to be*.

It is *I*.   That must be *they*.

In good informal English, however, practice on this point is divided. The general feeling seems to be that the subject form is more correct, but that the object form is more natural and human. In spite of the general schoolroom insistence on the "correct" forms, a great many cultured people definitely prefer "It is *me*" and "That must be *them*." This is a point on which we can't please everybody, so we might as well please ourselves. The only variations really to be avoided are, "It is *me*—I mean *I*," and "It was *her*—ain't my grammar awful?"

About the same sort of divided practice is found in such sentences as:

He is as tall as *I* (or *me*).
She is better than *he* (or *him*).

If you want to avoid argument, you can say "as tall as *I am*" and "better than *he is*." Otherwise, take your choice.

2. *Uses of the object forms.* The object forms, like the subject forms, give little trouble when used alone. Very few people would say "I saw *he*," "Give *she* the book," or "That belongs to *they*." But a good many people do use the subject forms erroneously when the pronouns occur in pairs or are coupled with nouns.

STANDARD	POPULAR
Between you and *me*.	Between you and *I*.
I saw John and *her*.	I saw John and *she*.

The popular use seems to grow out of a feeling that the subject forms are somehow more elegant. It is the natural, though unfortunate, result of being corrected for saying "John and *me* were there." Mistakes in both directions may be corrected by the simple rule that *the form of a pronoun that would be used if it stood alone should also be used if it is coupled with another pronoun or a noun.*

If this sounds too complicated, try the following rules:

a. *Always* use the forms *I, he, she, we,* and *they*, as subjects, whether they are used alone or joined with other words.

b. *Never* use these forms as anything but subjects, unless you are perfectly sure you know all about grammar.

3. *Uses of the possessive forms.* For the form used before a participle

see under **Gerunds,** pages 300–301. For other uses of the possessive forms see pages 343–44.

censor, censure, censer

A *censor* (if he isn't taking a census) prohibits a book or deletes a passage. To *censure* is simply to blame without taking restrictive action; *censure* may also be used as a noun meaning adverse criticism. A *censer* contains incense.

center around

To *center around* is less logical than to *center on* or *upon*, but it certainly occurs more frequently, even in highly respectable writing.

central

This word is often used in a rather gasping attempt to sound important. "Occupies a *central* position in relation to" means "is in the middle of." The expression "is central to" presumably means "is important to" when it means anything.

Chinaman, Chinese

Many Americans think of *Chinaman* as the normal noun for a Chinese national. But the Chinese people prefer *Chinese* as both noun and adjective, and consider *Chinaman* to be a rather insulting term, like *Wop* or *Hunky*.

cite, site, sight

To *cite* means to call attention to, to refer to, or to summon before a court. A *site* is a place where something is, or is to be, situated. *Sight*, aside from the meanings connected with vision, is often used colloquially to mean "a great deal": "that will take a *sight* of doing"; "not by a long *sight*."

Cities

When the name of a city is followed by the name of a state or country, it is set off by a comma. Ordinarily the name of the state or country is not mentioned unless it is actually needed for identification. Thus we would normally write, *Paris, Texas;* but our readers might consider *Paris, France* rather countrified.

Coining Words

To make up a new word is to *coin* it. Obviously, all of our words must have been coined by somebody, and you have as much right to coin as anybody else, but it isn't wise to overdo it.

If you feel like coining a word for a special occasion, and do it in a way that is clear to your audience (for instance, "She is very *Aunt Lucified*"), suit yourself and take your chances. But if you coin by depending on an inaccurate memory, or by making a bad guess at words that are already in existence (for instance, if you write *sensitivify* instead of *sensitize*), you might as well expect unfavorable criticism.

Collective Nouns

Such words as *group, family,* and *set* are singular in form, but refer to a number of people or things. They are called *collective nouns,* and there is often a question whether they should be used with singular or plural verbs and pronouns.

As a general rule, if you think of the group referred to as a unit, use singular forms:

My family *owns its* own home.

If you think of the members of the group as individuals, use plural forms:

The majority *are* driving *their* own cars.

Don't worry about borderline cases—practice varies, and some people will think you are wrong whatever you do. It is better to write in a way that is clear, even if it is open to criticism, than to twist a sentence until it is "correct" but awkward or wordy. Even a mixture like "The committee *has* decided to make up *their* own minds" is at least as good as "The committee has decided that each of its members will make up his or her own mind."

Colloquial

The term *colloquial* originally meant simply "conversational." Most modern books on usage agree that *colloquial* now means something like "appropriate to the conversation and informal writing of educated people." Unfortunately, the word seems to be used in many schoolrooms as a term of reproach, almost equivalent to "illiterate." There seems to be no reasonable excuse for this attitude. Much of our best writing is decidedly colloquial.

Colon (:)

The principal uses of the *colon* today are:

1. After the salutation of a business or formal letter: Dear Sir: (Many writers use the *colon* after the salutation in any letter. Others use a comma or dash in informal letters. *Please* don't use a semicolon.)

2. To introduce an explanation (as in the first line of this entry) or list:

The following men will report for shots tomorrow: Baker, Colwell, Cummings, Novak, and Serna.

3. To introduce a quotation of more than one sentence, especially in rather formal writing.

4. To separate figures for hours from figures for minutes (10:45).

5. Some publishers use *colons* to separate certain items in references to books, but their uses vary so much that it is hopeless to learn a general principle. Follow whatever form is prescribed for a given publication.

6. The use of *colons* to separate certain types of clauses is much less common than it used to be, which is probably just as well.

combine

The verb *combine* takes the stress on the second syllable, with the first slurred. In the noun *combine,* both syllables are pronounced distinctly, with a slightly greater stress on the first. *Combine* is the correct technical name for a reaping-and-threshing machine, and is in fairly good informal use to indicate a political or business alliance, especially if you disapprove of its purpose.

We can expect trouble from the Schmidt-Davis *combine.*

It is not in good use as a substitute for *combination* in other senses.

Comma (,)

A *comma* indicates a minor pause, and anybody who can read aloud with reasonable skill can put in most of the necessary commas by ear. This is especially true if he realizes that the purpose of a comma is to help the reader understand the sentence with as little effort as possible, rather than to conform to rules. The principal uses of the comma are as follows:

1. *To prevent a false connection of ideas.*

Dick took Mary, and Betty took Jane.

Without the comma a reader would first get the impression that "Dick took Mary and Betty." Of course he could straighten it out, but he would have to backtrack.

While we were out shooting, Dick found a purse.

We don't want to give the impression that we were shooting Dick, or even outshooting him. If the second clause read "*we* found a purse," there would be no reasonable chance of a misunderstanding, and the comma would be optional.

We had to work fast, for John wanted to get home.
Jim, put up the car.
When we went out to milk, the sun was just setting

2. *In pairs, to set apart something not in the main line of thought.*

He is, I realize, trying as hard as he can.
Mr. Davis, who has a lot of experience, thinks it won't work.
His decision was, in the opinion of most of his friends, a serious mistake.
He had, to some extent, failed in his efforts.

In the last sentence above, as in many others, the pair of commas is optional. Since the interruption *to some extent* is too short to be confusing, we could write the whole sentence with no punctuation but the period. But use *two commas or else none.* Either comma alone is worse than useless, since it breaks the main statement instead of setting off the interruption.

3. *To indicate the place for a necessary pause.* When a sentence is long enough to require a pause somewhere, a comma is useful to show where the pause should be. Compare the following sentences:

If John were here we could do it.
If only the president of the Board of Athletic Control were here, we could probably do it without too much trouble.

It would break no absolute rules to take the comma out of the second sentence and put it in the first. But a comma would not make the first sentence any clearer, and it is a sound principle not to use a punctuation mark unless it accomplishes something. On the other hand, it is rather hard to read the second sentence without a pause, and a comma shows the best place for the pause—between the two clauses. If you prefer, you may learn the rule that "An introductory adverbial clause should be set off by a comma unless it is short and intimately connected with the movement of the sentence."

4. *To separate members of a series.*

He ordered orange juice, cereal, eggs, toast (,) and coffee.

The question whether the comma is necessary before the *and* has been bitterly debated, but the plain fact is that usage is fairly evenly divided. Most English instructors (including this one) use the comma in such positions, and miss it when it does not appear. But except for trick sentences, the omission of the comma would probably not cause any real ambiguity once in a year's reading.

5. *Between successive adjectives.* Compare the two following sentences:

He was a young, healthy man.
He was a healthy young man.

In the first, both *young* and *healthy* modify *man.* They therefore form a series and should be separated by a comma. In the second, *young* modifies *man,* and *healthy* modifies the combination *young man.* There is no series, and no comma is required, as you can probably tell by reading the sentence aloud. In borderline cases it is usually better to leave the comma out.

6. *Conventional uses.* There are a few special situations in which commas are expected regardless of whether a pause is indicated.

a. To separate two geographical units, one of which is included in the other:

Lima, Peru   Seattle, Washington
Essex County, New York

b. To separate the day of the month from the year:

June 18, 1947

When no day is indicated, a comma after the month is optional:

June (,) 1947

c. In figures containing more than four digits, commas are used to set off thousands, millions, etc.:

10,000   3,487,291

In four-figure groups a comma is optional except in dates, where it is not used.

d. To set off a name from a following degree or title:

J. F. Smith, Ph.D.   Robert Clark, Jr.
John Aley, M.A., LL.D.   Matthew K. Reis, Colonel (,)
                                  USAR

7. *Commas with other marks.* A comma is placed within final quotes, but after parentheses. It is not used after an exclamation point or question mark; but it should be used after a period indicating an abbreviation exactly as if the abbreviated word were written in full.

Comma Fault; Comma Splice

When a comma is used to join two independent clauses that have no grammatical relationship, the result is a *comma fault* or *comma splice*: Applications for graduation are due by April 25, all seniors must meet this deadline.

For a full discussion, see *Run-on sentence,* pages 191–93.

common

Originally *common* meant "belonging to the community," hence "shared" (common property), or "frequent" (a common idea). Later it came to mean characteristic of the lower classes. ("His manners are rather *common.*") This led to some ambiguity: a *common taste* might indicate either a shared one or a low one. Probably for this reason the phrase "a common friend" seemed to some speakers insulting, and "a mutual friend" was substituted. Since *mutual* originally meant "having the same relation to each other," this was illogical, and it is still regarded as highly objectionable by many speakers. However, the phrase is now very *common* (in any sense you like) in standard use.

Common and Proper Nouns

Theoretically, a noun which designates a particular thing is *proper* and should begin with a capital; and a noun which can designate any member of a class is *common*, requiring no capital unless it begins a sentence. Actually our habits of capitalization are too complicated to be covered in any definition of reasonable length. The following kinds of nouns are usually considered *proper* and written with capitals:

1. Names and nicknames of people and animals: *Robin Hood, Billy the Kid, the Brown Bomber, Man o' War.*

2. Names of specific institutions, events, ships, classes, etc.: *Phoenix Union High School,* the *First National Bank,* the *Western Open,* the *Civil War,* the *Normandie,* the *Twentieth Century Limited, Geography 100.*

3. Names of specific geographic features: *Lake Superior,* the *Rocky Mountains,* the *Mojave Desert, Tonto Creek.*

4. Names of cities, states, countries, regions, etc.: *Springfield, Idaho, France,* the *Near East.*

5. Names of the inhabitants of such places: a *New Yorker,* the *Texans,* an *Irishman.*

6. Titles when used to designate individuals: *Major Brown* asked the *Colonel* to assign him another captain.

7. Names of the months, days of the week, and holidays: The first *Tuesday* after the first *Monday* in *November* is *Election Day.*

8. Brand names: *Frigidaire, Eversharp, Camels.*

9. Nouns designating the Deity: *God, Jehovah,* the *Almighty.*

All other nouns are usually considered *common,* and are written without capitals.

There has never been a perfect agreement about which nouns are to be capitalized, and there isn't now. The style sheets of newspapers and publishing houses show some differences. Borderline cases are not worth worrying about, since there is no final authority.

compare (to or with), contrast

To *compare* one thing *to* another is to point out similarities. To *compare* a thing *with* another is to examine or point out both similarities and differences. To *contrast* a thing *with* another is to point out differences.

Comparisons

The early prescriptive grammarians, looking eagerly for "common errors" they could criticize, found a bonanza in the subject of comparisons. The rules they invented are still found in many textbooks, and are followed (or at least believed) by varying numbers of standard speakers. Since there is much division in both theory and practice, I cannot pretend to do more than offer the following opinions:

1. *Incomplete comparisons*

   a. The theory that all comparisons must be completely expressed is ridiculous. Such sentences as "It is warmer in here" and "She is looking better today" are entirely satisfactory unless there is a definite reason for being more precise—obviously some incomplete comparisons may be ambiguous. Others are deliberately misleading. The advertiser who says, "Supreme tires give you 20 percent more mileage" hopes the reader will take the statement to mean that Supreme tires will outlast any others, though if the truth of his statement is challenged he can defend it by saying that he meant "more mileage than 'ordinary' tires at half the price." But if we criticize his sentence it should be on ethical rather than grammatical grounds.

   b. Expressions like *as big or bigger than* will do well enough in conversation. It is perfectly natural to start a sentence with "This is as big or bigger"; and if we do, there is no reasonable way to go on with it but by adding *than. As big as or bigger than* is unquestionably correct, but sounds affected to many people. In careful writing the recommended revision is to "This is as big as his, or bigger."

2. *Illogical comparisons*

   a. The theory that some adjectives should never be compared because their positive forms have an absolute meaning can be cheerfully disregarded, although it still has some adherents. *Straighter, blackest, more perfect,* and *most complete* are quite as well established as *more nearly straight, most nearly black,* and so forth—and they are shorter and more forceful. For the one exception that is worth considering, see **unique.**

   b. Such sentences as "He is *taller than any* man on his team" generally pass unnoticed (except in English classes). Strict logic certainly demands *taller than any other,* but most people apparently feel that the shorter form is satisfactory, since the meaning is clear. Expressions like *tallest of any* have been used by reputable writers for six centuries, and no simple judgment of them seems possible. "He is the *tallest of any man* on the team" would be better with the *of any* deleted; but "He has the *worst* temper *of any* man I have even known" can hardly be tinkered with. It must either be accepted as established idiom or completely recast. I should accept it.

3. *Case of pronouns after* as *and* than. If you are worried about whether to say "as tall as I" or "as tall as me," add *am,* and the *I* becomes

inevitable. Otherwise, suit yourself and let somebody else worry. The same principle applies to *taller than*. The idea that *as* and *than* can never be prepositions is supported only by impassioned statements, not by evidence. *Than* seems to be a preposition in the almost too correct "than whom"; and so does the second *as* in the familiar injunction, "Never use *as* as a preposition."

4. *Superlative when only two things are compared.* The idea that a man with only two sons can only have an *elder* son, not an *eldest* one is an unfortunate throwback to the time when English had three grammatical numbers—singular, dual, and plural. It would be just as logical to object to "It is bigger than any of the others," since here more than two things are being compared. Also, we do not ordinarily insist on the *former* and *latter* halves of a football game. Either degree may be used in dual comparisons, and the superlative is often more satisfactorily emphatic.

5. *As* and *so.*

a. Some generations ago it was standard practice to use *so . . . as* rather than *as . . . as* after negatives. Today the practice is quite evenly divided. Suit yourself.

H. L. Hunt is not *so* (or *as*) rich *as* J. Paul Getty.

b. The phrases *as far as* and *so long as* are often used as conjunctions with no implication of comparison:

As far as I know, we'll be leaving tomorrow.
As long as he's here, we might as well try to get the matter settled.

It is quite common and legitimate to substitute a *so* for the first *as* in each of these.

complected, complexioned

Originally, the only correct phrase was *dark-complexioned*. The substitute *complected* is a back formation, coined (probably independently by a number of different people) in error. It is now widely used, but is certainly not fully accepted as standard, and is often ridiculed.

complement, compliment

Complement always refers in some way to completeness.

The ship had her full *complement* of men.
Boyd's practical experience *complemented* his partner's theoretical training.

The normal order of a sentence is subject, verb, *complement.*
Compliment refers only to praise or respect.

He paid her a *compliment.*
He *complimented* Suzanne on her dancing.

Complex Sentence

A sentence containing at least one subordinate clause. See pages
143–44.

Compound Predicate

Two or more verbs having the same subject are sometimes called a
compound predicate.

He *lives* and *works* in New York.
She *has been* here for a long time and *ought to know* better.

Compound Sentence

A sentence containing two or more independent clauses and no subordinate clause is called a *compound sentence.* See pages 142–43.

Compound Subject

When two or more subjects take the same verb, they are called col-
lectively the *compound subject.*

He and Leroy were there.
Dorfmann or Adams will pitch today.

Compound Words

A simple word such as *take* may be combined with another word or
with a prefix or suffix to make a compound word—*overtake, retake, take-
over, unmistakable,* etc. It is sometimes difficult (and it is for most people
unimportant) to determine whether a given word is simple or compound.
The chief questions that come up concern whether a compound word
should be hyphenated (see **hyphen**) and how the plural forms of compound nouns should be written (see pages 120–21).

(in) connection with

One of the single words *about, in,* and *with* will usually do at least
as well as this phrase.

I want to see you *in connection with* (*about*) your request.
His experience *in connection with* the college was unfortunate.

(In the second sentence either *in* or *with* would be clearer, depending on the meaning intended.)

Connotation and Denotation

As a technical term in logic the *denotation* of a term is the class of things to which it refers, and the *connotation* is the sum of what the term tells about those things. Thus the denotation of *planets* is simply Mars, Venus, Mercury, and so forth; the connotation is the sum of qualities that distinguish them from stars and other objects.

In ordinary use denotation is the simple and direct meaning of a word and connotation is what is implied in addition. It is difficult to draw an exact line between connotation and denotation in this use, and ridiculous to be dogmatic about "exact connotation," since people react very differently to the same words. However, the terms are useful if not overstrained. If a girl is 5 feet 7 inches and weighs 111 pounds, she'd probably rather have you call her *slender* than *skinny*.

conscience, conscious

Your *conscience* is supposed to guide your moral decisions. *Conscious* means "aware."

consensus

Consensus by itself means "the general opinion" or "an agreement in opinion," so that "*consensus* of opinion" is theoretically repetitious and is avoided by many careful writers.

considerable

Considerable is a perfectly good adjective, but is often misused in two ways:

1. To modify a verb, usually *help:* "That helped considerable" (should be *considerably*).

2. As a condensation for *a considerable* amount: "He wants *considerable* for his car."

Consonants

See **Vowels and Consonants.**

Construction

A grammatical pattern is often called a *construction*. For instance, "Eustace caught the fish" is in the *active construction*, while "The fish was caught by Eustace" is in the *passive construction*.

contact

Many English teachers are almost fanatically opposed to *contact* as a verb, presumably because it is much used by salesmen, and English teachers usually don't like salesmen (possibly because they usually can't afford to buy whatever is being sold). I don't use it myself, but it is obviously here to stay, even in standard usage.

content, contented, contents

We can say that a man is either *content* or *contented* (both stressed on the second syllable), but only "a *contented* man." When there is a choice, *content* is rather more formal.

The nouns *content* and *contents* take the stress on the first syllable. *Content* is used for the intellectual makeup, as "the *content* of a course," and for the proportion contained, as "the sugar *content* of the blood." *Contents* is used in a more physical sense, as "the *contents* of a box" or "the *contents* of a book" (you can get an idea of the general *content* of a book by examining the table of its specific *contents*). *Contents* may be used with either a singular or plural verb.

Context

The *context* is the language that accompanies the particular word or passage that is being considered. It is often necessary to examine the context in order to determine even approximately what is meant by a given word or statement. Thus to quote out of context often gives a very false impression. If a man says, "According to the John Birchers I am not a loyal citizen," it is decidedly dishonest to quote him as saying "I am not a loyal citizen."

The word *context* is sometimes used to mean the situation as well as the surrounding language, but this extended use is likely to be confusing.

continual(ly), continuous(ly)

Careful speakers use *continual* to mean "frequently repeated," and *continuous* to mean "without interruption."

He was in Paris *continually* for ten years. (he made many visits during this period)
He was in Paris *continuously* for ten years. (he was there the whole time)

Contractions

Such contractions as *can't, doesn't, he'll, I'd,* and *won't* are completely standard but rather informal. Since they look more informal than they sound, many people feel that they detract from the dignity of serious writing. It's a matter of taste.

could

See **can, may.**

council, counsel, consul

A *council* is always a group (the city *council*). *Counsel* means advice or the lawyer who gives it. A *consul* is a government representative in a foreign city. A *councilor* is a member of a council. A *counselor* is a person who gives *counsel.* A lawyer is a *counselor,* but may act as *counsel* for the defense.

couple

Originally *couple* meant a set of two joined in some distinctive way, as a married *couple.* Now it is often used to mean either simply two or a vague small number which there is some reason to minimize.

We had a *couple* of drinks.
Could you let me have a *couple* of eggs?

In such uses as the above, the *of* is often omitted.

A *couple* fellows were over last night.

This usage is not standard.

Course Names

The names of specific courses, such as *Zoology 100,* are regularly capitalized.
It is not necessary to capitalize such words as *history* and *zoology*

when they refer simply to subjects, but it is natural and permissible to do so when they are listed along with such subjects as *English* and *French,* which must be capitalized.

The names of all college departments are capitalized.

credible, credulous

Credible means *believable; credulous* means *too ready to believe* (all suckers are *credulous*). While we're in the neighborhood, *creditable* means *deserving praise.* (See also **incredible, incredulous.**)

cunning, cute

Cunning used to mean "craft" or "crafty," and sometimes still does. *Cute* is an abbreviation of *acute,* and formerly meant "sharp." We can't stop the ladies from using them the way they do, but men should find other adjectives.

current

See **archaic.**

curriculum

The new plural *curriculums* now seems to appear at least as often as the Latin plural *curricula.*

Dangling Modifiers

The phrase at the beginning of the following sentence is called a *dangling modifier:*

Raising the foaming glass to his lips, the minister suddenly appeared at the door.

A careful consideration of customs and probabilities suggests that somebody other than the minister was raising the foaming glass—after all, the minister wasn't even in the room yet; but the author of the sentence is certainly leaving himself open to either misunderstanding or ridicule. He should have written, "Raising the foaming glass to his lips, Eric suddenly saw the minister at the door." The word which a phrase is intended to modify should never be taken for granted, but should be put in as close to the phrase as possible so that a reader will automatically make the intended association. Dangling modifiers usually, though not always, contain participles. A few other examples follow:

After doing the dishes, the floor was scrubbed.

Revised: *After doing the dishes, they* scrubbed the floor.

To be a good pitcher, the batters must be studied.

Revised: *To be a good pitcher, you* must study the batters.

While driving to Prescott, a tire went flat.

Revised: *While driving to Prescott, we* had a flat tire.

Notice that the dangling effect is often caused by an unnecessary shift to the passive construction.

dare

Though *dare* is now normally regular, the older *he dare* still occurs along with *he dares,* especially in negative sentences. The same is true of *need:*

He *dare* not ask my help, and he *needn't* think I am going to volunteer it.

Dash (—)

The main purpose of a *dash* is to indicate some kind of a break in thought. Its meaning is less specialized than that of most of the other punctuation marks. It is therefore very popular with those who don't want to bother to decide between more precise marks and equally unpopular with many instructors, who regard it as a lazy way of avoiding difficulties. It is now used far more, even in quite formal writing, than it used to be. One reason is that it is visually effective—it shows up well and indicates a break in thought even to a reader who knows nothing about theories of punctuation.

Some writers, principally women, use nothing but *dashes* in letters. They seem to feel that, aside from the trouble this habit saves, it gives an impression of agreeable informality. (A girl I used to know broke off her engagement because her fiancé used semicolons in his love letters. She felt that true passion could not be accompanied by such precise punctuation.) This is, of course, a matter of taste. In general, a short passage containing nothing but dashes may be quite effective if the impression desired is either intimate chattiness or the sort of headlong rush of events that some TV announcers aim at.

The use of too many dashes in long passages is likely to be boring. They give the effect of unconnected bits of information, rather than ideas accurately fitted together. The four best-recognized uses of the dash are:

1. To indicate a sharp break in the line of the sentence:

He was very—but why go into that?

2. To serve as informal parentheses:

His war experiences—he had served in the Pacific—had taught him a good deal.

3. To introduce a rephrasing or summary:

His family, his education, his business experience—all his background had prepared him for this.

4. To indicate that a sentence is unfinished:

"I don't really think—"

data

This is a Latin plural form meaning "the given facts." There is not much occasion to use the singular form *datum* except in the technical sense of "point of departure." In other senses we are more likely to say "one of the *data*" than "one *datum*."

Dates

The traditional form for *dates* in the United States is:

April 2, 1957

The months are not usually abbreviated in the body of a paper. In references and other places where saving space is important, *May, June,* and *July* are written in full, *September* is shortened to *Sept.,* and all the others are reduced to their first three letters. When figures only are used, the order is the same as when the date is written out. Thus April 2, 1957 would be shown as 4/2/57.

There is now a growing tendency to put the day before the month, a practice which has advantages. If you write:

2 April 1957

you keep the two sets of figures distinct. But if you use this order and abbreviate it, you should use either letters or Roman numerals for the month to avoid misunderstanding. During World War II the Army adopted the form 2 Apr 57 (using the first three letters of each month, with no period). Many people now use the form 2/IV/57. Since most of us are too lazy to write a big number like 29 as XXIX, it is quite easy to remember that 2/IV must mean the second of April, not the fourth of February.

Any of these forms is acceptable, but 4/2/57 is less likely to be misinterpreted than any of the others.

Dative Case

In Latin the *dative case* was a separate form, used primarily to indicate the indirect object of a verb. No useful purpose is served by talking about *dative cases* in English.

Defining Terms

If you use terms that might be confusing or ambiguous, explain what *you mean* by them. But don't assume that your meaning is the only legitimate one, or that your readers will throw aside the habits of years just to conform to your practice. See also pages 55–59.

Denotation

See **Connotation and Denotation.**

Dialect

Some writers on the language still believe that there is one standard of "pure English" and that all other varieties are dialects, usually regional or characteristic of national groups, as *Scottish dialect.* Modern linguists take the view that there is no one uniform standard, and that anyone who speaks English at all must speak either some one dialect or a mixture of several. The three generally recognized major dialects in the United States are *New England, Southern,* and *Western* or *General American* (though some linguists use a different division and terminology). All of these can be subdivided almost indefinitely. Some regions with particularly strong foreign backgrounds have special dialects almost unrelated to the major dialects which surround them, e.g., Pennsylvania Dutch.

different from (than, to)

The traditionally standard American usage is *different from. Different than* is frequently condemned, but has actually been in good usage for centuries, and shows no signs of disappearing. In simple comparisons, *from* is generally preferable:

This is *different from* that.

In such expressions as "This is *different than* I expected" or "He does it *differently than* John used to," *than* has its advantages. We could not substitute *from* alone, but would have to use *from what* and *from the way*.

Different to is standard British usage, but very rare in America.

Diphthong, Digraph, and Ligature

A *diphthong* (pronounced *dif'thong* or *dip'thong*) is a combination of two vowel *sounds* running together in the same syllable—for instance, the sound of *oi* in *coin* or of *i* in *bite* (pronounced *bah-eet,* with the *ah* and the *ee* running rapidly together). The so-called "long vowels" which serve as the names of the letters *a, e, i, o,* and *u,* and which appear in such words as date, meter, rice, pose, and cute, are all actually diphthongs, as you will see if you pronounce them slowly and carefully (for a few people long *e* is a pure vowel, but most of us begin it with a sound like the *i* in bit).

A *digraph* is a combination of two letters used to represent a single sound—for instance, the *ea* in *breath* or the *th* in *that* (the sound represented by *th* is just as simple as the sound represented by *f* in *fat*).

A *ligature* is a special character consisting of two letters joined—for instance, æ.

Unfortunately the three terms are often confused. It is not uncommon to hear digraphs called diphthongs or ligatures called digraphs. It is therefore important to make sure that you understand how a given writer or speaker is using each term.

If changes in English spelling had kept up with changes in pronunciation, most of this confusion could be avoided; but we have to get along with what we have.

disinterested, interested, uninterested

An *interest* may be either a matter of curiosity (an *interest* in botany) or a definite share (an *interest* in a mine). *Interested* may mean having either kind of interest. The word for "not curious" is *uninterested*. *Disinterested* means "having no share in the matter and therefore unbiased."

A judge or referee should be *disinterested* but not *uninterested*. A student should be *interested;* but when he is bored he should call himself *un-*, not *dis-*.

Division of Words

The best general rule for dividing words at the end of a line is, "When in doubt, don't do it." It is easier to read a paper with a fairly irregular right-hand margin than one with many divided words. When a word is obviously composed of several parts, the division should come between the parts (*re-store*, but *rest-ing*). Otherwise, the division should reflect pronunciation (*cam-el* but *cha-meleon*). Double consonants are usually split, unless they come at the end of a word to which an inflectional ending as distinguished from a suffix is added (*pas-sage* but *pass-ing*).

There are so many borderline cases that even the most elaborate set of rules is not completely reliable. Never divide a word in the middle of a syllable, and go by pronunciation, not appearance. *Walk-ed* is as bad as *thro-ugh*, though *add-ed* is permissible because the *-ed* is pronounced separately. Also, never leave a single letter on either line: both *a-bout* and *man-y* are considered wrong.

don't

As a contraction for *do not, don't* is appropriate except in very formal writing. As a substitute for *doesn't*, it is widely used and sometimes defended, but a great many people who are broad-minded about speech in general find this use particularly irritating.

Double Comparatives

Double comparatives and superlatives, such as *more dearer* and *most unkindest* were once in good use, but are now generally considered illiterate.

Double Negative

In older English, double (not to mention triple and quadruple) negatives were common even in literature; and the statement that "two negatives make an affirmative" is not accurate, no matter how often it has been repeated. It is true, however, that some types of double negative are no longer standard.

1. A speaker who applies two negatives to *different* words usually means to strengthen the negative idea rather than to reverse it; and his intention is usually perfectly clear to the audience:

I have money.

I have *no* money.
I *haven't no* money.

It is silly to say that the third sentence "really means" the same thing as the first. But it is quite accurate to say that it is not standard English. Most educated people carefully avoid clear-cut double negatives of this type.

2. There are some words in English that have a negative implication without an obviously negative form, such as *but, hardly,* and *only.* Look at these three sentences:

There are*n't but* two of them
He has*n't* made *hardly* any effort.
There are*n't only* two days left.

The first of these is standard, in spite of theoretical objections. The second is a careless slip, which should be corrected in revision. The third is practically illiterate.

doubt

Doubt that means quite as much as *doubt but that* or *doubt but what.* When the more formal usage is also shorter and simpler, it might as well be used.

dove, dived

Both forms are common in standard use; but *dived* is seldom questioned, and *dove* is often criticized.

draft, draught

Both forms are pronounced *draft,* and are interchangeable in most uses. *Draught* is rapidly disappearing in America.

drought, drouth

Interchangeable. *Drouth* seems to be gaining.

due to

Many English instructors object strongly to *due to* as a connective ("*Due to* the lack of rain, the crops were in poor condition"). Nevertheless, such uses appear frequently in standard writing. They are a rather natural development of the undoubtedly correct use: "The poor condition of the crops was *due to* the lack of rain." In other words, *due to* has developed exactly like *owing to,* but rather later.

As a matter of effective style, *due to* is as good (aside from prejudice) as *owing to* or *because of;* but a simple *because* is often preferable to any of the three, since it leads naturally to a more direct statement:

> We could not get anything done, *due to* (or *owing to,* or *because of*) the absence of the president.

Because is always better than *due to the fact that.*

each

When *each* is the subject, it takes a single verb.

> *Each* of the houses *has* its own candidate.

When *each* merely modifies the subject, it does not affect the form of the verb.

> The four *boys each make* their own decisions.

effect

See **affect.**

e.g.

E.g. means "for example" (from Latin *exempli gratia*). There is not much point in using it except when space is precious.

either

The usual American pronunciation is *eether.* The pronunciation *eyether* is legitimate if it comes naturally; but if you deliberately change to it you will probably lose more admirers than you will gain.

Either usually refers to choice between two. When the reference is to more than two, *any* or *anyone* is preferable.

Either normally takes a singular verb, and is referred to by a singular pronoun.

elder, eldest

These old forms of *older* and *oldest* have practically passed out of use except in such set phrases as *elder statesmen* and (very formally) *eldest son.*

Ellipsis (. . .)

The principal use of the *ellipsis* is to indicate that something has been omitted from quoted material. This makes it possible to leave out parts that are not important to your purpose. It is never permissible to shorten a quotation without indicating that something has been left out.

> *Original:* The bill, which had been hotly debated for several days, finally passed by a vote of forty-two to thirty-nine.
>
> *Quotation:* According to Hofstetter, "The bill . . . finally passed by a vote of forty-two to thirty-nine."

Some careful writers use a fourth period when the material omitted comes at the end of a sentence in the original.

> *Original:* He died twenty minutes later, in spite of all our efforts to save him. We buried him the next day.
>
> *Quotation:* J. F. Buchsbaum says: "He died twenty minutes later. . . . We buried him the next day."

Some writers use the ellipsis for other purposes, such as to indicate a decided break in thought, or to show that sentences of their own are unfinished. There is nothing wrong with doing this if you like the effect, but there is no reason for learning rules about it.

Elliptical Constructions

An elliptical expression is one in which one or more words are implied rather than directly stated. There are two common and legitimate types:

1. Omission of one or more words to avoid repetition.

John went one way, Dick (went) the other (way).
She sings better than Mary (sings).

The word omitted need not be in exactly the same form as the word expressed. "She sings better than you (sing)" is as correct as "She sings better than Mary."

The rule that all comparisons must be completely expressed need not be taken seriously. "I feel better today" is just as good as "I feel better today than I did yesterday," unless the speaker wishes to emphasize a contrast between the two times. The *as . . . than* construction has also been given more attention than it is worth.

He is *as tall or taller than* John. (in standard use, in spite of theoretical objections)
He is *as tall as or taller than* John. (theoretically correct, but hardly attractive)
He is *as tall as* John, *or taller.* (correct *and* natural)

2. Omission of elements which are obvious because of either the situation or the neighboring words.

(I) am leaving tomorrow.
(You had) better not drive so fast.
While (he was) in the Army Jake learned a good deal about radios.
Two, please.

Obviously, an element should not be omitted unless the meaning is clear without it. In "Two, please" the situation should tell us whether the request is for tickets or doughnuts. But it is rather silly to theorize that this is a sentence with both subject and verb "understood." We need be concerned only with whether it is clear and appropriate.

else

There are still a few people who write *somebody's else* as a matter of flaming principle; but *somebody else's* is now almost universal in standard English.

emigrant, immigrant

Both words refer to the same person, but from different viewpoints. An *emigrant* from Austria is an *immigrant* when he gets to America. The *e-* comes from the same word as *ex-*, meaning out, the *im-* is a modification of *in*. Since most migration is in this direction, we have many more occasions to use *immigrant*.

emigrate

See *immigrate.*

en-, in-

The prefix *in-* sometimes has the general meaning of *in* or *on,* sometimes a negative meaning (*inanimate, inedible*). *En-* is a variant for the first of these only.

Some words are spelled only with one or the other of these forms—*encourage, enforce, infect, insist.* Others may be spelled either way, with usage quite evenly divided.

enclose, inclose
endorse, indorse

If you are quite sure that one form is correct, use it and don't worry about whether it is "preferred." If you are not sure, look it up.

enthuse

Enthuse is what is called a "back formation." People familiar with the noun *enthusiasm* assumed that it must have developed from a verb *enthuse,* so they used the verb—coining it without knowing that they were doing so.

A great many people, including this writer, do not like the word, but it is obviously more economical than "be enthusiastic" and often appears in standard English.

envelop, envelope

The verb has no final *e* and is pronounced *en-vel'-up.* The noun has a final *e* and takes the stress on the first syllable, which is usually pronounced *en,* but sometimes *on.*

equally as

If one thing is *as good as* another, the two are *equally* good. The combination *equally as* is seldom necessary.

etc.

An abbreviation for *et cetera,* which is equivalent to *and so forth.*

1. Notice that the *t* comes before the *c.*
2. This form should be used only when there is a real need for saving space. Most instructors dislike it in the body of the paper.

3. If you do not abbreviate, *and so forth* is usually preferred to *et cetera* written in full.

4. There is no justification for the form *and etc.*, which invites, and usually receives, ridicule.

euphemism, euphuism, euphony

A *euphemism* is a pleasant or colorless term substituted for one regarded as unpleasant. *Pass away* for *die* and *social disease* for *syphilis* are examples. One trouble with the process is that the substitute often becomes the normal direct term, and a further euphemism is developed. During the nineteenth century this verbal delicacy was carried to lengths now generally regarded as ridiculous.

The current standard tendency is to use the direct and simple word unless there is a real social taboo, as there is about some of our four-letter words.

The best advice is probably to call a spade a spade whenever you can do it simply and naturally. If you do it with a sense of great daring you will probably be considered young rather than sophisticated.

Euphuism is the name given to a very elaborate and artificial style that characterized some writing in the Elizabethan period.

Euphony means simply the quality of "sounding well." Since we don't all have the same tastes, it is hard to be successfully dogmatic about this subject; but if you write a sentence that is difficult to read aloud, or has too strong an unintentional rhythm, or has a sound effect inappropriate to the subject, you may be told that it is not *euphonious*.

everybody, everyone

Everybody and *everyone* are interchangeable. In their usual meanings they are written as single words, but when the second element is stressed they are divided.

Almost *everybody* was there.
Almost *everyone* was there.
Almost *every body* of water in the state is low.
Almost *every one* of the pieces was broken.

Everybody and *everyone* should be used with singlar verbs, but may be referred to by plural pronouns.

Everybody is expected to bring *his* (or *their*) own tools.
Practically *everybody is* coming, but *they aren't* all staying.

For other compounds with *every,* see **any and its compounds.**

ex-

Ex-, meaning "former," may be used as a hyphenated prefix with anything reasonable:

ex-husband   ex-schoolteacher   ex-senator

except, accept

Except means "leave out"; *accept* means "receive" or "agree to."

Exclamation Point (!)

The *exclamation point* may be used to give emphasis to a whole sentence or to a particular word.

Ouch, that hurts!
Ouch! That hurts.
Ouch! That hurts!
I should say not!

It is usually considered as ending a sentence, and is thus followed by a capital letter. It may be enclosed in parentheses to call special attention to a word within a sentence.

He had seventeen (!) hats and half a dozen overcoats.

If there is the slightest doubt about using an exclamation point, leave it out. Too many of these marks are likely to give an effect of gushing.

excuse, pardon

The choice between these words is, of course, a matter of taste and habit. On the whole, *excuse me* has the better standing as a social term. *Pardon me* seems to be considered more elegant by some speakers, but for this very reason is regarded as rather ridiculous by many others, who use it only when they want to be slightly sarcastic. *I beg your pardon* is often used to mean "I disagree." *Pardon* alone sounds very small-townish to many ears.

expect

Expect, in the sense of "suppose," is a normal British idiom, but has hardly been naturalized in America.

falls

We usually say, "The *falls* are 30 feet high," but we may speak of "a *falls*." There is no logic whatever in this combination of practices, but it is convenient.

famed

Famed is often used in newspapers as a substitute for *famous*, presumably because it is shorter. In other types of writing there is usually room for the extra letter.

farther, further

Farther is never used as a verb, and almost never in the sense of *additional* or *additionally*: otherwise the two forms are interchangeable.

He will do his best to *further* your interests.
They made no *further* effort.
It is *further* (or *farther*) along in the book.
They walked *farther* (or *further*) into the woods.

faze

Faze is a respectable, though slightly informal, word meaning to embarrass or disconcert. It may also be spelled *feaze* or *feeze*, but not *phase*, which is an entirely different word.

feel (bad or badly, good or well)

"He *feels bad*" is generally preferred to "he *feels badly*."
"He *feels good*" generally refers to a mental attitude.
"He *feels well*" refers to the state of his health.

fewer

See **less**.

fiancé, fiancée

One *e* for a man and two for a woman. The accent mark is beginning to disappear. Usually pronounced something like *fee-on-say.*

Figures of Speech

The two most important *figures of speech* are *metaphors* and *similes* (which see). The passion for classifying which resulted in the development of special terms for subvarieties of metaphors (*hendiadys, metonymy, synecdoche,* etc.) and for almost every other use of language that was not completely straightforward (from *anacoluthon* to *zeugma*) has now abated considerably.

fine

In spite of objections, *fine* is in widespread standard use to modify verbs.

That works *fine.*

first rate, first-rate

With or without a hyphen, *first rate* is in standard use to modify a noun (a *first rate* play), but not to modify a verb (he did *first rate*).

fish

The usual plural is *fish*, though *fishes* may be used either to individualize as in the song title "The Three Little Fishes" or to indicate separate species, as in "Bass and trout are the two *fishes* that I most like to catch." In the latter use, *kinds of fish* is more usual than *fishes.*

fix

Fix is now standard in the sense of "repair" or "arrange satisfactorily" as well as in earlier meanings. As a noun meaning "predicament" it is still considered very informal; but since comparatively few people ever use *predicament, fix* will probably soon be fully accepted in this use also.

folk, folks

In the sense of "family," British usage calls for *folk.* American usage calls for either *folks* or some entirely different word. In the sense of people in general, *folks* is folksy.

Foreign Plurals

The tendency now is to use English plurals for words of foreign origin whenever both English and foreign forms are current. For the formation of the most common plurals, see page 119.

Foreign Words in English

There was a time when it was rather generally felt that foreign terms added a touch of grace to English. Now the tendency is to feel that a foreign word should be used only when there is no satisfactory English substitute (*geisha, samovar*). Exceptions may reasonably be made in fiction when a foreign flavor is desired, or when addressing a selected audience who may be expected to know the foreign words.

Formal English

A generation ago "Formal English" was often regarded as the only really "correct" English. Now the tendency is to use the word *formal* literally, to indicate an attitude rather than a "level."

former, latter

These two words are not exactly obsolescent, but they are certainly used much less than they used to be. The current tendency is to use either *first* and *second* or *first* and *last* when comparing two units. A football game never seems to have a *latter* half, though a book still may. Neither now has a *former* half. Moreover, if you refer to Smith and Jones in one sentence, it is usually better to repeat the names in the next sentence than to call one of them the *former* and the other the *latter*.

Fragments

A group of words punctuated as a sentence, but lacking either the subject or the main verb, is called a *fragment*—unless the instructor thinks that the lack is both intentional and satisfactory. See pages 189–90.

freshman

Only the singular form is used as a modifier (the *freshman* class). As nouns we use one *freshman*, several *freshmen*. A capital is not required, but may be used when the *Freshman Class* is mentioned as a specific organization.

full, -ful

When *full* is used as the last half of a word it is shortened to *-ful* (*careful, spoonful*).

Function Words

Words which have no definite meaning of their own, but are used merely to fill out a grammatical pattern, or to indicate the particular way in which other words are used, are called *function words.* Auxiliary verbs and connectives are most often used in this way. In the sentence "He has money," *has* is equivalent to *possesses,* and is a "full" word. But in the sentence "He has gone," *has* merely indicates the time of the main verb, and is a function word. The words italicized in the following sentence are all function words:

The wife *of the* gardener works *more* rapidly.

Compare this with:

Johnson's wife works faster.

It is impossible to draw a clear line between function words and "full" words, and useless to split hairs about them. It does little good to attempt to analyze function words logically. We simply have to develop the accepted habits, and the less we think about them the better. They are hard on foreigners simply because a logical approach to them will not work. We could just as well say "attorney *of* law" and "doctor *at* medicine," but we don't.

funny

Except in very formal English, *funny* is a perfectly good word for "odd."

further

See **farther.**

Fused Sentence

In a *fused sentence,* two statements that could stand separately are joined without punctuation or a connective: I have to break that date I am studying for an exam. See also *Run-on sentence,* pages 191–93.

Gender

It is often said that English has "natural gender," while many other languages have "grammatical gender." For instance, in French the word for *pencil* is masculine and the word for *pen* is feminine. Actually, *gender* is a purely grammatical phenomenon, and English has none. We use some words only to refer to female beings, or as things personified as female, but we do not have special forms of adjectives to modify them. If we refer to an actress as *she,* it is because the actress is a woman, and not because the word *actress* is feminine. If the term *gender* were dropped entirely in discussing English grammar, nothing would be lost.

Genitive Case

Another term for the possessive case, always used in referring to Latin and German, and preferred by some grammarians in referring to English. If you use it, notice that the middle vowel is *i,* not *e.*

genteel

This word formerly meant "well bred." Now it usually means something like "trying to act well bred and not making it."

gentleman

There was a time when a man of assured social position was regularly referred to as a *gentleman;* to call him a *man* was almost insulting. The general feeling now is that *man* is good enough for anybody, and should be used unless you are specifically calling attention to certain (or perhaps uncertain) desirable qualities, as in "That *man* is a real *gentleman.*"

Gerunds

Some grammarians call present participles *gerunds* whenever they are used as nouns. By so doing they can distinguish between the two following sentences:

I don't like Betty's working. (I disapprove of Betty's activity)

I don't like Betty working. (I don't like Betty when she works)

In the first they call *working* a gerund modified by *Betty's*; in the second they call it a participle modifying *Betty*.

This theory is ingenious rather than sound. In Latin the gerund *operandum* is obviously different from the participle *operantem*, but in English the one form *working* serves both purposes and might as well be called a participle all the time. The fact is that both expressions are in good use in the first meaning, with the plain form gaining ground. Moreover, since the supposed distinction between the two will not be caught by one reader in a hundred, it is clearly not a very dependable basis for communication. We can therefore forget about the "gerund" and notice only the following points:

We automatically use the possessive form:

1. When the participle indicates an accomplishment rather than a temporary activity:

He likes *Betty's* cooking.

2. When the participle is used as the subject:

Schlegelmeyer's pitching won the game.

Otherwise we may take our choice.

get, got, gotten

The verb *get* has a very wide range of meanings. The simple sentence "I *got* him," for instance, might mean "I engaged him," "I killed him," "I understood him," or several other things. *Get* also enters into a bewildering variety of combinations. We may *get up* or *down, hot* or *cold, sick* or *left. married* or *beaten, away* or *away with something*. We may *get going*. We don't *get coming*, but we may *have got it coming*. Possibly one reason so many teachers have a strong prejudice against *get* is that it is very hard to explain.

Some of the uses of *get* are definitely informal, some are not standard, and some are slang. But it would be hopeless to attempt a complete analysis—there is too much disagreement about which is which. Only a few of the most debated uses will be discussed here.

1. It is often said that *got* is redundant when used with *have*, whether to indicate possession or necessity.

Have you *got* any apples? (Have you any apples?)
He has *got* to do it. (He has to do it.)

It is true that *got* does not add anything to the theoretical meaning of these sentences; but it is also true that *have* is used so often as an auxiliary that it is likely to seem a little bare when used alone. Since we regularly say, "Have you found any apples?" "Have you sold any apples?" and so forth, it seems natural to say, "Have you got any apples?" rather than to vary the pattern by using *have* alone.

To indicate necessity, *has got to* strikes many people as more satisfactorily emphatic than *has to*. Both idioms are certainly standard, no matter how often they are criticized.

The practice of leaving out the *have* and using *got* alone in these meanings is not recognized as standard, though many standard speakers who think they are saying "I've got" often sound as if they were saying "I got to go" or "I got enough now."

2. The past participle *gotten* has disappeared in British usage, but is a permissible form in American usage in the sense of "become" or "procured." Thus we can say either "He had *got* tired of it" or "He had *gotten* tired of it," "He has *got* the tickets" or "He has *gotten* the tickets." It is also permissible in many verb-connective combinations, as "It had *got* (or *gotten*) away from him." But *gotten* is never used to indicate either necessity (He has *got* to do it) or simple possession (He has *got* a farm in Pennsylvania). It is not necessary to memorize rules about this. If you can't trust your ears, remember that *got* can be used in any sense, and avoid *gotten*. But *forgotten* is the only standard past participle of *forget*.

girl friend

See **boy friend.**

good, well

In standard usage *good* is used only to modify nouns and pronouns. There is no logical reason why "He pitched *good*" should be any worse than "He pitched *fast*," but so much classroom time has been spent objecting to the extended use of *good* to modify verbs and other modifiers that it has become an important shibboleth.

Well may be used as an adverb or an adjective. As an adverb, its meaning is *ably*:

The plan was *well* constructed.
He drove *well*.

As an adjective, *well* has several meanings:

It is *well* to avoid discussion of the bond issue.
All's *well* that ends well.
He is now a *well* man.

In the first sentence, *well* means *advisable*; in the second, *pleasing* or *satisfactory*; in the third, *healthy*.

good and

In the sense of *very*, *good and* has an informal flavor, but is definitely established in standard English.

good-bye, good-by

The form with the final *e* is older, but both are now standard. With either spelling the hyphen is optional.

graduate

The passive construction ("He *was graduated* from Cornell") has been almost completely replaced by the active ("He *graduated* from Cornell"). However, if you like the academic flavor of the former, it is still permissible and will impress some people favorably.

grounds

In the sense of *reason(s)*, *grounds* may be either singular or plural:

What were the *grounds*?
The only *grounds* was cruelty.

guess

Guess, in the sense of "suppose" is now standard throughout most of this country. Some Southerners (who say "reckon") and some Britons (who say "fancy") object to it; but the schoolroom opposition throughout most of the country has about died out.

had better, had rather; would better, would rather

Had better, had rather, and *would rather* are all standard. *Would better* is decidedly questionable, though often used with conscious pride. *You better* (with the *'d* omitted) is not standard.

You *had better* get in the house.
I *would rather* (or *had rather*) kill a man than a dog.

half

A *half* is more specific than *half a*.

He ran *a half mile*. (880 yards)
He ran *half a* mile. (Approximately)

Similarly, *a half dollar* is a coin, while *half a dollar* is a sum.

The double construction *a half a* is common speech, but is generally considered careless or ignorant in writing.

hanged, hung

In legal language, murderers are *hanged* when they are executed, and many careful users of standard insist on *hanged* in this sense even in ordinary English. But the tendency to use *hung* in all senses is so strong and general (not to mention sensible) that "He was *hung* for murder" is now, on the evidence, in standard usage, though it is very likely to be criticized.

happen to be

Happen to be is a perfectly good idiom when there is a reason to bring out the element of chance:

I just *happened to be* working late when he called.

When there is no reason to emphasize chance, some form of *be* is usually better.

In other words, don't substitute "He *happened to be* hungry" for "He *was* hungry" unless you want to bring out an idea of rarity or coincidence. *Happened to be* for *was* is not only wordy, but often sounds apologetic or uncertain.

hardly

"I *have hardly* any left" means just as much as "I *haven't hardly* any left," and is more generally admired.

he or she (his or her)

The use of the double pronoun is overfussy. Ordinary *he* or *his* will do for a reference to mixed as well as purely male company. In a sentence like "Neither John nor Mary liked _____ assignment," the best way to fill the blank is with *their*.

height (not heighth)

Maybe the form with the extra *h* ought to exist in standard English, to go along with *width*, *breadth*, and *length*; but it doesn't.

help but

Such expressions as "I can't *help but* admire him," are criticized on theoretical grounds; but they have been in standard use for a long time and still are.

high school

High school may always be written as two separate words. Some writers hyphenate the combination, or even write it as a single word, when they use it to modify another word.

He went to *high school.*
A *high school* (or *high-school* or *highschool*) text.

It is usually capitalized when it refers to a specific school:

He went to the *Richfield High School* for two years. (Some newspapers would say *Richfield high school.*)

Historical Present

We are likely to be more interested in something that is still going on than in something that has already happened. Consequently there is a fairly general tendency to make past events seem more vivid by talking about them in the present tense. When a respected authority does this, we call it the *historical present:*

There *is* a silence in the great hall. The audience *is* tense, expectant. Then Washington *rises* to speak. . . .

If a less respected person does the same sort of thing, we call it vulgar:

I *play* an interesting hand last week. The bid *is* four spades and I hold. . . .

There is no justice.

A special (and paradoxical) use of the historical present is to refer to fiction and drama. We usually say that the historical Richard II *died* in 1400, but Shakespeare's Richard II *dies* in Act V.

There is no justice at all.

home

In spite of theoretical objections, "He is *home*" is established in both literary and conversational standard usage, along with "He is *at home*." On the other hand, "He is *to home*" is good colloquial English only in limited areas.

homey, homely

The British call a girl *homely* as a compliment, implying that she would be a nice, comfortable person to have around the house. We don't. Both we and the British may speak of a club as having a nice, *homely* atmosphere, but Americans are morely likely to substitute *homey* or (better) *homelike*.

Homonyms

Words with the same sound but different meanings are called *homonyms* (*sun, son; sight, cite, site*). Sometimes *homonyms* have the same spelling, in spite of different origins. Thus the verb *rock* (sway) comes from an Old English word; the noun *rock* (stone) comes from an unrelated French word. On the other hand, the same original word may have developed different spellings in different meanings. Thus we call the *flower* (best part) of the grain simply *flour*, though we have not found it necessary to develop a special spelling of *cream* in similar senses (*cream* of the crop, *cream* of wheat).

hope, hopes

We often use the plural where the singular would be at least as reasonable, especially with *high*.

His *hopes* were high.
He had high *hopes* of accomplishing something.

But the phrase *in hopes of* is not a standard variation of *in* (*the*) *hope of*.

however

The chief difficulty with *however* is in the question of what punctuation to use with it when it joins two clauses. Standard practice usually follows the following rule: separate *however* from the rest of the clause to which it belongs by a comma, and from the other clause by a semicolon.

They will make every possible effort; *however,* we should not expect too much.
Most people think of oranges as sweet and lemons as sour. This is not always true, *however*; there are sour oranges and sweet lemons.

When *however* in the sense of "nevertheless" occurs within a clause instead of between two clauses, it is set off by a pair of commas:

The president, *however,* decided on a different policy.

When *however* means "no matter how," it is not separated from the word it modifies:

However little he knows about a subject, he always expresses an opinion.

Hyphen (-)

1. *At the end of a line.* The *hyphen* is used to mark the division in a word carried over from the end of one line to the beginning of another.
   a. The division must be between pronounced syllables:

thought-less, but never *thou-ght* or *walk-ed*

   b. There must be at least two letters before and after the *hyphen*:

scar-ing and *ac-cuse,* but not *scar-y* or *a-cross*

   c. Double consonants are usually divided unless they come at the end of a simple word to which an ending is added:

com-mittee or *commit-tee* and *let-ting,* but *bless-ing*

d. In doubtful cases, the tendency is to put as many letters as possible after the *hyphen* without distorting the pronunciation:

hy-phen   *re-store*   *res-piration*

2. *With prefixes.* Prefixes are usually hyphenated when:

a. The root word begins with the vowel with which the prefix ends:

pre-eminent   *anti-intellectual*

b. The root word begins with a capital letter:

pre-Christmas   *un-American*

c. Confusion with another word might result:

re-mark (mark again), *remark*
super-vision (Superman has it), *supervision*

d. *Ex-* is used in the sense of *former:*

ex-professional   *ex-wife*

3. *To make compound words.*
a. Two-word numbers from *twenty-one* to *ninety-nine*, fractions (*five-eighths*), and words indicating relation by marriage (*brother-in-law*, etc.) are treated as permanent compounds.
b. Groups of words used as a unit to modify a following noun may be hyphenated in such uses.

He lived in the *eighteenth century.*	An *eighteenth-century* poet
He kept to the *middle of the road.*	A *middle-of-the-road* policy

Such hyphens may be omitted when there is no possible ambiguity (we could say "An eighteenth century poet"), but are very useful in indicating just which connections are closest. Compare:

The middle-of-the-road policy satisfied nobody.
Johnson had to leave in the middle of the road-policy debate.

c. In many words there is a variety in practice. *Tax payers, tax-pay-*

ers, and *taxpayers* are all in use. If you have to guess, the form with two separate words is probably the safest.

ibid.

Ibid. is an abbreviation of *ibidem,* a Latin word meaning "in the same place." It is used principally in footnotes, and refers to the work mentioned in the *immediately preceding* footnote. It should be underlined or printed in italics.

[1]Archibald A. Hill, *Introduction to Linguistic Structures* (New York, 1958), p. 126.
[2]*Ibid.,* p. 173.

Notice that *ibid.* is separated from the page number by both a period and a comma.

-ics

Nouns ending in *-ics* are usually treated as singular when they refer to a subject of study, but as plural when they refer to activities or qualities:

Tactics is a difficult subject. *His tactics* are sound.
Acoustics is the science of sounds. *The acoustics* are bad.

Idiom

The most frequent meaning of *idiom* is an expression which departs from the normal pattern of a language, or has a meaning that is not quite what you would expect, considering the meanings of the individual words.

He *had better* be there.   They will be *on hand.*

We learn these *idioms* by simple exposure, not by grammatical theory, and they are *hard* on foreigners.

The term *idiom* is also used in a quite different sense, to mean the characteristic expression of a language or dialect. Thus we might say that the English *idiom* is more direct than the German, or that a certain character speaks in the *idiom* of Brooklyn.

i.e.

I.e. is an abbreviation of *id est,* a Latin phrase meaning "that is." It is used chiefly when space is important, as in compact reference works.

if, whether

All of the following variations are acceptable:

I don't know *if he is coming*
        if he is coming or not.
        whether he is coming.
        whether he is coming or not.
        whether or not he is coming.

If the clause is used as a subject rather than a complement, we would use one of the forms beginning *whether:*

Whether (or not) he is coming hasn't been decided yet.

immigrant

See **emigrant.**

immigrate, emigrate

Immigrate means "migrate to." *Emigrate* means "migrate from."

Imperative Mood

In commands and requests with no expressed subject ("Be quiet," "Please come here"), the verbs are often said to be in the *imperative mood.* There seems to be no reasonable way of making mistakes in such constructions.

Impersonal Style

In many types of writing it is inappropriate for the writer to call attention to himself when he can reasonably avoid it; yet there are times when he must make a clear distinction between his personal opinions and established fact. About the best general principle to follow is to *be* as impersonal as is reasonable, but not to *pretend to be* more impersonal than you are. "It is the opinion of the writer of the present paper" is a very roundabout way of saying "I think."

imply, infer

Imply and *infer* are complementary terms. To *imply* is to indicate something without saying it directly. To *infer* is to gather more than has been directly stated.

His words *implied* that he did not trust me.
I *inferred* that he did not trust me.

in, into

The piano is *in* the next room.
They went *into* the next room.

These two sentences show the general difference between *in* and *into*. *In* primarily indicates mere location (in time, in space, or figuratively); *into* indicates a change of position or condition. When in doubt it is usually better to use *in*. "They went *in* the next room" is in good general usage, while "The piano is *into* the next room" is typical only of a few regional dialects.

The choice between *into* and *in to* can be determined by the natural pronunciation.

He came into (*in'to*) some money.
He came *in to* play.

in-, un-

Both *in-* and *un-* may be used as prefixes meaning *not*. There is no satisfactory general rule on which prefix should be used. Only *un-* is used with English roots (*unsung, unworkable*), but either may be used with Latin roots.

in back of

Many schools texts describe the phrase *in back of* as objectionable for one reason or another. Some of these prefer *back of*, and some insist on *behind*. But *in back of* goes naturally with *in front of*, and is definitely established in standard usage.

incidentally

This adverb is formed from the adjective *incidental*, not directly from the noun *incident*. The very common misspelling *incidently* has no standing whatever.

incredible, incredulous

Incredible means *unbelievable; incredulous* means *unbelieving*.

Indicative

An unnecessary term in English. See **Mood** if you are really curious.

Indirect Discourse

In indirect discourse, a writer puts into his own words the words of another or his own words from the past. No quotation marks are used.

I answered that I thought his daughter was very pretty.

When the subordinate clause is introduced by a verb of *thinking* in the past tense, the subordinate verb (or first auxiliary) is put in the past tense:

I thought I had answered the question.

The same principle no longer applies rigidly to verbs of *saying:*

He said he believed it would work.

or

He said he believes it will work.
Either is acceptable.

Indirect Questions

A question reported in a statement, but not quoted exactly, is called an *indirect question,* and does not require a question mark.

Original question: When are they coming?
Quoted question: He asked, "When are they coming?"
Indirect question: He asked when they were coming.

individual

For *each individual* read *everybody;* for the *majority of individuals* read *most people.* In fact, whenever you come across a writer who uses *individual* when he could just as well say *man* or *person,* it might be a good idea to change authors and read another book. *Individual* is occasionally useful as an adjective (*individual* portions) or even as a definitely technical noun (for instance, when the *individual* is contrasted with *society*); but it is far more often the first symptom of a creeping inflation of the vocabulary. A precautionary attitude is indicated, in order that exposure to this practice may not ultimately be reflected, with adverse results, in the stylistic characteristics of the individual. (This means "Look out or you'll be doing it yourself.")

infer

See *imply.*

Infinitive

In some languages the *infinitive* is a special form of the verb, not used alone to make a definite statement, and not limited as to person or number (hence the name). English has no exact equivalent of this form, but the term *infinitive* is often used to designate:

1. The plain form of the verb when it comes directly after another verb:

He will *go.*   They must *try.*

2. The phrase consisting of *to* plus the plain form:

To drive so fast is dangerous.
That is a silly thing *to do.*
He is going *to be* there.

Only the *to go* construction is called an *infinitive* in this book. As the examples above indicate, an *infinitive* may be used as a noun (*to drive* . . . is), as a modifier (thing *to do*), or as part of a verb phrase (is going *to be*). It may also be used in such sentences as:

He asked his friend *to do* that.

However, it is never used alone as the main verb of a sentence ("The Johnsons *to be* here today"). See also **Split Infinitive.**

inside (of)

Inside the house   The *inside of* the house

In expressions of time rather than space, *inside of* is used without the preceding *the* (*inside of* two months). More formal equivalents are *within* and *in less than.*

Intensive Pronouns

The compound personal pronouns (*myself*, etc.) are often called *intensive* when they are used to emphasize ("He did it *himself*") rather than to show "reflexive" action ("He cut *himself*").

Intensives

Words intended to increase the force of following words (such as *extremely, terribly,* and *very*) are called *intensives.* Our general tendency to exaggerate tempts us to overuse intensives, and thus to weaken them. Such words as *awfully* and *terribly* have pretty well lost their original meaning and are now practically synonymous, with considerably weakened force. *Quite,* which originally meant *completely,* now often weakens rather than strengthens the word it modifies. Other intensives tend to have the same effect unless they are pronounced with a strong stress.

inter-, intra-

Inter- means *between; intra-* means *within.* Thus *intercollegiate* sports are between different colleges, while *intramural* sports take place "within the walls" (*muros* is Latin for *walls*) of a single college.

Intransitive Verbs

See **Transitive and Intransitive Verbs.**

invite

Not standard as a noun.

Irony

Irony might be defined as a method of implying the opposite of what is actually said with a little more restraint than is characteristic of *sarcasm.* Suppose your roommate has borrowed your last clean shirt on the night of the junior prom. If you say, "You're a real pal!" you are being sarcastic. If you remark with apparent calmness, "There's nothing like having a bosom friend" you are being ironical. Never use *irony* unless you are either sure he'll get it or sure he won't.

We also speak of the *irony of fate* or *of events* when something happens that seems to make light of all human efforts or experience. When a star tackle breaks his leg playing ping pong or a man dies of thirst just an hour before a heavy rain, it is kinder to say "ironical" than "funny."

-ise, -ize

If you have to guess between an *-ise* and an *-ize* ending, the best rule of thumb is the following:

1. When the part of the word before the ending is complete or nearly so, add *-ize*.

apologize   characterize   memorize   standardize

2. When the part before the ending doesn't look much like a word all by itself, add *-ise*.

advise   despise   disguise   franchise   surprise

Many words are spelled with either ending.

Italics

See **Underlining.**

its, it's

Like all pronouns, *it* forms *its* possessive with no apostrophe. *It's* is legitimate only as a contraction of *it is.* If you remember that the apostrophe must be used to show the omission of the second *i* in *it is,* you may figure out that the possessive form does not need one.

it's me, it's I

In spite of almost frantic opposition, *it's me* has become the normal form in standard English. *It's I* is also permissible if you can say it without feeling self-conscious or overvirtuous, but it isn't worth a special effort, since it will probably lose you more admirers than it will gain. The same is true of *it's we.*

The expressions *it's her, it's him,* and *it's them* are not quite so well established, probably because we can usually substitute *it's Helen,* or *Jack,* or *the Smiths.*

Insistence on using the subject forms of any of these pronouns is now an indication rather of petty snobbery than of "good English."

-ize

See **-ise**

Jargon

Jargon means a form of language that is for some reason unintelligible. It is now most frequently used to indicate a kind of shoptalk which not only mystifies outsiders but often fools the speakers into believing that they are saying something much more important than they actually are. We can forgive a young doctor for saying "lacerations and contusions" for "scratches and bruises"— after all, he may have enough trouble collecting his fees, with the aid of big words. It is not so easy to forgive people who say things like "His failure to provide optimum motivation for his classes was traceable to the deficiencies of his preparation in subject matter areas, which resulted in an incapacity to provide adequate stimulation through the broadening of their intellectual horizons." This really is not a very good way to say "He bored his classes because he didn't know enough to teach them anything."

job

There are still people who think that *job* is less dignified than *position*. On the other hand, many employers feel that an applicant for a *job* might be willing to work, whereas a seeker after a *position* might be looking merely for a comfortable place.

It is still definitely slang to call a car or a girl "a nice *job.*"

judgment, judgement

The spelling without *e* in the middle is "preferred"—largely because it is so unnatural that people who know it are proud of their knowledge. The other spelling is now definitely established also. The same statements apply to *acknowledgment, acknowledgement.*

kind, sort

1. *Kind of* and *sort of* are both often used informally for *rather* or *somewhat:*

I feel *kind of* sorry about that.

Like many colloquial expressions, they look more informal than they sound, and sometimes seem rather undignified in writing.

2. *Kind of a, sort of a.* In such expressions as *a sort of a* handyman and *some kind of a* story, the *a* after *of* could certainly be dropped without affecting the meaning, and is often criticized as incorrect; but it is clearly established in standard usage.

3. Such expressions as *these kind of apples* and *those sort of people* have been in standard use for some seven centuries, and will probably continue in spite of frequent protests that *this kind* and *that sort* are required by the rules of agreement. It is just as well to "correct" these phrases in revision if you notice them.

lady

A generation ago it was generally considered almost insulting to call a woman a *woman*, unless she definitely belonged to what used to be called "the working class." It is now generally felt that *woman* is good enough to designate anybody, and that *lady* should be used only to indicate certain admirable qualities. Thus a speaker might reasonably make the following remarks about the same friend:

Helen is the tallest *woman* in the club.
You can always depend on Helen—she's a *lady*.

last, latest

Last may mean either *final* or *most recent*. *Latest* means *most recent*.

last, latter

Latter is used only in referring to a group of two units or two parts. *Last* must be used when there are more than two, and may be used when there are only two. We can say either the *latter half* or the *last half* of the month, but always the *last day*. (See also **former, latter**.)

lay, lie

The following expressions are standard.

present:	I *lie*	in bed.
past:	I *lay*	
present perfect:	I have *lain*	

present:	I *lay*	the book down.
past:	I *laid*	
present perfect:	I have *laid*	

"I lay down" may sound like "I laid down," and the fact that the past form of one verb is the present form of the other may seem unfair; but it really does not take a superhuman effort to master the standard uses, and enough people think the difference is important to make the effort it does take worthwhile.

l.c.

L.c. is an abbreviation for *lower case,* and means "use small letters instead of capitals."

lead, led

The noun *lead* is pronounced *led* when it refers to a metal, otherwise *leed.*

The present tense of the verb is spelled *lead* and pronounced *leed.* The past tense is spelled and pronounced *led.*

learn, teach

Such expressions as "That will *learn* him" and "The teacher *learned* them to spell" are not standard. Use *teach* and *taught.*

leave

As a synonym for *let, leave* is standard in the expression "*Leave* (or *let*) him alone," but not in such expressions as "Let him go."

However, Damon Runyon's very popular stories of Broadway characters started a widespread fad for a sort of slumming use of such expressions as "*Leave* us not be hasty." If you say things like this you are supposed to indicate by your tone that you really know better.

less, lesser

Less may be used in place of *fewer* in referring to numbers, as well as in comparing size or quantity.

There were *less* (or *fewer*) than ten members present.

Lesser is a rather formal equivalent of *smaller,* now little used.

let's, let us, let's us

Let's began as a contraction of *let us,* but in speech now usually has a different meaning.

Let us do it. *Permit us to do it.*
Let's do it. *I suggest (or urge) that we do it.*

In very formal usage (as in "Let us pray") the full form is used with the second meaning, and many people never use the contracted form in writing. There is, however, a growing tendency to recognize that it is not only legitimate but an aid to clarity. Misguided insistence on the full form is perhaps responsible for driving innocent speakers who want to be clear to the definitely nonstandard *let's us*.

liable

See **apt to.**

lie

See **lay, lie.**

Ligature

See **Diphthong.**

like, as

The idea that *like* should never be used to introduce a clause has no sound basis in either theory or actual usage; but a good many people believe it firmly, and are much disturbed by such sentences as:

He did it *like* I told him.
He acts *like* he is tired.

If you want to avoid their criticism. substitute *as* in the first sentence and *as if* in the second.

like for

In such sentences as "I'd *like for* you to see them," the *for* is sometimes condemned as redundant; but the construction has been standard for centuries.

likely

See **apt to.**

loan

Loan is now completely established as a verb in business transactions, but not otherwise:

The bank *loaned* (or *lent*) him four hundred dollars.

Many people whose general usage is standard would also say:

She *loaned* him a book.

Many others would insist that only *lent* is permissible in this sentence. If you don't mind criticism, suit yourself. If you do, use *lent*.

Localism

A word, expression, or pronunciation which is current in only a limited region is called a *localism*.

locate

Locate is a convenient word for "Find (or explain) the position of." It is seldom advisable in any other use. *Is located* seldom means any more than simple *is*.

loose, lose

Perhaps the best way to keep these straight is to remember that the verb *lose-lost* has only one *o* in both tenses; and that the expression "*loose* as a *goose*" rimes to the eye as well as to the ear.

lot, lots

Such expressions as "a *lot* of money" and "*lots* of friends" are standard, though a bit informal. Notice that the first of these contains two words (not *alot*).

mad

In America, *mad* normally means *angry*, not *insane*. When insanity is suggested, it is usually of a mild and often pleasant kind:

Such delightful people—quite *mad*, of course.
We were in a *mad* rush to get off.

madam

"Dear *Madam*" is the feminine equivalent of "Dear Sir," and may be used in a letter to any woman, married or unmarried. In speech, the contraction *ma'am* is generally preferred among friends, though *madam* is generally used by store clerks and waiters.

madame, mademoiselle, mesdames, mesdemoiselles

These are French words, and may be reasonably used to refer to French women. Otherwise, they are appropriate to advertisements in women's magazines, and common in small-town newspaper reporting.

Malapropism

Mrs. Malaprop (from *mal à propos*—inappropriate) is a character in Sheridan's *The Rivals;* she knew a good many big words but had very vague ideas about what they meant. If you use a word which sounds something like the one you are reaching for but has a very different meaning, you commit a *malapropism.* Example:

He proved it by *seductive* (for *deductive*) reasoning.

man, woman

In a more genteel age it seems to have been felt that to call men and women *men* and *women* implied that they were not ladies and gentlemen. This feeling has now largely disappeared. It is still conventional to *address* a group as "ladies," "gentlemen," or both; but we now usually *refer* to them as *men* and *women.*

may

See *can.*

may can

The fact that *can* is a defective verb, lacking both participles and the infinitive, is a ridiculous nuisance. We have to say:

I *can* today.
I *could* yesterday
I may *be able to* tomorrow.
I used to *be able to* do it, but I *can't* any more.

We really ought to be grateful for the constructions *may can* and *used to could,* which have been invented to make up some of the deficiencies, but the unfortunate fact is that they are not standard in writing anywhere, and are respected in speech only in certain limited areas, mostly in the South.

maybe, may be

Maybe is written as a single word only when it means *perhaps*.

Messrs.

This is an abbreviation for the French *messieurs,* and can be used as the plural of *Mr.* (*Messrs.* Smith and Alford). It is now dropping out of general use, and there seems to be no reason to mourn its passing. See also **Miss, Mr., and Mrs.**

Metaphors and Similes

A *simile* is a fully expressed comparison:

He is *as big as a moose.*

A *metaphor* is an expression which is not literally accurate, but which suggests a quality, perhaps more vividly than a simile:

He is *a moose.*

Mixed metaphors, in which the implied comparison changes without warning, are often ridiculous ("the hand that rocked the cradle has kicked the bucket"). It seems a little hasty, however, to condemn all mixed metaphors on principle. Hamlet's "to take arms against a sea of troubles" has worn very well.

Metaphorical uses of words are often so satisfactory that they become standard, and what was originally an imaginative suggestion becomes a new literal meaning—for example, "The *head* of any *body* needs a good *staff* to *carry out* his *plans.*"

Meter

The *er* spelling is now more common than the *re* in all senses.

In referring to verse, *meter* designates the rhythmical pattern.

Specific *meters* are usually indicated by a pair of words, the first showing of stress pattern (or in Greek or Latin the time pattern) of the foot, the second showing the number of feet in the line.

The most common types of feet in English are:

iambic—*along*   dactylic—*easily*
trochaic—*many*   anapestic—*in a rush*

A *spondee* (*manlike*) may be substituted for a dactyl, but is seldom the basic foot of a meter.

The number of feet is shown by compound words consisting of Greek numerals followed by *-meter*.

dimeter—two feet	pentameter—five feet
trimeter—three feet	hexameter—six feet
tetrameter—four feet	heptameter—seven feet

Thus a poem in iambic pentameter has a basic pattern of five iambic feet:

A bóok of vérses únderneáth the boúgh

might

See **can, may.**

mighty

In such phrases as "a *mighty* nice girl," *mighty* is often condemned on the double grounds of perversion of meaning and misuse of the parts of speech. Perhaps it is a bit informal for some types of writing, but some mighty fine people have been using it for a long time.

Miss, Mr., and Mrs.

In standard English these three words are fully satisfactory only when followed by proper names. The last two are used only in their abbreviated forms. Only *Miss* has a plural, and that is dropping out of ordinary use (most of us would say *The Miss Smiths* rather than *The Misses Smith*). The whole situation is very curious, and quite different from what we find in most other languages. We simply do not have any fully acceptable way of addressing strangers.

In French, for instance, you can call a stranger *Madame, Mademoiselle,* or *Monsieur,* whichever happens to be appropriate, without being either rude or overpolite. Even if you know (or are supposed to know) the person's name, the forms are perfectly acceptable. This is very handy if you are not quite sure of the name, or if it is too long to be convenient. But in English we almost have to choose between saying "Mr. Titherington" or "Hey, you!" Of course we can put in a *sir* or *ma'am,* but we don't often begin sentences with these words except in situations prescribed by discipline. The following suggestions for addressing people whose names you do not know are offered:

1. If it doesn't seem reasonable to call a man "Mac" or "Pardner," say *Sir* rather than *Mister*.

2. *Ma(d)am* stands higher than *Miss*, and should be used in all borderline cases.

The French plurals *mesdames* and *messrs.* (for *messieurs*) seem to be established in the society pages of newspapers, where they save a good deal of space; but most of us can get along without them elsewhere.

Mixed Construction

We often forget how we have started a sentence, and finish it on a different pattern. The first two of the sentences below are satisfactory; but the third, which changes from one pattern to the other, is an example of a *mixed construction*.

My father practices law, and I want to too.
My father is a lawyer, and I want to be one too.
My father practices law, and I want to be one too.

There are many varieties of mixed construction, and anybody is apt to slip into one in a hurried first draft. The way to catch them in revision is to be sure that you consider each sentence as a whole, and notice how the parts fit together.

Mode

A variant of the grammatical term *mood*.

Money

Sums of *money* should be expressed in figures when you want them to be easy to pick out (as in a business letter) or when it would be quite cumbersome to write them in words ($183.67). Otherwise, they should usually be written out, especially if they are round sums. There are no reliable rules.

The practice of writing out sums in words and then repeating them parenthetically in figures has now been generally abandoned except in certain legal forms.

Mood

Latin has three sets of verb forms, called respectively the *indicative*, the *subjunctive*, and the *imperative mood*. Some grammarians call the *infinitive* a fourth mood. Since English has only one set for all purposes, the term *mood* is unnecessary. However, there are a few idiomatic expressions which may be traced back to the time when English did have separate moods. These are discussed under **Subjunctive.**

moral, morale

Moral is connected with morals. *Morale* (rimes with *pal*) means "spirit."

The student body may not be particularly *moral*, but its *morale* is high.

most

Almost is often shortened to *most* in conversation. This is not advisable in writing, but if you do it, do it firmly and don't write *'most*.

muchly

Much can do anything that *muchly* can, and do it better.

must

The use of *must* as a noun ("This book is a *must*") and a modifier (*must* legislation) is quite recent; but on the evidence it *must* now be called standard.

mutual

See **common.**

myself

This is normal for emphasis ("I saw it *myself*") or for reflexive action ("I cut *myself*"), but should not ordinarily be used simply as a substitute for either *I* or *me*.

naive

Pronounced *nah-éev,* and now usually spelled with only one dot over the *i*. *Naive* is both French and English. *Naïf* is purely French, and quite unnecessary in English. The word means "unsophisticated" or "unworldly," often with a suggestion that the unworldliness is not quite bright.

need

In most uses *need* is a perfectly regular verb. However, in questions and negative statements, when *need* is followed by the plain form of another verb, we may use *need* instead of *needs* even with a singular subject:

> *Need* he ask that?
> He *need* not try that again.

It is now more usual to say:

> *Does he need to* ask that?
> He *doesn't need* to try that again.

neither

The usual pronunciation is *nee'ther*. *Neye'ther* is all right if it comes naturally, but is not worth practicing.

Neither should be followed by *nor* rather than *or:*

> *Neither* John *nor* his brother has been here.

Notice that *has* is singular.

nice

Nice is a word with a curious history. It meant first *ignorant,* then *silly,* then *precise,* and finally became a general expression of approval. It is a useful word when you want to be a little vague, or when you are too lazy to figure out exactly what you do mean, and it is often quite satisfactory in conversation. In writing, a more definite word is usually preferable.

no (in compounds)

See **any and its compounds.**

no use

The following variations are all standard:

> *It* is *no use trying* to help him.
> *It* is (of) *no use to try* to help him.
> *There* is *no use* (in) *trying* to help him.

It is not used with *in,* and *there* is not used with either *of* or *to;* but since there seems to be no temptation towards these combinations, it (or there) is no use worrying about them.

Nominative Absolute

Phrases like those italicized in the following sentences are usually called *nominative absolutes:*

That job finished, he turned to the next one.
Her husband being away, she could eat exactly what she liked.

They are called absolute after the ablative absolute in Latin. It would be hard to prove that they are nominative, since examples with the six pronouns that have separate nominative forms (I, he, she, we, they, who) occur only when specially manufactured for textbooks: He having finished his task, the class was dismissed. I have been trying unsuccessfully for years to find one in normal speech or writing.

Nominative Case

In English the only discoverable traces of the *nominative case* are the six pronoun forms, *I, he, she, we, they,* and *who,* which can just as easily be called the *subject forms.* The statement that "nouns used as subjects must be in the nominative case" is a meaningless carryover from Latin grammar.

none, no one

None was originally the negative form of *one,* and always took a singular verb. Now it seems natural to think of it as the opposite of *some,* and to use it with a plural verb. Take your choice.

None of them *has* (or *have*) any real interest in it.

No one is rather more emphatic than *none.* It always takes a singular verb.

No one of these books *is* very useful by itself.

Nonrestrictive Clauses

Another term for *amplifying* (or *descriptive* or *nonessential*) clauses. Amplifying clauses add information but do not provide essential identification:

Gene Jones, who was in town today, bought a new car.

They are always set off by commas.

not—Position in Sentence

Many teachers are fond of saying that such a sentence as "I *don't think* I can go" is illogical, because you *do* think (at least occasionally), and should therefore say "I think I cannot go." Unfortunately, the same teachers are likely to say "I don't like your attitude" and "I don't have enough time," though they do occasionally like and have other things. Their attitude might therefore be described as micro-logical or (more informally) as nit-picking. Unnecessary precision is often offensive as well as troublesome. Unless a real ambiguity results, *not* may be put wherever it seems natural. So may other words with a negative meaning or implication.

not as—not so

In completely expressed negative comparisons, either *as* or *so* may be used. *As* is now more usual.

This is not *as* (or *so*) good as the other.

In incomplete expressions *not as* implies a specific comparison, while *not so* is synonymous with *not very*.

He is not *as* old [as somebody].
He is not *so* [very] old.

notoriety, notorious

Notoriety normally means a sort of cheap substitute for fame, and *notorious* means "well known for unworthy reasons." Neither word is complimentary unless used by somebody who thinks that any advertising is good advertising.

Noun and Verb Stress

There are a good many pairs of nouns and verbs which are identical in their written forms, but are pronounced with a different stress.

NOUNS	VERBS
con'-trast	con-trast'
in'-sult	in-sult'
rec'-ord	re-cord'

The unstressed syllable is often slurred. When the noun may be stressed either way, there is more prestige in pronouncing it like the verb. I don't know why Adele's *perfume'* should be more fragrant than Sally's *per'-fume,* or Kent's *re-search'* more scholarly than Brook's *re'-search,* but they seem to be.

nowhere near

As an emphatic substitute for *not nearly, nowhere near* is standard. *Nowheres,* with or without a following *near,* is not.

number

When *number* is preceded by *the* it usually indicates a definite (though perhaps unspecified) number, and takes a singular verb:

The *number* of people who still believe in magic *is* amazing.

A number of is usually equivalent to *many* and takes a plural verb:

A *number* of the trees *were* damaged by the storm.

Number

There are two grammatical numbers in English, *singular* and *plural.* Most nouns have separate forms for the two numbers, and all the pronouns except *you* and *who* are limited to one number or the other. *Number* has disappeared from adjectives except in the pairs *this-these* and *that-those.* The only traces left in verbs are *am, was,* and the *-s* form of the present tense. See **Agreement.**

Number Forms of Nouns

Ordinarily there is no problem in choosing between the singular and plural forms of nouns. However, there are a few peculiarities in the uses of nouns indicating number, quantity, and measurement.

1. Such hyphenated compounds as the following are always used as modifiers, and therefore never take the plural form:

a *six-foot* tackle   a *forty-acre* pasture
three *two-quart* jars   ten *five-dollar* bills

2. When nouns indicating *number* are preceded by a word indicating plurality, they are usually put in the singular form. When they are not so

preceded, the plurality-of-their-plurality can only be shown by their endings:

Three *hundred* came. Hundreds came.
She has two *dozen* eggs. She has *dozens* of eggs.

3. Traces of this same distinction can still be found in nouns indicating *quantity* and *measurement,* but in standard usage these are now usually put in the plural even when preceded by a plural number, except in hyphenated compounds.

ten *tons* of coal (sometimes ten *ton*)
He was six *feet* tall. (sometimes six *foot*)

Numbers

Types of numbers. The numbers *one, two, three,* and so forth are called *cardinal numbers.* The numbers *first, second, third,* and so forth are called *ordinal numbers* because they name the order of things.

Types of numerals. The ordinary figures 1, 2, 3, and so forth are called *Arabic.* When the letters, I, V, X, L, C, D, and M are used to indicate numbers, they are called *Roman numerals.* Roman numerals are not used with perfect consistency (for instance, 9 may be indicated by IX, VIIII, or VIIIJ) but the most usual system is indicated below.

1–I	18–XVIII	110–CX
2–II	19–XIX	. . .
3–III	20–XX	
4–IV	21–XXI	140–CXL
5–V	. . .	. . .
6–VI	30–XXX	400–CD
7–VII	. . .	. . .
8–VIII	40–XL	500–D
9–IX	. . .	. . .
10–X	50–L	600–DC
11–XI	. . .	. . .
12–XII	60–LX	900–CM
13–XIII	. . .	. . .
14–XIV	90–XC	1,000–M
15–XV	. . .	. . .
16–XVI	100–C	1955–MCMLV
17–XVII	. . .	

You will notice certain principles in this system:

1. The basic letters stand for 1, 5, 10, 50, 100, 500, and 1,000.

2. No letter occurs more than three times in a row.

3. The normal procedure is to put the letters in descending order of size. Thus 1873 is represented by MDCCCLXXIII.

4. To prevent a letter from coming four times in a row, the numbers 4 and 9, 40 and 90, 400 and 900 are indicated by a kind of subtraction. Thus IV means 1 from 5, or 4; XC means 10 from 100, or 90.

5. Although small letters may be used for Roman numerals, capital letters are now more common.

6. Except for carving dates on banks built to look more or less like Roman temples, Roman numerals should seldom be used alone. However, they are useful when different kinds of numbers to indicate different levels are needed, as in outlines (II, A, 3), to distinguish volume numbers from page numbers of books, and so forth.

When to use words. Apparently there used to be a feeling that figures were a rather undignified substitute for words, and perhaps not quite legal. Formal documents gave even dates as "One thousand seven hundred and fifty-three," and businessmen played safe by writing out the words and then putting the figures in parentheses. This attitude has nearly disappeared, but words are generally used in the following situations:

1. At the very beginning of sentences:

Fifteen men, 26 women, and 13 children were on the boat.

2. When round numbers are used approximately:

It will cost you a thousand dollars for the round trip, and fifty dollars a day while you are there.

3. When small numbers are used in such a way that there is no reason to think a reader will want to find them rapidly (some people define "small" as under 100, others as ten or less):

It is only nine miles to Phoenix, but it is sixty-three (or 63) to Wickenburg and 196 to Flagstaff.

4. To indicate hours, when not followed by A.M. or P.M., or by the exact minute:

He came at seven o'clock and stayed until half past ten.
He came at 7 A.M. and stayed until 10:32.

When to use figures. In the following situations figures rather than words should be used:

1. For large numbers—see (3) above.

2. For small numbers when you wish to indicate that they are precise and not approximate. If you write "$5.00" your reader knows you have given him the exact figure. "Five dollars" might mean $4.98 or $5.15.

3. Whenever you have reason to think that a reader might want to find the numbers rapidly. Thus you might normally write *five* and *seven,* or even *nineteen* and *sixty-two.* But if you are dealing with percentages or temperatures, in such a way that your reader might reasonably be more interested in your numbers than your words, make it easy for him to find the numbers. Figures are easy to pick out.

Punctuating figures. Decimal fractions (including cents) are set off from whole numbers by a period (6.73%; $18.75).

Minutes are usually set off from hours by a colon, though a period is sometimes used (6:32 A.M. or 6.32 A.M.).

Ordinarily, figures larger than 999 are separated by commas into groups of three, beginning from the right (17,388; $13,466,791.46). But dates are punctuated only by separating the day of the month from the year (June 29, 1954), and street numbers are not punctuated at all (12473 Seventh Avenue). Some stylebooks require the use of commas only when the number contains more than four figures ($1750 but $17,500). This is not yet usual except in advertising.

Plurals of figures. The plural of a figure may be indicated by either *'s* or simple *s* (three 9's or three 9s).

O, oh

In very formal writing, *O* is a sign of direct address ("*O* king, I hear and obey"), and *oh* is an exclamation, though often a very mild one. Most people now use *oh* for both purposes:

Oh John, will you come over here?
Oh, I don't think so.
Oh! I never thought of that.

obsolete

See **archaic.**

of

Of is often added unnecessarily to other connectives:

He looked *out* (*of*) the window.
He stepped *off* (*of*) the porch.
His place is *outside* (*of*) the city limits.

Of these, *off of* is rather generally regarded as substandard. The others are now generally accepted.

The mistaken writing of *of* for *'ve* is a very common error:

He might *of* done it. (should be *might've* or *might have*)

Omissions

If a subject or verb is omitted a potential sentence becomes a fragment. If something else is omitted the result may be:

1. A logical contradiction:

[other]
Jim was older than any boy in the block.

∧

Without the *other* this says that Jim was older than Jim.

2. An unacceptable grammatical construction:

[had]
Allen had heard and Pete seen the bear.

∧

3. An obvious blank:

She had three children, a son in the Army and a married daughter in San Francisco. [Who and where is the third?]

4. Complete ambiguity when something is clearly missing but the reader can't tell what:

He looked for the knife was no longer there.

Everybody sometimes leaves out words. If you leave out many, make a practice of reading your papers aloud before handing them in—and be careful to read *only* the words that you actually see.

on, on to, onto, upon

When *on* and *to* are separate words that just happen to come together, they are written separately.

He went on to say more.

The single word *onto* may be used in a way that parallels *into*; that is, it indicates motion with the result of being *on* something. Theoretically, "He jumped *on* the porch" implies that he was already there when he jumped; while "He jumped *onto* the porch" indicates that he got there by jumping. Actually, *on* is now ordinarily used in both meanings, and is always the safer choice in doubtful cases. Such expressions as "He stood onto the porch" are not standard.

Upon is still a perfectly good word, but it is never required in place of *on*.

one

The use of *one* as an indefinite pronoun is becoming distinctly rare in American English. In spite of the efforts of generations of teachers, we normally say "*We* normally say" or "*You* normally say," instead of "*One* normally says."

The repetition of *one* ("*One* should do *one's* best, shouldn't *one*?") and its use as a substitute for I ("After all, *one* has had some experience in these matters") sound intolerably affected to most Americans.

only

It is often preached in schoolrooms that *only* inevitably modifies the word that immediately follows it, so that "He *only* wants ten cents" means something quite different from "He wants only ten cents." This simply is not true. Put *only* where it sounds natural, and only change its position if it is ambiguous.

opt, option

Option is a useful technical term in business. Otherwise, whenever a man has an *option,* he has a *choice,* which he would be well advised to *choose.* If there is any sound reason for ever using *opt* as a verb, it has never been made clear to me.

-or, -our

In American usage *-or* is always acceptable in place of the British *-our*, though in a few words (*glamour*, the *Saviour*) the *-our* ending is still often used.

Ordinal Numerals

The words *first, second, third,* and so forth are called *ordinal* numerals, while *one, two, three,* and so forth are called *cardinal* numerals.

Such forms as *firstly* and *secondly* are never necessary.

Such abbreviations as *1st* and *2nd* should be used only where there is a real need for economy of space.

ought

In standard English, *ought* is never preceded by *had*. The negative form is *oughtn't to*, not *hadn't ought to*.

out loud

Out loud is considered more informal than *aloud*, as well as more emphatic. Both are in standard use.

over

When *over* is used as a prefix, the compound word is regularly written without a hyphen; *overactive, overcareful*, etc.

Overloaded Sentences

It is all right to put several ideas in a single sentence if:

1. They are closely related.
2. The relation is clearly shown.
3. The whole sentence is not so complicated as to put an unreasonable strain on a reader's attention.

A sentence that fails to meet any one of these conditions is overloaded. It should be either strengthened so that it will carry the load better or split into parts.

pair

After a number the plural may be either *pair* or *pairs*; otherwise it is usually *pairs*:

He bought three *pair* (or *pairs*) of shoes.
All the *pairs* were well matched.

pants, trousers, slacks, breeches, levis, denims, shorts, *etc.*

We consider a garment with two sleeves definitely singular, but we seem to be permanently confused about garments with two legs, or even leg-holes. All of the words in this list normally take plural verbs unless preceded by "pair of," though the people who sell them sometimes speak of *one pant* and *two pants*. For some reason the word *pants* seems to be regarded as rather undignified in serious writings. All the others are completely standard.

Paradox

A *paradox* is either an apparent contradiction or something which has the opposite effect from what might be expected.

He is so efficient that he never gets anything done.
The better I know him the less I know about him.
The more he eats, the thinner he gets.
She was so good she made him worse.

pardon

See **excuse.**

Parentheses ( )

1. *For insertions. Parentheses* are used to insert illustrations, definitions, or other information not a part of the main structure of the sentence but useful for a clear understanding.

In two states (Idaho and Nevada) such laws have already been passed.
His collection of incunabula (books printed before 1500) is one of the largest in the country.
Her long theatrical career (she first appeared on the stage in 1902) was now drawing to a close.

In informal writing, commas or dashes may often be used satisfactorily in place of parentheses.

2. *With other punctuation.* A parenthetical expression does not affect the other punctuation of a sentence in which it is inserted. Any mark required at the point of insertion should be placed *after* the second curve:

The room contained a table (borrowed from the neighbors), three chairs, and a phonograph (probably Edison's first model).

3. *Parentheses and brackets.* In academic writing, parentheses are used only for insertions in a writer's own sentence. Insertions in quoted material should be put in brackets ([ ]).

Participles

A *participle* is a word derived from a verb but functioning on the borderline between verb and adjective. *Present participles* are always formed by adding -*ing* to the plain form. *Past participles* are formed in various ways, of which the following are examples:

> He has *broken* it.
>   *begun*
>   *made*
>   *finished*

You will notice that *broken* and *begun* are special forms, used only as *participles,* while *made* and *finished* are identical with the forms for the past tense.

Any participle may be used as a part of a verb phrase or as an adjective.

The horse *was running.*	He *had broken* the dish.
The *running* horse suddenly swerved.	He had a *broken* arm.

Sometimes a participle is so close to the borderline between verb and adjective that it might be called either:

She had been *smiling* and happy all morning.

Had been smiling looks like a verb phrase. *Smiling and happy* looks like a pair of adjectives. Argument is useless—take your choice.

Any *present participle* may also be used as a noun ("*Running* is a strenuous sport"), although some people call it a *gerund* when it is so used. Comparatively few *past participles* are used as nouns (the *slain,* the *wounded*), and they are not called anything fancy.

Participles are not supposed to be used alone as verbs. Few of us make the mistake of using present participles in this way. Such expressions as "Annie *doing* me a favor" strike us as incomplete. But the substitution of the past participle for the past tense is a very common error:

Annie *done* (should be *did*) me a favor.
We *seen* (should be *saw*) him yesterday.

Such expressions are very common in some dialects, and they are certainly used by millions of intelligent and admirable people. But the prejudice against them is so strong that it is worth whatever time it takes to learn and practice the standard usage.

party

Party is established in legal usage (the *party* of the first part, one *party* to the dispute, etc.). As a substitute for *person* it is not now generally admired.

passé

Out of date, out of style. *Passé*, is passé, or ought to be.

passed, past

Passed is a form of the verb *pass.*

He *passed* the test.
He had *passed* a good deal of time there.
The bill was *passed* by the Legislature.

Past indicates former time rather than the action of passing.

In the *past* this was often done.
All his *past* efforts were failures.

Passive Constructions

A *passive construction* represents the subject as the receiver rather than the performer of an action. It is therefore appropriate when the performer is unknown, vague, or comparatively unimportant. Otherwise an active construction is usually preferable.

1. *The impersonal passive.* We often want a sentence to tell what happened rather than who did it. Sometimes we can choose between an *active construction* with a pronoun subject and a *passive construction*:

ACTIVE	PASSIVE
They *make* several good cars in England.	Several good cars *are made* in England.
You *can open* it with a screwdriver.	It *can be opened* with a screwdriver.
We *use* the passive construction.	The passive construction *is used.*

In each of these pairs the passive is rather more formal. In the following examples it would be hard to find a natural active construction:

The crops *are ruined.*   The meadow *was flooded.*

2. *Passive with unknown agent.* When the performer of an action is actually unknown, the passive is the normal construction:

Smith's grocery store *was robbed* last night.

3. *Passive with unimportant agent.* When the speaker is more interested in the receiver of the action than in the performer, the passive is appropriate:

My brother *was bitten* by a dog.

4. *The weak passive.* Unless there is a definite reason for using the passive, an active construction is usually preferable. "John saw Tom" is two words shorter than "Tom was seen by John," and is also more direct and forceful. It is especially unfortunate to begin a sentence containing several clauses with a passive construction, since one passive often leads to another, and a discouraging tangle is likely to result. Compare the following sentences:

ACTIVE	PASSIVE
Ponsonby suggested that Sanders ask the contractor to submit a new bid.	It was suggested by Ponsonby that the submission of a new bid by the contractor be requested by Sanders.

There are people who write whole books in this style.

5. *The cautious passive.* The frequency of the passive construction in military and bureaucratic correspondence is caused partly by official policies of impersonality, but owes something also to the fact that passive statements can be made without indicating exactly who is responsible. The passing of the buck is thereby greatly facilitated—not to mention that the recipient of such communications is often reduced to gibbering frustration, and effectively prevented from making a further nuisance of himself.

peeve, peevish

Peevish is an old and standard word. *Peeve* is a back formation. As a verb it is decidedly informal; as a noun it is slang.

people

A generation ago the use of *people* as a plural of *person* was still frequently condemned. It is now unquestionably standard.

per cent, percent

Per cent may be written as one word or two. The literal meaning is "to the hundred." Thus *ten per cent* equals one tenth. The noun *percentage* originally meant a fixed proportion:

He gets a *percentage* of the profits.

Percentage is often shortened to *percent,* and is sometimes used to indicate merely a part, with no exact proportion to the whole:

A small *percentage* (or *percent*) of them will always have trouble.

Since this is a mere pretense at exactness, it offers no real advantage over "a small fraction," or even "a few."

"Perfect" Constructions

Verb phrases consisting of some form of *have* followed by the past participle of the main verb are called *perfect* constructions. Here *perfect* has its original meaning of "completed," and does not imply unusual virtue or quality.

He *has finished* the job.	Present perfect.
He *had finished* the job when I got there.	Past perfect.
He *will have finished* the job by Tuesday.	Future perfect.

It is often said that these three constructions are used to show action completed in the present, past, or future. Actually, the future perfect is very little used, since *he will finish* conveys just about the same information as *he will have finished.* The past perfect gives little trouble, though it is often replaced by another construction: "He finished before I came" is equivalent to "He had finished when I came." But the present perfect is almost impossible to explain—we simply have to get used to it. It does not always indicate completed action. "He has worked there for twenty years" implies that he is still working there, while "He worked there for twenty years" implies that he has left. Moreover, we say "He has already done it" but "He did it yesterday." A foreigner should simply believe us if we tell him this. We couldn't possibly explain why.

Period (.)

1. *At the end of a sentence.* The principal use of a period is to mark the end of a statement. When there is any doubt about whether the final mark should be a period or one of the other end marks (exclamation point or question mark), the period is usually the better choice.

2. *With abbreviations.* Periods are also used to indicate abbreviations: Sept.; Mr.; Prof. J. D. Hasting; P.S.

a. When an abbreviated form is pronounced as spelled, it is considered an informal word, and is not followed by a *period*:

The *Doc* gave me a health *exam* this morning.

b. Periods are not usually used with abbreviations consisting entirely of capital letters (*FHA, CIO*).

c. British publishers follow the theory that a period indicates that something has been omitted after it occurs and therefore should not be used when the abbreviation ends with the final letter of the original word. They therefore use *Dr, Mr,* and so forth. This practice is not usual in this country.

3. *As a decimal point.* The period (or something that looks very much like it) is used to indicate decimal fractions and to set off cents from dollars (17.89 miles; 3.5%; $16.95). This period is not used when cents are indicated without the dollar sign ($0.38 or $.38; 38¢).

4. *To indicate omission.* Three periods (. . .) are called an *ellipsis,* and are used to show an omission of one or more words.

5. *With quotation marks.* The period is usually put within final quotes, even if it does not logically belong there:

I heard him mumble something about "not my fault."

Person

There are three grammatical *persons.* The first represents the speaker;

the second, the person spoken to; and the third, the person (or thing) spoken of.

The pronouns *I* and *we* are in the first person. *You* is in the second. The others, and all nouns, are usually considered to be in the third.

Verbs may be said to be in the same person as their subjects, although *am* and the *-s* form are the only ones in which the physical indication of person has remained.

phone

This shortened form of *telephone* is now in general use except in decidedly formal writing. No apostrophe is needed.

photo

Photo is not as thoroughly established as *phone*, probably because a short form is less needed. It is not much shorter than *picture*, and not as short as *snap* or *shot*.

Phrase

In this book any closely related group of words which does not contain both a subject and a predicate (and is therefore not a clause) is called a *phrase*.

In the morning   Driving down the street   Must have been

place

Place is a good word, but the combinations *any place, every place, no place,* and *some place* are not generally considered improvements over *anywhere, everywhere, nowhere,* and *somewhere.*

plan to and plan on

Plan to do it is unquestionably standard. *Plan on doing it* is also widely used, but is often criticized.

plenty

Standard usage requires an *of* after *plenty* before a noun:

I have *plenty of* potatoes.

The use of *plenty* as an intensifier ("He was *plenty tired*," "He worked *plenty hard"*) seems to be spreading, but is still generally considered substandard.

P.M.

See **A.M. and P.M.**

Possessive Forms and Of Phrases

1. The *possessive form* is used to show not only ownership but a number of other relations.

> He bought *Walter's* house.
> The ball hit the *pitcher's* foot.
> *Elmo's* brother is here.
> *Sheila's* picture does not do her justice.
> They worked hard for the *Senator's* election.
> *Hemingway's* novels have been very popular.
> Give me a *dollar's* worth.
> He can do it in a *week's* time.
> I don't like *Betty's* (or *Betty*) working so hard.

See also **Gerunds,** pages 300–301.

2. Theoretically, any relation that can be shown by the possessive form of a noun can also be shown by a phrase consisting of *of* and the plain form. Thus we can choose between:

Ed Ryan's home	The home of Ed Ryan
Aristotle's father	The father of Aristotle
The ship's crew	The crew of the ship

Frequently the choice is completely a matter of personal taste, but two general tendencies are noticeable:

a. Possessive forms are usually restricted to living things, or at least things (like ships) that can be personified. This is by no means absolute. There are a number of set phrases like *a day's work, a stone's throw,* and *an hour's time* that are in very common use; and it certainly cannot be proved that "The *house's* roof leaks" is incorrect. But most of us would probably say "The *roof of the house* leaks."

b. Single personal names are more likely to be used in the possessive form than with an *of* phrase. Although we may say "The home *of Ed Ryan*," we generally say "*Ed's* home" or "*Ryan's* home," rather than "The home *of Ed*," or "The home *of Ryan*." Also, we do not usually say

"The father *of John*," though we might say "The father *of John Fink*," or "The father *of John Fink and Edna*."

3. *The double possessive.* With nouns referring to persons, we sometimes combine the possessive form and the *of* phrase.

A friend *of my father's*
That speech *of Lincoln's*
What business is that *of John's*?

This seems to have originated as a combination of the ideas of "possession" (in its broadest sense) and of selection from a group. Thus "a friend *of my father's*" indicates one of a number of people who are my father's friends.

practicable, practical

A plan or theory that can be put into practice may be called either *practicable* or *practical*. A thing that can be used is almost always called *practical*. A person is always called *practical*.

pre-

Pre- is followed by a hyphen when the word to which it is joined begins with an *e* or a capital letter (pre-eminent, pre-Romantic). Otherwise there is no hyphen (prearrange, prefabricate).

Predicate

The *predicate* of a sentence consists of everything in the sentence except the subject and its modifiers. The verb alone is sometimes called the *simple predicate*.

predominant(-ly), predominate

The adjective is *predominant*, the adverb *predominantly*, and the verb *predominate*. The erroneous form *predominately* results from confusing the verb and adjective.

prefer

In comparing two things, you *prefer* one *to* the other.

Prefix

A *prefix* is a word or word element that can be placed before another word to make a new word with a changed meaning:

*de*moralize *inter*collegiate *over*take *re*-examine

prejudice, prejudiced

The noun is *prejudice,* the modifier *prejudiced.*

He has a *prejudice* against women.
He is *prejudiced* against women.

Prepositions

The idiomatic use of prepositions is much too complicated a subject to be discussed briefly, but two points may be made.

1. A *preposition* at the end of a sentence is legitimate except where it is unnecessary, and admirable if it avoids an inversion involving *which* or *whom.* Thus "That is the one I was looking at" is (at the very least) as good as "That is the one *at which* I was looking." But "That is the house where I live" is damaged by adding *at* at the end.

2. Economy suggests that two prepositions should never be used where one will do the job, but usage varies (see **of**). I record, but cannot explain, the fact that I might say a boy fell *out* or *out of* a window, but only *out of* a tree.

pretty

In the sense of *moderately, pretty* is usually said to be "established in informal use." It is certainly established, and has been used pretty often by many writers not usually considered informal.

preventive, preventative

Preventive was the original form. *Preventative* began as a mistake (probably under the influence of *representative*); but it has been used so often that it should now be considered a variant form rather than an error.

principal, principle

Principle is always a noun, and usually means something like an underlying truth, a rule of conduct, or an inherent quality:

The *principles* of science should be followed.
He is a man of high *principles.*
The *principles* on which it works can be found in the shop manual.
In *principle,* I abhor it.

Principal is used as a noun when it refers to a sum of money or to a person (the *principal* of a school, the *principals* in a law suit).

As an adjective, the form is always *principal.*

Principal Parts of Verbs

The plain form (*take*), the past tense (*took*), and the past participle (*taken*) are called the *principal parts of a verb*, because in irregular verbs they have to be learned individually, while the other two forms (*takes* and *taking*) can be derived regularly from the plain form.

prior to

There is no law against using this phrase (or *previous to*) instead of *before*, but it is hard to think of a good reason for doing so.

privilege

Notice that this ends in *-ege* (pronounced *ij*).

Profanity and Obscenity

Fifty years ago people wrote *jeepers, gosh dang it, blankety-blank*, or *heck* when they were thinking of something else. Only the last one has survived as a rather improbable quotation from athletes interviewed for the sports sections. Since the original words behind these euphemisms have pretty well lost their shock effect, it seems advisable to use them only when you think they have a definite artistic value.

As for the biological four-letter words, the best principle is to be matter-of-fact but not daring—you won't scare your instructor, but you may bore him.

professor

Professor is spelled with a single *f* and a double *s*. The formal written abbreviation is not used with a last name alone.

Prof. Richard Jones   *Prof.* C. E. Jones   *Professor* Jones

The informal abbreviation *prof* is not followed by a period and should be used with reasonable discretion.

Progressive Constructions

Very roughly, we may say that the simple forms (*calls, called,* and *will call*) indicate the time of an activity only in a general way, and that the progressive forms (*is calling, was calling,* and *will be calling*) place it more specifically. Thus *he calls* usually indicates a habit extending through the present, while *he is calling* usually indicates a specific action taking place right now. For this reason the simple forms are sometimes called "indefinite" and the progressive forms "definite." However, the distinction is by no means uniform. It varies with different verbs, with different tenses, and with different contexts.

Verbs indicating *perceptions* are used more often in the simple tenses than are most other verbs. Thus we say, "I *hear* it now," or "I *see* it now" (perception), but "I *am* listening now" or "I *am looking* now" (effort).

Verbs indicating states of mind or attitude are also likely to be in the simple tenses, probably because the speaker usually thinks of his attitude as continuing. We rarely say "I *am liking,*" "I *am loving,*" "He *is hating,*" or "They *are knowing*" unless we wish to emphasize that we are feeling strongly right now ("I *am* simply *loving* this dance"). Similarly, "I *admire* him" indicates a general attitude; "I *am admiring* him" indicates a temporary, active appraisal.

In the past and future, the progressive forms often indicate action already going on at the time of another event, while the simple forms indicate action starting at or after the other event.

He *was doing* it when they came.
He *did* it when they came.

He *will be resting* when you get there.
He *will rest* when you get there.

When no second event is mentioned, the simple and progressive forms are more nearly interchangeable in the past and future than in the present.

What is he doing now?   He *is working* (not "He *works*").
What will he do tomorrow?   He *will work* (or *will be working*).
What did he do yesterday?   He *worked* (or *was working*).

In some situations the progressive forms somehow imply inevitability rather than a personal decision, and are therefore more polite than the simple forms.

Want to go fishing tomorrow? Sorry, I'll *play* tennis. (this sounds like a direct refusal)
Sorry, I'll *be playing* tennis. (this implies that I can't help it, and really am sorry)

Why weren't you here last night? I *bowled.* (presumably by choice)
I was bowling. (caught in the fell clutch of circumstance)

A number of other differences could be added, but these are enough
to show that our uses of these forms depend on an erratic set of habits
rather than any fixed principles. Actually, most native speakers have little
trouble in making appropriate choices, though intelligent foreigners who
try to follow rules are often hopelessly confused. It is easy to forgive them.

Pronouns, Antecedents, and Referents

1. *Pronouns and antecedents.* One of the main uses of pronouns is to
avoid repeating nouns. Thus we can say, "I asked John how *his* sister was
getting along, and *he* said *she* was feeling much better." This is obviously
neater than saying, "I asked John how John's sister was getting along,
and John said John's sister was feeling much better." The noun to which
a pronoun refers is called its *antecedent* (literally, "going before"). In the
sentence above, *John* is the antecedent of both *his* and *he,* and *sister* is the
antecedent of *she.* But the pronoun *I* has no antecedent, any more than
the noun *John* has. Both words stand directly for persons, instead of
referring to other words previously used. The pronouns *I, we,* and *you*
are regularly used without antecedents, and all other pronouns may be.

Whenever we use a pronoun to stand for a noun, we must be careful
to do it in such a way that our audience knows just what noun it is supposed to stand for:

I saw Fred and Annette yesterday, and *he* looked tired. (clear)
I saw Fred and Dave yesterday, and *he* looked tired. (ambiguous)

It is better to repeat a noun than to leave your audience guessing.

The pronoun *it* is often used to refer to the idea contained in a group
of words, rather than to any one word:

They argued about whether they would go fishing, but finally decided
that *it* was too much trouble.

This, that, and *which* (sometimes called pronouns) are used in similar
ways:

Dick suggested that we try to find one second hand. We decided that
that was a good idea.
He was driving at fifty miles an hour, *which* is dangerous on that road.

This sort of reference is satisfactory unless:

a. The group contains a single word that might be mistaken for the antecedent.

Ambiguous: He was doing sixty on the Apache Trail, *which* is never
safe.

The reader can only guess whether the speed or the road itself was dangerous.

b. The reference is to an idea implied but not expressed.

Confused: My father practices law, and *that* is what I want to be.

In this sentence *that* is apparently intended to refer to *lawyer*, which
isn't there to refer to. If *be* were changed to *do,* then *that* would refer to
practice(s) law, and the sentence would be satisfactory.

Since it is almost impossible to avoid some vague or ambiguous references in a first draft, you should watch for them when you are revising.
It isn't enough for *you* to know what every *it, this, that,* and *which* stands
for. Unless your reader knows too—automatically and at the first glance
—your sentences need tightening up.

2. *Agreement of pronouns.* In some languages pronouns have to
"agree" with their antecedents: that is, they have to match *words* that
have previously been used. But in English we have a choice between the
pronoun that matches the word and the one that best expresses the idea.
For instance, we can say either:

Everybody in favor should raise *his* hand. (because the word *everybody* is singular)

or

Everybody in favor should raise *their hands.* (because the idea expressed by *everybody* is plural)

Some people have a theory that a plural pronoun should never be used
with *everybody,* but there are sentences in which it can hardly be helped,
such as "*Everybody* went to the dance, and I think *they* all had a good
time."

When we want to refer to a group noun as a unit, we usually use a
singular pronoun:

The jury gave *its* verdict.

But when we want to refer to a group noun with an emphasis on the individuals of which the group is composed, we usually use a plural pronoun:

The jury left *their* seats.

There are a great many sentences in which either a singular or a plural pronoun may be used, and arguments about which is better simply cannot be settled, unless one is definitely clearer than the other. In older English it was customary to make the pronoun match the preceding *noun*; now it is becoming more usual to make it fit the *idea*. About all we can say is that both methods are in good standing, although some people are prejudiced one way or the other.

The same principle applies to such sentences as "I want each of you to do (*his* or *your*) best." Take your choice. You will find authorities on both sides.

pronunciation

Notice that the second syllable is *-nun-*, not *-noun-*.

Proper Adjectives

Adjectives formed from proper nouns are called *proper adjectives* and are begun with capital letters: *French* cooking, *Shakespearian* sonnets, etc. However, when they come into common use in a meaning which has little to do with their origin, they may be begun with small letters. Thus we regularly write *French* cooking, because we definitely associate it with France; but we may write either *French* or *french* windows, because here the emphasis is on the shape rather than the origin. When in doubt, it is safer to use the capital letter.

Proper Nouns

See **Common and Proper Nouns**

proposition

Proposition is a standard word in mathematics, philosophy, and business, and at least a useful word in social relations when it means the opposite of *proposal*. It is not recommended as a general substitute for *plan* or *affair*.

Used as a verb, *proposition* is definitely substandard linguistically, and usually implies a request that is substandard morally.

proved, proven

The verb to *prove* began as a perfectly regular one, and *proved* is always correct. *Proven* got into the language by mistake. However, it has been in for a long time and is now established, though it is not used nearly as often as *proved*.

provided, providing (that)

In such sentences as "He will start tomorrow, *provided that* he can get materials," *providing* may be substituted for *provided*, and *that* is optional after either word. *If* will do quite as well as any of them, but provisions are frequent in legal and quasi-legal languages: ". . . provided that nothing herein contained shall prejudice the rights . . . and further provided that . . ." I'd use *but*, myself.

psychology, psychiatry, *etc.*

There is probably no very good reason for putting these words here, since people who spell them "physcology" etc. would hardly be able to find them here. However, if you happen to find this entry by accident, you might notice how they are spelled.

public

Public may take either a singular or a plural verb.

Punctuation

Punctuation was developed as a method of helping readers to understand the relations of written words. If used in this way, it can obviously be helpful. Unfortunately, we sometimes forget the original purpose of punctuation, and treat it as if it were an end in itself; the "rules of punctuation" often appear to be just as arbitrary as the "rules of grammar," and even more mysterious. Quite naturally, many readers cheerfully disregard much of the punctuation they encounter, and have very vague ideas about what marks to use when it is time to write.

There is something rather peculiar about trying to teach punctuation by giving students passages incorrectly punctuated, or not punctuated at all, and telling them to "punctuate this correctly." In the first place, if a passage can be clearly understood without the "correct marks," a student may reasonably decide that it does not really need them; and his idea that punctuation is a system of arbitrary obstacles rather than of helpful hints is likely to be strengthened. In the second place, there are usually several equally "correct" ways to punctuate any but the very simplest passages. It might be reasonable to say, "Punctuate this so it will make some kind of sense." But there is usually not enough time available for a fair consideration of all reasonable variants; and at any rate such exercises are appropriate only for students who have already learned a good deal about the subject.

In order to punctuate intelligently we must find out what sort of effect each of the marks may be expected to have in guiding a reader's association of ideas. Then we can use the marks, like the words themselves, as a means to an end. We may miss our aim at times, as we sometimes do in the choice and arranging of our words; but this approach is more promising than trying to remember whether a given comma is used in accordance with Rule 19a.

It is true that a few perfectly arbitrary habits are widely and rather uniformly practiced. For instance, we are expected to separate a city from a state by a comma (*Atlanta, Georgia*) although the meaning would be as clear without the mark, and most of us would not pause between the two words if we read them aloud. But such rigid rules are not as numerous as students are often led to believe, and they are certainly not as important as an understanding of how the marks can be used as actual aids to communication.

Uses of the following marks are discussed under separate entries in this INDEX:

Apostrophe (')	Hyphen (-)
Brackets ([])	Parentheses ( )
Caret (∧)	Period (.)
Colon (:)	Question Mark (?)
Comma (,)	Quotation Marks (" ")
Dash (—)	Semicolon (;)
Ellipsis (. . .)	Underlining (_____)
Exclamation point (!)	

A study of these entries should be reinforced by some practice in reading good contemporary prose with careful attention to how each mark is used and whether or not it seems to be effective. Only when you have learned what the marks do *to* you as you read can you expect them to do similar things *for* you when you write.

purist

A *purist* is a man who takes pride in using words exactly as they are defined in an out-of-date dictionary.

Question Mark (?)

1. *In direct questions.* The question mark is required after a direct question:

> What is the approximate population of each of the three largest cities in New England?

It is *not* used after an indirect question.

> He asked what she was going to do.

2. *In requests.* The question mark is optional after a request phrased as a question.

> Will you please fill out the enclosed form?
> Will you please check the information in your files, fill out the enclosed form, and return the information to me tomorrow.

There is no fixed rule, and the question mark and period in the two sentences above could be reversed. But a period after a very short question may seem rude unless the situation calls for a direct order. The longer the question, the more appropriate the period.

3. *With other marks.* When a question mark is used with quotation marks, its position depends on whether the sentence as a whole or only the quoted part is a question:

> Are you sure he said "The test will cover only the second chapter"?
> She heard him ask, "Where are our seats?"
> "Who cares?" he remarked and went on with his work.
> Did he say "What time is it?"
> His first question was, "What are the dates of the French Revolution?"; I didn't hear the other one.

Notice that a question mark within quotation marks is not followed by a comma, a period, or a second question mark, but is followed by a semicolon if the structure of the sentence requires it.

questionnaire

Notice the double *n*.

quite a

Such expressions as *quite a bit, quite a few, quite a while,* and *quite a good player* are definitely standard, though rather informal. Some people who use them freely would object to *quite a man* as slangy.

Quotation Marks (" ")

1. *To indicate quotations. Quotation marks* (also called *quotes*) are used to indicate the exact words used by a speaker or previous writer. Double quotes are the usual form, although the practice of using single quotes is gaining ground. For quotations within quotations the forms should alternate:

John answered, "I distinctly heard Peggy say 'That is mine.'"
John answered, 'I distinctly heard Peggy say "That is mine."'

Notice that closing marks should not be omitted even when two sets come together.

In academic writing, quotations of more than four lines are usually indicated by indenting and single spacing in typed papers, and by simply indenting in longhand papers, rather than by the use of quotes. This keeps the reader from forgetting where the quotation began, and reduces the necessity for quotes within quotes.

2. *In titles.* In informal writing, titles of books, magazines, and so forth are often put in quotes. In academic writing such titles are put in italics (or underlined to indicate italics), but quotes are used for titles of poems, stories, or articles of less than book length.

Mrs. Frank's "Heartache on the Campus" first appeared in *The Woman's Home Companion.*

3. *For words used as words.* In informal writing, words discussed as words rather than used to express meaning may be put in quotes:

He was confused by such terms as "protocol" and "implemented."

In academic writing such words would usually be italicized.

4. *The apologetic use.* It is not advisable to use quotes apologetically:

He was "bawled out" by the first sergeant.

Either say *bawled out* without the quotes or find some such substitute as *severely reprimanded.*

5. *Quotation marks used with other marks.* When a comma or period follows a quoted passage, it is put within the final quotes, regardless of its relation to the sentence as a whole. Other marks are put within or without, depending on the construction of the whole sentence.

> She heard him say "This way," and a moment later, "Here it is."
> He may have said "I dislike her"; but can you really believe that he said "I despise her"?

It used to be generally taught that quoted material should be set off from the rest of the sentence by commas as well as quotation marks. Such commas are now often omitted:

> "The main thing," said Larry, "is to find a place that is still open."
> "The main thing" said Larry "is to find a place that is still open."

A comma should not be used with quotes when a pause would be distinctly unnatural:

> "Very truly yours" sounds better to me than "yours very truly."

raise, rear

We used to be taught that only animals were *raised*—children were *reared.* Perhaps it is a result of progressive education, but now children are generally *raised,* too.

raise, rise

When the subject shifts its whole position, it *rises.* When it moves anything else, including part of itself, it *raises.*

He *rises*	from his seat.	He *raises*	his hand.
rose		*raised*	
has risen		*has raised*	

rarely ever

Rarely and *hardly ever* are synonymous. For emphasis, they are often fused into *rarely ever* in speech, but this combination cannot be considered standard in writing.

re-

In long-established words the prefix *re-* has a number of meanings difficult to analyze (*rely, remove, repeat, reverse,* etc.). Its most frequent meaning, and the only one used in new formations, is *again.* It is separated by a hyphen whenever this meaning has to be distinguished from another:

We must *re-mark* the boundaries. (not *remark*)

A hyphen is also used between *re-* and a word beginning with *e*: *re-emphasize.*

real, really

Real is often used in standard English to modify other modifiers: "a *real* nice time"; "He did that *real* well." On the other hand, such expressions are often severely condemned. *Really* is an unquestionably standard substitute.

reason is because, reason why

Such sentences as the following are often criticized as containing unnecessary repetition of an idea:

The *reason I failed* was *because* I misunderstood the first question.
That is the *reason why* he did it.

You can avoid criticism by rewriting the sentences as follows:

The *reason* I failed was *that* I misunderstood the first question.
That is the *reason* he did it.

or

That is *why* he did it.

However, if you think *reason . . . because* and *reason why* are satisfactorily emphatic, you will have plenty of good company.

receipt, recipe

You always get a *receipt* (*re-seat'*) for a payment; but the directions for making cookies may be called either a *receipt* or a *recipe* (*ress'-i-pee*).

reckon

See **calculate.**

Redundancy

A word or phrase which repeats an idea already expressed, without adding anything useful, is called *redundant*. The words italicized in the following sentences are all worse than useless.

Where is he *at?*
The consensus *of opinion* is that Richards hasn't a chance.
The trial is set for 3 P.M. tomorrow *afternoon.*
He said that if he was elected *that* he would clean out the corrupt crowd *of dishonest people* at City Hall.

Reflexive Pronouns

In such sentences as "He hurt *himself,*" the compound pronoun may be called *reflexive.*

regard, regards

The two expressions *as regards* and *in regard to* are often jumbled into *in regards to.*

regardless

The *-less* makes this word sufficiently negative:

He will do it, *regardless of what you say.*

The form *irregardless* (probably influenced by *irrespective*) is a double negative that is only used humorously. Even if the user is serious about it his audience is likely not to be. The triple negative *disirregardless* has now begun to appear, and we may hope for *undisirregardless* in the near future.

Relative Clauses

Clauses used as adjectives:

He is the man *who bought our car.*
A girl *we know* owns six dogs.

See pages 158–59.

remember

Memory is often followed by *of*. In standard usage, *remember* is not.

I have a faint *memory of* reading that book.
I faintly *remember* (no *of*) reading that book.

respectfully, respectively

Respectively means "in the order listed," and has nothing whatever to do with *respectfully*.

Restrictive and Nonrestrictive Clauses

In this book the terms "identifying" and "amplifying" clauses are used. See pages 157–58.

reverend

The rules for the "correct" usage of *reverend* are highly formalized:

1. It is properly used only as a title, not as a substitute for *minister* ("The *reverend* told me" may be common, but it is not standard).
2. It is not used with a bare last name—*Reverend John Smith* or *Reverend J. E. Smith*, but not *Reverend Smith*.
3. It is even better with *the* before it: *the Reverend J. E. Smith*.
4. Best of all is *the* before it and *Mr.* after it. This combination makes the first name or initials unnecessary: the Reverend Mr. Smith. However, local ground rules vary a good deal.

The original meaning of *reverend* was "to be revered." *Reverent* is a different word, meaning simply "revering," and may be used of laymen as well as ministers.

Rhetorical Questions

A *rhetorical question* is one to which the speaker expects no answer, unless he is planning to supply it himself.

rhyme, rime

Rime is the earlier spelling, and seems to be returning to favor after a long period in which *rhyme* (resulting from a mistaken belief that the word was related to *rhythm*) was the usual one.

right

Right in the sense of *very* is used in conversation by many standard speakers throughout the country, but many people consider it too informal for writing.

role

Role (a part in a play) is now usually spelled without the circumflex accent (*rôle*).

Roman Numerals

See **Numbers.**

round, around

See **around.**

Run-on sentence

A sentence is said to be *run on* when two statements are run together without punctuation or a connective (a *fused sentence*) or with only a comma between them (*comma fault, comma splice*):

He never showed up for the exam he was up all night.
We never got to see the movie, there was too long a line of people waiting to get in.

said

As a modifier, *said* is appropriate only in legal phraseology (*said* property, the *said* defendant).

saint

For a particular *saint*, the abbreviation is usually *St.* (*St.* John); for several saints, SS. (SS. Matthew and Mark).

Sarcasm

See **Irony.**

Seasons

The *seasons* (*spring, summer, fall* or *autumn,* and *winter*) need not be capitalized.

seem

Can't seem to is often condemned as illogical—we could not substitute *appear* as we could in *doesn't seem to*. However, it is very handy, and definitely standard in conversation, though it rarely appears in print.

seldom

Seldom, by itself, means "hardly ever." There is therefore no need for *seldom ever*.

semi-

A prefix meaning *half*. No hyphen is needed unless the main word begins with an *i* or a capital letter.

Semicolon (;)

A *semicolon* is read like a period, rather than like a comma; but where a period indicates a complete break in thought, a semicolon suggests that the groups of words it separates are parts of a larger whole. Semicolons are rather formal marks, and are seldom absolutely necessary; however, they are convenient for several purposes:

1. *To separate members of a series that contain internal commas.* Compare the two following sentences:

Dinner included meat, bread, vegetables, and fruit.
Dinner included meat, flown in from the continent; bread, freshly baked that afternoon; fresh vegetables; and several kinds of fruit, including some quite strange to me.

With nothing but commas, the second sentence would be rather bumpy; the semicolons show where the main pauses come, and so make it easier to read.

2. *To separate independent clauses when they are rather long and contain internal commas:*

A good many people have tried, but nobody has succeeded.
A good many people, some of them very well prepared, have tried; but nobody, according to the best records available, has succeeded.

3. *To separate independent clauses when no connective is used:*

Some traffic officers think the new code will help; others doubt this.

This sentence could be broken in two, or a comma and *but* could be substituted for the semicolon. A comma alone would not be sufficient.

Usually these words belong to the second clause, and are therefore preceded by a semicolon and followed by a comma.

set, sit

Such expressions as "Let's *set* (should be *sit*) awhile" and "We *set* (should be *sat*) there for hours" are widely used, especially in the country, but are not generally accepted as standard.

Sit is seldom misused, though people who have been warned against *set* sometimes go too far and say "*Sit* (should be *set*) this on the table."

shall

See *will and shall.*

Shifting Viewpoint

It is all right to shift from one person or tense to another if you do it on purpose in order to accomplish something. But if the shift was made simply because we forget how you started, then one is likely to have a sentence as confused as this one. And unless you are sure you are writing for thousands, you had better keep the same audience in mind throughout. Otherwise you are likely to be explaining the obvious in one paragraph and leaving out essential points in the next.

should

See *will and shall.*

sic

Sic is Latin for *thus.* It is used, in brackets, to indicate that a mistake in quoted material was made by the original author and not in copying:

"He was born in Brooklin [*sic*] in 1873."

sick at, sick to

The usual standard expression is *sick at my stomach,* though *sick to* is current in some regions. The English have solved this problem by deciding that *sick* all by itself means nauseated, and using *ill* as the general term. Even in America we usually *become ill,* though all but the most formal can also *get sick.* It is now old-fashioned, if not provincial, to *take sick.*

sight

See *cite.*

similar to

Similar to is longer than *like* and means no more. Besides, *like* is seldom misspelled, while *similar* often is.

similes

See **Metaphors and Similes.**

site

See *cite.*

slow, slowly

Slow may be used to modify verbs as well as nouns, though it sounds awkward in some positions. We could say "He walked *slow*" or "He walked *slowly*," but only "He *slowly* walked to the corner." It is hard to explain why "He *slow* walked to the corner" is wrong, but it is.

Though often criticized in classrooms, *so* is standard:

In purpose clauses:	He came home early *so* he could work in the garden.
In result clauses:	He has lived here a long time, *so* he knows almost everybody.
As an intensive:	There are *so* many new people here.

The following expressions are not universally admired:

So you're tired. *So* I should do your work for you? *So* what?

so-called

So-called is likely to sound peevish at best, and ridiculous when the calling is accurate. Describe a man as a *so-called mastermind* if you must, but don't call him a *so-called lawyer* if he *is* a lawyer, even if you don't think he should be.

some, somewhat

Since *some* was originally singular, there is nothing illogical in such expressions as *some day* and *some lucky man,* though half-informed purists sometimes object to them. In the sense, of "moderately," *somewhat* is the generally preferred form in written English—"He felt *somewhat* better" —though many cultivated speakers would substitute *some* in conversation. As a strong intensifier (going *some, some* speech), *some* is slang.

See also **any and its compounds.**

sometime, some time, sometimes

When the idea is "at a certain (or uncertain) time," write *sometime.* When the idea of duration is present, write *some time:*

He went there *sometime* in 1952 and stayed *some time.*

Sometimes means occasionally.

sooner . . . than

If you remember "no *sooner* said *than* done" you won't be tempted to write "He had no *sooner* gone to bed *when* he remembered he had not put the car in the garage."

sort

See **kind.**

specie, species

These words are not the singular and plural of the same word. *Specie* (*spee'she*) means coin as distinguished from paper money. *Species* means kind, especially as a biological term. It has the same written form in the singular and plural, and most people pronounce it *spee'sheez* in both numbers, though some pronounce the singular *spee'shiz.*

Split Infinitive

A Latin infinitive cannot be split because it is a single word. An English infinitive can be split and sometimes should. In such a sentence as "I want *to* actually *see* him do it," it would be impossible to move *actually* without either changing the meaning or weakening the force. However, most split infinitives are awkward and weaken rather than strengthen the sentences in which they occur. Such a sentence as "I want *to* eventually *get* to Philadelphia" would be improved by putting *eventually* almost anywhere but where it is. In revising papers, suspect every split infinitive, and leave only those that you are sure you can defend.

Squinting Modifiers

A *squinting modifier* is one that "looks both ways"—that is, it could reasonably be understood as applying either to the preceding or the following element.

> He asked me *while I was in New York* to visit his sister.
> *Revised:* He asked me to visit his sister *while I was in New York.*
> *While I was in New York* he asked me to visit his sister.
>
> He advised me *secretly* to go to the police.
> *Revised:* He *secretly* advised me to go to the police.
> He advised me to go *secretly* to the police.
>
> She told Algernon *after a few minutes* to get a taxi.
> *Revised:* *After a few minutes* she told Algernon to get a taxi.
> She told Algernon to get a taxi *after a few minutes.*

stationary, stationery

Paper, envelopes, and so forth are called *stationery* and are sold at a station*er's*. In all other uses the form is *stationary*.

statue, stature, statute

Statue means a carved figure. *Stature* can mean either the physical height of a person (He was a man of medium *stature*) or *standing* in the figurative sense (His professional *stature* made him an obvious choice for chairman). *Statute* means a law or rule formally enacted. *Statute law* is often contrasted with *case law,* which is based on judicial decisions rather than legislative enactment.

Strong Verbs

Such verbs as *sing* and *break,* which form their past tenses by a change in the vowel, and *without* adding a *d* or *t*, or changing a *d* to a *t* are called *strong*. All regular verbs, which add a *d* or *ed,* are *weak,* and so are such verbs as *make* and *think.*

The terms *strong* and *weak* are useful in discussing Old English, but much less satisfactory than *regular* and *irregular* in Modern English.

Stylebooks

A *stylebook* gives the rules on capitalization, punctuation, and other mechanical details to be used by a particular newspaper, publishing house, or other organization. It may include rules (usually antiquated) on grammar and even style. Probably no two stylebooks have ever been in complete agreement, and certainly no stylebook has ever covered all possible cases.

A stylebook may be very useful in getting a number of people to write with comparative uniformity; but if it is taken too solemnly it can lead to wasting endless time on trivial decisions.

Subjunctive

Three kinds of expressions are often said to be in the "subjunctive mood":

1. Wishes, such as "God bless us." This causes no trouble except when we try to explain it, and the simplest way to do that is to say that it is short for "*May God bless* us." It is quite true that our ancestors could have used a subjunctive form of *bless* without the *may*, but that was when there was a subjunctive form to use.

2. Expressions of willed action, such as "They insisted that he *try* again" and "They requested that he *be* given another chance." There is no trouble in understanding these, and no good reason for insisting on their use. They can be explained as short for *should try* and *should be*, which are now more common and quite as respectable.

3. Conditional expressions such as "If he *were* here," and "If it *be* true." With verbs other than *to be* there is no longer a question of form in the past tense. In the present tense, "If he *call*" is now obsolete, since it seems to most people like a simple mistake in agreement, and "If it *be*" is on its last legs. This leaves "If I *were*" and "If he *were*" as the only real excuse for preserving the theory of a subjunctive mood.

such (a)

Sentences like "He is *such* a little boy" and "They are *such* exciting things to think about" are standard, even though they are criticized in some textbooks as involving incomplete comparisons. After *no, such* is standard, *such a* is not: *no such* thing.

Suffix

An ending, other than an inflection, that can be added to a word to give it a new meaning or function: *-able, -ation, -ish, -ly, -ment, -ous,* and so forth.

suite

Suite (pronounced *sweet*) is now most frequently used to indicate a set of connecting rooms or a set of matched furniture. The original meaning is "following," which is retained in the sense of "staff of assistants" and in the musical term for a series of dances.

sure, surely

The adverbial use of *sure* is established in such fixed expressions as *sure enough* and *sure as fate*. Many standards speakers use and defend it either alone or at the beginning of a sentence:

"Will you do it?"
"*Sure*" or "*Sure* I will."

Others don't. As a direct modifier of a verb, *surely* is more generally admired:

He *surely* did a lot of work on that.

suspect, suspicion

In standard English, *suspicion* is used only as a noun. *Suspect* is used both as a noun (pronounced *sus'pect*), meaning "a person under suspicion," and as a verb (pronounced *sus-pect'*): "We *suspected* (not *suspicioned*) he was there."

Synonyms

Words that have approximately the same meaning are called *synonyms* (*couch, davenport, sofa; begin, commence, start*). It is obviously important to choose the *synonym* which will come closest to conveying your exact meaning.

It is often said that no two words are exact synonyms. Whether or not this can be proved, it is much closer to the truth than the rather widespread idea that any synonym of a word can be substituted for it at any time—and probably should be, just for the sake of variety. It is better to repeat an accurate term than to vary it with a less accurate one.

Synthetic

See **Analytic and Synthetic.**

Tense

The word *tense* comes from the Latin word *tempus*, meaning "time," but the relation between time and tense has become very irregular. English has only two clear-cut tenses—the present and the past—and each of these may be used to indicate any of the three natural divisions of time—the present, the past, and the future.

TENSE	TIME	
present	*past*	I *see* it now.
	present	It *is* cold at Valley Forge. (historical present)
	future	We *play* in Denver next week.
past	*present*	I didn't know he *was* there right now.
	past	We *found* them yesterday.
	future	If you *tried* tomorrow, you might catch him.

If you think this is illogical, you are perfectly right; but we are used to such expressions, and they don't usually cause much trouble unless we think about them too much and pretend that they are all perfectly reasonable. The fact is that tense is only one of our ways of indicating time. We also indicate definite time by such words as *yesterday* and *tomorrow* and comparative time by words like *before* and *after*.

Still another way of showing time is by verb phrases like *will go* and *have gone*. Many (but not all) grammarians say that some of these phrases are also tenses; they usually say that English has six tenses, about as follows:

	SIMPLE	PROGRESSIVE	EMPHATIC
Present	he calls	he is calling	he does call
Past	he called	he was calling	he did call
Future	he will call	he will be calling	
Present perfect	he has called	he has been calling	
Past perfect	he had called	he had been calling	
Future perfect	he will have called	he will have been calling	

The first three are said to represent the absolute divisions of time, and the three "perfect" tenses to show relative time: before the present, before the past, and before the future. ("Perfect" in this conection means "completely finished," and has nothing to do with virtue.)

At first glance this arrangement seems logical and reasonably complete, but the more we study it, the more suspicious we become. It would be hard to prove, for instance, that the difference between *called* and *has called* is any greater than that between *called* and *was calling*; yet *has called* is listed as a different tense from *called,* and *was calling* merely as a different form of the same one. Moreover, a number of combinations indicating various aspects of time are left out entirely: *used to call, is going to call,* etc.

On the whole, the evidence seems to show that the main reason we talk about six tenses in English is that there really were six in Latin (you can count them: *vocat, vocabat, vocabit, vocavit, vocaverat,* and *vocaverit*). It is perfectly certain that there were only two tenses in Old English, the present and the past. Since then we have developed a number of verb phrases, some of which are used as substitutes for the missing tenses. You can call them tenses if you want to, but they are not called that in this book.

than

See **Comparisons,** 1b, 2b, and 3; also **then, than.**

that

See **this and that.**

their, there, they're

Their is the possessive form. *They're* is the contraction for *they are.* *There* is used in all other senses.

them

As a modifier (*them* apples), *them* is not standard.

then, than

Remember that *then* rimes with *when,* and that *than* has nothing to do with time.

there is or are

There is never considered the subject of a sentence; a verb following it therefore agrees with the following subject; "There *is* a man at the door"; "There *are* three men here." When *there* is followed by a compound subject of which the first member is singular, the verb may be either singular or plural: "There *is* (or *are*) a man and three boys on the raft." If both members of the compound subject are singular, the verb may be either singular or plural.

they

The impersonal use of *they* ("*They* say he's rich," "*They* make good cars in England") is rather informal, and occurs more often in speech than in writing; but it is certainly standard.

this and that

1. The use of *this* and *that* and their plurals *these* and *those* as substantives and adjectival modifiers seldom causes trouble unless the reference is vague. See **Pronouns, Antecedents, and Referents.**

2. The use of *this* and *that* as adverbial modifiers ("even *this* short a piece"; "not *that* important") is often questioned, but has been well established for centuries.

3. *This here* and *that there* are pleasantly emphatic forms, but unfortunately not standard unless divided by a noun:

this desk *here*   *that* fellow *there*

These here has the same lack of status. *Those there* does not seem to occur, its place being filled by *them there*, which is considered even lower on the scale.

4. For many centuries *that* has been used to indicate something comparatively remote in time or space, with *this* indicating something nearer at hand, and *it* noncommittal as to time or distance. These distinctions are still generally followed in regard to space, but a tendency has lately developed to use only *this* in regard to time.

He said we ought to try one more round. *This* (formerly *it*) seemed like a good idea at the time.
Last month I saw her with Dick. *This* (formerly *that*) surprised me very much until I discovered that Dick had a new Jaguar.

The tendency apparently comes from an effort to be dramatic by bringing everything into the foreground. It sounds to many of us rather frantic, and it certainly blurs some useful distinctions.

5. For the use of *that* in relative clauses see page 157; in other subordinate clauses, page 159.

though, although

Though and *although* are completely interchangeable except in the combination *even though*, which now has the special emphasis that *although* used to have. The simplified spelling *tho* and *altho* (like *thru*—see next entry) are now used by many standard writers, though seldom allowed to appear in print.

through

The simplified spelling *thru* is heartily approved by some people, detested by others. Suit yourself, but if your instructor doesn't like it, you probably won't convert him.

till, until

These words are interchangeable. Use whichever you think sounds best in a given sentence, but notice that *until* has only one *l*, and *till* is NOT spelled *'til*.

Title of Paper

The title of a paper should be appropriate, short, and modest. Also, it should be considered a label attached to the paper, not a part of it. Usually it is best to write the paper before naming it. Then look for a few words that indicate the central idea. "An Accident at the Factory" is better than "A Serious Industrial Accident at the W. F. Hamline Furniture Factory." Let the reader find out for himself how good the paper is. If you put words like *amusing* or *exciting* in the title you may arouse his resistance.

If you do put down the title first, remember that your first sentence can't lean on it. If your title is "Why I Don't Like Strawberries," you can't begin "These berries. . . ." You have to say "Strawberries" to explain, without the title, what you are talking about.

today, tomorrow, tonight

All these words are now usually spelled without a hyphen.

Topic Sentences

A topic sentence is one that expresses the main idea of a paragraph. It may or may not actually appear in the paper, but it should always appear in a good outline. In other words, any paragraph that cannot be summarized by a clear topic sentence has something wrong with it. See also pages 181–85.

toward, towards

Variant forms—take your choice.

Transition

Each paragraph should be a reasonably complete unit in itself, but the relation of ideas between succeeding paragraphs should be made clear to a reader. Often the connection (called *transition* or "going across") is made almost automatically by including in the first line of the new paragraph a word or phrase which ties it to the preceding one:

The success of *this* effort suggested the next step.
On the following day he tried a different approach.
Undiscouraged by *such* a reception, he continued his efforts.

Not every paragraph needs such a link with what has gone before, but it is well to remember that a connection that is perfectly clear in the mind of the writer may not be in the least clear to a reader unless it is specifically stated. Unless you are quite sure that the circumstances make the connection unmistakably clear, it is better to play safe and insert a connecting word or phrase—or even a whole sentence.

Transitive and Intransitive Verbs

Compare the two following sentences:

The man *saw* John
The man *was John.*

In the first, *the man* and *John* stand for different people. The verb *saw* is said to be *transitive* (literal meaning, "going across") because it carries over the action from one to the other. And the complement, *John,* may be called the *direct object* because it receives the action of the verb.

In the second, the *man* and *John* stand for the same person. The verb is said to be *intransitive* because it does not carry over any action from one to the other, but simply links them. Since the complement refers to the subject it may be called the *subjective complement* (or a number of other things), but not a direct object. If we change this sentence to read "The man was there," *was* is no longer a linking verb, but is still intransitive.

This classification of verbs is quite important in some highly inflected languages, but in contemporary English:

1. Almost all verbs can be used both ways.
2. In many sentences it is impossible to prove which way a verb is used.
3. In such cases it makes little difference what it is called.

The nonstandard uses of such verbs as *lay, learn, rise,* and *set* cannot be explained on the basis of this classification, since all four of these verbs are classified as both transitive and intransitive—though not in all uses.

transpire

This word *is* in the dictionaries. It should be allowed to remain there, undisturbed.

trite

Trite comes from a Latin participle, *tritus,* which means "worn out." Trite expressions are worn out because they've been overworked: *fresh as a daisy, sadder but wiser, first and foremost, last but not least, the long arm of the law, goes without saying, kiss of death, beat a hasty retreat.*

try and

"*Try and* get that finished tonight" is much more encouraging than merely "*try to* get it finished," since *try and* implies success while *try to* leaves the betting even. (It is only fair to add that many teachers disagree with this analysis, and condemn *try and.*)

twice

The only *t* or *t* sound in *twice* is at the beginning.

type

As a rough synonym for *kind* or *sort, type* is legitimate when it indicates a reasonably definite model:

this *type* of automatic ejector
a vehicle of the *jeep type*

When the meaning is less specific, *kind* or *sort* is generally preferable:

that *kind* of thing
a person of that *sort*

The use of *type* as an adjective, without a following *of*, invites ridicule:

I don't care for that *type* book.
He is a very *high-type* fellow.

un-

See **in-, un-.**

Underlining

Underlining in longhand or typescript is the equivalent of italics in print. The principal uses of *underlining* in college papers are:

1. To indicate the titles of books, periodicals, and newspapers (but not of articles, poems, etc. contained in such publications).

I have read reviews of Hemingway's Old Man and the Sea in The Saturday Review and The New York Times.
Kipling's story "Rikki-tikki-tavi" first appeared in The Jungle Book.

2. To indicate that words are being considered simply as words, and not for their meaning:

The expression the more the merrier is easier to understand than to explain.

I would use therefore rather than so in that sentence.

3. To give special emphasis:

It is never safe to leave a loaded gun in a car.

Underlining for emphasis should be used sparingly or it loses its effect. It is better to underline a few key words than a whole sentence. When you are in doubt about underlining, don't.

unique

This word originally meant "the only one of its kind." Such expressions as *very unique* and *most unique* are therefore weaker than the simple *unique,* and are also often condemned as illogical by people who know the original meaning of the word. Perhaps we should recognize that this word, like hundreds of others, has lost much of its original force, and is now often used to mean simply "unusual." But its unique value seems worth preserving.

uninterested

See **disinterested.**

Unrelated Ideas

When a sentence contains two or more ideas, the relation between them should be made clear to the reader. Look at the following sentences:

He had played left tackle at Minnesota and he weighed 169 pounds.
Although he only weighed 169 pounds, he had played left tackle at Minnesota.
Although he had played left tackle at Minnesota, he was now down to 169 pounds.

There is a big difference between being good for his size and worn down from his past—and the writer shouldn't leave the reader guessing.

until

Only one *l.* Interchangeable with *till.*

upon

See **onto, on to, upon.**

used to, didn't use to

This expression is now used only in the past tense: "They *used to* live there." The *d* is not pronounced, but should be written, except in the negative "didn't *use* to." For *used to could,* see **may, can.**

very

The schoolroom theory that *very* should not be used to modify participles is a silly bit of pedantry. *Very pleased* is quite as good as *very much pleased.* However, *very* has been used so much that it is just as likely to weaken as to strengthen an expression. Radio announcers seem to realize this, and try to strengthen *very* by doubling it. Anybody else who uses *very very* should be condemned to listen to radio announcers until he begins to scream.

vice, vise

A bad habit is spelled *vice.* The tool may be spelled either way.

Voice

Latin verbs have two sets of forms called *voices,* active and passive. Thus *voco* means *I call,* while *vocor* means *I am called.* In English all the special forms of the passive voice have disappeared, and their places have been taken by combinations of the verb *to be* and past participles. We may therefore drop the term *voice* and speak simply of active and passive constructions.

When a verb tells what the subject does, we call it active:

A horse pulled the cart.

When it tells what was done to the subject, we call it passive:

The cart was pulled by a horse.

It is usually better to use active verbs, but passive ones are sometimes useful, especially when the subject is unknown, vague, or comparatively unimportant. See **Passive Constructions.**

Vowels and Consonants

The English alphabet is traditionally divided into vowels and consonants, as follows:

A, *e, i, o,* and *u* are vowels.

Y is a vowel except when pronounced as in *yes.*

W is a vowel when it follows another vowel in the same syllable, as in *draw.*

Y and *w* are consonants except in the uses mentioned above.

All the other letters are always consonants.

The table below indicates the long and short values of the vowels:

	LONG	SHORT
a	f*a*te	f*a*t
e	m*e*te	m*e*t
i	b*i*te	b*i*t
o	n*o*te	n*o*t
u	c*u*be	c*u*b

This classification, which is based on the letters themselves rather than on the sounds they erratically represent, is worse than useless for a discussion of English phonetics. It is given here solely because it may be of some help in understanding spelling rules about the doubling of consonants and so forth. A full treatment of vowel and consonant sounds would require far more space than is available here.

vs.

This is an abbreviation of Latin *versus,* meaning "against," used mainly to indicate the opponents in sporting events. The standard pronunciation is *ver'sus,* though *vee ess'* is now often heard.

wait for, on

In most of the country to *wait on* a person implies service, and simple expectation is expressed by *wait for.*

wake, waken, awake, awaken

Waken and *awaken* are always regular, and *wake* and *awake* may be. The irregular past forms *woke* and *awoke* are also standard; in British use so is the past participle *woken.* All four verbs are freely interchangeable, and preferences differ.

want

1. The idea that *want* properly means "lack," and should never be used as a substitute for *wish* seems (fortunately) to be dying out.

2. As a substitute for *ought to, want to* is generally considered substandard.

3. The standard construction after *want* is the simple infinitive:

I *want* you *to get* up early. (not "I *want for* you *to get*" or "I *want that you should get*")

4. In spite of both their economy and pleasantly idiomatic flavor, such expressions as *want off*, *want on*, and *want out* are generally condemned in schoolrooms, and cannot (yet) be considered standard.

way, ways, away, the way

1. In such sentences as "It was (*a*)*way* over his head," *way* and the older *away* now occur about equally often in standard writing.

2. In expressions like "a long *way(s)* off," *ways* is much more common in standard speech, but *way* is almost universal in writing, or at least in print.

3. Such sentences as "He did it *the way* he was supposed to" are very common in standard speech, possibly because they avoid the uncomfortable choice between the weak *as* and the forbidden *like*. They appear also, but less frequently, in standard writing.

we

Aside from its definitely personal use, *we* is often used impersonally. (*We* often use *we* impersonally.)

Some editors also use *we* instead of *I*. Whether this is modesty or the very immodest belief than an editor is a host in himself would be hard to determine.

Weak Verbs

See **Strong Verbs.**

weather, whether

The *wh-* in *whether* suggests its relation to such words as *where*, *when*, and *which*. The simple *w-* in *weather* fits in nicely with *warm*, *wet*, and *windy*. The popular compromise (spelling both words *wheather*) results only in being wrong all the time.

well

See **good.**

what all

In expressions like "*What all* are we supposed to do?" and "They have dogs, cats, hamsters, and I don't know *what all*," the *all* may be considered a grace note of Southern speech. It seldom appears in writing except when the local flavor of dialogue is represented.

(is) when, where

There is a general and natural tendency to use *when* and *where* clauses as definitions:

A debate *is when* two sides argue.
A junction *is where* two roads come together.

Since such definitions are usually clear, it is unfortunate that they are very generally condemned as illogical; but they are so condemned, and will probably be marked wrong.

where at

Where implies *at* which or *at* what place. An extra *at* is therefore unnecessary.

whether, if

See *if, whether.*

which

Amplifying clauses are regularly introduced by *which* rather than *that*:

The Carfrae Hotel, *which* has the best restaurant in town, is on Townsend Avenue.

Identifying clauses are more often introduced by *that*, but *which* is permissible if you like the sound better:

Here is a book *that* (or *which*) I think you may find useful.

while

Aside from being a convenient short way to indicate "during the time when," *while* may be used to indicate a mild opposition.

Jim was in favor of going by train, *while* Tom rather preferred the bus.

This usage is often condemned on theoretical grounds, but it has a long and respectable history.

who, whom

If you find the choice between *who* and *whom* troublesome, follow these rules:

1. Use *whom* in such set phrases as "to *whom* it may concern."
2. Say "the man it belongs to" and "the boy we were talking about" rather than "the man to *who(m)* it belongs" and "the boy about *who(m)* we were talking."
3. Remember that *who(m)* can often be omitted or replaced by *that* or an explanatory noun.
4. Whenever you are in doubt, use *who*.
5. Don't give *whomever* a thought. *Whoever* is in standard use in all constructions.

who's, whose

Who's is a constraction of *who is,* and therefore needs the apostrophe. The possessive form *whose,* like all other pronoun possessive forms, is written without an apostrophe.

Whose with Inanimate Objects

Who and *whom* are used only of people, but *whose* is sometimes used to refer to things, simply because neither *that* nor *which* has a possessive form.

That is the train *whose* whistle we heard.

Of course we might say "That is the train of which we heard the whistle," but this would seem more like a balancing act than a natural sentence.

will *and* shall; would *and* should

A few grammarians still cling to the theory that the "simple future" and the "future of determination" are expressed as follows:

SIMPLE FUTURE		FUTURE OF DETERMINATION	
I shall	we shall	I will	we will
you will	you will	you shall	you shall
he will	they will	he shall	they shall

This is an oversimplification of British usage; and as regards current

American usage it must be considered a pious wish rather than a description. Practice varies considerably, but the general tendency is about as follows:

1. In future statements the usual form is *will* (or *'ll*) with any subject, regardless of how determined the speaker is. "I *shall*" and "We *shall*" for the "simple future" are permissible but not necessary.

2. In questions, *will* is again the normal form with any subject, unless permission or consent is asked:

> *Will* we have any left? (*Shall* is possible here, but even less common than in statements.)

If permission or consent is asked, *will* is abnormal with *any* subject, but *should* is established as an alternate for *shall*.

> *Shall* (*should*) we go?
> *Shall* (*should*) he turn on the light?

3. The separate "future of determination" has practically disappeared except in the drafting of constitutions ("The purpose of this organization *shall* be," etc.). Orders are written, "You *will* proceed," not "You *shall* proceed."

Shall still occurs in such sentences as "I am determined that he *shall* have a chance," but the more usual expression is now "I am determined for him to have a chance."

Would and *should* sometimes serve simply as the past tenses of *will* and *shall* after verbs of saying, thinking, etc.

> They *will* go.   He said they *would* go.
> *Shall* we go?   We asked if we *should* go.

In other uses, *should* is much more common than *shall* after *I* and *we*. Such sentences as the following are frequently used:

> I *will* be finished tomorrow—at least, I *should* think so.

The difference between the past and present forms often has nothing to do with time:

> *Will* you pass the butter? (I expect you to)
> *Would* you pass the butter? (it would be a favor)

I *shall* do it. (definite statement)
I *should* do it. (either a conditional statement, or a statement about duty rather than performance)
Should we go? (asking for an opinion)
Shall we go? (asking for a definite decision)

Of course not all speakers make such distinctions.

wire

As a substitute for *telegram* and *telegraph, wire* is now standard.

-wise

For centuries *-wise* has been used with a limited number of nouns to form adverbs indicating position, direction, or manner. In some but not all it alternates with *-ways: crosswise* or *crossways, lengthwise* or *lengthways,* but only *clockwise* and *fanwise.* There is now a widespread tendency to use it freely in forming new compounds, particularly with abstract nouns, in the different sense of *in regard to* or *as the* _____ *is concerned.* Such combinations as *careerwise* and *publicity-wise* can be defended as economical, and theoretical objections to them are on rather shaky ground; but they do set a good many teeth on edge. Since their value, public-relations-wise, is definitely limited, it may be wise, success-wise, to avoid them. If you must use them, make your own guesses about hyphens.

Wordiness

It is not necessary to reduce every sentence to the very smallest number of words that can possibly be used to express the ideas it contains; but it *is* important to use reasonable economy. If you are in the habit of saying things like "each and every one" for "each" or "in this modern day and age" for "now," you may reasonably expect your instructor to write "deadwood" instead of "goody-goody," and "D" instead of "B+."

would have

Would have is a standard phrase, but is sometimes misused in two situations:

1. In contrary-to-fact conditions:

If Sheldon *had* (not *would have*) come, he could help us.

2. As a duplicate indication of past time in such sentences as:

He *would have* liked to have seen that.

This sentence could be revised to either "He *would have* liked to see" or "He *would* like to *have* seen."

ye for the

The Old English letter for the *th* sound was thorn (þ). This disappeared from ordinary use, but many people continued to write þ for *the*. Unless they closed the top of the thorn very carefully, it looked more like *y* than anything else, and early printers often used *ye* to represent *the*. It was still pronounced *the* by the people who used it, but later generations, finding it in old books, misunderstood and mispronounced it. It is recommended only for those who like very dubious antiques.

ye for you

In older English, *ye* was the subject form and *you* was the object form. Now *you* is used for all purposes. In those dialects where *ye* still appears, it is an all-purpose variant rather than a special subject form.

you

You is the normal indefinite pronoun in American usage:

How do *you* get to the post office?
You never know what the legislature will do.

All efforts to establish *one* as the normal form seem to have failed, though we sometimes use such substitutes as *a fellow, a man,* or even *a person.*

you all

In the South, *you all* is a polite plural, usually pronounced *you-all'* or even *yawl*. In the North it is pronounced *you'all* and used only in ignorance.

When a Yankee hears one Southerner say to another, visibly alone, "Won't *you all* come over this evening," he assumes that *you all* is used in the singular. What it actually means is "Won't you come over, and of course bring your family, and if there happen to be any odd cousins around of course they will be welcome too." It would be rude not to make the invitation completely general.

Perhaps it is natural that a mere Northerner cannot understand all this.

your, you're

Your is the possessive form. *You're* is the contraction for *you are.*

INDEX

Items in the Index to Usage are not indexed here because the Index to Usage is alphabetically arranged and cross referenced.

	M 1	M 2	M 3	M 4
Mechanics	Abbreviations 247–248	Capitalization 267–268	Division of Words 288, 307–309	Margins, Spacing, etc. 21, 240
P 2	P 3	P 4	P 5	P 6
Brackets 265	Caret 268	Colon 272	Comma 272–275	Dash 284–285
P 12	P 13	P 14	**Word Form and Choice**	W 1
Question Mark 353	Quotation Marks 354–355	Semicolon 360–361		Adjective and Adverb Confused 250–251
W 7	W 8	W 9	W 10	W 11
Jargon 316	Specific Word Needed Use Dictionary	Substandard Word Use Dictionary	Unsuccessful Slang 33–35	Wrong Word Use Dictionary
S 5	S 6	S 7	S 8	S 9
Fused Sentence 191–194	Omission 333–334	Overloaded Sentence 335	Reference of Pronouns 348–350	Run-on-Sentenc 191–194
S 15	S 16	S 17	S 18	**Paragraph and Whole Compositio**
Voice 52	Unrelated Ideas 374	Weak Passive 339	Wordiness 381	
C 6	C 7	C 8	C 9	C 10
Paragraph Length 14–15	Shifting Viewpoint 361	Title of Paper 16, 370	Topic Sentence 370–371	Transition 371

M 5	M 6	M 7	Punctuation	P 1
Numbers	Spelling	Underlining		Apostrophe
330–332	Use Dictionary	373		259–260

P 7
Ellipsis
291

	W 3	W 4	W 5	W 6
	Agreement: Subject–Verb	Case	Cliche'	Shop Talk
	252–254	268–270	372	33

Sentence Structure	S 1	S 2	S 3	S 4
	Dangling Modifier	Double Comparison	Double Negative	Faulty Parallelism
	283–284	288	288	195

S 10	S 11	S 12	S 13	S 14
Sentence Fragment	Shifted Construction	Split Infinitive	Squinting Modifier	Subordination
189–190	194	363	364	133, 144, 155

C 1	C 2	C 3	C 4	C 5
Letter Form: Business	Letter Form: Social	Organization of Paper	Paragraph Coherence	Paragraph Division
214–215	213–214	8–13 17–19 173–181	181–185	14–15

Research Paper	R 1	R 2	R 3	R 4
	Bibliographical Entry Form	Footnote Form	Footnote Needed	Mechanical Form
	228–231	238–239	237	240